T0134449

Human–Computer Interaction Series

Editors-in-Chief

Desney Tan
Microsoft Research, Redmond, WA, USA

Jean Vanderdonckt
Louvain School of Management, Université catholique de Louvain,
Louvain-La-Neuve, Belgium

The Human–Computer Interaction Series, launched in 2004, publishes books that advance the science and technology of developing systems which are effective and satisfying for people in a wide variety of contexts. Titles focus on theoretical perspectives (such as formal approaches drawn from a variety of behavioural sciences), practical approaches (such as techniques for effectively integrating user needs in system development), and social issues (such as the determinants of utility, usability and acceptability).

HCI is a multidisciplinary field and focuses on the human aspects in the development of computer technology. As technology becomes increasingly more pervasive the need to take a human-centred approach in the design and development of computer-based systems becomes ever more important.

Titles published within the Human–Computer Interaction Series are included in Thomson Reuters' Book Citation Index, The DBLP Computer Science Bibliography and The HCI Bibliography.

More information about this series at http://www.springer.com/series/6033

Andrea Resmini · Sarah A. Rice ·
Bernadette Irizarry

Editors

Advances in Information Architecture

The Academics / Practitioners
Roundtable 2014–2019

 Springer

Editors
Andrea Resmini
Department of Intelligent Systems
and Digital Design
Halmstad University
Halmstad, Sweden

Sarah A. Rice
Seneb Consulting
San Jose, CA, USA

Jönköping Academy for Improvement
of Health and Welfare
Jönköping University
Jönköping, Sweden

Bernadette Irizarry
Velvet Hammer Design
Los Angeles, CA, USA

ISSN 1571-5035 ISSN 2524-4477 (electronic)
Human–Computer Interaction Series
ISBN 978-3-030-63207-6 ISBN 978-3-030-63205-2 (eBook)
https://doi.org/10.1007/978-3-030-63205-2

© The Editor(s) (if applicable) and The Author(s), under exclusive license to Springer Nature
Switzerland AG 2021
This work is subject to copyright. All rights are solely and exclusively licensed by the Publisher, whether
the whole or part of the material is concerned, specifically the rights of translation, reprinting, reuse
of illustrations, recitation, broadcasting, reproduction on microfilms or in any other physical way, and
transmission or information storage and retrieval, electronic adaptation, computer software, or by similar
or dissimilar methodology now known or hereafter developed.
The use of general descriptive names, registered names, trademarks, service marks, etc. in this publication
does not imply, even in the absence of a specific statement, that such names are exempt from the relevant
protective laws and regulations and therefore free for general use.
The publisher, the authors and the editors are safe to assume that the advice and information in this book
are believed to be true and accurate at the date of publication. Neither the publisher nor the authors or
the editors give a warranty, expressed or implied, with respect to the material contained herein or for any
errors or omissions that may have been made. The publisher remains neutral with regard to jurisdictional
claims in published maps and institutional affiliations.

This Springer imprint is published by the registered company Springer Nature Switzerland AG
The registered company address is: Gewerbestrasse 11, 6330 Cham, Switzerland

Foreword

Information Architecture: The First 300,000 Years

Does This Book Feel Heavy to You?

Perhaps not as heavy as it should. What you hold in your hands now is a milestone: cut from the raw earth, hewn and chipped at, carved and shaped, set down in place as a marker of distance traveled. Such milestones are infrequent and distinct—that's what makes them useful markers.

In this case, the distance traveled is the distance between nothing and something: from scraps of ideas pasted together into makeshift frameworks to formalized language, practices, dialectics, and an emerging cultural identity as a global community of practice across societies, cultures, languages, and forms—much of it led by the unique voices you will encounter in this book.

But I'm Getting Ahead of Myself

Information architecture—the structural design of bodies of information to align them with human psychology and behavior—wouldn't exist in the form we know without these people, their ideas, and their stories. But information architecture has no origin story of its own, because the origin of information architecture is intimately bound to the origin of humanity itself.

Compared to every other species on the planet, the human animal's mastery of information is undeniable and unparalleled. Gifted with the remarkable processing power of the human nervous system—a mystery so deep in its complexity it challenges our notions of complexity's limits—humans developed the ability to do more than simply sense and respond to their environments, but to reshape their understanding of the world based on the information latent in those experiences.

When the human mind first turned experience into information, combing meaning out of the constant flow of sensory and emotional inputs, taking conscious control of its own understanding of the world, true sentience—the essential quality of human consciousness—was born. So was information architecture.

At the deepest psychological level, association and juxtaposition drive the meaning we bring to, and take from, our experiences. These deep processes are the "associative engine" behind both our extraordinary capacity for intuition and our propensity to fall into the predictable psychological traps of bias and prejudice. This is the messy, high-speed, unconscious realm of Daniel Kahneman's System 1; it is also the dream logic of Freud and the mythic, archetypal landscape of Jung. This is where the enduringly common human experiences are written that gave Joseph Campbell's hero his thousand faces.

This fundamental process of association and juxtaposition is the essence of the craft of information architecture. The field in which information architects operate is the ancient, unconscious wiring of the human mind—the part that shapes the conscious mind's experience almost invisibly. Every fracture in our culture wars is the result of clashing, incompatible information architectures: one individual drawing a very different meaning from the world than another, based on a very different internal understanding of the world. Every individual human consciousness shapes, and is shaped by, its own information architecture.

It is through this web of conceptual association that we give meaning to and make sense of our world. But it is also through information architecture that we consciously, intentionally sculpt that meaning according to our own designs.

Because the power of information architecture doesn't just apply at the individual level. When we needed to communicate our accumulated understandings to one another—replicating a bit of one person's associative matrix in the mind of another—we assigned sounds to ideas and markings to the sounds and we called it language. And the structure of the languages themselves was built on association too, as onomatopoeia seeped into our phonemes and crude visual renderings of a person, a tree, the sun became letters, icons, ideograms.

Arthur C. Clarke wrote famously that "Any sufficiently advanced technology is indistinguishable from magic." If so, then information architecture was the first such magic. In the competition for resources, amidst predators and competitors alike, information architecture afforded humanity, to borrow a phrase, an invisible competitive advantage. Not just in the obvious areas of hunting, gathering, and coordinating groups of people toward achieving an objective, but also in the areas of healing, care, and the mutual support necessary to keep a tribe healthy, sane, and most importantly, together.

Information Architecture Enabled All of It

Wherever and whenever humans have created associations to convey meaning, they have been practicing information architecture. It is present in every area of intellectual endeavor, every activity of communications, governance, science, and technology. It provides the underpinnings for marketing, advertising, industrial design, graphic design, political propaganda, law, organizational theory, and many, many other fundamental aspects of human society and civilization. Behind every one of these acts, across the vast millennia of human existence, lies an act of information architecture. No human mind was ever changed without it.

Through these tools, we orchestrated ways to share associations at scale, transmitting through families and tribes entire bodies of knowledge about how to live, treat one another, navigate hazards physical and spiritual, and thrive. Culture, art, music, religion, tradition, social custom: all the various glues that hold humans and human societies together draw their power from the associations they impart.

These associations, which encapsulate our understanding of ourselves and our world, which capture our hopes and fears and flaws and perfections, which shape our lives even as we shape them, are the raw materials of the information architect. If semiotics defines the signposts by which humans conceptually navigate the world, information architecture defines the streets, highways, alleys, and traffic laws that govern our journey.

Every major shift in our understanding has been, at its heart, a shift in our information architectures. It is worth noting that, at the human scale of observed phenomena on planet Earth, Newton's equations provide exactly the same results as Einstein's. But the underlying information architecture, the meaning behind the variables and the implications of their relationships, was completely different. And thus, Einstein revolutionized physics.

It is worth noting that Linnaeus's famed taxonomy, encompassing the entirety of known life on Earth, was created to facilitate sense-making and communication among (all too) human naturalists, not to capture some essential truth about the nature of life itself; the fact that Linnaeus's morphological observations track closely (but not exactly) to genetic lineages is a happy validation of Darwin's ideas but beside the point of Linnaeus's great project.

Likewise, it is worth noting that Roget's great project, the thesaurus, was conceived not to give a hand to writers in a tight spot, but to encompass all human knowledge in a single, unifying, orderly structure. Melvil Dewey would propose a similar, yet wholly different structure for organizing published information in physical form, again designing for human use. Each of these was a work of information architecture, though none of their creators could have claimed the title.

It is thus that information architecture grew, invisibly, incrementally, and in isolated pockets of activity driven by human necessity. This ancient and most human practice—part art, part craft, and part simply primal instinct—was finally framed and named in the closing years of the twentieth century, as we grappled with creating structural and hypertextual representations of our own human understanding, instantiated in our burgeoning new digital information environments. The invisible world of information that our ancient forebears inhabited had grown so thickly visible as to occlude the physical world itself, as in the immersive worlds of the web, massively multiplayer games, and virtual worlds.

Among information architects it is a well-known phenomenon: Once someone has been introduced to the basic concepts of information architecture, or IA, the way you see the world is forever changed. You start to see the mechanics of IA, the patterns of association and juxtaposition, underlying more and more facets of your own daily experience, until it becomes reflex. It truly is an acquired condition for which there is no cure, because we have spent our lives immersed in information-saturated environments, with architectures implicit or explicit all around us.

Anchored in no particular intellectual tradition, having no theory of its own, the nascent discipline grew piecemeal, lashed together from captured bits of insight like a driftwood raft. Driven by the practical concerns of industry, the practice's self-taught scholars adapted what they could use from across disciplines and discarded what they couldn't. The task before the field of IA is therefore in no small part one of rediscovery and reclamation of its own lost history.

That process of reclamation—part discovery, part synthesis, part pure creative invention—has led the authors represented in this volume to unexpected intellectual destinations far and wide. Here you will see represented viewpoints on how information architecture plays out in academia and in industry alike; on how it intersects with the ideas and ideals of feminism, diversity, equity, and inclusion; on how it influences, informs, and in some ways can't help but dictate our very understanding of both space and time.

It would be simple, perhaps too simple, to characterize the information architects as merely keepers of language and order: boxes and labels for ideas. But there are those who believe language is imbued with something like the power of magic, the ability to draw into reality what was previously only fantasy through instantiation in words. In my own career, I certainly have been touched by the power of naming things, and I would be the last to discount its powerful influence over human affairs.

And yet there are also those who assert the limitations of language to capture and express the nuance of lived experience. And it does seem true that the more we attempt to categorize, compartmentalize, and hierarchicalize our world, the more some indescribable something seems to slip through our fingers. This is no more evident than in the funhouse reflections of ourselves fed back to us by our artificial intelligences, which amplify our innate predilections, predispositions, and simple blind spots to comical, grotesque, and sometimes destructive proportions.

It becomes plainly apparent that these simple linguistic webs of association, on which our AIs must draw in order to reach their conclusions, bear very little resemblance to the realities of our world. And it will be up to humans to interpret those realities and express them in the form of structures that AIs can consume and thereupon behave in ways that do not cause harm. This work will fall to the only people who can do it. This is the work of the information architects.

What the machines have taught us is that when we pass down the way we classify and frame the world and all its phenomena, we also pass down our foibles, our prejudices, our ideas about what's right and normal and acceptable and justifiable in this world. It's all right there, dancing in the architecture. We have discovered that the same structural practices used to reveal truth can also obscure it, and those practices used to enlighten and empower are the same ones used to keep people in ignorance and fear.

The meaning we assign to individual human experiences and individual human lives through the structures and processes we create has consequences that can be lifelong, or can be matters of life and death. This work necessitates an expert class of uncommon open-mindedness, clarity of thinking, and compassion. Information architecture must exist because we need it to exist if we are to survive in an information-rich world.

The most remarkable, most extraordinary thing is that despite all our variations, and all the possible architectures each of us could possess, no cultural divide in history has proven entirely insurmountable. No tribe, no nation, no cluster of humans identifying together under any banner, has been immune to defectors, expatriates, cultural importation and exportation alike, radical hereticism in the face of overwhelming social pressure, and yes even love against cultural taboo and across tribal divides.

Information architecture—the ability to choose the meanings we make—makes it all possible. Because without it, we have no shared understanding. And without that, we can't get anywhere together.

So we keep moving forward, we keep seeking truth, we keep creating that shared understanding, and we keep teaching what we have learned along the way, marking the journey one milestone at a time.

Oakland, CA, USA   Jesse James Garrett
October 2020

Preface

> *Information architecture is an intervention. It disturbs an established system.*
>
> —Peter Morville, *Intertwingled.*

The information landscape has grown more complex, porous and connected—the information challenges brought on by the smartphone revolution, pervasive computing, the Internet of Things, and artificial intelligence demand a more focused, human-centered attention from governments, organizations, and individuals. The 'move fast and break things' ethos that pervades industry-led fields has by and large left all of us who inhabit the current information environment exposed, defenseless, confused, and exploited. Are today's practitioners, researchers, and educators prepared to solve current and future challenges?

Advances in Information Architecture revisits information architecture's efforts to transform itself in 2013 with the publication of *Reframing Information Architecture*, reports on subsequent developments, and bridges the academic and practitioner communities with the goals of critically contributing to the maturation of the field, to ensure that the societal demands for more humane spaces are met, and that concerns with privacy, security, diversity, inclusion, and sustainability are better addressed.

The book details pivotal moments in the conversation on the practice of information architecture in the early 2000s; traces the shift from classical information architecture to contemporary information architecture; presents and discusses the insights and developments from the Academics and Practitioners Information Architecture Roundtable between 2014 and 2019; and explores recent contributions to information architecture theory and practice, illustrating the ways today's creators are extending yesterday's ideas to grapple with the systemic challenges ahead.

What Is the Focus of the Book?

Advances in Information Architecture reports on the Academics and Practitioners Information Architecture Roundtable and the role it has played in three core areas: education, critique, and the maturation of the field. It copiously draws from the corpus of work that has emerged from the Roundtable over the past eight years. The collection couples invited contributions that pinpoint key events and shifts in the practice, with interviews that reflect on the evolution of the field from the 1990s to the end of the 2010s.

What Contributions Does the Book Contain?

Advances in Information Architecture is the result of a decade long global conversation. As its editors, we were committed to being equitable and inclusive. The bulk of the contributions found in *Advances in Information Architecture* are the product of the peer-review processes for the Academics and Practitioners Roundtable. We recognize this effort is impacted by the structural limitations and inequities within the field, but sought nonetheless to include as diverse an ensemble of voices as we could, and firmly believe this book adds its contribution, as small as it might be, to further the discussion on how to dismantle these limitations and inequities within the field. We know it had this effect on our own editing process.

Who Should Read This Book?

Advances in Information Architecture will be of interest to academics researching information architecture, teaching courses in information architecture, or crafting curricula in information architecture. Practitioners from the field and those who practice information architecture as part of other disciplines, including service designers, strategic designers, user experience designers, and project or product managers, will also find the book interesting and beneficial.

Los Angeles, USA   Bernadette Irizarry
Jönköping, Sweden   Andrea Resmini
San Jose, USA   Sarah A. Rice
February–October 2020

Acknowledgements

In no particular order, Sarah, Bern, and Andrea want to extend their gratitude to:

Jesse James Garrett, for accepting our invitation to write the foreword, and for doing so with gusto.

Megan Stowe, for her editorial help.

Raffaella Isidori, Bertil Lindenfalk, Luca Rosati, Flàvia Lacerda, Jason Hobbs, Dan Klyn, Megan Stowe, and Brittnee S. Alford for their hard work reviewing, editing, proofing, and generally making this book as good as it could be. It goes without saying that any error, inaccuracy or factual mistake you might still encounter is entirely the editors' fault.

Arturo Jimenez, Ylce Irizarry and Clai Rice for their creativity and generous counsel. Daniel Kauffman, Jordan Abrams, and Joshric Aurea for getting us out of trouble.

The Roundtable organizers, for working tirelessly year after year to ensure there is a Roundtable to attend: Keith Instone, Jason Hobbs, Terence Fenn, Stacy Surla, Dan Zollman, Jeffrey Pass.

Everyone who has attended a Roundtable, be it once, a few times, or every year since 2013, for being the life and blood of the conversation.

Chairs, co-chairs, and organizers of the ASIS&T Information Architecture Summit first and of the IA Conference then, for supporting the Roundtable and helping make it happen over the years. Kevin Hoffman deserves a special mention for believing in the importance of the Roundtable back in 2012, when it was still nothing more than a wacky idea.

Helen Desmond and Jayanthi Krishnamoorthi at Springer, for their invaluable help in making the book you're reading a reality.

Spouses, offspring, and pets, for their patience and understanding.

Contents

Architectures

Futures

Contents   xvii

Editors and Contributors

About the Editors

Andrea Resmini is associate professor of experience design and information architecture in the Department of Intelligent Systems and Digital Design at Halmstad University and the Director of Innovation and Research at the Center for Co-production, Jönköping Academy for Improvement of Health and Welfare at the School of Health and Welfare, Jönköping University. An architect turned information architect, Andrea is a two-time past president of the Information Architecture Institute, a founding member of Architecta, the Italian Society for Information Architecture, the editor in chief of the *Journal of Information Architecture*, and the author of *Pervasive Information Architecture* (2011) and *Reframing Information Architecture* (2014).

Sarah A. Rice is the founder and CEO of Seneb Consulting and is an information architect with over two decades of strategy and consulting experience, architecting complex information experiences for companies such as Google, Sony, PayPal, Microsoft, eBay, Princess Cruises, and NetApp. She has also taught information architecture to interaction design students at California College of the Arts. She holds a Master's degree in Library and Information Science with continuing interest in data science and visualization. She is a past Information Architecture Institute board member, ran the Institute's premier conference on Information, Design, Experience and Architecture (IDEA) three years running, and has organized the Academic/Practitioner Roundtable since 2015. She has a passion for ethics in information environments, leading her to create and speak about the Ethics Canvas for Information Professionals regularly at industry conferences.

Bernadette Irizarry a creative leader with roots in graphic design and sculpture, Bern is the founder and CEO of the Los Angeles-based design consultancy, Velvet Hammer. Bern has built and led cross-disciplinary teams for over 20 years, holds two patents in color selection and served as an organizer for the Academics and Practitioners Roundtable from 2016–2019. Dedicated to growing diversity in technology and design, she currently sits on the Board of Advisors for AIGA Los Angeles, and co-founded the Los Angeles Chapter of Ladies that UX.

Contributors

Marcia J. Bates Department of Information Studies, University of California at Los Angeles (UCLA), Los Angeles, CA, USA

Jesse James Garrett Oakland, CA, USA

Adam Greenfield London, UK

Atsushi Hasegawa Concent, Inc., Tokyo, Japan

Marsha Haverty Autodesk, Inc., Portland, OR, USA

Bernadette Irizarry Velvet Hammer Design, Los Angeles, CA, USA

Dan Klyn University of Michigan School of Information, Ann Arbor, MI, USA; The Understanding Group (TUG), Ann Arbor, MI, USA

Peter Morville Semantic Studios, Charlottesville, VA, USA

Simon Norris Nomensa, London, UK

Jeffrey R. Pass Booz Allen Hamilton, McLean, VA, USA

Andrea Resmini Department of Intelligent Systems and Digital Design, Halmstad University, Halmstad, Sweden;
Jönköping Academy for Improvement of Health and Welfare, Jönköping University, Jönköping, Sweden

Sarah A. Rice Seneb Consulting, San Jose, CA, USA

Asha R. Singh UXPA DC, Washington, DC, USA

Stacy Merrill Surla University of Maryland, College Park, MD, USA; MetaMetrics Inc., Durham, NC, USA

Christina Wodtke Stanford University, Stanford, CA, USA

Dan Zollman Dialogue for Design LLC, Cambridge, MA, USA

Introduction

Bernadette Irizarry, Sarah A. Rice, and Andrea Resmini

This book has been long in the making. Some seven years. It started out as yet another volume of proceedings from yet another conference, it quickly transformed into a much broader reflection on some of the big questions the field of information architecture was grappling with, and has ended up being neither and much more.

This is why the book you have in your hands is called *Advances in Information Architecture.* It originates from the Academics and Practitioners Roundtable and its sessions that ran yearly between 2014 and 2019 as part of the ASIS&T Information Architecture Summit first and then of the IA Conference. It reflects on the role the Roundtable has played in the discourse on information architecture in the past eight years, but it does not stop there. While the book's roots are deeply intertwined with the goals and perspectives of the different Roundtables, from education to critique to ethics and inclusion, and the need to reframe information architecture for the twenty-first century, its branches have stretched out to become a global, community-wide effort reflecting on what information architecture has been, what is it now, and what could or should it be moving forward.

This figurative tree of information architecture intends to mark the landscape and be visible from afar: it is a boundary marker, a stake in the ground if you will, a

---

B. Irizarry (✉)
Velvet Hammer Design, Los Angeles, CA, USA
e-mail: bern@velvethammer.com

S. A. Rice
Seneb Consulting, San Jose, CA, USA
e-mail: rice@seneb.com

A. Resmini (✉)
Department of Intelligent Systems and Digital Design, Halmstad University, Halmstad, Sweden
e-mail: andrea.resmini@hh.se

Jönköping Academy for Improvement of Health and Welfare, Jönköping University, Jönköping, Sweden

© The Author(s), under exclusive license to Springer Nature Switzerland AG 2021
1

A. Resmini et al. (eds.), *Advances in Information Architecture*,
Human–Computer Interaction Series, https://doi.org/10.1007/978-3-030-63205-2_1

reclamation of what happened before as a necessary part of the foundations of the field, and an opening for its future.

To accomplish this goal, the book presents insights from both practice and research in information architecture framed within the context of academic reflection and accountability. The chapters vary in format and type and include: original contributions of authors who presented their work and ideas at one of the Roundtable sessions between 2014 and 2019; novel contributions developed from shorter sessions presented at either the 2014–2019 Roundtable or other related industry or academic events; interviews with industry leaders, researchers, and scholars working in information architecture; and reprints, with edits, of four seminal articles published between 2000 and 2014 that illustrate key moments and turning points in the collective history of the field.

All contributions, both the revised and adapted versions of the original peer-reviewed papers and presentations that were accepted at the 2014–2019 Roundtables, and the ones specifically written for inclusion on the book, have been blind peer-reviewed for acceptance.

The interviews introduce key figures from the global information architecture community who have either been instrumental to the success of the Roundtable over the years or whose critical voice, professional activity, or theoretical reflections have contributed to the advancement of the field. All interviews were conducted during the late spring and summer of 2020 as ninety-minute semi-structured remote interviews: they were recorded, transcribed, edited for length, clarity and pace, proofed and approved by the editors and the individual interviewees.

The article reprints preserve the original text as much as possible. Still, notes have been added where necessary to clarify individual points that might have lost their significance or meaning due to the passage of time or the lack of context; headings and paragraphs have been at times reflowed to follow the book's conventions; paragraphs only relating to in-context conversations being had at the time have been excised; texts have been further proofed and visible typing errors corrected.

A Book in Three Parts

Structurally and logically, the book is divided into three parts that mirror and reinforce the intent of tying the foundations of information architecture with its future: Part I, Prologues, catches up to the present; Part II, Architectures, illustrates the practice and the research in information architecture as it is today; Part III, Futures, shows how information architecture contributes to address those topics, from artificial intelligence to sustainability to equality, that are of critical importance for our current and future lives in information environments.

A foreword by Jesse James Garrett and an afterword in the form of an interview with Richard Saul Wurman bookend the volume.

Contributions and interviews represent a concerted and conscious effort to be global in nature, and the book offers viewpoints from South and North America, Europe, Africa, and Asia.

Part I—Prologues

Part I of the book provides a critical reassessment of the history and development of the field of information architecture through the lens of the reframing initiated by the Academics and Practitioners Roundtable, selected interviews with early pioneers, and an overview of the individual Roundtables between 2014 and 2019. Part I, Prologues, comprises nine chapters.

In *Classical to Contemporary*, Andrea Resmini, Halmstad University, structures the conversation on reframing information architecture through the lens of Van Gigch and Pipino's Meta-modeling Methodology and offers a critical reflection on how to pragmatically identify the shift from classical, "pre-iPhone," information architecture to contemporary, "post-iPhone," information architecture.

In *Big Architect, Little Architect*, a reprint of a seminal article originally written in 2000, Peter Morville, Semantic Studios, differentiates between strategic and tactical information architecture. *Big Architect, Little Architect* is referenced a conspicuous number of times in contributions and interviews within the book.

In *Information Architecture Front and Center*, Bernadette Irizarry and Sarah A. Rice interview Keith Instone, information architect and user experience consultant, to discuss his encounter with information architecture at Argus Associates in the early 1990s, the struggle with enterprise culture, and the importance of creating bridges between the practice and academia.

In *To IA or Not IA*, a reprint of an article originally written in 2006, Adam Greenfield, writer and urbanist, expresses his dissatisfaction and disappointment with the lack of academic rigor, curiosity and long-term vision the field was grappling with in the early 2000s.

In *On Being Magpies*, Andrea Resmini enters in conversation with Andrew Dillon, University of Texas at Austin, to discuss his early involvement with the field, the role of academia in shaping it, and what are the major obstacles to a consolidated, visible presence of information architecture in research and higher education.

In *The Memphis Plenary*, a reprint of his 2009 ASIS&T Information Architecture Summit closing plenary, Jesse James Garrett, coach and author, states that information architecture is at a critical impasse, one in which it is impossible to identify "bad information architecture" because the field lacks a language of critique, and suggests that the job role of the information architect, or rather its non-existence, is partially responsible for it.

In *Towards a New Information Architecture*, a reprint of a 2014 article, Christina Wodtke retells the history of the field, from its heyday to its decline and unexpected resurgence, detailing how the "big information architecture" and "little information architecture" communities met, how information architecture was smallified in the wake of interaction design and user experience, and how it is today more than strategic in a world where making sense of too much data is a social imperative.

In *Bandleaders in the Idea Business*, Andrea Resmini interviews Lou Rosenfeld, Rosenfeld Media, to reflect on the early days of classical information architecture,

Rosenfeld's frustrations with the information architecture community, the problem of intangibility, and good team playing.

In *The Academic and Practitioners Roundtable 2014–2019*, Sarah A. Rice and Bernadette Irizarry provide a detailed history of the various editions of the Roundtable, describing topics, sessions, participants, deliverables, and outcomes.

Part II—Architectures

Part II of the book illustrates current developments in contemporary information architecture, post-reframing, through a diversity of contributions that vary in terms of approach, application, industry, and context, and with interviews that discuss the role of information architecture in mature public and private settings from around the world. Part II also comprises nine chapters.

In *She Persists*, Bernadette Irizarry interviews information architect Abby Covert to discuss her role in the global community of practice, information architecture as a skill set that can be applied to any field, maturity models in information architecture practice and the impact they have on the field's survival.

In *Information Architecture for Industry Events*, Jeffrey Pass and Asha Singh illustrate in case study format the efforts undertaken at a number of American events to architect more diverse and inclusive experiences for attendees and speakers, detailing the outcomes of a series of workshop series focusing on diversity, inclusion, safety, and accessibility, and concluding by providing a series of actionable steps to improve industry events and their organizational bodies.

In *Teaching Information Architecture in South Africa*, Sarah A. Rice interviews Terence Fenn, University of Johannesburg, to understand how information architecture was instrumental to rethinking a postcolonial model for design school pedagogy in post-Apartheid South Africa.

In *Inversion Within Information Architecture*, Simon Norris, Nomensa, introduces the concept of inversion as a way to work from the flows of big data up to the user experience, and ties it to the level of analysis framework to provide a robust tool for architecting complex and pervasive information architectures.

In *Information Architecture Do (道)*, Atsushi Hasegawa, Concent, situates information architecture as a profession in Japan discussing the traditional division of labor from the perspective of Edward Hall's distinction between high- and low-context cultures, presents the traditional Japanese educational method called "do (道)," discusses Seigow Matsuoka's editorial engineering as a "do" form, and introduces a possible "do" approach to information architecture and information architecture education.

In *In Search of: Information Architecture*, Dan Klyn, The Understanding Group, applies a classical information architecture model to a contemporary information architecture problem space, comparing Joyce's *Ulysses* to Wurman's *The City: Form and Intent* to articulate the characteristics of a masterwork in information architecture.

In *Institutions are People and Leadership is Key* Sarah A. Rice interviews Flávia Lacerda, Federal Government of Brasilia, Brazil. Lacerda, who introduced the Meta-modeling Methodology in information architecture discourse, speaks about the changing landscape of information architecture education and practice in Brazil and its role for Brazilian public governance.

In *The Organization and Exploration of Space as Narrative*, Andrea Resmini, Halmstad University, analyzes space and narrative in video games as an instance of the information architecture of digital experiences, with the intent of providing an example of how contemporary information architecture can be employed to critique different types of information environments.

In *Keepers of Structure*, Sarah A. Rice interviews Nathaniel Davis, Method-Brain, to discuss the importance of models and modeling in information architecture as a way to convey structure throughout the conceptualization, definition, and implementation of products and services.

Part III—Futures

Part III of the book is dedicated to what is on the horizon for information architecture. The interviews and contributions discuss the impact on society of developments in technology, consider the changing cultural landscape, offer insights into the role that information architecture could play in shaping a better future, and suggest venues for key areas that professional practice and academic research and inquiry could investigate together and in their respective competencies. Part III comprises five chapters.

In *There is No AI without IA*, Sarah A. Rice interviews Carol Smith, Carnegie Mellon University, to discuss the complex interdisciplinary interplay that teams have to negotiate to produce human-centered results where technology is a primary concern, the role of information architecture in the design of artificial intelligence systems, and what really makes a system "smart."

In *Towards a Feminist Information Architecture*, Stacy Surla, University of Maryland and MetaMetrics Inc., reframes and extends information architecture from a feminist perspective, stressing the importance of defining "the user" in novel and more inclusive ways, investigating feminist approaches in related disciplines such as human computer interaction, information science, and interaction design, and outlining a preliminary feminist agenda for information architecture.

In *Information Architecture in the Anthropocene*, independent information architecture and user experience consultant Dan Zollman discusses how information architecture practitioners work in a morally and politically challenging climate where pervasive, systemic problems require considering the consequences of design work for social justice and sustainability. Zollman explores what these systemic problems mean for the profession, and concludes offering three approaches to addressing these that apply processual and relational interpretations to the practice of information architecture.

In *Acts of Architecture*, Andrea Resmini interviews Andrew Hinton, Honeywell Connected Enterprise, to talk about the role of embodiment in information architecture, Gibson's concept of environment and its application to both physical and digital information spaces, and the way the field needs new tools and new methods to address today's challenges.

In *Concepts for an Information Architecture of Time*, Marsha Haverty, Autodesk, and Marcia Bates, UCLA, present a structure and a vocabulary for discussing time in relation to information architecture. They elaborate on performance rhythms, show through examples how these rhythms both arise out of and influence human behavior, and argue that addressing performance rhythms will become critical as information systems expand in intelligence and autonomy.

Bernadette Irizarry is a creative leader with roots in graphic design and sculpture, Bern is the founder and CEO of the Los Angeles-based design consultancy, Velvet Hammer. Bern has built and led cross-disciplinary teams for over 20 years, holds two patents in color selection and served as an organizer for the Academics and Practitioners Roundtable from 2016 to 2019. Dedicated to growing diversity in technology and design, she currently sits on the Board of Advisors for AIGA Los Angeles, and co-founded the Los Angeles Chapter of Ladies that UX.

Sarah A. Rice is founder and CEO of Seneb Consulting and is an information architect with over two decades of strategy and consulting experience, architecting complex information experiences for companies such as Google, Sony, PayPal, Microsoft, eBay, Princess Cruises, and NetApp. She has also taught information architecture to interaction design students at California College of the Arts. She holds a Master's degree in Library and Information Science with continuing interest in data science and visualization. She is a past Information Architecture Institute board member, ran the Institute's premier conference on Information, Design, Experience and Architecture (IDEA) three years running, and has organized the Academic/Practitioner Roundtable since 2015. She has a passion for ethics in information environments, leading her to create and speak about the Ethics Canvas for Information Professionals regularly at industry conferences.

Andrea Resmini is associate professor of experience design and information architecture in the Department of Intelligent Systems and Digital Design at Halmstad University and the Director of Innovation and Research at the Center for Co-production, Jönköping Academy for Improvement of Health and Welfare at the School of Health and Welfare, Jönköping University. An architect turned information architect, Andrea is a two-time past president of the Information Architecture Institute, a founding member of Architecta, the Italian Society for Information Architecture, the Editor-in-chief of the *Journal of Information Architecture*, and the author of *Pervasive Information Architecture* (2011) and *Reframing Information Architecture* (2014).

Prologues

Classical to Contemporary: An M3-Based Model for Framing Change in Information Architecture

Andrea Resmini

Abstract This chapter frames the ongoing epistemological evolution of information architecture as a shift, under the pressure of social and technological change, from the "classical" information architecture of the 1990s and early 2000s to a "contemporary" information architecture. It then establishes a differentiation between the two, modeled in accordance with the conceptualization of innovation in fields of knowledge offered by Van Gigch and Pipino's Meta-Modeling Methodology.

Introduction

"Reframing Information Architecture" was the title of the first Academics and Practitioners Roundtable which was held in 2013 as one of the pre-conference workshops organized as part of the 14th ASIS&T Information Architecture Summit in Baltimore, United States. The goal of that Roundtable was twofold: reprise the conversation between the practice of information architecture and its research and education side that was started in 2010 in a breakaway session at that same conference (Instone & Resmini, 2010); and strategically tie that conversation to a recast of the epistemological statute of the field in order to support the maturation and development of information architecture as a whole (Hobbs et al., 2010).

As a result of that first Roundtable and of the global conversation it instigated and gave form to, the current, contemporary understanding of information architecture has by and large left behind "the illusion of the web as a library" (Resmini, 2014, p. v). Conversely, so too "has the idea that library and information science is the only relevant body of knowledge for the discipline" (Lacerda et al., 2019).

Both in the practice and in research and education, this has opened the field to new methodological and conceptual contributions coming from a host of different

A. Resmini (✉)
Department of Intelligent Systems and Digital Design, Halmstad University, Halmstad, Sweden
e-mail: andrea.resmini@hh.se

Jönköping Academy for improvement of Health and Welfare, Jönköping University, Jönköping, Sweden

© The Author(s), under exclusive license to Springer Nature Switzerland AG 2021   9
A. Resmini et al. (eds.), *Advances in Information Architecture*,
Human–Computer Interaction Series, https://doi.org/10.1007/978-3-030-63205-2_2

disciplines, architecture and systems thinking among others, and has vastly broadened the seminal concept of what the "information spaces" that the field is vested in are: information architecture has been slowly moving "away from the single artifact, the website, to consider the entire product or service ecosystem (…) some parts of which might not be online or might not even be digital at all" (Resmini, 2014, p. v), and strategic and organizational problems that are far removed from the idea of producing "blueprints for the web" (Wodtke, 2003).

The 2013 Roundtable resulted in the publication of a book by the same name in 2014, documenting the event and presenting eleven contributions that illustrated the changing nature of information architecture practice and research. One of the chapters, *Information Architecture as an Academic Discipline*, written by Flávia Lacerda and Mamede Lima-Marques, appropriated and reinterpreted Van Gigch and Pipino's Meta-Modeling Methodology (Van Gigch & Pipino, 1986), often shortened to M3, as a way to frame the debate on how to advance information architecture in the context of disciplinary discourses (Lacerda & Lima-Marques, 2014).

Lacerda and Lima-Marques's contribution introduced a way to approach the dialog between practice, academia, and the larger context they live in, which has become the backbone of the meta-conversation involving the relationship between the practice and theory of information architecture in all seven consecutive years, 2014–2020, during which the Roundtable has run as part of the Information Architecture Summit first and then of the Information Architecture Conference, its successor since 2019.

The Meta-Modeling Methodology

The M3 is a systemic, conceptual framework to understand innovation processes in any field of knowledge as social constructs (Fig. 1). It is structured around three individual levels of inquiry that create a system of flows and stocks (Meadows, 2008) that influence each other via input and output processes while operating at different speeds.

At the meta level, that of epistemology and the slowest to change, we have the fundamental concepts and frameworks that structure the worldview of any given knowledge-based community. Epistemology concerns itself with the theory of knowledge and looks at what differentiates valid "episteme," knowledge, from "doxa," opinion. This level is the locus of paradigm shifts: for example, from Aristotelian to Scholastic impetus when discussing motion (Kuhn, 1962, p. 120), or from a geocentric universe to Copernicus' heliocentric cosmology (Floridi, 2014, p. 87).

While Kuhn's conceptualization of paradigms and paradigm shifts has been thoroughly criticized (Percival, 1979; Cohen, 2015), it is difficult not to recognize the weight carried in the practice of design by his intuition that until "that scholastic paradigm was invented, there were no pendulums, but only swinging stones, for the scientist to see" (Kuhn, 1962, p. 120). One has only to consider current usage of the term "artificial intelligence" as a de facto retronym for already-consolidated terms such as "machine learning," "natural language processing," or even "algorithm,"

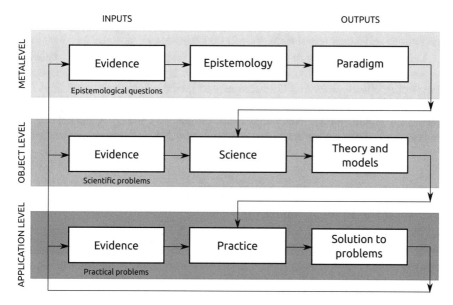

Fig. 1 The M3 as adapted by Lacerda and Lima-Marques (2014)

to concede Kuhn's articulation some standing ground, especially in fields such as the new media design practices where the semantic of the language and its shifts represent part of the direct outcomes of the creation process (Hinton, 2014).

At the object level, that of science, we have the theories and models that are used "to describe, explain and predict problems and their solutions" (Lacerda & Lima-Marques, 2014). The object level is the level where systematic study of the world happens through observation and experimentation and where knowledge is organized and stratified. This is where, for example, Darwin's theory of evolution or Anderson's "long tail" (2004) reside in the M3.

At the application level, that of practice and the fastest to change, we have solutions to everyday problems encountered in a field. This is where practitioners operate as they exercise their craft: surgeons, shopkeepers, and of course designers. It is where we find repeated performance of one or more skills or activities and where the concrete application of concepts from the meta level and theories from the object level happens.

These three levels feed into each other through the aforementioned system of stock and flows, inputs and outputs: through time and accumulation, the "solutions to problems" at the application level become "evidence" for the object level. Here, they might change theories and become evidence for the meta level, producing in the long-term epistemological change. This means that the "guiding" role of the epistemology level, which acts as a set of constraints that establish what is valid but also "acceptable" knowledge in a specific historic moment, thus ruling out certain conceptual framing in favor of others, is counterbalanced and slowly undermined by a constant trickling up, bottom to top, of practices that first make it to the object level, where they are validated, and then possibly to the meta level, where they challenge the current understanding of what domain knowledge is.

The M3 allows addressing "the existing gap (…) in Western culture between 'episteme' (science and 'knowledge that'), which is highly valued and respected, and 'techne' (technology and 'knowledge how'), which is seen as secondary' (…) by making them part of a systemic process" (Lacerda et al., 2019), a rather important part of the ongoing efforts to reconcile the different views and goals that the practice and the research and education camps in information architecture express as of today.

Classical and Contemporary Information Architecture Through the Lens of the M3

In the discourse related to the evolution of the field of information architecture, and of its reframing, a period of rapid transition to a different conceptualization can be retrospectively identified as beginning around the years 2008–2009, and made to roughly coincide with the commercialization of the Apple iPhone and the subsequent introduction of the App Store. It is in these years that a coherent and continuative conversation begins across multiple venues (Alfrink, 2007; Rosati & Resmini, 2007; Hinton, 2008; Potente & Salvini, 2008; Hobbs, 2008; Wodtke, 2009; Resmini & Rosati, 2009) that consciously and deliberately transcends the original formulation of information architecture as a way for "understanding and conveying the big picture of a web site" (Rosenfeld & Morville, 1998, p. 14).

This period of transition follows what could only be called a period of epistemological crisis for the field (Resmini, 2013), roughly affecting the years between 2004 and 2006, one that coincided with the initial wave of interactive web application, the so-called Web 2.0 popularized by Tim O'Reilly (2004) and his Web 2.0 Summit, and the widespread diffusion of folksonomies (Quintarelli, 2005).

Revising and extending earlier seminal work by Ronda León (2008), Resmini and Rosati (2011) posit that it is possible to distinguish three initial knowledge streams contributing to the genesis of information architecture: an information design one, rooted in Wurman's work from the 1970s onward (Wurman, 1989, 1997); an information systems one, which became prevalent in the 1980s; and an information science one, that of Rosenfeld and Morville, which operated a "synthesis" and became mainstream, and dominating, in the 1990s. Resmini and Rosati then define "classical information architecture" the information architecture of the years between the early 1990s and the early 2000s, and call "pervasive or ubiquitous information architecture" the information architecture that emerges from the period of crisis outlined above (2004–2006), pointing at contributions such as Morville's "Ambient Findability" (2005).

This chapter, benefiting from an additional decade of research and insights, maintains the idea of an epistemological reframing of information architecture having happened in the 2000s, but adopts the more reasoned iPhone-related chronology

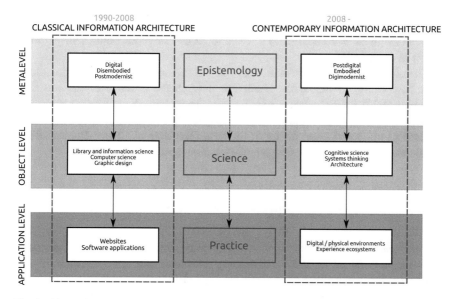

Fig. 2 Classical and contemporary information architecture as M3 structures

detailed above; suggests "contemporary" as a more neutral and suitable term for the original "pervasive and ubiquitous" period; and establishes a differentiation between classical and contemporary information architecture modeled in accordance with the conceptual framing of the M3 (Fig. 2).

Classical Information Architecture (1990–2008)

At the meta level, classical information architecture corresponds to a digital-centered view of the world, which is disembodied, kept behind screens, and still rooted in the cultural dominant of the time, postmodernism (Resmini & Lindenfalk, 2021). This is for example visible in the conceptual construction of the object of design as an individual, authored artifact, the website (Kirby, 2009), but also in its acceptance of "open and ambiguous structures" (Beardon, 1994) as part of its own philosophical foundations (Bowker & Star, 1999).

At the object level, that of theory, the relevant components are being borrowed primarily from library and information science and, to a lesser degree, from computer science and visual and graphic design. An interesting juxtaposition here can be seen in the absence, in the practice, of any relevant information systems component (Resmini & Rosati, 2012), something that will lead later more business- and information technology-oriented commentators to distinguish between "web information architecture" and "enterprise information architecture," this latter representing an evolution of the research and practice threads of the 1980s (Leganza, 2010).

At the application level, information architecture is primarily focusing on websites, with software applications, either desktop or remote, being a very limited subset of the practice.

The classical information architecture period sees practicing information architects "cho(osing) to define the discipline through the artifacts of the practice" (Resmini, 2013), that is websites, creating an epistemological conflation that resulted in constraining the entire field to be nothing more than its incidental outcomes and, because of the practice-led nature of the field (Hobbs et al., 2010; Hobbs, 2019), spilled over into academic research and education, stifling development.

Contemporary Information Architecture (2008–)

From a conceptual point of view, contemporary information architecture, post-iPhone-revolution information architecture, does not represent a discontinuity. In this sense, it is not a Kuhn-type paradigm shift (1962), where the currently dominant paradigm is made incompatible with emerging phenomena and a new, different paradigm is adopted in response. It is rather an acknowledgment that not only were practitioners of information architecture extending their applicative reach to domains extraneous to those considered "valid" during the classical period, but that a parallel reflection, as pointed out earlier in the chapter, was happening in research in information architecture and affecting the object and meta levels of the M3.

Contemporary information architecture sees its meta level center on postdigital, rather than digital, experiences (Jenkins, 2011; Berry & Dieter, 2015). Postdigital is here the concretization of Negroponte's far-seeing prediction of the upcoming banality of digital, written for Wired in 1998: as digital and physical increasingly blend (Benyon, 2014), they form a continuous information space in which people move from a mobile app to a store, from a real-time display to a card reader, from a website to a classroom, without ever worrying, as long as everything works, whether something is digital or physical. Because of the new relevance that the physical world, its context, and its affordances assume in the meta level, embodiment becomes a necessary concern of information architecture and embodied experiences a relevant part of its conceptualization. For example, when considering the information architecture of a Disney park (Arango, 2017) or when establishing how a voice interface should contextualize conversations (Grochow, 2020).

Postdigitality and embodiment, together with the anonymous mass co-production of information possible in the post-iPhone world, create in turn the conditions for supplanting postmodernism as the cultural dominant. Kirby (2009) calls this new cultural dominant digimodernism, a product of the effects of computing on society and culture. Digimodernism is characterized by anonymous co-creation and ownership, evanescence, haphazardness, and unfinishedness. For example, a social media platform such as Instagram is by definition an empty information architecture that requires contributions from its user base in the form of photos, comments, and social signifiers such as likes or stars. It is also evanescent, since its content is in continuous flow, it "does not endure (and) it has no interest as a reproducible item" (Kirby, 2009, p. 52), and thus unfinished and haphazard, in the sense that its "future development (…) is undecided. What it will consist of further down the line is as yet unknown. This feels like freedom; it may also feel like futility" (ibid.).

At the object level, contemporary information architecture adds theories and methods borrowed from disciplines that address the increased complexity of its object of design to the theories and methods of the classical period. These have so far included, for example, architecture and urban planning (Arango, 2018; Resmini & Rosati, 2011), systems thinking (Morville, 2015), cognitive science (Hinton, 2014).

At the application level, practitioners engage with a vast array of experience ecosystems (Resmini & Lacerda, 2016; Lindenfalk & Resmini, 2019) that deal with both organizational (Merholz, 2019) and social (Hobbs, 2008) issues, and with digital/physical environments (Mandelli et al., 2011; Rosati, 2020).

Beyond Reframing

We're right out of the starting block, not at the finish line – a friend

The framing of information architecture through the lens of Van Gigch and Pipino's Meta-Modeling Methodology is not a point of arrival, but rather the formalization of the conversation started by Lacerda and Lima-Marques in 2014 and continued at the Academics and Practitioners Roundtable between 2015 and 2019.

The M3 has been an immensely valuable tool for the information architecture community: it has allowed all actors involved to press their points in a systematic way while being aware of the mutual relationships between each other's respective expertise and roles, and their relative weight at specific crossroads in the conversation. Still, it should be treated for what it is: a model.

Classical information and contemporary information architecture, and their different characteristics at the meta, object and application level as outlined here, are also not meant to be taken as absolute categories. They represent a secondary, hopefully useful abstraction whose goals are to illuminate, under its own light of course, why information architecture today should be practiced, judged, criticized, and theorized differently than in the 1990s, and so facilitate a critical, reflective conversation on the development of the field.

References

Alfrink, K. (2007). *Playful architectures.* Proceedings of the 3rd ASIS&T European Information Architecture Summit. https://www.slideshare.net/kaeru/playful-ias-euro-ia-summit-2007.
Anderson, C. (2004). The long tail. *Wired.* https://www.wired.com/2004/10/tail/.
Arango, J. (2018). *Living in information.* Two Waves Books.

Arango, J. (2017). *Three placemaking lessons from the magic kingdom*. UX Collective. https://uxd esign.cc/3-placemaking-lessons-from-the-magic-kingdom-4263deb29b2f.

Beardon, C. (1994). Computers, postmodernism and the culture of the artificial. *AI & Society, 8,* 1–16. https://doi.org/10.1007/BF02065174.

Benyon, D. (2014). *Spaces of interaction, places for experience*. Morgan & Claypool.

Berry, D. M., & Dieter, M. (2015). *Postdigital aesthetics*. Palgrave Macmillan.

Bowker, G. C., & Star, S. L. (1999). *Sorting things out*. The MIT Press.

Cohen, M. (2015). *Paradigm shift*. Imprint Academic.

Floridi, L. (2014). *The fourth revolution*. Oxford University Press.

Grochow, J. M. (2020). A taxonomy of automated assistants. *Communications of the ACM, 63*(4), 39–41. https://dl.acm.org/doi/10.1145/3382746.

Hinton, A. (2008). *Linkosophy*. Closing plenary at the 9th ASIS&T Information Architecture Summit. https://andrewhinton.com/2008/04/15/linkosophy/.

Hinton, A. (2014). *Understanding context*. O'Reilly.

Hobbs, J. (2008). *Hotel Yeoville*. Proceedings of the 9th ASIS&T Information Architecture Summit. Also in Kurgan, T. (2013). *Hotel Yeoville* (pp. 85–88) (as "Bridging the Divide"). Fourthwall Books.

Hobbs, J. (2019). *Re: The future of information architecture*. http://jh-01.com/content/?p=374.

Hobbs, J., Fenn, T., & Resmini, A. (2010). Maturing a practice. *Journal of Information Architecture, 2*(1). http://journalofia.org/volume2/issue1/04-hobbs/.

Instone, K., & Resmini, A. (2010). Research and practice in IA. *Bulletin of the American Society for Information Science and Technology, 36*(6).

Jenkins, S. (2011). Welcome to the post-digital world, an exhilarating return to civility. *The Guardian*. https://www.theguardian.com/commentisfree/2011/dec/01/post-digital-world-web.

Kirby, A. (2009). *Digimodernism: How new technologies dismantle the postmodern and reconfigure our culture*. Continuum.

Kuhn, T. S. (1962). *The structure of scientific revolution*. University of Chicago Press.

Lacerda, F., & Lima-Marques, M. (2014). Information architecture as an academic discipline—A methodological approach. In A. Resmini (Ed.), *Reframing information architecture*. Springer.

Lacerda, F., Lima-Marques, M., & Resmini, A. (2019). An information architecture framework for the Internet of Things. *Philosophy & Technology, 32*, 727–744. https://doi.org/10.1007/s13347-018-0332-4.

Leganza, G. (2010). Trends in information architecture practices. *Forrester*. https://www.forrester.com/report/Trends+In+Information+Architecture+Practices/-/E-RES56375.

Lindenfalk, B., & Resmini, A. (2019). Mapping an ambient assisted living service as a seamful cross-channel ecosystem. In M. Pfannstiel & M. Rasche (Eds.), *Service Design and Service Thinking in Healthcare and Hospital Management: Theory, Concepts, Practice* (pp. 289–314). Springer.

Mandelli, E., Rosati, L., & Resmini, A. (2011). Architettura dell'informazione e design museale [Information architecture and museum design]. *Tafter Journal*. http://www.tafterjournal.it/2011/07/01/architettura-dell'informazione-e-design-museale/.

Meadows, D. H. (2008). *Thinking in systems*. Chelsea Green Publishing.

Merholz, P. (2019). *Org design is largely information architecture*. Proceedings of the First Information Architecture Conference—IAC19. https://www.slideshare.net/peterme/org-design-is-largely-information-architecture.

Morville, P. (2005). *Ambient findability*. O'Reilly.

Morville, P. (2015). *Intertwingled*. Semantic Studios.

Negroponte, N. (1998). Beyond digital. *Wired*. https://web.media.mit.edu/~nicholas/Wired/WIRED6-12.html.

Percival, W. K. (1979). The applicability of Kuhn's paradigms to the social sciences. *The American Sociologist, 14*(1), 28–31. http://www.jstor.com/stable/27702355.

Potente, D., & Salvini, E. (2008). *Apple, Ikea and their integrated information architecture.* Proceedings of the 4th ASIS&T European Information Architecture Summit. https://www.slideshare.net/davidepotente/apple-ikea-and-their-integrated-ia-presentation.

O'Reilly, T. (2004). *What is Web 2.0.* O'Reilly. https://www.oreilly.com/pub/a/web2/archive/what-is-web-20.html.

Quintarelli, E. (2005). *Folksonomies: Power to the people.* Proceedings of the ISKO Meeting Milano 2005. http://www.iskoi.org/doc/folksonomies.htm.

Resmini, A. (2013). The architecture of information. *Etudes de Communication, 41*(2), 32–56.

Resmini, A. (2014). *Reframing information architecture.* Springer.

Resmini, A., & Lacerda, F. (2016). *The architecture of cross-channel ecosystems.* Proceedings of the 8th International ACM Conference on Management of Emergent Digital EcoSystems (MEDES'16).

Resmini A., & Lindenfalk B. (2021). Mapping experience ecosystems as emergent actor-created spaces. In A. Hameurlain, A. M. Tjoa, & R. Chbeir (Eds.), *Transactions on Large-Scale Data- and Knowledge-Centered Systems XLVII* (vol. 12630). Lecture Notes in Computer Science. Springer, Berlin, Heidelberg. https://doi.org/10.1007/978-3-662-62919-2_1.

Resmini, A., & Rosati, L. (2012). A brief history of information architecture. *Journal of Information Architecture, 3*(2). http://journalofia.org/volume3/issue2/03-resmini/.

Resmini, A., & Rosati, L. (2009). *Information architecture for ubiquitous ecologies.* Proceedings of the International ACM Conference on Management of Emergent Digital EcoSystems (MEDES'09) (pp. 196–199).

Resmini, A., & Rosati, L. (2011). *Pervasive information architecture.* Morgan Kaufmann.

Ronda León, R. (2008). *Arquitectura de Información: análisis histórico-conceptual* [Information architecture: A historical-conceptual analysis]. No Solo Usabilidad. http://www.nosolousabilidad.com/articulos/historia_arquitectura_informacion.htm.

Rosati, L. (2020). *Come l'architettura dell'informazione plasma l'esperienza: La storia del Vietnam Veterans Memorial.* https://www.lucarosati.it/blog/architettura-informazione-esperienza.

Rosati, L., & Resmini, A. (2007). *From physical to digital environments (and back): Seven laws of findability.* Proceedings of the 3rd ASIS&T European Information Architecture Summit. https://www.slideshare.net/vector/towards-a-crosscontext-ia.

Rosenfeld, L., & Morville, P. (1998). Information Architecture for the World Wide Web. O'Reilly & Associates.

Van Gigch, J. P., & Pipino, L. L. (1986). In search of a paradigm for the discipline of information systems. *Future Computing Systems, 1*(1), 71–97.

Wodtke, C. (2003). *Information architecture: Blueprints for the web.* New Riders.

Wodtke, C. (2009). *Social spaces: Lessons from radical architects.* IDEA Conference 2009. https://www.slideshare.net/cwodtke/social-spaces-lessons-from-radical-architects/.

Wurman, R. S. (1989). *Information anxiety.* Doubleday.

Wurman, R. S. (1997). *Information architects.* Graphis.

Andrea Resmini is associate professor of experience design and information architecture in the Department of Intelligent Systems and Digital Design at Halmstad University and the Director of Innovation and Research at the Center for Co-production, Jönköping Academy for Improvement of Health and Welfare at the School of Health and Welfare, Jönköping University. An architect turned information architect, Andrea is a two-time past president of the Information Architecture Institute, a founding member of Architecta, the Italian Society for Information Architecture, the Editor-in-chief of the Journal of Information Architecture, and the author of *Pervasive Information Architecture* (2011) and *Reframing Information Architecture* (2014).

Big Architect, Little Architect

Peter Morville

First came the primordial soup. Thousands of relatively simple single-celled web sites appeared on the scene, and each one was quickly claimed by a multi-functional organism called a "webmaster." A symbiotic relationship quickly became apparent. Webmaster fed web site. Web site got bigger and more important. So did the role of the webmaster. Life was good.

Then, bad things started to happen. The size and complexity and importance of the web sites began to spiral out of control. Mutations started cropping up.

Strange new organisms with names like interaction designer, usability engineer, customer experience analyst, and information architect began competing with the webmaster and each other for responsibilities and rewards. Equilibrium had been punctuated[1] and we entered the current era of rapid speciation and specialization.

Survival of the Fittest

As all of these new life forms struggle to define their roles and relationships in a competitive environment, the dialog can become quite heated. Consider a recent

---

[1] Punctuated equilibrium. http://pespmc1.vub.ac.be/PUNCTUEQ.html.

According to Peter Morville, the article "was named after one of the first books (he) ever read: *Big Dog, Little Dog* by P. D. Eastman."

Originally published July 7, 2000 in the "Strange Connections" column of the Argus Center for Information Architecture website (Morville, P. (2000). Big Architect, Little Architect. Argus Center for Information Architecture. https://argus-acia.com/strange_connections/strange004.html). Footnotes added where necessary to clarify or contextualize parts of the conversation.

P. Morville (✉)
Semantic Studios, Charlottesville, VA, USA
e-mail: morville@semanticstudios.com

© The Author(s), under exclusive license to Springer Nature Switzerland AG 2021   19
A. Resmini et al. (eds.), *Advances in Information Architecture*,
Human–Computer Interaction Series, https://doi.org/10.1007/978-3-030-63205-2_3

posting on the CHI-Web Mailing List in which Jared Spool, a dominant member of the usability engineer genus attacked[2] the customer experience genus, stating:

> I personally think the current "customer experience" movement is a crock of sh*t. I think it's all a FUD (fear, uncertainty, and doubt) campaign to get executives to shift their consulting dollars. (*) "i" omitted in consideration of communications decency filters

These battles can be very upsetting or very humorous, depending upon your perspective at the time (i.e., if you're the one being attacked, you're less likely to think it's funny).

Before we take any of these struggles too seriously, we need to remember a couple of facts:

1. Evolution (so far) has not led to a single-species world. There will be room (and need) for many types of web design professionals.
2. The food supply (i.e., money available to support the increasing number and complexity and importance of web sites) will continue to grow rapidly for the foreseeable future.

So, we all need to lighten up.

The Role of the Information Architect

This brings me to the central and very serious topic of this article. I have recently witnessed attempts to curtail the role of the information architect, with the obvious sinister objective of reducing our precious food supply. This is not funny.

It all began in March, when Jesse James Garrett created a very good visual model[3] to illustrate the elements of user experience.

As with all good tools, shady people quickly found ways to subvert Jesse's visual for their own evil purposes. Despite the fact that Jesse explicitly states on the visual itself that "(t)his model does not describe a development process, nor does it define roles within a user experience development team," I have seen people trying to squeeze the role of information architect into the box for information architecture on Jesse's visual.

These people say things like:

> We don't need to involve the information architect yet. Their role doesn't begin until after we've defined user needs, site objectives, functional specifications, and content requirements. See, look at Jesse's diagram.

or

---

[2]The original comment is still available via the Wayback Machine at https://web.archive.org/web/20011222162657/www.acm.org/archives/wa.cgi?A2=ind0006e&L=chi-web&D=0&P=183.
[3]Garrett, J. J. (2000). The Elements of User Experience. http://www.jjg.net/elements/pdf/elements.pdf.

The information architect shouldn't be involved in the design of navigation systems. That's the interaction designer's job.

We must challenge these *architect-in-a-box* threats or face a future nearly as bad as the prospect of being stuck into little blue folders.[4]

In Defense of Diversity and Fuzziness

There is a core to the practice of information architecture that involves the structure and organization of information systems that provide intuitive access to content and applications. However, interpretations of the role of the information architect vary depending upon the organizations, the projects, and the people involved.

At one end of the spectrum, the Little Information Architect may focus solely on bottom-up tasks such as the definition of metadata fields and controlled vocabularies. At the other end, the Big Information Architect may play the role of "an orchestra conductor or film director, conceiving a vision and moving the team forward," as described by Gayle Curtis, Creative Director at vivid studios.

While this diversity and fuzziness drives some people crazy, I think it's a good thing. In the rich, dynamic environment of web design, it would be foolish to draw thick black lines between and around professional roles and responsibilities.

Some projects require a Big Information Architect. Others require a little information architect. The best work comes out of collaboration between information architects and interaction designers and other professionals of all shapes and sizes. By working together to design useful and usable web sites, we can ensure that our food supply continues to grow. Evolution is not a zero-sum game.

Peter Morville is a pioneer of the fields of information architecture and user experience, and his bestselling books include Information Architecture for the World Wide Web, Ambient Findability, Search Patterns, and Intertwingled. He has been helping people to plan since 1994, and advises such clients as AT&T, Cisco, Harvard, IBM, the Library of Congress, Macy's, the National Cancer Institute, and Vodafone. He has delivered conference keynotes and workshops in North America, South America, Europe, Asia, and Australia. His work has been covered by *Business Week*, *NPR*, *The Economist*, *The Washington Post*, and *The Wall Street Journal*. His latest book is *Planning for Everything*.

---

[4]Morville, P. (2000). Little Blue Folders. Strange Connections. Argus Center for Information Architecture. https://argus-acia.com/strange_connections/strange003.html.

Information Architecture Front and Center: In Conversation with Keith Instone

Bernadette Irizarry and Sarah A. Rice

Keith Instone is a user experience consultant with roots in human computer interaction. Instone's career spans practice and research, and includes stints at Argus Associates and IBM. He has taught computer science at Bowling Green State University and helped develop Michigan State University's experience architecture program. He currently sits on the Board of Michigan UXPA and was an organizer of the Academic/Practitioners Roundtable from 2014 to 2018.

B. Irizarry (✉)
Velvet Hammer Design, Los Angeles, CA, USA
e-mail: bern@velvethammer.com

S. A. Rice
Seneb Consulting, San Jose, CA, USA
e-mail: rice@seneb.com

© The Author(s), under exclusive license to Springer Nature Switzerland AG 2021
A. Resmini et al. (eds.), *Advances in Information Architecture*,
Human–Computer Interaction Series, https://doi.org/10.1007/978-3-030-63205-2_4

Q: You are a long-standing and dedicated member of the information architecture community, but many people may not know you began your career as a computer scientist. What brought you to information architecture? How did you get started?

It started during the early days of the Web, when I became interested and focused on web usability. There was this cool thing called the Internet and most folks were happy enough to just make things flash. I thought it would be a good idea to apply the human computer interaction principles that I had learned on personal computer software. I met Peter Morville and Lou Rosenfeld when they started writing their Web Architect column for O'Reilly's *Web Review Magazine*. By chance, they lived nearby in Michigan, so we spent time together and I started to understand who these librarians were and why they cared about the same things that I cared about as a computer scientist. At the time I didn't know librarians and computer scientists had anything in common. As we talked more and I understood their background and their point of view, I realized I was talking about the user interface and they were talking more about the things that were behind the interface; asking how to organize all that information that then becomes part of the user interface.

I started working with them at Argus Associates where we figured out how those two areas related. It was like chocolate and peanut butter, usability and information architecture. We worked with clients on consulting projects and we invented stuff together. For example, I was doing some card sorting that they had never done before. So we would sell card sorting to clients and convince them that they needed it, and invest three weeks into doing it as part of our discovery process. And then we would take it to the next level, figuring out how to do card sorting not just with text but with pictures. We would learn about users' models by giving them different pictures and having them sort them in different ways, and that gave us insights that would then guide the rest of what we were trying to build. My work at Argus got me deeply embedded in information architecture and I committed myself to the discipline. It seemed like something very important.

Q: After Argus, you took a job at IBM. Tell us about those years: what was information architecture like inside such a large enterprise?

I worked at IBM for 10 years. At least one third of my job was representing information architecture throughout IBM to different people as we were working on different projects. I was constantly holding up the mantle and talking about information architecture—when we were talking strategy, when we were talking design, when we were talking operations. I kept it in focus, while others would only be concerned with it for a little while.

I was championing information architecture every single day. I was working on navigation for the IBM website, and became the navigation guy. The key was to advocate for information architecture all the time so not just when it was time to worry about the navigation, but also when we were having strategic discussions around which projects to undertake. I would point out that a certain project would make business sense but was going to be really hard to do because I understood how our information systems were organized. For example, someone might want to build a new marketing website just for small and medium businesses. I knew we did not have much content specifically for small and medium business and if they did that project, when it was time to figure out what content would go on this website, there would be little. IBM only had large collections of content for large enterprises. I could see the gaps we had in our information and could advise that we wait for the marketing department to create content to fill the gap. We could then come back to it later and propose that project.

Over the course of my career, I continued to focus on information architecture, but I noticed that everything changed again. The world was focused on applications, interaction rich web applications came onto the scene. I found myself tapping into my roots in HCI and focusing more on interaction. I was applying concepts from desktop application design to web apps. The information architecture was still important, but our user interfaces became richer, so it wasn't just about clicking on links and organizing content into buckets. Now we were worrying about dragging and dropping and the other things that users could do. I knew that the information architecture was still important, but other people were less focused on it. They were interested in how to build drag drop interfaces and it seemed less important to focus on what they're dragging and dropping.

Q: Were these shifts in focus an issue for the enterprise?

There have been periods of time where the way we organize or manage information was a really important concern to the business, and people would focus on it. But then they'd lose interest after the taxonomy, the content management system, or the navigation was implemented. The focus on drag and drop was an example of the pendulum swinging farther in the other direction.

At IBM there was some magical thinking going on, that information systems would be maintained with no real effort on anyone's part. After a couple of years when things started to fall apart, they would focus on it again with a project, and focus on the "thing that would solve it." They would believe that it would naturally maintain itself but it would fall apart again over time. I was called in to clean up the mess over and over. I tried to explain to people what was happening and how to avoid the messes in the first place.

Q: You have been involved in the development of information architecture via your own research and teaching interests, and more recently in the Roundtable. From your point of view, how has the field changed?

Today, I introduce myself to others as a user experience consultant, but information architecture has been at the core of my career. Part of my answer has to do with terminology. User experience is the term that everybody else is using. I've been reading up on startups, and many books say that you need to worry about your users, you need to do design thinking, and all of the other usual recommendations. That's the modern view of product management. All of these books tend to use the term "user experience." They're not explicitly mentioning information architecture that often, but I see it embedded in all the things that they do. They talk about drawing a conceptual map of competitors, or they mention enterprise architecture systems.

In the early days, information architecture became the term for the person who was the generalist that sort of did everything. Similar to how "webmaster" was the generic term that applied to the one who did magical things, incomprehensible things that got done in connection with the internet or the web site; nobody understood it, but whoever was in that role was the magician that could do everything. The information architect took on that role for a while.

Nowadays, that generalist is the user experience designer, for better or for worse. That doesn't mean that information architecture isn't just as important, it means that we're starting to take all those skills and techniques and folding them into one thing. It seems that only a few organizations and projects that are information heavy enough where they can devote the people to doing information architecture full time.

I stay connected to information architecture by working with people on the Roundtable, or going to information architecture conferences. This lets me stay close to it, even if I'm not doing it every day. For a couple of months out of the year, I feel like I'm really immersed in the theory and the science of it, and for the other ten months, I take what I learned and go out and practice it.

Q: The role of information architecture has changed. Do you view that as a good or bad thing?

Like most things, it is good and bad. Abby Covert's book[1] is an awesome thing, because it introduces the concepts of information architecture to a broad audience so that they can apply it widely. But in a professional context, some organizations would be better off if they didn't spread information architecture out among multiple generalists who apply a little bit at the strategy phase and a little bit at the design phase and then a little bit at the operations phase when things tend to break. Instead, the organization would benefit from recognizing and declaring that information architecture

---

[1]Covert, A. (2014). *How to Make Sense of Any Mess*. http://www.howtomakesenseofanymess.com/.

and the value it brings is important. As a result, they will have somebody focus on it all the time. When organizations are more focused, they can be strategic, instead of reactionary. Being reactionary means that everything becomes a buzzword, and people will gravitate to the latest buzzword, instead of an established practice or discipline. We've seen this with "digital transformation" or "design thinking" as it moves into becoming part of management consulting speak to get people's attention. Once that happens, the other types of information architecture thinking are forgotten, as well as the doing.

How we as a community deal with it is most concerning to me. Some of us will need to stand up for information architecture as a field of study, promote ourselves a little bit more, make the business case a little bit more, and sometimes be a little bit more critical of organizations that need it but don't use it. For example, if a company releases some artificial intelligence (AI) that's a disaster, it's extremely biased and bad things happen—instead of just saying it was stupid technologists or it was a bad business decision, we could point out that it's in part because you were treating information architecture as this side thing. You weren't doing it early on when you were designing your algorithms. Maybe that's happening inside some organizations now. What we really need is to participate with all the groups who are creating a consortium of artificial intelligence technologists in order to talk about ethics. We're not at that table.

Information architects have been so busy heads down doing the work, which is important, that we haven't had enough energy or momentum to talk about how to do the work at scale. We're not acting as a profession.

Q: How have we failed to act as a profession?

I see evidence of this in three different ways. First, we haven't codified our ethics in some way, and that's not acting as professionals. Second, we haven't formed an industry consortium where we have businesses put money in a pool behind an information architecture purpose. This is how a lot of work gets done in technology. Businesses like Google, Facebook, and financial institutions get together and they share money, that's how we make movement at a higher level. Third, let's look at academia. We've got some fields of study at different universities, but it's scattered. There could be more information architecture classes as well as information architecture majors and disciplines. One metric we've used is how many PhDs in information architecture are there in practice. It is a proxy for how much we are a profession, how much we are a field of study, how important we are in academic disciplines—likewise, in industry. As information architects we're good at practicing information architecture. We're good at doing it ourselves, helping our colleagues on our team also do it when we need to distribute the work. But we have a long way to go as a profession.

Q: When you look at other disciplines, for example interaction design, user experience or service design, both the practice and the academy have developed robust programs. Information architecture programs seem fewer and far between. Why?

There is a combination of factors at play. When I was in academia, before I joined Argus, I was doing research in human computer interaction. We called it human computer interaction in part because there were a whole bunch of grants from governments to fund human computer interaction. Then, up popped digital libraries, and there were digital library projects. The reaction in academia with the faculty where I worked was to figure out how to get grants. We looked at our human computer interaction work and found topics that related to digital libraries. For example, when we worked with hypertext, we could quickly rewrite a grant proposal to mention digital libraries. And so, suddenly we were in the digital library research business.

Another factor is the competition among different disciplines. Human computer interaction was already established from the computer science perspective. Library science had started, and continues to develop, iSchools.[2] Academic research that we would call information architecture, they might call information-something-else. Maybe they call it information management, information science, or informatics. It became difficult to get everyone in the same room at the same time. There were politics, different academic paths, and conflicting schedules. Our Roundtable was often scheduled at the same time as the iSchool conference, and both events focus on "information."

In many ways, we have hitched our wagon to the user experience wagon, so when we approach a company, or when an academic teaches user experience they're also going to teach information architecture, and that can be ok. It hasn't been as easy to hitch on to design thinking or service design wagon, and they have also gained steam. Right now, we don't seem to have our own wagon to push, at least, not one that's had much momentum.

It's hard to say why that happened. Maybe all the government grant agencies got together at some point when they were figuring out what to fund, and we didn't have a compelling enough pitch. Again, since a lot of what we do as information architects touches so many things and it is sort of a hidden layer. At some point they would have said, well, we're funding "information management," that's close enough. And we're funding user experience, and human–computer interaction, those are close enough too. We will just make a sub-category underneath all these other things for information architecture. This is not what we're doing right now, for this interview and this book: we're putting information architecture front and center and making a category underneath for human–computer interaction, service design and design thinking and see what happens.

There are times I work for a startup when I don't need to spend time thinking about information rich environments and I will fold information architecture activities into other phases of the work. But when I'm working with a large Fortune 10 company, and the focus is on an overall employee experience that is information rich, then, I will make the case for differentiating information architecture and not hiding it underneath those other labels. It will be a line item that the project manager cares about, or I might advocate for a group of five or six people within the company to be dedicated to information architecture and work as a community of practice.

---

[2]iSchools or Information Schools, university programs committed to the study of people, information, technology and science.

Q: You mentioned we have been heads down doing the work, do you think this may have been short-sighted? The nature of information has changed dramatically since the 1990s, when the prevailing opinion was that Library and Information Science was sufficient to provide the basis for information architecture. Digital information is now embedded everywhere—remediated constantly, 24/7—and we live a connected, always-on life. Did we anticipate back then that we would need to look outside of Library and Information Science?

You are right. When I was working in the pre-internet days, we thought about information as something we'd put on a physical device, like a CD, to be mailed to people through the postal service, in different cities and buildings. Everything was separated and standalone. Then came the Web, starting with websites. The approach we adopted was that the CD just got a whole lot bigger and, bonus point, we didn't have to mail it out. But it was still a web site. It was still self-contained. When mobile devices came out, the web site shrank in some ways. The screen got small, which introduced limitations, but everything else expanded in so many other ways. People could be on the move and access the site. They could connect services to one another to make them more relevant. Our information environments all became connected. Such pervasive information architectures[3] address the whole ecosystem. Organizations had to think of their content. It wasn't sitting on a CD, it wasn't really sitting on a website. It was all over the place, it was connected, and people were experiencing it in different ways. The next move was to personalize it, and write algorithms to help make 10,000 paragraphs of text more meaningful. It changed the game.

The question becomes then how do you define the role that takes care of that level of information? Information is so involved in everything. We don't just belong in marketing. We don't just belong in sales. We don't just belong in operations because information is in our blood. What is the name of a role for somebody who deals with the blood that goes through the whole system? When, before, we were just thinking we were an arm, or a leg, or a story system, or a kiosk.

As a practitioner, I've been able to swivel, and move and adapt. From one day to the next I could tweak my business card and no harm is done, but for an academic program, it's hard. I was involved early on at Kent State, which offered an information architecture degree. Currently, it is labeled a user experience degree, which makes perfect sense from a teaching marketing perspective and from what the practitioners need. It also means that information architecture is not as strong in the academy, which a discipline needs to be.

Q: You were an adjunct professor at Bowling Green State University. Were you teaching information architecture?

I've never taught information architecture, but I've been teaching around it as well as interacting with a lot of people who are teaching information architecture. I spent a couple of years working with the folks at Michigan State to develop their undergraduate program in experience architecture. They carefully chose "experience

---

[3] Resmini, A., and Rosati, L. (2011). *Pervasive Information Architecture: Designing Cross-Channel User Experiences*. Morgan Kaufmann.

architecture" as a new term because they were inventing something new from a branding perspective. It's also important to know that the program was coming out of the Writing and Rhetoric department. They have a strong professional writing program, and they were finding that good professional writers go into technical communication. Here is a new career path into user experience jobs—it is interesting when you start with rhetoric and writing versus starting with library science, computer science, or marketing.

They developed a curriculum that was built upon their professional writing, and content strategy was core to it. They partnered with the design program to teach some interaction design and visual design. They had to teach their own technical classes because they couldn't work out a deal with the computer science department to teach just enough database concepts to be useful. I was helping their PhDs in English teach computer science because I have a computer science background.

After a couple years they had a curriculum that was very project based. We took a step back, noticed a gap in their program—information architecture. Even though they had a strong content foundation, they had visual design, they had jumped over information architecture. It was a big hole in the middle. They also had a gap in their curriculum around theory. We ended up creating a class with two parts: information architecture methods and information architecture theory. It was a good combination, because we could talk about modeling as well as the theory of information.

It was interesting to see that, left to their own devices, information architecture was not in their first iteration. The students were learning it because they were doing projects with the parking department to develop a new parking application, they were doing card sorting and they were doing all the little things, but they weren't getting at the core of the larger information architecture theory.

Curriculum development is the closest that I've been recently to teaching information architecture. I've been working on how I as a practitioner can help professors teach better. It's an underlying theme of the Roundtable. How do we get these two worlds to collaborate together because that's part of how we advance the field of information architecture. I don't think I have any concrete answers except that it's hard.

Q: Why is it hard?

Because often in industry we're on the hamster wheel, we're going really fast, we have these tight deadlines and when we do user research in industry it's very quick and dirty. Our goal is just to make this awesome product better. If we actually learn anything about human behavior, then that's just by accident. We focus on the business or marketing goal, for exmple what do we need to do to get people to buy more cars. On the research side, we want to understand why people buy things at all, why fifteen products are better than five products. Should we price it high, price it low. In academia, we want more. We seek to generate core knowledge that's reusable for lots of things. In industry, even if we discover that core knowledge we can't share it because it's proprietary. Academics focus on teaching, and how to best introduce the subject to people and keep them engaged. The only time a practitioner is likely to talk to an academic is when they are teaching a senior class and their students are graduating, because we want to hire people. I've also found some practitioners believe that academics may not be teaching the right stuff, or students don't know what is useful out in practice, but they have no interest in working with academics to improve the situation.

Q: You mentioned that bridging practice and academia as one of the underlying themes of the Roundtable. As someone who has been involved with the Roundtable since its inception, would you reflect a bit on its history and its evolution?

It was important to me and Andrea Resmini to see if we had enough practitioners interested in the more academic topics. We had done some things informally, and we had also held a joint session at the Information Architecture Summit.[4] People were consistently showing interest. There was a need, and the biggest challenge was to figure out a way to engage people. We decided the best way was to pick a day at a conference where a lot of smart people were showing up anyway. We would ask them to show up early, dig in deeper into a topic, and spend more time discussing it.

We did that, then some of the things we worked on would bleed into the rest of the conference program. For a couple of years, we had a great time, but not everyone knew about it, so we started approaching the conference's program committee and asking for a panel slot on the schedule so we could share our results with others.

The Roundtable helped me professionally to get into the details, to think about things. I remember going home after the Roundtable and thinking about the conversations there for the following thirty days. Then, on the 30th day, I would wake up and say "Ah, now I understand what Jason Hobbs was saying." Or, "now I understand why Dan Klyn will not quit talking about ducks and buildings".[5] It took about thirty days for my brain to process it, but then I got it. I'm not clear on how I'll use it the other eleven months, but I know that I will.

We focused on theoretical topics for the first Roundtable and it has stayed the same over the years. There's been a core of us who work on these big picture ideas. We will commit to having at least one day of the year where we think deeper thoughts and spend time with others who don't complain that we're just navel gazing because we're talking about ethics or theory. People have accused us of "defining the damn thing" all over again. We are going much deeper than just a dictionary definition of the work we do and what we think is important. This is what gets me coming back every year, because I know that I will learn a lot in that one day that I'm going to be able to leverage.

Q: Do you think the Roundtable has been successful?

I've seen the community going deeper into the topics that we discuss. For example, in 2015 we talked about a language of critique and, a couple of months later, Christina Wodtke wrote an awesome article about critique. I know that the Roundtable helped her to do it and as a result, there are more people talking about critique. There were

---

[4]At the 11 ASIS&T Information Architecture Summit. See Instone, K. and Resmini, A. (2010). Research and practice in IA. *Bulletin of the American Society for Information Science and Technology*, Vol. 36, No. 6.

[5]Klyn, D. (2013). *Dutch Uncles, Ducks and Decorated Sheds.* https://www.slideshare.net/danfnord/dutch-uncles-ducks-and-decorated-sheds-reframing-ia.

conference keynotes and books that went deeper into topics that had been Roundtable discussions a couple of years before.

Where we seem to have failed is in reaching people to let them know that the field is so much deeper now. We have not reached decision-makers, or CIOs. We most definitely haven't reached back into academia. We keep inviting them to the Roundtable, but since we're at a practitioner conference, most of us haven't been able to attend academic conferences where they are talking about information architecture.

I have conversations with people who want to understand the information architecture boom and they only talk about wireframes; I tell them that we've reframed the conversation. I can point to that body of knowledge that we have accumulated. That makes it easier for people to admit that they had not been paying attention. They talk about buying the "polar bear book"[6] and "doing information architecture on the side." But they are not aware of *Pervasive Information Architecture*,[7] or *Understanding Context*.[8] *Reframing Information Architecture*[9] was definitely a great accomplishment. It adds to the list of things that we can reference when talking about all the advances in discipline that have happened over the last ten years.

Q: Do you think the work of reframing information architecture is finished?

About a year ago, the IBM CEO said artificial intelligence cannot succeed without information architecture, and that got some of the people in our community excited. I knew that the IBM definition of information architecture is not the same as ours, so I considered it half a victory. At least they were using our label, but it wasn't quite exactly what we mean by information architecture. They use terminology like data architecture, enterprise architecture or network architecture. Again, when information is in our blood, we're going to have lots of different uses for it. Also, "architecture" itself can be a vague term.

Sometimes when I talk to folks "architecture" is that umbrella term that includes design. Other times it's the architecture that happens before design. I noticed that in my evolution as an information architect at IBM working with information at a large scale, I realized that I was acting like an urban planner. The whole ecosystem of websites was like a huge city, with slums on one side and high rises on the other, with highways cutting through the middle of things. Having the term "architecture" in what we do, helped me see that bigger picture. If I was just going to be an information designer I wouldn't have even been thinking that way. There's power in the term "information" and extreme power in "architecture." Put them together and we've got a double loaded term that we have to wrestle people over.

---

[6]Rosenfeld, L., Morville, P., and Arango, J. (2015). *Information Architecture for the World Wide Web and Beyond* (4th ed). Referred to since its first edition as "the polar bear book" based on the polar bear illustration that appears on its cover.

[7]Resmini, A., and Rosati, L. (2011) ibid.

[8]Hinton, A. (2014). *Understanding Context*. O'Reilly.

[9]Resmini, A. (2014). *Reframing Information Architecture*. Springer.

Q: You mentioned urban planning and its relationship to architecture. Some in the information architecture community point to it as a model for information architecture. Urban planning's focus on the system, the relationship between the buildings, streets or green areas; how people will flow through paths …

… or how the policies that determined it can impact what's built. If the policies are screwed up then individual buildings are gonna suck. I remember hearing these ideas from Andrea Resmini, using urban planning as a way to better understand and tackle complex information, similar to the more systemic, European way of doing architecture—this fascinated me.

I grew up in the software development world of computer science—which is all build, build, build. Code, code, code. Slowly, I was learning that there was more to do either before, or in addition, or as part of a bigger picture—I was learning from others to look at things more holistically, focus on things at the system's level. Some building or coding will happen as a result of that focus, but don't start with building, and not for the sole purpose of building. That's different from a startup, for instance, that has already figured out that they're going to develop an app. They start there and work their way backwards to figure out how to make that app a reality. I would enter the conversation and help figure out what they needed to be doing in the first place. They had already made a bunch of assumptions on a business model. I would help them focus on the information architecture while thinking about the business model, waiting until it's time to do the navigation and other things. It was enlightening for me.

Q: You shared that the profession needs to step up its game. Would you be in favor of some sort of certification? An IA certification that states you possess a certain expertise, provides a title and what that entails?

I think it's worth trying, even if we try and fail. The benefit is that we will have learned something, we will have taken the time to figure something out. If we even had certification that provided a small amount of benefit, it would be better than what we have now, which is nothing. We could learn from our mistakes and do better. I notice that built environment architects have similar discussions around how to certify someone to be "good." If you take all the tests that will only certify that you were a good built environment architect from twenty years ago, it wouldn't mean that you're a good built environment architect today. These architects are struggling with how to tell if other professions are actually prepared to do a good job and not have people die as a result of their work.

By figuring out how we certified this fast moving, hard to get your hand around thing called information architecture, we could learn something—that others built environment architects and the library scientists and others might take notice of and want to emulate. That's my hope at least. The biggest problem is finding people who want to take the risk, invest the time, knowing that it's like creating a startup. It will most likely fail, but could get acquired later on.

Q: What do we need to be saying in a book titled "Advances in Information Architecture" to summarizes what took place between 2014 and 2019 at the Academics and Practitioners Roundtable?

I'd like to see a book that serves multiple audiences. For the more advanced practitioner, who has never been able to participate in the Roundtables, they can read the book to catch up and practice information architecture in the best way possible known today.

The second goal for the book would be for it to serve as a reference. I've got plenty of books on my shelf that I read once and I put them down and I never check into them again. The most useful ones are the ones that I keep opening up all the time. Sometimes you need the handbook, other times, you need to simply read and get caught up. I would also want a mix of familiar voices and new voices and to pull from different academic areas. It needs to answer the question: what do I need to know for information architecture?

In the past I would have said, "Why even bother with a stupid book, it's better to do it in these other ways." I've come to realize, however, that things change fast. There are so many Medium articles out there, and they have all become somewhat disposable. It feels like fast food knowledge. We want something that will last longer, and a book is a good way to encapsulate information architecture's body of knowledge. That way, we can say, here are the ten books that you have to have on your shelf if you want to understand what information architecture is. When I go to a talk, and hear the speaker only references two of those ten books, I want to be able to raise my hand and say, great talk, you're 20% of the way there. And then list out the other eight books that they need to reference. This book should be one of those "must reads."

Bernadette Irizarry is a creative leader with roots in graphic design and sculpture, Bern is the founder and CEO of the Los Angeles-based design consultancy, Velvet Hammer. Bern has built and led cross-disciplinary teams for over 20 years, holds two patents in color selection and served as an organizer for the Academics and Practitioners Roundtable from 2016 to 2019. Dedicated to growing diversity in technology and design, she currently sits on the Board of Advisors for AIGA Los Angeles, and co-founded the Los Angeles Chapter of Ladies that UX.

Sarah A. Rice is founder and CEO of Seneb Consulting and is an information architect with over two decades of strategy and consulting experience, architecting complex information experiences for companies such as Google, Sony, PayPal, Microsoft, eBay, Princess Cruises, and NetApp. She has also taught information architecture to interaction design students at California College of the Arts. She holds a Master's degree in Library and Information Science with continuing interest in data science and visualization. She is a past Information Architecture Institute board member, ran the Institute's premier conference on Information, Design, Experience and Architecture (IDEA) three years running, and has organized the Academic/Practitioner Roundtable since 2015. She has a passion for ethics in information environments, leading her to create and speak about the Ethics Canvas for Information Professionals regularly at industry conferences.

To IA or Not IA

Adam Greenfield

Some of my more regular readers, and certainly anyone who knows me personally, will be aware that for the last few years, I've been more or less backing away from public identification with the information architecture (IA) community. I no longer identify myself professionally as an information architect, that is to say, and I'm no longer so terribly interested in attending or presenting at information architecture-centric events.

Given how very much this community has given to me, though, I feel like I owe folks an explanation for my increasing alienation … even if nobody's asked for one. If I'm able to express myself correctly, it should shed some light on why I have been so reluctant to endorse, let alone embrace, the various events and causes to which more than a few of you have invited me to lend support over the last few years.

Please bear in mind, as you read the following, that in this case all the usual disclaimers are utterly sincere. I really do respect the hell out of the parties involved, and equally, I mean this criticism—however blunt—to be both constructive and useful.

A lot of this distance is a healthy, and probably inevitable, structural consequence of the field's reaching maturity. The stirring challenges of those first couple of years are now largely resolved, and to the extent that those challenges were constructed as dialectics, most of them broke against the "big IA" viewpoint I was personally most invested in. Practitioners in the field, by and large, now spend their time and energy not in abstract definitional debates but in the nitty-gritty, day-to-day details of managing information flow in the large-scale enterprise. Given that this was never anything I found particularly captivating, it's understandable why I'd look elsewhere for inspiration.

Originally published on Adam Greenfield's v-2.org website on October 4 2006.

A. Greenfield (✉)
London, UK

© The Author(s), under exclusive license to Springer Nature Switzerland AG 2021
A. Resmini et al. (eds.), *Advances in Information Architecture*,
Human–Computer Interaction Series, https://doi.org/10.1007/978-3-030-63205-2_5

But some of it is due to what I cannot help but see as a revenge effect. The early champions of information architecture—and here I'm explicitly thinking of Christina Wodtke, Lou Rosenfeld, Jesse James Garrett, and the Peters, Morville and Merholz—were successful beyond any reasonable expectation in creating a welcoming, nurturing community. We all owe them a debt of gratitude for that; so, in my opinion, do the literally tens of millions of people who have used sites designed or improved by IAs who came up under their tutelage. Their contribution cannot be overstated and will not be forgotten.

But the less salutary flipside of nurturance is an environment in which pointed criticism is rarely heard or countenanced. It's not that there weren't expressions of divergent viewpoints at the various IA events and gatherings I've been to over the years; of course there were. It's that the field has seemed (to me, at least) more interested in being supportive and in welcoming all contributions—even long past the historical moment when this made sense—than in imposing a more rigorous quality control.

More concretely: I want you to go and at least have a glance at this article,[1] recently published as the lead article on Boxes and Arrows (B&A), which remains the IA community's premier source for professional development materials. Put with maximum bluntness—and with all due respect to its author, who was doubtlessly writing in good faith—the problem with the article is that it presents as an "interesting new idea" a concept that has been extensively investigated, considered and published elsewhere.

There is prior art here, in other words—and not a little, either. Author, editorial staff, and (perhaps most worrisomely) the commenters on the article seem entirely unaware of two decades of published work on the problem in the HCI field. From the perspective of a serious practitioner, both article and communal response are nothing but noise; the comments worry me most because, in a sense, they represent the collective intelligence of the IA field, and because nobody seems willing or able to point out the piece's essential vacuity.

(Ironically, this is in part nothing but a knowledge management issue—ironic because the fields are so closely interrelated that for years Yahoo actually listed IA as a subcategory of KM.)

Nor is the piece, or B&A itself, the only example of this. For a community that claims as its domain the structuration of information in the service of a human user, IA as a body seems startlingly uninterested in the much deeper and more interesting challenges that emerge around mobile and ubiquitous encounters with information. After years in which many of us tried to argue that IA potentially constituted a powerful, general skillset applicable to situations far beyond the Web, it seems as if that "beyond" extends only as far as corporate intranets and the like. And this strikes me as a failure, locally and globally.

---

[1]The article mentioned here is Howard, R (2006). Ambient Signifiers: How I Learned to Stop Getting Lost and Love Tokyo Rail: Boxes & Arrows. Archived version available at the Wayback Machine. https://web.archive.org/web/20061108024650/, https://boxesandarrows.com/view/ambient_signifi.

Now, before you leap to remind me: I know that both B&A and the various IA summits and retreats are almost entirely volunteer efforts. I know that it takes an enormous amount of energy to keep up with developments in one's own field, let alone the other streams flowing alongside. And nobody is more dismayed than I by the sour bleating self-appointed experts emit when they feel that the benisons of their knowledge have been insufficiently appreciated. So, I'm sure not trying to score points here, and to the extent that people are personally hurt or offended by my comments, I apologize.

But that leaves the question of why so very many articles and presentations in the field seem predicated on the assumption that IA is something coextensive with Web technologies, most especially as used in the enterprise. I, at least, cannot take seriously, and do not want to take part in, a community where one not-terribly-interesting flavor of current practice trumps intellectual curiosity and the will to learn and grow.

Another way of looking at all of this is to say that the community has voted with its feet, that the people who are and who do IA at this point in time have made it clear where their interests lie. I once argued that IA is "whatever we say it is," and so it is—simply with a different "we" in the driver's seat. But given my feeling that the mobile and ubiquitous context offers individual information architects the prospect of a vastly expanded, more influential and, frankly, more important field of inquiry and practice, if IA is as a whole not interested in what's going on here, then I am afraid that I am not interested in it. I hope those of you in IA from whom I have learned so much will understand and forgive my feelings.

Adam Greenfield is a writer and urbanist based in London.

On Being Magpies: In Conversation with Andrew Dillon

Andrea Resmini

Andrew Dillon is currently the V. M. Daniel Professor of Information at the School of Information, University of Texas at Austin, where he served as dean between 2002 and 2017. He was one of the prominent scholars who actively participated in the building of the field in the late 1990s.

A. Resmini (✉)
Department of Intelligent Systems and Digital Design, Halmstad University, Halmstad, Sweden
e-mail: andrea.resmini@hh.se

Jönköping Academy for Improvement of Health and Welfare, Jönköping University, Jönköping, Sweden

© The Author(s), under exclusive license to Springer Nature Switzerland AG 2021
A. Resmini et al. (eds.), *Advances in Information Architecture*,
Human–Computer Interaction Series, https://doi.org/10.1007/978-3-030-63205-2_6

Q: That bio could only be described as terse. Would you mind if we start from what is missing from those few lines that we should know? And how did you and information architecture cross paths?

I suppose I have made a career in information, and that's more by accident than by any intent.

As a graduate student in psychology I became really interested in the actual utility of psychology to shape meaningful acts or behaviors in the world. I was not particularly interested in clinical or industrial work that most of my fellow graduates pursued, and I was troubled by the great disparity between what seemed to me a very rich theoretical landscape expressed in textbooks and classes, and the practical application of this on the lives of people. From what I could tell, psychology rarely went beyond what common sense might have easily predicted or explained.

As luck would have it, I ended up doing my master's thesis with Dr. Jurek Kirakowski at University College Cork in Ireland. He was one of the first faculty members in Ireland interested in what was called Human–Computer Interaction or Human Factors, and he set me on my path to considering design, and particularly the design of interactive information systems, as one area where human behavior was going to be important to understand. I became very interested in user interface design, as we called it then, and in how the scientific understanding of language, perception, and skill development could be used to help companies develop more usable systems. The umbrella term at the time was "information," because it was all information technology.

I went on to do a PhD in England, where I had a great six or seven years at Loughborough University, pursuing my doctoral studies part-time while working with a group of social scientists in the Human Sciences and Advanced Technology (HUSAT) Research Institute. We were doing applied research on the design of everything from kitchen appliances and car interiors to CAD systems for British Aerospace or design tools for European software companies. It was fascinating, captivating, stimulating, and all new. Here was a chance to really apply and test the value of psychology in real world contexts.

My interests solidified around hypermedia and hypertext, which were just emerging at that time, and I started conducting research in that area for my PhD, trying to understand how people navigated large and unstructured document spaces, or determining if we could design information representations that would increase comprehension or performance. From there, I accepted a postdoc at Indiana University, in their psychology department and related Institute for the Study of Human Capabilities where I concentrated on individual differences in human cognition. I returned to England after this, rejoining the HUSAT Institute, but within a year or so I accepted a full-time faculty position back in Indiana. I was young and imagined I would spend a few more years in the US before returning to Europe, but In Indiana I made connections with the computer science program at the School of Library and Information Science and started to feel quite at home there. I spent roughly eight very productive years helping found the School of Informatics, and overseeing the development of a new Master's degree in HCI. I then had the opportunity to come to Texas to lead the development of the School of Information here, and I took it. Twenty years later, I'm still here.

Back when I was a student, we couldn't have predicted the information infrastructure that has emerged, but the same two questions consistently remain on the table: how does this impact people and what can we do to shape this emerging infrastructure so that it can better augment and complement the way people want to live. Of course, we've also seen a lot more, including the cynical side of information manipulation both from commercial and political interests. There's no end to issues we must address, there's no end to the questions, there's always a sense that we could design this differently and that we certainly could do better. It is important that we do not focus on technological advances, as they're inevitably going to happen and they tend to capture people's attention. What's vital is to understand the human response to new technologies so that we can shape better information infrastructures. In some ways, I think the rest of the world has caught up with the importance of information architecture by smashing right into it. Many are now beginning to reflect back on the emerging information infrastructure we have put in place, and have started asking fundamental ethical and political questions. Information architecture, it seems to me, is at the core of these concerns with our emerging world, even though it might not be the term people use, I sense there is a growing acknowledgement that the issues of concern to us are ultimately of concern to everyone.

Q: What about your history with information architecture and the information architecture community? You were one of the early academics involved in the definition and development of the field. How did it all start?

It is sort of intriguing. I was a bit of a cynic early on when I first heard the term "information architecture." This would have been around 1998–1999. I thought it was a catchy, trendy term for what I was doing and since I was really a scientist, I did not have time for labels. Then in 2000 I attended a CHI conference in Europe: as luck had it, on my way back I was flying in through Boston. Lou Rosenfeld had organized this Information Architecture Summit, under the auspices of ASIS&T, the American Society for Information Science and Technology, and he invited me to be on a panel. The Summit was to take place at the conference facilities of Boston airport: travel-wise, that made it easy for me to participate, and on such turns of luck are futures changed.

I didn't give the topic much thought: I knew a few of the people attending, and my plan was to simply engage in discussion and tell them how I thought information architecture was basically HCI. Yes, it was a nicer name that made us all feel rather good about ourselves, but I went to the panel thinking how short lived the term was going to be since it competed with existing disciplinary names and didn't really offer anything distinctive to warrant separation. And at the end of the weekend, I had changed my mind. Just like that. The enthusiasm of the group, the excitement about the very same issues that I was interested in, often in isolation at Indiana, the fact they were clearly framing problems in a distinctive non-HCI way, terminologically, and just the excitement that here was a group of quite different people all feeling they wanted a community, proved intriguing. I left then thinking there was something in this "information architecture" term that could be powerful.

I went back to Indiana and started talking to colleagues: what is this information architecture thing, what do we mean by that label and could we sort of create a cohesive discipline around it? I attended an event Lou Rosenfeld and Peter Morville organized in La Jolla, under the patronage of the Argus Institute for Information Architecture, to further explore the theme and, of course, the ASIS&T Information Architecture Summits continued for many years (even though summits were supposed to be one-off gatherings to address hot topics).

By the time of the Argus meet, information architecture was generating a lot of interest and there was much discussion on what it all meant. Were we engaged in "big information architecture" or "little information architecture"? These terms meant different things to different people. From my point of view, there was only "big information architecture": I was big picture all the way. I just believed we were architecting a form of existence into the world that was going to touch everybody on the planet, everybody living within these spaces within a few decades. We just had to think about these things on a grand scale. You don't ask your architect to worry about the plumbing: they know you need plumbing, but their role is to consider the building systemically. They need to think about the building as part of the local environment and about its long-term survivability. They have to think about how that space interacts with larger spaces around it and about the experience of people within the new space that's been created for them. They have to think about its look and feel as much as the mechanics, and this requires a big orientation to do properly.

I still believe that the architecture metaphor has limitations. But it does convey this notion of "bigness," this idea of thinking in design terms and in terms of lived experience. I ended up giving several talks on "big information architecture" and I was keen on pushing it as part of the curriculum development at the schools I was in. I agreed to write a column on information architecture for ASIS&T that ran in their Bulletin for five or six years. I also tried to get more information architecture into the ASIS&T conference, and to engage more of my colleagues with information architecture, however it was becoming clearer that the information architecture community that was emerging didn't really want to be part of this other, more traditional, professional association. That's why the Information Architecture Summit became an independent annual event, and a very successful one too. The end result was a new, mostly profession-oriented information architecture community which didn't overlap with the more academically oriented community that ASIST&T represented. Meanwhile, it also became clear that the bifurcation, the "big information architecture" versus "little information architecture" split, would not easily be resolved.

The problem was, and is, that having its own conferences and gatherings is a natural thing for a discipline to do, but an intellectual discipline won't survive unless it has firm roots in the academy, and I think we never quite resolved that for information architecture. If your field doesn't have the sort of scholarly credentials the academy expects, it means you're not going to have an established, accredited process to turn graduates into professionals, or PhDs into researchers and professors. In the long run, the lack of a recognized research and education path has an impact on any profession as well. Normally, this is a slow process, so it's not determined yet for information architecture, but in my view we didn't use our first decade as best as we might have to lay solid foundations for such a process. Colleagues who are in the professional world, they're perhaps less concerned with this, they have their own concerns and the academic side is a secondary concern at best. For me, as an academic, the education side was and is a crucial identity issue. Information architecture clearly has a core set of ideas and practices that unified lots of work that may not have existed in one single discipline and I still believe there's an opportunity to scope this out. It still hurts to think that we haven't made the discipline more visible to others.

Q: Have we lost a once in a lifetime opportunity there?

I don't believe so. User experience has eaten some of that space, for sure, but also offers us some clues. While it could be argued it is a lump-them-all-together kind of term, and one that doesn't invite very nuanced distinctions between individual practices, user experience has gained traction even in academia. Interestingly, many of the students who come to us seem to consider being an information architect or a user experience designer as two sides of the same professional identity. That would probably not have been true twenty years ago. So, at the speed at which academia moves, maybe we're right on course and we're emerging on schedule. But if I look back, it's clear we never gave much thought to making history. We never thought we were even creating a field. And then the initial excitement got blown out of the water in the dotcom bubble burst. The economy tanked and for a while there was no work in information architecture, which I suppose suited the cynics who did not care for the label, but then when the economy returned, information architecture came back. There was a second wave which has sustained itself over time, and I always tell students that it is very important to be aware that there is a long-standing professional identity we need to manage: people may become very concerned with labels, and sometimes a label gets eradicated because of an economic shift. It's interesting and telling that information architecture was not eradicated: it tells me that the term remains meaningful and the profession is valid. There is a core set of qualities that will survive most economic upturns and downturns, and this is an identity worth retaining.

Q: The relationship between academia and practice is the primary reason behind the Roundtable, this book, and the book before it, "Reframing Information Architecture." All the same, as you were saying, it is not infrequent to find practitioners who don't seem to care too much about the educational or research parts: the link between the formalities of education and research in information architecture and the continuous survival and development of a healthy practice, and vice versa, are not immediately apparent to them. It isn't now and it wasn't back in the early 2000s, judging by what you and others were saying and writing at the time. So while on one hand you may well have been vindicated, because if anything information everywhere, system-wide "big information architecture," is what has been changing the world in the past twenty years, on the other we haven't yet solved that education/research/practice conundrum, have we?

No, we haven't. It is a conundrum because if you don't codify your knowledge and find a way of representing it, if you don't have an identity wrapped around some professional ways of being and doing, a discipline fritters away, blown about by events outside its control. I recognize that when we look at academic disciplines, they can seem stodgy, limited and slow moving. A group gets together, starts their own conference, formalizes regulations for membership, organizes research, curricula, structures its own scholarly output in a venue such as a journal and so on. These all take time. Professions move more nimbly, and in the early part of this century the mood in the information architecture camp was even that information architecture didn't have to do those things, that's not what we were about.

At the time I probably didn't appreciate enough how important professional structures were, in and out of academia. That's not to say that I think the only solution is an association with membership dues, that's a pretty dated model in some respects, but those structures first emerged and stayed around in many intellectual arenas because they help establish and consolidate an identity. I suspect there is real value here that we might have been too quick to dismiss in our embrace of the new. This is one part of it. The other part is that you cannot really establish much that's meaningful and sustainable unless you have a body of knowledge that you can claim, conceptually, theoretically, and practically, as yours. What makes you a biologist, what makes you a doctor, what makes you an information architect. This body of knowledge may not necessarily be exclusively yours: plenty of knowledge, theoretical and practical, is shared across fields. But we didn't succeed terribly well in codifying that kind of knowledge structure within information architecture, partly because we were magpies. We pulled bits from psychology, bits from design, bits from computer science, librarianship etc. and brought them to the nest, hoarded broadly but then reflected sparsely.

This cross-fertilization is a truism for quite a few of early twenty-first century disciplinary movements, but information architecture really needs to become more reflective. A set of core principles and understandings needs to be in place: not everybody has to agree on what is the canon, but a sense of collective engagement with the idea of a core has to be in place so that academics can take up what is normally their responsibility, building that up into a body of knowledge which forms the basis of education and drives new research. I suspect now that if we were asked to say who are the top ten information architecture academics in the United States or the world, we'd struggle. Moreover, I'm not sure many faculty yet identify themselves that way. And I think that's also part of the challenge.

Q: This fluidity you mention is most definitely a part of the troubles information architecture is facing in higher education and academia. In the practice, information architecture, user experience, or information systems can be lumped together or even be confused with one another to no great loss overall. Academia, or an academic career if you will, is built around precise Aristotelian boxes: that something is distinctly identified as information systems rather than computer science matters for publications, funding, curricula, and ultimately space. How are we solving this problem?

The set of concerns centering on information, even as a term, has been broadening and broadening in these past years. I helped create a School of Information at a time when university administrators were scratching their heads telling me one cannot call a school that, because everybody *does* information. I found that a mean-ingless criticism: we all communicate and educate as well, but we do have schools of communication and education, so why should information be any different? What we provide here is information architecture, designing and studying the impact of information spaces on people, anything from literacy and usability up to privacy and policy, there are information impacts resulting from this emerging information architecture.

My response would keep administrators quiet for a while, but then new people would come in and the questions would come up again. We're a great school but a small one. We still know that every time a new president or a new provost comes in, they'll scratch their head at some point and come over to visit us and ask "what is it you guys do over here?" I doubt they ever go to the School of Computer Science and say that. I doubt they ever go to the School of Liberal Arts and ask that. But they all come to the School of Information and raise that question. We still have some miles to go before we can convince everyone that information architecture forms a legitimate area of inquiry or scholarship. This concern will outlast me: I'll probably be retired before we even get close to resolving it. As we said, academia works slowly.

These concerns are identical to those you mention in terms of establishing cred-ibility and identity for an epistemological space for information architecture within academia, something I think is really important. I'm still wrestling with that, as an academic and as administrator, but it's clear higher education is still presenting students a skewed perspective in which we do not insist as much as we should on the structural soundness of human experiences. What sort of world are we creating where we get to shape all sorts of experiences for people without addressing what it means to be human or what's good for them, where we do not consider systemi-cally how designs can be manipulated and exploited for someone's advantage? These are clearly, to me, information architecture problems. Which also means that user-centeredness is probably a key to make the role of information architecture more concrete to those who take decisions.

I have a minor obsession with the term "user-centered design" and how it now means many different things to different people. We've never actually really codified it. It is particularly fascinating to think that it emerged in the 1950s from a coalition of interests, early human factors and industrial design, architecture and product design, as an attempt to systematize this idea of the human in the loop being considered part of the design challenge. It predates computing concerns by a decade or more. Architects in the 1960s, maybe using slightly different turns of phrase, were constantly arguing how to systematically address human issues in design. Those arguments actually parallel the arguments we have now, and I'm not sure that we've made a huge amount of progress in that time. We should think of user-centeredness as a core value for information architecture. I would advocate that strongly. Values, to me, are a key component of being a professional.

Q: One could argue that being human-centered is epistemologically inevitable for any type of design activity, after all we don't know what it means to be an octopus, but also that design has explicitly and repeatedly stated a concern for human-centeredness. I'm thinking of Leonardo's Vitruvian man or, more recently, of Le Corbusier's Modulor.

That's part of our identity but the key to being user-centered is not just to acknowledge we ultimately design for people, of course we do, but that we put the concerns and interests of people first. This is a meaningful difference. It doesn't matter whether the idea came from architecture or from industrial engineering. Human-centeredness is one of the core ideas which the community should find a way of articulating. If you design to extract a transaction from a customer, or just to reduce error in a control process, you are not really being fully user-centered, you are customer-centered, or system centered, and there is a real difference. I think there is a value choice we have to make, and obviously not everyone wants to make it. This book and these conversations, and the work you have done so far, are part of the effort. To me, it's fundamental, it's overdue, and it's exciting that we are doing it. It would be nice if we had all reached agreements on this much earlier on in the emergence of the field, but in a way we couldn't have. These are just naturally long drawn out processes. If you look at the history of any field you see similar patterns. Psychology had its own birth pangs, as did computer science.

Q: It sure feels like a slow process. You mentioned reflectivity. In his 2009 closing keynote at the ASIS&T Information Architecture Summit in Memphis, Jesse James Garrett asked the audience how we knew his work was good. He argued we didn't really know; we just took his word for it. A powerful rhetorical artifice, but also a strong argument in favor of critique if there ever was one. Critique, quality, what is good information architecture have all been topics of discussion at the Roundtable since it began in 2013: we've definitely made progress, but a complete frame has yet to emerge and what is there is primarily conceptual in nature. If we look at the history of design or architecture, the conversations around the artifacts, Breuer's Wassily chair or Starck's Juicy Salif, have traditionally been the focus. We don't center the conversation on what Zaha Adid said in an interview, but rather on the Eli & Edythe Broad Art Museum she designed in East Lansing. Is it good or bad? What are the artifacts of information architecture we should discuss? How should they be discussed? Or is this the wrong approach and we should figure out an entirely different narrative to support that reflective deepening of the conversation you mentioned?

Jesse's point is fascinating. What is "good?" You can point to an award-winning chair now and tomorrow, and it won't change. It's an artifact and it won an award. It might go out of fashion but its qualities as a chair can be recognized over time. We have a challenge. Information architectures shift so rapidly. When we show students the Amazon's homepage from 1994, they don't go "oh that's great." If you show anybody an award-winning design or something that we thought was quite brilliant in 2005, it might now look like it came straight out of the ark. This has even become its own thing, a staple of conference talks: someone shows you an old, tragic-looking web page and everyone laughs. What gets often drowned in that laughter is a more in-depth conversation on why that tragic web page may happen to have represented a major breakthrough at the time. Part of the issue is that I don't think we've even resolved whether we should point to a visible instance or to the process. The latter might be innovative forever, even if the output is not.

Q: That's probably part of the educational gap you mentioned before. We cannot seem to identify correctly what rules we should judge by and so we stop at the low resolution of an image or the odd formatting of a piece of text. It could also be said that, if we consider the epistemological level of the field in accordance with the M3,[1] the digital/physical information architectures we design today are transient, unfinished, and volatile. This is not that dissimilar to what service design theory has wrestled with, and we could glean much from how we've been critiquing expressive art forms such as film, music, or dance. If we can critique a ballet, in itself and in its relationship to the concept and history of "ballet," we should be able to critique a contemporary information architecture. And of course, any such language we devise will evolve over time: not many in 1908 would appreciate or even understand Tarantino's "Pulp Fiction" or Nolan and Joy's "Westworld." No diegetic gaze back then, no scrambling of the timeline. Still, there is a continuously developing body of knowledge we can refer to and that allows us to reflectively appreciate breakthroughs, as you said, or historically situate a specific movie. We similarly understand that early incunabula are not "good books" by today's standards, that the aptly named "boneshaker" might have been an ingenious device but not a "good bicycle," and that the modernist, Corbusian house, a machine to live in, has plenty shortcomings and we probably wouldn't want to live in one, but we understand the validity of what the attention to air, light, heating, and rational spaces meant at the time.

Yes, absolutely spot on. Movies are a fascinating example. A movie from the 1920s or the 1930s will certainly challenge us: the special effects were much more primitive; action scenes, pace, language were all very different; the sense of scale or depth, or even the light they were able to capture with a camera introduced what we would now see as limitations to what they could do. But we can still appreciate the power in the story and how innovative that might have been in shooting a certain scene, because the viewing of that film is an experience.

There is obviously a language or a way of framing the quality of experiences that recognizes the constraints of time which we operate under. We don't have that yet in information architecture, and I don't know that we can borrow that kind of rhetoric from the languages of critique for more experience-oriented fields. Rather than looking for the physical instantiation we should probably ask ourselves which are the elements that constitute a dynamic experience in space. Here the parallel with performance-like experiences could really help. The way we talk about this does hinder our ability to reflect back and get closer to answering Jesse's question about what makes a good information architecture. That's a fundamental question, even if we know that "good" is a loosey goosey term that will also be redefined.

Movies seem also to suggest, as maybe music also does, that some artifacts push beyond the boundaries of the fashion or culture of the time they're created and stand out in a way that we can think about their qualities, whatever they are, independently of that. Those with scientific backgrounds in the community would probably object that if we're going to resort to criticism as a source of insight, we're doomed, and that

---

[1]Lacerda, F., & Lima-Marques, M. (2014). Information architecture as a discipline—A methodological approach. In A. Resmini (Ed.), *Reframing information architecture*. Springer.

art criticism means eternal disagreement rather than shared, testable, standards. It is an understandable position, but an unfair one. Are the Beatles the most important musicians in the history of pop simply because they sold more than anybody else?[2] That's a pretty crass kind of measure as well. I don't have a solution, but aligning a language of critique and a language of science is going to prove a real challenge.

Q: For my part, I clearly consider all sorts of design activities, including information architecture, as arts and crafts endeavors. The built environment is my primary key, with its foundations in phenomenology, embodiment, spatiality, and placemaking. In this sense, the "architecture" part of information architecture is definitely not just a metaphor, it is an accurate description of what we do, even though we use more abstract raw materials than bricks and mortar, primarily information, to build spaces and create places. I'm at peace with the idea that criticism is what we need, with all of its shortcomings. As you said, it's not like knowing someone had a billion downloads on Spotify tells me anything for certain in terms of how important that song will be in the history of music. Both approaches have their place in a healthy conversation, as do different ways of assessing value and schools of thought, but we're most definitely missing the former while we have some of the latter thanks to human-computer interaction and related fields.

Acknowledging each other's existence would be a first step. We have ways to evaluate performances across disciplines which aren't science and that are not firmly rooted in peer evaluation: the humanities, the arts, we know how to gauge contributions in those spaces which are critique based. If I have to reflect and try to answer Jesse's question, how would I know that he has done good information architecture work? I've heard him talk. I've read some of his work. I've listened to him argue and I formed my evaluation that way. None of that is based on any external acknowledgment such as awards, nor can I point to design evidence. That's much more elusive. That's not necessarily wrong as you say, but the question he raised speaks to the uneasiness that exists in the community about establishing our credentials and giving ourselves equal authority to other disciplines. As an academic, one way to get there is by consolidating our epistemology, what we claim about the world and the role of information architecture in it. We'll argue about these things: every field does, but it's part of maturing and a process that perhaps we might want to pursue a little more actively.

Q: What are the core ideas you consider important to consolidate information architecture as its own field? What are we missing?

Well, since I'm a psychologist I would say that there are some fundamental basics about the way humans grasp the world that we have to build on.

I do believe as you do that we're part craft, design, but I also think we're part science, and I actually think those two ways of problem solving are not terribly far apart, as I try to teach students. If you're designing, at some point you'll take a leap,

---

[2] Even more poignantly, if we consider album sales, Garth Brooks is the second best-selling artist of all time. Bob Dylan is 45th, two positions behind the Backstreet Boys. Source: Clark, T. (2020). The 50 best-selling music artists of all time. Business Insider. https://www.businessinsider.com/best-selling-music-artists-of-all-time-2016-9.

maybe from a set of requirements or maybe from a very fuzzy concept, and think of a solution. What is that leap? How do you make that jump? I sure can't teach you how to "create." This is the step you yourself take based on your entire life experience. Science, psychology can provide you with guidelines for what you should rule in or rule out in making the leap. If you design against the principles of visual closure or the limitations of short-term memory, your solution is likely to be less useful, less acceptable, or less desirable. These principles aren't going to serve you for every possible solution in every possible situation, but they help acquiring the necessary experience, the craft, that over time allows one to distinguish between good and bad information architecture. This is not to say that we should suddenly become an annex of psychology, but there are rules and principles of how people respond to information that we should know about.

Should we worry about the design of organization-level structures? I think we should. I consider that a fundamental area of application for information architecture: how do contexts of use evolve and what are the dynamics of a group adopting, using, and sharing these information spaces. Principles of sociology and organizational theory can be brought into facilitate that necessary leap from requirements to solutions.

What belongs in here is not just an understanding of user-centered design, it is a methodological understanding of design processes in general, of how far structured methods can take you, and of the layered nature of information architecture. Designers bring to the process a form of codified knowledge about design which is different from the one I bring as a social scientist. Additional disciplinary contributions would add more perspectives. An information architecture curriculum would need to codify these different languages and approaches into a coherent vision. What I most surely wouldn't do is spend a lot of time arguing about what goes in and what moves out. It's not as if we can aspire to having an absolutely clear-cut curricular identity for information architecture that would work everywhere. We'll always have disagreements, but maybe it wouldn't be as hard as it might have been twenty years ago.

Q: If it might not be as hard, what's standing in our way then?

If we talk about the academy, then people, administrators. But they're a barrier because the real issue, the real challenge is attracting into a field sufficient people from outside who can recognize what we do. One of the strengths or probably the greatest strength of our school, and any school like ours for sure, even though I can only speak to ours in particular because it was designed this way, is that we might have twenty faculty and thirteen or fourteen different PhDs: we have sociologists, historians, philosophers, designers, computer scientists. People ask "how did that happen?" and I say "by design," it was intentional. For prospective candidates, it's not their background or their disciplinary box that matters: it's the questions they ask and how they go about answering them.

Within an academic environment, this has its challenges. We still have endless discussions with junior faculty who say they come from a certain tradition, publish only in certain journals, and who are worried about how their work will be evaluated by those who might have different touchpoints. We tell them they'll be evaluated on their own strengths, that they shouldn't worry about trying to fit into what they imagine are the top two or three journals in the field, but this is not common practice nor an established way of looking at one's career in academia. It also collides with other academic fields where senior faculty can typically point junior faculty to the top five journals and tell them go on, publish there and you'll get tenure. Our approach is more along the lines of "just do some interesting work and share it with the world: we're going to recognize you for that, do it and let's worry about how to explain it in five years." It still doesn't eliminate the stress that derives from having to bravely chase one's goals for five years with the end line looming close enough to have one asking constantly "am I making progress or am I going to be out of a job?". Infrastructure and leadership are vital here, they exist to create a better space, and while we've done, I believe, a pretty good job at Texas, it's inevitably slow work. I've now spent fifteen or sixteen years of my life helping create this kind of environment. It's also fifteen years where the legitimate question could be "where were you in the information architecture community?" and the answer is I was on the underside, building infrastructure. It's still, I believe, extremely important work for the reasons I mentioned, but not that obvious in the eyes of the field at large.

Q: I couldn't agree more. And we covered some of what you have been doing and some of what has happened, so maybe this interview will help answer that question, if it ever comes up. I have one final curiosity: suppose you could peer into a magical crystal ball. What does the future of information architecture look like?

It's pure blue skying, but I would say the potential and possibilities are huge. "Big information architecture" is a very meaningful label for a set of concerns, of methods, of practices, and of beliefs that wrap around a set of values that matter enormously for today's world. I hope enough people are beginning to understand that the creation of the information infrastructure that everybody on the planet will exist in very shortly happens to be a pivotal moment for our existence and it's vital that we get it right. It is a precious human space that will carry all sorts of implications for how we live, and that must be designed for correctly. As we get a chance to shape it, we should address fundamental issues of equality and fairness. Information and its architecture should augment us in a way that enhances our better tendencies rather than our negative ones. That would imply an even bigger information architecture, shifting even more away from doing the building to actually concerning itself with ethical and perhaps even moral issues. That's something that we may have to wrestle with going forward.

In a more practical sense, the world is realizing now that information architecture is fundamental to existence on this planet. The world at large may not use our terms, they may not understand that information architecture exists as we see it, but they recognize the changes. In forty years, there's not going to be anybody left on this planet who remembers a time when there wasn't a pervasive information architecture of that kind. Not often can you point to moments like this in human history: we might end up being forgotten by history, some weird anomaly that a postgraduate student will unearth two hundred years in the future and remark: "You know, two hundred years ago there were these people talking about information architecture like it needed to be understood and shaped." By then, information architectures are going to be such an integral part of everyday life that they're taken for granted, and people then will have a hard time envisioning that there was a time people were wrestling with this and doubting information architecture was "a thing" or if it was "big" or "little."

We're entering that phase now and the opportunity for us as a discipline is there. Are we still going to argue amongst ourselves? Yes. Will we find out in ten years that young information architects still worry about whether their identity or the professional role is recognized and understood? I suspect as much. But can we now take a leadership role in helping to alleviate some of that? I think we should and, judging by this conversation, we are. Just remember we're magpies.

Andrea Resmini is associate professor of experience design and information architecture in the Department of Intelligent Systems and Digital Design at Halmstad University and the Director of Innovation and Research at the Center for Co-production, Jönköping Academy for Improvement of Health and Welfare at the School of Health and Welfare, Jönköping University. An architect turned information architect, Andrea is a two-time past president of the Information Architecture Institute, a founding member of Architecta, the Italian Society for Information Architecture, the Editor-in-chief of the Journal of Information Architecture, and the author of *Pervasive Information Architecture* (2011) and *Reframing Information Architecture* (2014).

The Memphis Plenary

Jesse James Garrett

I recognize that being chosen to deliver the closing plenary is an honor, and I do not intend to repay that kindness by giving you a product demo.

I will not be participating in five-minute madness this year. You may consider this my 45-min madness.

This is a different kind of talk for me. First of all, I have no slides! I kind of feel like I'm working without a net here. I can't throw in the occasional visual pun to keep you guys paying attention. Secondly, I have no idea how long this talk is. I just finished it just before this began, so basically when I'm out of things to say, I'll stop talking. Hopefully that will be sooner than you expected, and not later. Third, I've decided not to take questions at the end of this talk. My preference would be that if you have questions, don't pose them to me. Pose them to each other. Publicly, if you can.

So if I run short, we'll just go straight into five-minute madness and then we'll all get to the bar that little bit sooner.

Okay, now: first-timers, please stand up.

[audience applauds]

I don't think we do enough to recognize the importance of new voices in this community, and at this event. Those of you who were here last year may recall my comments from five-minute madness last year, where it seemed like maybe I was a little bit too hard on the first-timers for not being more active participants. What I was really trying to do was scold the old-timers for not doing more to make the

Jesse James Garrett's closing plenary address, delivered March 22 2009 at the 10th ASIS&T Information Architecture Summit 2009 in Memphis, Tennessee.

Recordings of the plenary are available at http://boxesandarrows.com/files/banda/ia-summit-09-plenary/Jesse_James_Garrett.m4a (audio) and at: http://theuxworkshop.tv/10th-annual-ia-summit-plenary-speech-jesse-james-garrett/ (video).

J. J. Garrett (✉)
Oakland, CA, USA
e-mail: jjg@jjg.net

© The Author(s), under exclusive license to Springer Nature Switzerland AG 2021
A. Resmini et al. (eds.), *Advances in Information Architecture*,
Human–Computer Interaction Series, https://doi.org/10.1007/978-3-030-63205-2_7

first-timers feel welcome, and so I hope that those of you who are first-timers this year have been made to feel welcome by this community.

Now, before you sit down, I want to apologize to all of you, because there's a great big chunk of this talk that is not going to mean very much to you—because I'm a ten-timer and I've got some things to say to my fellow ten-timers. So, I'll just get that out of the way. I hope you've enjoyed the rest of the conference—and now you can sit down.

So yeah, in case you guys haven't heard, this is the tenth IA Summit. I don't know if word got around about that. This is my tenth IA Summit. Anyone who was at that first Summit will recount for you the strange energy in that room: academics and practitioners eyeing each other warily, skeptical of what the other had to contribute. There was turbulence. (Hi Peter!) But it was productive turbulence.

I can't say I've seen much turbulence at these events since then. Which ought to make all of us nervous, because the opposite of turbulence is stagnation.

In his opening keynote, Michael Wesch quoted Marshall McLuhan: "We march backward into the future." When I saw this quote, it reminded me of the old quip that generals are always fighting the last war—which is why I think we've been stagnating. What war is the field of information architecture fighting?

The war we still seem to be fighting is the war against information architecture itself as a valid concept, as a meaningful part of design practices.

Almost everything you see about the IA community and IA practices—the mailing lists, the conferences, the professional organizations, the process models, the best practice patterns—they're all optimized to answer two questions: Is this stuff for real? And is it valuable? And the answer to both questions is always, invariably, an emphatic "yes."

IA is real. And IA is good. And that's what we all agree on: some IA is better than no IA. But is there such a thing as "bad IA"? I mean, is it possible for an information architecture professional to do a thorough, responsible job, following all the agreed-upon best practices, and still come up with a bad solution?

I don't think anybody knows the answer to this question. Because we're still fighting the last war. We're still trying to defend the answer to that question: is IA good? Is IA valuable?

Now, if you are about my age (and most of you seem to be, which I'll come back to in a minute), your grandparents grew up in the Depression. And if your grandparents are like mine, this was an experience that shaped their behavior for the rest of their lives. They save everything: any little bit of leftover food, or a loose scrap of fabric, or a button or a screw. They save everything, because the notion of scarcity was deeply imprinted on them when they were young and became such a fundamental part of their worldview that decades later they're still hoarding all this stuff even though the Depression's been over... well, it took a break anyway.

Here are some of the most common terms from past IA Summit programs: taxonomy, thesaurus, controlled vocabulary, metadata, faceted classification, navigation, content management—and then there was that one year with all the talks about tagging. Like my grandparents, we cling to these things because they are what saved us. They are the tools by which we proved that yes, IA is real, and it is valuable. But that war is over. We won. And now it's time to move on, because those comfortable, familiar things represent only part of what information architecture can be.

So it's time to leave the nest. Thank you, Lou and Peter. Thank you, library science. For getting us off to a great start. For giving us the tools and knowledge to win a place for IA in the world. There will still be a place for library science in IA, but it's only a part of our larger destiny.

Thank you to ASIST. Thank you to Dick Hill, and Vanessa and Jan and Carlene. This field would not be where it is without your efforts at these events, year after year. But I'm curious—show of hands: who here has ever been to any ASIST event other than an IA summit? [audience raises hands] Who here is an ASIST member? [audience raises hands] A smattering at best. ASIST has been sort of a benevolent host organism for the incubation of IA, but the relationship between ASIST and IA beyond IA Summit hasn't really gone anywhere.

Okay, I'm debating how to do this… Name the five best-known information architects. [audience calls out various names] Now: name a work of information architecture created by one of these people. [silence] Is that a sign of a mature profession?

The names you know are notable for what they say about their work, not for the work itself. They're not known for the quality of their work (and I'm including myself in this category).

Moreover, do you know good IA when you see it? And can different people have different ideas about the qualities of a good solution or a bad one, based on their philosophical approach to their work?

One thing I'm really surprised we don't have yet, that I had expected to see long before now, is the emergence of schools of thought about information architecture.

Will there ever be a controversial work of information architecture? Something we argue about the merits of? A work that has admirers and detractors alike?

We have lots of ways of talking about our processes. In fact, if you look back at these ten years of the IA Summit, the talks are almost all about process. And to the extent that we've had controversy, it's been over questions of process: Is documentation necessary? If so, how much? Which deliverables are the right ones? Personas, absolutely essential, or big waste of time?

What we don't have are ways of talking about the product of our work. We don't have a language of critique. Until we have ways to describe the qualities of an information architecture, we won't be able to tell good IA from bad IA. All we'll ever be able to do is judge processes.

Another thing that you'll notice from looking back over ten years of the Summit is that talks are ephemeral. I was at all those summits, and I remember maybe a tenth of what I saw—and I saw less than half of what was on the program. I'm known for being down on academia a lot of the time, but they do have one thing right: you have to publish in order to create a body of knowledge.

I think I'm pretty good at what I do. But you guys are going to have to take my word for it. Because you don't know my work. You only know what I say about my work.

I think I'm pretty good at what I do. I hope I'm getting better. I hope that my best work is still ahead of me. But I'm not sure. And I'm not sure how I would know. I've been coming to the Summit for ten years, and I've been doing this work, in some form or another, for close to 15. And as I've watched my professional peers settle down, get married, start families, become managers, I've found myself wondering about creative peaks.

In the field of mathematics, they say that if you haven't made a significant contribution by the age of 30, you never will. It's a young person's game. 33 is young to be publishing your first novel, but it's old to be recording your first album.

When do information architects hit their creative peaks? Let's assume that I'm at about the median age for this group. Just assume most of you are my age, and there are about as many older than me as younger than me.

Now, if I'm at about the median age for an information architect now, when will that change? Will the median age keep going up, as this group of people ages? Presumably, at some point I'll be one of the oldest guys in the room.

Alternately, what if information architecture is something that you don't really get good at until you've been doing it for 20 years? Then we really have something to look forward to, don't we?

Here's another thing I thought we'd be hearing more about by the time of the tenth IA Summit:

You guys heard of this thing called neuromarketing? Man, this stuff is cool. They take people, they hook them up to MRIs—you know, brainwave scanners—and then they show them TV commercials. And they look at what parts of their brains light up when they watch these TV commercials. Then they do a little bit of A/B testing, and they can figure out how to craft a TV commercial that will elicit things like a feeling of safety. Or trust. Or desire.

So yeah, my first reaction when I saw this stuff was: Wow, I gotta get my hands on some of that! We've only just scratched the surface of what we can do with eyetracking and the marketers have already moved on to braintracking! But then my second reaction was: Wait a minute. What are we talking about here? A process designed to elicit specific patterns of neural activity in users? Back in the 50s, they called that "mind control"!

Now in a lot of ways, we're already in the mind control business. Information architecture and interaction design both seek to reward and reinforce certain patterns of thought and behavior. (Just ask anybody who's tried to wrestle any 37 signals app into functioning the way they want to work, instead of the way Jason Fried thinks they ought to be working.)

So there's always been an ethical dimension to our work. But who's talking about this stuff? Who's taking it seriously?

I don't hear anybody talking about these things. Instead, what everybody wants to talk about is power, authority, respect. "Where's our seat at the table?" Well, you know, there are people who make the decisions you want to be making. They're called product managers. You want that authority? Go get that job. Don't ask them to give that authority to you.

"When are we going to get the respect we deserve?" I'll tell you how it's going to happen. Somebody in this room, right now, at some point in the future is going to be the CEO of some company other than a design firm. They'll develop all of those right political and managerial skills to rise to that level of power. And they will institute a culture in their organization that respects user experience. And then they're just going to start kicking their competitors' asses. And then gradually it will happen in industry after industry after industry. That's how it will happen. But it will take time.

I had the thought at one of these summits a few years ago that we would know we had really arrived as a profession when there were people who wanted to sell us stuff. Because, you see, I grew up in the United States, where you don't exist unless you are a target market.

And here at this event this year we have companies like TechSmith and Axure and Access Innovations and Optimal Workshop. And we thank them for their support. But where's Microsoft? Where's Adobe? Where's Omni?

We aren't a target market for any but the smallest companies. The big ones still don't understand who we are. We're still a small community, struggling to define itself.

In 2002, in the wake of the last bubble burst, I wrote an essay called "ia/recon".[1] In that essay, I tried to chart what I saw as a way forward for the field out of the endless debate over definitions. In the essay, I drew a distinction between the discipline of information architecture and the role of the information architect, and I argued that one need not be defined by the other.

Seven years later, I can see that I was wrong. The discipline of information architecture and the role of the information architect will always be defined in conjunction with one another. As long as you have information architects, what they do will always be information architecture. Seems pretty obvious, right? Only took me seven years to figure out.

But that's okay, because what is clear to me now is that there is no such thing as an information architect.

Information architecture does not exist as a profession. As an area of interest and inquiry? Sure. As your favorite part of your job? Absolutely. But it's not a profession.

Now, you IxDA folks should hold off for a moment before Twittering your victory speeches—because there's no such thing as an interaction designer either. Not as a profession. Anyone who claims to specialize in one or the other is a fool or a liar. The fools are fooling themselves into thinking that one aspect of their work is somehow paramount. And the liars seek to align themselves with a tribe that will convey upon them status and power.

There are no information architects. There are no interaction designers. There are only, and only ever have been, user experience designers.

I'd like to talk about each of these three words, in reverse order, starting with "design." Now, this is a word that I have personally had a long and difficult history with. I didn't like this word being applied to our work for many years. I thought it placed us in a tradition—graphic design, industrial design, interface design—where

---

[1]Garrett, J. J. (2002). ia/recon. http://jjg.net/ia/recon/.

our work did not belong. I also saw the dogmatism endemic to design education as poisonous and destructive to a field as young as ours. I still find the tendency of "designers" to view all human creative endeavor through the narrow lens of their own training and experience to be contemptible and appallingly short-sighted.

But I'm ready to give up fighting against this word, if only because it's easily understood by those outside our field. And anything that enables us to be more easily understood is something we desperately need.

Now, let's talk about that word "experience." A lot of people have trouble with this word, especially paired with the word "design." "You can't call it experience design!" they say. "How can you possibly control someone else's experience?" they demand.

Well, wait a minute—who said anything about control? Treating design as synonymous with control, and the designer as the all-powerful controller, says something more about the way these designers think of themselves and their relationship to their work than it does about the notion of experience design.

"Experience is too ephemeral," they say, "too insubstantial to be designed." You mean insubstantial the way music is insubstantial? Or a dance routine? Or a football play? Yet all of these things are designed.

The entire hypothesis of experience design (and it is a hypothesis at this point) is that the ephemeral and insubstantial can be designed. And that there is a kind of design that can be practiced independent of medium and across media.

Now, this part makes a lot of people uncomfortable because they're committed to the design tradition of a particular medium. So they dismiss experience design as simply best practices. "What you call experience design," they say, "is really nothing more than good industrial design." Or good graphic design. Or good interface design.

This "mediumism" resists the idea that design can be practiced in a medium-independent or cross-media way. Because that implies that there may be something these mediumist design traditions have been missing all along.

If our work simply recapitulates what has been best practice in all these fields all along, why are the experiences they deliver so astonishingly bad? And let's face it, they are really bad.

One big reason for it has to do with this last word, one which I think has been unfairly maligned: the word "user." You guys know the joke, right? There are only two industries in the world that refer to their customers as users. One is the technology business and the other is drug dealers. Ha ha, get it? Our work is just as dehumanizing as selling people deadly, addictive chemicals that will destroy their lives and eventually kill them! Get it? It's funny because it's true.

No, it's not. I'm here to reclaim "user." Because "user" connotes use, and use matters! We don't make things for those most passive of entities, consumers. We don't even make things for audiences, which at least connotes some level of appreciation. The things we make get used! They become a part of people's lives! That's important work. It touches people in ways most of them could never even identify. But it's real.

Okay, time for another show of hands: who here has "information architect" or "information architecture" in your title, on your business card? Raise your hand. [audience raises hands] Almost as many as we had ASIST members.

Okay, now let me see those hands again. Keep your hand up if there is also someone in your organization with "interaction design" or "interaction designer" in the title.

[hands go down]

Almost every hand went down. I see one hand, two hands. Three, four… five.

This is what the interaction design community recognizes—and what the leadership of the IxDA[2] recognizes in particular—that the IA community does not.

In the marketplace, this is a zero-sum game. Every job req created for an "interaction designer" is one less job req for an "information architect" and vice versa. And the more "interaction designers" there are, the more status and authority and influence and power accrues to the IxDA and its leadership.

They get this, and you can see it play out in everything they do, including refusing offers of support and cooperation from groups they see as competitors, and throwing temper tantrums about how other groups schedule their conferences. Meanwhile, the IAs are so busy declaring peace that they don't even realize that they've already lost the war.

This territorialism cannot go on, and I hope the IxDA leadership sees an opportunity here for positive change. These organizations should be sponsoring each other's events, reaching out to each other's membership, working together to raise the tide for everyone.

There is no us and them. We are not information architects. We are not interaction designers. We are user experience designers. This is the identity we must embrace. Any other will only hold back the progress of the field by marginalizing an important dimension of our work and misleading those outside our field about what is most important and valuable about what we do. Because it's not information, and it's not interaction.

We're in the experience business. User experience. We create things that people use.

To use something is to engage with it. And engagement is what it's all about.

Our work exists to be engaged with. In some sense, if no one engages with our work it doesn't exist.

It reminds me of an artist named J. S. G. Boggs. He hand-draws these meticulously detailed near-replicas of U.S. currency. It's gotten him in trouble with the Secret Service a couple of times. They're near-replicas—they're not exact, they're obviously fake. They're fascinating and they're delightful, in and of themselves, as objects.

But here's the catch: For Boggs, the work isn't complete until he gets someone to accept the object as currency. The transaction is the artwork, not the object that changes hands. As he sees it, his work is not about creating things that look like currency it's about using art as currency. It's the use—the human engagement—that matters.

Designing with human experience as an explicit outcome and human engagement as an explicit goal is different from the kinds of design that have gone before. It can be practiced in any medium, and across media.

---

[2]The Interaction Design Association. http://ixda.org/.

Show of hands: Who here is involved in creating digital experiences? [audience raises hands] Okay, hands down. Now: who's involved in creating non-digital experiences? [audience raises hands] More hands than I thought.

Now, do we really believe that this is the boundary of our profession? And if we don't, why are there so many talks about websites at conferences like this one?

Don't get me wrong, I love the web. I hope to be working with the web in 10 years, in 20 years. But the web is just a canvas. Or perhaps a better metaphor is clay—raw material that we shape into experiences for people.

But there are lots of materials—media—we can use to shape experiences. Saying user experience design is about digital media is rather like saying that sculpture is about the properties of clay.

That's not to say that an individual sculptor can't dedicate themselves to really mastering clay. They can, and they do—just like many of you will always be really great at creating user experiences for the web.

But that does not define the boundary of user experience design. Where it really gets interesting is when you start looking at experiences that involve multiple media, multiple channels. Because there's a whole lot more to orchestrating a multi-channel experience than simply making sure that the carpet matches the drapes.

We've always said we were in the multimedia business. Let's put some weight behind that. Expanding our horizons in this way does not dilute our influence. It strengthens it.

So if we're all user experience designers, and there are no more information architects, but there is still such a thing as information architecture, what does it look like?

Well, let's take a closer look at engagement, and think about the ways we can engage people. What are the varieties of human engagement?

We can engage people's senses. We can stimulate them through visuals, through sound, through touch and smell and taste. This is the domain of the traditional creative arts: painting, music, fashion, cooking.

We can engage their minds, get them thinking, reasoning, analyzing, synthesizing. This is where fields like scholarship and rhetoric have something to teach us.

We can engage their hearts, provoke them in feelings of joy and sadness and wonder and rage. (I've seen a lot of rage.) The folks who know about this stuff are the storytellers, the filmmakers, and yes, even the marketers.

And we can engage their bodies. We can compel them to act. This is the closest to what we've traditionally done studying and trying to influence human behavior.

And that's really about it. Or at least, that's all that I've been able to think of: Perception, engaging the senses. Cognition, engaging the mind. Emotion, engaging the heart. And action, engaging the body.

Mapping out the interrelationships between these turns out to be a surprisingly deep problem. Every part influences every other part in unexpected ways. In particular, thinking and feeling are so tangled up together that we practically need a new word for it: "thinkfeel."

There are a few other factors, sort of orthogonal to these, that influence experience:

There are our capabilities: the properties of our bodies, the acuity of our senses, the sharpness and flexibility of our minds, the size of our hearts. Our capabilities determine what we can do.

Then there are our constraints, which define what we can't do. The limits on our abilities, whether permanent—someone who's having a hard time reading because they have dyslexia—or temporary—someone who's having a hard time reading because they've had five bourbons.

Finally, we have context. And I have to admit that I'm cheating a bit on this one because I'm packing a lot of different factors up into this one category. There's the context of the moment: babies crying, dogs barking, phones ringing. (Calgon, take me away!) Then there's personal context: the history, associations, beliefs, personality traits of that individual. And there's the broad context: social, cultural, economic, technological.

But these three—capabilities, constraints, and context—are really just cofactors, shaping and influencing experience in those big four categories: perception, cognition, emotion, and action.

Our role, as user experience designers, is to synthesize and orchestrate elements in all of these areas to create a holistic, cohesive, engaging experience.

So how do we create user experiences that engage across all of these areas? Where can we look to for expertise? Where's the insight? Where are the areas for further inquiry?

Perception is already pretty well covered. We've got visual designers and, sometimes, animators. In some cases, we've got sound designers. We've got industrial designers, working on the tactile aspects of the products we create.

Action, again, is pretty much what we were doing already. I defined action as engagement of the body, which may sound strange to many of you when I say that we've really been doing this all along. But if you think about our work, when we talk about behavior, we are always talking about some physical manifestation of a user's intention—even when that manifestation is as small as a click. (And the interaction designers claim to own behavior anyway so I say let them have it.)

Because the real action is in these last two areas, cognition and emotion. This, to my mind, is the manifest destiny for information architecture. We may not have fully recognized it before because the phrase "information architecture" puts the emphasis on the wrong thing.

It's never been about information. It's always been about people: how they relate to that information, how that information makes them think, how it makes them feel, and how the structure of that information influences both things. This is huge, unexplored territory.

We must acknowledge that as user experience designers we have a broader place in the world than simply delivering value to businesses. We must embrace our role as a cultural force.

Here's Michael Wesch quoting Marshall McLuhan again: "We shape our tools, and then our tools shape us." Think about that for a second. "We shape our tools, and then our tools shape us." When McLuhan said "we," and when he said "us," he was talking about the entire human race. But not everybody's a shaper, right? The shapers are the people in this room, the people in this field. We shape those tools and then, the experiences that those tools create shape humanity itself. Think about the responsibility that entails.

I believe that when we embrace that role as a cultural force, and we embrace that responsibility, this work—user experience design—will take its place among the most fundamental and important human crafts, alongside engineering and architecture and all kinds of creative expression and creative problem-solving disciplines.

At last year's five-minute madness, I said that the experts who give talks at events like this one were making it up as they went along. But, I said, that's okay, because we all are.

I take that back. We aren't making it up as we go along. This is not a process of invention. This is a process of discovery.

What we are uncovering about people, about tools and their use, about experiences—it's always been there. We just didn't know how to see it.

This discovery phase is far from over. Ten years isn't nearly enough time. There's more that we can't see than is apparent to us right now.

For my part, and for you as well, I hope there's always more for us to discover together.

Thank you all very much.

Jesse James Garrett is a design leadership coach whose career in human-centered design includes co-founding the first UX consultancy, Adaptive Path, and writing the foundational book *The Elements of User Experience*, whose iconic five-plane model has become a staple of the field. His work has been published in more than a dozen languages and he is a frequent keynote speaker on making designers and organizations more human-centered in their work.

Toward a New Information Architecture: The Rise and Fall and Rise of a Necessary Discipline

Christina Wodtke

> *There is a tsunami of data that is crashing onto the beaches of the civilized world. This is a tidal wave of unrelated, growing data formed in bits and bytes, coming in an unorganized, uncontrolled, incoherent cacophony of foam. None of it is easily related, none of it comes with any organization methodology....*
>
> *R. S. Wurman (1996).*

Act One: The Birth of a Practice

When the internet was first becoming a thing, it was very different than it is now. It wasn't very interactive. To be honest, it barely had any interface design either. The great bulk of websites were just walls of text arranged into a semblance of order by tables with the borders turned off. Interactivity was clicking "bookmark," "set as homepage" or submitting a "contact us" form. But what the Internet did have was information. Everybody put everything they had up on the web, from help pages to marketing brochures.

It was a mess, and someone had to make it all make sense. So, while most software interaction designers declined to play with the very limited set of tinker toys the internet offered, others stepped up to fight the "tidal wave of data" Wurman was describing. And they became the first Information Architects (IAs).

These early IAs were not trained in web design; nobody was. They came from a variety of backgrounds, from library science (Lou Rosenfeld and Peter Morville) to journalism (Jesse James Garrett) to painting (me), graphic design (Erin Malone), cognitive psychology (Andrea Gallagher), anthropology (Peter Merholz), landscape

Originally published on Medium on February 16, 2014 (https://medium.com/goodux-badux/tow ards-a-new-information-architecture-f38b5cc904c0). *This is a revised version.*

C. Wodtke (✉)
Stanford University, Stanford, CA, USA

© The Author(s), under exclusive license to Springer Nature Switzerland AG 2021
A. Resmini et al. (eds.), *Advances in Information Architecture*,
Human–Computer Interaction Series, https://doi.org/10.1007/978-3-030-63205-2_8

Welcome to Amazon.com Books!

One million titles, consistently low prices.

(If you explore just one thing, make it our personal notification service. We think it's very cool!)

SPOTLIGHT! — AUGUST 16TH
  These are the books we love, offered at Amazon.com low prices. The spotlight moves EVERY
  day so please come often.

ONE MILLION TITLES
  Search Amazon.com's million title catalog by author, subject, title, keyword, and more... Or take
  a look at the books we recommend in over 20 categories... Check out our customer reviews and
  the award winners from the Hugo and Nebula to the Pulitzer and Nobel... and bestsellers are
  30% off the publishers list...

EYES & EDITORS, A PERSONAL NOTIFICATION SERVICE
  Like to know when that book you want comes out in paperback or when your favorite author
  releases a new title? Eyes, our tireless, automated search agent, will send you mail. Meanwhile,
  our human editors are busy previewing galleys and reading advance reviews. They can let you
  know when especially wonderful works are published in particular genres or subject areas. Come
  in, meet Eyes, and have it all explained.

YOUR ACCOUNT
  Check the status of your orders or change the email address and password you have on file with
  us. Please note that you **do not** need an account to use the store. The first time you place an
  order, you will be given the opportunity to create an account.

Fig. 1 Amazon's 1994 original homepage and its wall of links. *Source* Asbury & Asbury (2011)

architecture, theater, and more. We were entrepreneurs more than anything else, all excited by this brave new world. We dove in and cobbled together a way to make sure all this information could be found and understood (Fig. 1).

It sounds like we all worked together, doesn't it? Far from it. Information architecture (IA) was invented in geographic silos with little sharing of knowledge until the first Information Architecture Summit in 2000. Which means it had already formed factions.

The wisdom of the library science's retrieval and organization approach was captured by Lou Rosenfeld and Peter Morville in their wildly popular "Information Architecture for the World Wide Web" book (1998). It was an insightful and well written book and it was published under the O'Reilly seal of approval. That meant wide adoption. It provided a model of how to organize complex information-rich sites used from Ann Arbor (where Argus, the first consulting firm specializing in IA, plied its trade) to the East Coast.

But while Lou and Peter were using the library arts at Argus to bring order and sense to the volumes of printed materials being transferred to the net, California was riding a two-headed boom-beast. You all know about the dotcom boom. But do you recall there was also a consultancy boom? All the traditional companies rushed to the internet to try to avoid being disrupted. None of them really understood technology, so they looked for turnkey solutions. The new consultancies needed an internet process to sell! So, they quickly rolled out an information architecture model loosely based on Richard Saul Wurman's book "Information Architects" (1996). It resembled what we now call user experience design (UXD) and focused on understanding and clarity over retrieval and navigation. Harder concepts for a new field, but critical ones.

This information architecture turned out pretty darn well for the Sapients and Viants and MarchFirsts and Methods, at least until the dotcom crash took them down and with it went the memory of what they had created. While most folks practicing information architecture today remember Argus, few recall the bold innovation of Clement Mok's Studio Archetype, where Peter Merholz and many other early West Coast information architects were minted.

The Californian view of information architect as leader/conductor/architect was supported by the other practitioners featured in Wurman's "Information Architects": Lynne Styles, Paul Kahn, Maria Guidice, and Nathan Shedroff. Giudice and Shedroff had both worked for Wurman at the Understanding Company. They trained a generation of information architects who believed it was their job to lead the design team to bridge business and user needs (Fig. 2).

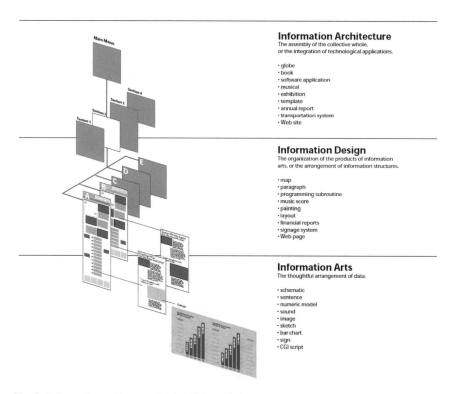

Fig. 2 Information architecture (Mok 1996, p. 99)

So, when the two tribes met, the terms "Big IA" and "Little IA" were coined to describe the split between these two definitions of information architecture (Morville 2000). Little IA was concerned with metadata, taxonomies, and controlled vocabularies. Library stuff! Big IA was concerned with the entirety of the effort, that it was coherent and complete. Architecture-Wurman stuff!

And though we were a house divided, we were a strong house.

> Now for the good news: There is a dune on the beach. There is a breakwater in the ocean that is clearly emerging in these last fleeting moments of the twentieth century. The breakwater is indeed breaking up the tsunami of data and focusing it in a more organized way to answer our questions and concerns. There is a new breed of graphic designers, exhibition designers, illustrators, and photographers, whose passion it is to make the complex clear.
>
> R. S. Wurman, Information Architects.

The information architects thought everything would be okay. We joked about "defining the damn thing" to the point of turning into its own acronym, DTDT. We founded the Information Architecture Institute to support the growth of the field and made sure it embraced the big and small nature of IA:

- The structural design of shared information environments;
- The art and science of organizing and labeling web sites, intranets, online communities and software to support usability and findability;
- An emerging community of practice focused on bringing principles of design and architecture to the digital landscape.

But this is not about giving a history lesson. This is Chekov's gun. Information architecture had a potentially fatal tension. And it will go off in the second act.

Act Two: The Smallification of Information Architecture

Peter Morville's "Big Architect, Little Architect" article made room for both approaches to information architecture, but also acknowledged an interesting new diagram that would eventually change how information architecture was perceived (Fig. 3).

Jesse James Garrett's "Elements of User Experience" diagram gave each individual design discipline a spot in the user experience firmament. And look how crisp the boundaries are! What a thick gray wall separates us information architects from our brother interaction design!

This diagram was followed by his bestselling book by the same name (2002): the book not only introduced information architecture to a new generation, but also defined it for them. If you started your career with that book, then information architecture is primarily concerned with organizing content and creating navigation. It's an extremely good book, and Garrett (an information architect himself) does not do a disservice to information architecture's core nature. In fact, many folks would argue he brings a much-needed clarity to the definition of the role. But there were

The Elements of User Experience

Jesse James Garrett
jjg@jjg.net
30 March 2000

A basic duality: The Web was originally conceived as a hypertextual information space; but the development of increasingly sophisticated front- and back-end technologies has fostered its use as a remote software interface. This dual nature has led to much confusion, as user experience practitioners have attempted to adapt their terminology to cases beyond the scope of its original application. The goal of this document is to define some of these terms within their appropriate contexts, and to clarify the underlying relationships among these various elements.

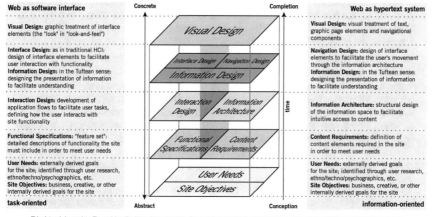

| Web as software interface | Concrete | Completion | Web as hypertext system |

Visual Design: graphic treatment of interface elements (the "look" in "look-and-feel")

Visual Design: visual treatment of text, graphic page elements and navigational components

Interface Design: as in traditional HCI: design of interface elements to facilitate user interaction with functionality
Information Design: in the Tuftean sense: designing the presentation of information to facilitate understanding

Navigation Design: design of interface elements to facilitate the user's movement through the information architecture
Information Design: in the Tuftean sense: designing the presentation of information to facilitate understanding

Interaction Design: development of application flows to facilitate user tasks, defining how the user interacts with site functionality

Information Architecture: structural design of the information space to facilitate intuitive access to content

Functional Specifications: "feature set": detailed descriptions of functionality the site must include in order to meet user needs

Content Requirements: definition of content elements required in the site in order to meet user needs

User Needs: externally derived goals for the site; identified through user research, ethno/techno/psychographics, etc.
Site Objectives: business, creative, or other internally derived goals for the site

User Needs: externally derived goals for the site; identified through user research, ethno/techno/psychographics, etc.
Site Objectives: business, creative, or other internally derived goals for the site

task-oriented — Abstract — Conception — **information-oriented**

This picture is incomplete: The model outlined here does not account for secondary considerations (such as those arising during technical or content development) that may influence decisions during user experience development. Also, this model does not describe a development process, nor does it define roles within a user experience development team. Rather, it seeks to define the key considerations that go into the development of user experience on the Web today.

© 2000 Jesse James Garrett   http://www.jjg.net/ia/

Fig. 3 The elements of user experience (Garrett 2002)

consequences to putting information architecture into a small box not many could have foreseen.

At this point in time, the web had become interactive and interaction designers had arrived in force, starting their own association, the Interaction Design Association (IxDA) in 2003. As the mailing lists devoted to information architecture became contentious and rude (the ASIS&T managed SIG-IA) or closed (the Information Architecture Institute members-only forum), the IxDA list offered an open-to-all, free alternative. The interaction designer camp brought along their passion and experience from software design, and many of the folks who might have defined themselves as "Big Information Architects" found it easy to move back and forth, learning exciting new things and playing with new toys: gestural interfaces! Voice commands! And they stayed in the new camp. Many who might have become the next generation of information architects became the first generation of internet-focused interaction designers. Which would have been fine, except it seems like you can't be both.

Sadly, humans are related to chimpanzees and share some of their worst tendencies. One is to break into tribes and go to war to slaughter each other. Rather than work together, the Information Architecture Institute and the newly formed IxDA focused on competing on what they saw as their unique value rather than focusing on intersections of common interest. They spoke of differences rather than sharing common goals. They chose the word *OR* over the word *AND*.

Garrett gave a talk at the Information Architecture Summit that sought to tear down the boundaries, but was widely misheard to say "Information architecture is dead, long live user experience." It's well worth reading his original words, so carefully chosen. He points out that

> (i)n the marketplace, this is a zero-sum game. Every job req created for an 'interaction designer' is one less job req for an 'information architect' and vice versa. And the more 'interaction designers' there are, the more status and authority and influence and power accrues to the IxDA and its leadership.
>
> They get this, and you can see it play out in everything they do, including refusing offers of support and cooperation from groups they see as competitors, and throwing temper tantrums about how other groups schedule their conferences. Meanwhile, the IAs are so busy declaring peace that they don't even realize that they've already lost the war. This territorialism cannot go on, and I hope the IxDA leadership sees an opportunity here for positive change. These organizations should be sponsoring each other's events, reaching out to each other's membership, working together to raise the tide for everyone.

He asked us to come together under the umbrella of the user experience designer:

> We are user experience designers. This is the identity we must embrace. Any other will only hold back the progress of the field by marginalizing an important dimension of our work and misleading those outside our field about what is most important and valuable about what we do.

He was right. I'm not sure he was heard.

"You are all user experience designers" was meant to heal. But the interaction designers just went back to their camps and the last of the information architects updated their business cards. I should be clear: the information architecture organizations did not reach out either, but focused even harder on defining a difference that was irrelevant to making good work. All the organizations were so focused on what they were not, it's not surprising many practitioners embraced a more inclusive definition: user experience design (Fig. 4).

Another devastating event to information architecture had occurred around this time: the rise of Google. Much of "Little IA" was concerned with retrieval. Many of the techniques that were not about navigation were focused on fixing search.

Fig. 4 The Google homepage in 1998

Information architecture had become synonymous with controlled vocabularies and best bets. But Google gave everyone the belief that the retrieval problem was solved. And while that has proven to be far from true in smaller information environments like intranets, the idea that humans could handcraft anything that could compete with a learning algorithm seems laughable. Suddenly library science seemed as relevant as ... libraries.

So, information architecture was both made small and made unnecessary.

Google fixed search.

No one navigates.

You don't need information architecture for software-as-a-service sites, you need interaction design.

You don't need information architecture.

In California, the title disappeared and information architecture seemed like a strange fad left over from the dotcom boom like Pets.com.

And where was I? I promised this was personal. At the end of act one, I had written "Information Architecture: Blueprints for the Web" (2003), and took the "Big IA" route. I tried to balance user research, interaction design and "Little IA" into a coherent whole. It sold very well. But the day it was published, I was working at Yahoo as an interaction designer. When the second edition came out, I was a product manager at LinkedIn. Titles have never seemed very important to me, but I was mistaken. I should have fought for information architecture at Yahoo, since that's really what I was doing. I was working on search, and making sure that tsunami of data was understood and harnessed.

Although by LinkedIn I was a product manager and not a designer of any kind of user experience, I still sought to bring order and understanding in a new data tsunami: the social stream. Information architecture is a way of thinking for me. It is a way of approaching any problem: thinking about products, making sense of the world around me. There will be no third edition of that book. I love information architecture, but I've moved on to other kinds of work. Not because information architecture was lacking but because I am a happy dilettante. I was never a specialist, but someone who loved the chaos of those early Wild West days of the web, and I still seek the next frontier.

No matter what I do though, I will think like an information architect.

Act Three: The New Information Architects

I call this new breed of talented thinkers Information Architects and this book was created to help celebrate and understand the importance of their work—a work which inspires hope that as we expand our capabilities to inform and communicate that we will value, with equal enthusiasm, the design of understanding.

Richard Saul Wurman Information Architects.

This year Peter Merholz stated that "UX stunted IA's growth" and started a firestorm of argument. Some people accused him of just making trouble to make trouble. While making trouble is not out of character for him, he isn't wrong either. Information architecture has taken a long time to find its feet after the one-two punch of interaction design and user experience (And I haven't even brought up content strategy!) No amount of "let's be friends" will change the fact that information architecture has stagnated in the years following the rise of user experience. He's also not wrong that we need information architecture and information architecture thinking more than we ever have.

But.

Information architecture is not dead. Thank goodness. Because no matter whether you think your digital product has "content" or not, the world is made of data. And somebody needs to make that world of data make sense to the humans who live in it. In fact, I'm even going to argue it's making a comeback.

Jesse James Garrett asked in his plenary where the great works of information architecture were. I say they are just showing up now. They are not pseudo-libraries or pseudo-buildings. They are understanding spaces made of information. They are new works that make data dance. They make the impossibly complex clear. Take Foodpairing, for example. Foodpairing is an online service that breaks ingredients into their unique flavor components, and then creates relationship trees that help chefs discover brave new combinations that delight the tongue.

Like the Netflix recommendation algorithm (Madrigal 2014), Foodpairing takes apart something we thought we knew, then reinvents our understanding by revealing hidden relationships. First we understand, then we eat. Bernard Lahousse, who started Foodpairing in 2006 with his partner Peter Coucquyt, does not know he is an information architect. He may consider himself a bio-engineer and a gastronome, but he is definitely an information architect, because he is helping us understand more deeply and through organization something we thought we knew (Fig. 5).

Lahousse gave a talk about Foodpairing at an interaction design conference. When I commented on Twitter that the talk was an information architecture talk, one person replied "why? It's not about controlled vocabularies or metadata." That is like saying a talk on mapmaking isn't a design talk because it doesn't mention Photoshop. Taxonomies, controlled vocabularies, those are just tools. Metadata is just a material. Information architecture is about making meaning out of piles of facts. Who cares how you do it, or in what medium? (Fig. 6).

The new IHOP menu is another example of how understanding the data and understanding the humans who need to consume it can lead to design and business wins. It was made by an information architect, Abby Covert, who knew her point of view and tools could be applied to more than a website.

The new information architects look rather like the very oldest: Dan Klyn is obsessed with Richard Saul Wurman's legacy (we all should be!) and is driving us to determine "what good means" (Klyn 2013) in different contexts; Abby Covert is experimenting with new forms of communication, such as children's books (2014), to find better ways to make the complex clear; Andrea Resmini is exploring the physical

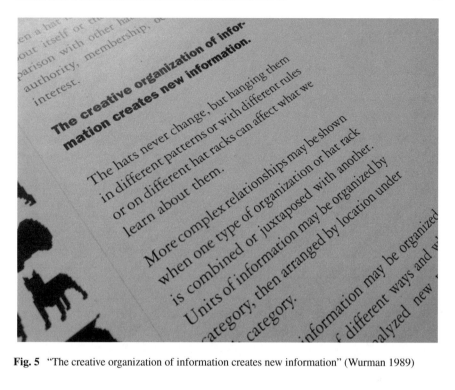

Fig. 5 "The creative organization of information creates new information" (Wurman 1989)

environment and ambient information (2013); Andy Fitzgerald made taxonomies a sensible approach to mobile (2013).

Medium does not matter, tools do not matter, but the goal does: to transform the chaos of data into the order of information. This is a discipline involved in inventing solutions to new problems as they arrive. And new problems are snowballing.

In 2009, Dan Brown pointed toward a new relevance for the information architect in a post-Google world. Just as furniture makers had to choose between making patterns for IKEA or continuing to hand craft furniture for a shrinking—but appreciative—market, so information architects must decide if they will handcraft best bets or create the rules for making them. Peter Morville, one of the "my two dads" of information architecture moved on to search. Search is far from solved. It and recommendation engines—the push to search's pull—provide more than enough of a fun rule space to keep IAs busy for many years to come.

As well, there is a new data crisis. Karl Fast points out that we are drowning in small data problems such as email and photos. We are producing information at such a pace we can no longer make sense of it. We are the tsunami. There is no data more precious or more personal. We need the next generation of information architects to make our lives make sense (Fig. 7).

Information architects are in the understanding business. Understanding is their north star, and organization and clarification are their tools. We may have a new

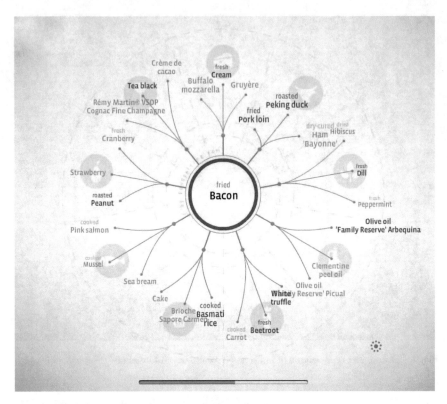

Fig. 6 Foodpairing

tsunami of data. But we also have information architects ready to help. Let us never forget how much we need them.

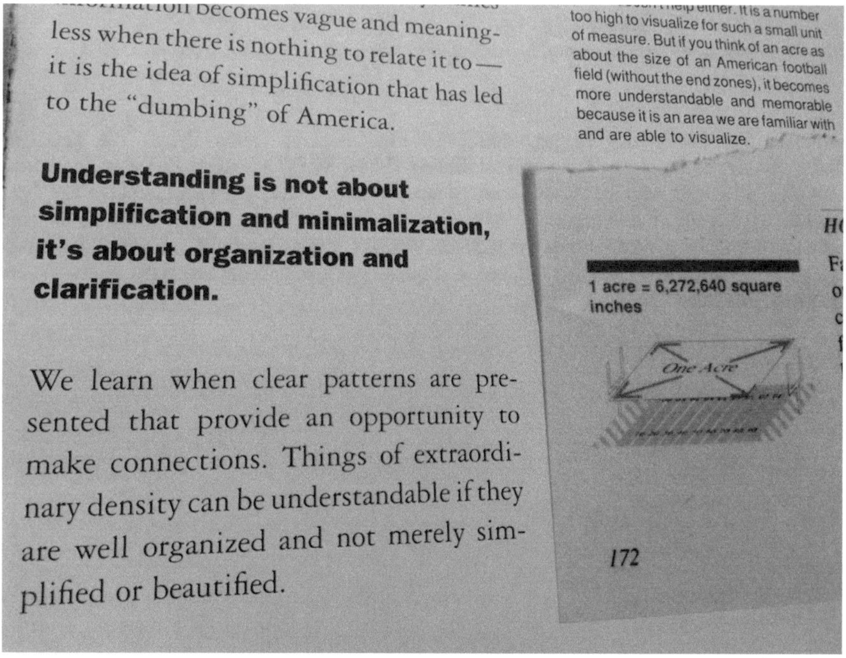

...ormation becomes vague and meaningless when there is nothing to relate it to —
it is the idea of simplification that has led
to the "dumbing" of America.

...elp either. It is a number
too high to visualize for such a small unit
of measure. But if you think of an acre as
about the size of an American football
field (without the end zones), it becomes
more understandable and memorable
because it is an area we are familiar with
and are able to visualize.

Understanding is not about simplification and minimalization, it's about organization and clarification.

1 acre = 6,272,640 square inches

One Acre

We learn when clear patterns are presented that provide an opportunity to make connections. Things of extraordinary density can be understandable if they are well organized and not merely simplified or beautified.

172

Fig. 7 "Understanding is not about simplification and minimization" (Wurman 1989)

References

Asbury & Asbury. (2011). *Web originals.* http://asburyandasbury.typepad.com/blog/2011/09/web-originals.html.

Brown, D. (2009). *Designing rules.* https://www.slideshare.net/brownorama/designing-rules-ia-summit-2009.

Covert, A. (2014). *What do you mean?* http://youtu.be/j7lMCMMWGZA.

Fitzgerald, A. (2013). Taxonomy for App Makers. 14th ASIS&T Information Architecture Summit. http://www.slideshare.net/andybywire/taxonomy-for-app-makers.

Garrett, J. J. (2002). *The elements of user experience.* New Riders.

Klyn, D. (2013). What good means. UX Strat 2013. https://alt.understandinggroup.com/wp-content/uploads/2013/09/DK-UXSTRAT.pdf.

Madrigal, A. C. (2014). How Netflix reverse-engineered Hollywood. *The Atlantic.* http://www.theatlantic.com/technology/archive/2014/01/how-netflix-reverse-engineered-hollywood/282679/.

Merholz, P. (2014). *UX stunted IA's growth.* https://www.peterme.com/2014/01/26/user-experience-has-stunted-information-architecture/.

Mok, C. (1996). *Designing business: Multiple media, multiple disciplines.* Adobe Press.

Morville, P. (2000). Big architect, little architect. Argus Center for Information Architecture. https://argus-acia.com/strange_connections/strange004.html.

Resmini, A. (2013). Ghost in the Shell: Navigation, meaning and place-making in information space. In A. Slavic, A. A. Salah & S. Davies (Eds.), *Classification and Visualization. Proceedings of the International UDC Seminar 2013.* Ergon.

Rosenfeld, L., & Morville, P. (1998). *Information architecture for the World Wide Web.* O'Reilly.

Wodtke, C. (2003). *Information architecture: Blueprints for the web.* New Riders.

Wurman, R. S. (1989). *Hats. Design quarterly. No. 145.* MIT Press.
Wurman, R. S. (1996). *Information architects.* Graphis Inc.

Christina Wodtke has helped grow companies like LinkedIn, Yahoo, Zynga, The New York Times and numerous startups throughout Silicon Valley. She's the author of the business fable book Radical Focus, which uses the power of story to build a new approach to OKRs, The Team that Managed Itself on creating high-performing autonomous teams, and Pencil Me In, on using drawing to make better businesses and products. She is currently a teacher at Stanford University in their HCI program in Computer Science, and speaks worldwide about humanity, teamwork, and the journey to excellence.

Bandleaders in the Idea Business: In Conversation with Lou Rosenfeld

Andrea Resmini

Lou Rosenfeld co-authored "Information Architecture for the World Wide Web", the "polar bear book", now "Information Architecture for the Web and Beyond". A central figure in the field, Rosenfeld is one of the founders of the Asilomar Institute for Information Architecture, later the Information Architecture Institute, and the person who started the Information Architecture Summit (now the IA Conference). He now heads Rosenfeld Media, a company he started and which produces user experience books, conferences, and workshops.

A. Resmini (✉)
Department of Intelligent Systems and Digital Design, Halmstad University, Halmstad, Sweden
e-mail: andrea.resmini@hh.se

Jönköping Academy for Improvement of Health and Welfare, Jönköping University, Jönköping, Sweden

© The Author(s), under exclusive license to Springer Nature Switzerland AG 2021
A. Resmini et al. (eds.), *Advances in Information Architecture*,
Human–Computer Interaction Series, https://doi.org/10.1007/978-3-030-63205-2_9

(Photo: by M. J. Babic)

Q: What better question to ask Lou Rosenfeld than how it all started?

Usually, when people ask me this sort of question, I talk about going to library school in the late 1980s at the University of Michigan. In 1988 I was a year out of undergraduate school after a history degree, and I wasn't really sure what to do. I waited tables, delivered Yellow Pages, worked in child care, sold sofas, did some landscaping. Fun jobs like that. I finally made up my mind to go back to graduate school—but where?

I had an idea for a business: an apartment listing service, something that I thought was badly needed in Ann Arbor, a college town. I didn't want to be a programmer or get a computer science degree and the local library school, which had just been renamed the School of Information, seemed just fine and proved to be a good choice, as it seemed that databases of books couldn't be all that different from databases of apartment listings. Little did I know.

My introduction to the information revolution was my online database searching class. We were using 2400 baud modems to dial into commercial databases at $300 an hour. Online searching was brand new and, given the cost, very stressful, but things changed very quickly during my two years at the School of Information. Soon we were working with a revolutionary new technology, CD-ROMs, and we got our own computer lab, where I got a job.

As I was young and male, and happened to be technology savvy relative to many of the people there, including the faculty, it was assumed that I was pretty smart, and I was afforded a lot more opportunities while in the program. I graduated in 1990 and, after a summer as a Hypercard programmer—probably my favorite job ever, I was hired by our new dean to be the School of Information's in-house technologist. I also did some work for the university library system, and eventually got to work on an interesting project involving personalized filtering of Usenet postings.

During these years, I was exposed to HCI, a variety of early remote collaboration technologies, and ultimately much of the pre-Web Internet—stuff like FTP, Telnet, and WAIS. Soon I was a Gopher master for the University of Michigan libraries and a PhD student at the School of Information.

I started teaching courses there on how to use those early Internet tools to find information on and, ultimately, create topical guides to the Internet. This was pre-Yahoo and it's how I met Peter Morville: he was one of my students.

And while I'd given up my idea for an apartment listing service, my entrepreneurial streak was intact. I started a company with a professor at the School, Joe Janes, as something of a hobby. We'd teach teachers and librarians workshops on how to find information on the internet. They were blown away by how much information was stuffed into their computers.

As the Web took off, we brought Peter into the company full-time. And things just kept getting busier. I really hated academia at that point; I'd been there forever. I didn't want to be a professor, so when I had to choose between staying in the PhD program or growing Argus, I obviously decided to do the latter.

We created a web design collaboration with a group of local tech companies that had complimentary skills. Argus took on information architecture, project and client management, and the others tackled the programming and graphic design. This was in 1995. At that time, I told Peter that by 1997 we should be out of that stressful, crazy collaborative arrangement, because information architecture as a stand-alone service was going to boom. I was spot on, and by 2000 Argus was a forty-person consulting firm, with most of the staff with library and information science backgrounds. It got probably a bit weird for them early on, since they found themselves to be consultants all of a sudden, making good money and being treated well.

We worked with big clients. We almost helped the Borders[1] Group create the world's first online bookstore before Amazon got there, but Borders just didn't get the Web. We had more success with such companies as AT&T and Ford. Peter and I also decided to write about the work we were doing. I had been a regular columnist for a few magazines at that point, including an O'Reilly publication called *Web Review*. That relationship led to the "polar bear" book, which was written in 1996–1997 and came out in its first edition in 1998.

When we wrote that first edition, Peter and I felt like we had a couple of chips on our collective shoulders. One was that we wanted to prove to the world that library science had critical value in the information revolution. The other was proving to the library world that there was much-needed value in their work outside of libraries. In some respects, I think we had actually more success with the former than the latter, which is shocking. I'm still kind of sad about that.

---

[1] Borders was a book and music retailer based in Ann Arbor, Michigan, operating more than 600 stores in the US in the early 2000s. It went bankrupt in 2011 and parts of its assets were acquired by Barnes & Nobles.

Q: Argus Associates closes its offices in 2001.[2]

Argus hit the wall in 2001. We went from forty people to shutting down operations in six months. It was terrible. Projects disappeared and we just couldn't go on. We went our separate ways and I became an independent consultant for a good ten years, doing information architecture work for large organizations. Peter and I wrote the second edition of the "polar bear," which kept selling great but was definitely changing and becoming a totally different book: the first edition had been designed for people creating websites; the second edition was for all those people who saw their websites becoming bloated garbage that just kept expanding.

My work at the time was mostly helping organizations such as PayPal, Caterpillar, the CDC, with their information architecture challenges. What I was seeing was that half the reason I was being hired was psychological: we bring in a consultant and the more we pay him the better we feel about ourselves. I started feeling like an information therapist: these people, these organizations, were just venting about their information challenges, and these were often organizational challenges and problems of silos, fragmentation, and so forth.

On most days, I felt like I wasn't doing anything significant: I was getting paid but I was not having an impact. And I'm not necessarily the right person, or have the right personality, to be that type of consultant. I'm interested in what *I'm* doing, I'm a little narcissistic that way. Around 2004 I got consumed by the idea of starting a publishing house because I felt O'Reilly, New Riders and Wiley were all only dipping their toes into publishing titles that appealed and were useful to our community. I briefly considered working as an acquisition editor, talked to a bunch of these publishers, but the whole system seemed insane and I'm an entrepreneur: I'd already started one successful business, so I said alright, I'll do it myself.

I had a conversation with Tim O'Reilly, one of my heroes, who congratulated me for going into publishing and told me that what I probably didn't realize was that most publishers are frustrated authors. I'm not sure about others, but I sure was. Even at O'Reilly, which is a great company, the approach was that books are a commodity: publish as many as you possibly can and know already that only one out of some very large number really succeeds. It's like throwing a bunch of ideas up against the wall to see which one sticks: you don't market your books, you hope the authors will; you don't really develop them, you just hope the authors can write; and sometimes you don't even edit the final copy, you just print it and send it to the stores. And I hate that model and wanted to do something different, I wanted to put to practice some of the principles I was learning, and that meant going my way.

Since one thing I'm good at is knowing a lot of people and, for the most part, not having them hate my guts, enough prospective writers signed up with me even though I had no idea what I was doing as a publisher. We went on to publish our first book, Indi Young's "Mental Models," and I slowly started building Rosenfeld Media from a hobby to a company that could not only pay me but pay other people's salaries.

---

[2]Higgins, R. W. (2001). Argus Associates, Inc. closes shop. Information Today. http://newsbreaks. infotoday.com/NewsBreaks/Argus-Associates-Inc-Closes-Shop-17629.asp.

At the time, a lot of work went into the creation of design systems for how we laid out each book, into the covers, into actual usability tests and studies of how people would interact with both the digital version, a PDF at the time, and the paper version. We had color prototypes printed with Lulu, which was very expensive at the time but was worth every dollar because it allowed us to actually study how the book worked.

Still, my philosophy for publishing was that I wasn't in the book business: I was in the idea business. So, the natural follow-up step was to figure out how we could use the company as an infrastructure to bring the growing network of experts I was working with to the organizations that needed to hear their ideas. We kept working on refining their points using iterative processes, moving their ideas from a kernel into well-polished books, presentations, or workshops, and finally conferences.

Q: When the Roundtable was started in 2013, it was a conscious effort to push the envelope and move the conversation beyond the polar bear book[3]. The intent was to acknowledge the ongoing social and technical changes, from smartphones to the internet of things, but especially give a platform for discussion to those many within the community who were working more with digital/physical experiences, organizational change, app-based or multi-device strategies, rather than with just websites. A vast part of the community, and an even larger part of those outside the community, seemed to be stuck in a diminutive frame of mind in which information architecture was only labels, navigation, and a website's taxonomy. And hence small.

When we did the fourth edition of the polar bear book—Jorge Arango, Peter Morville, and I—O'Reilly suggested to subtitle it "for the web and beyond." We actually resisted the idea initially, but in hindsight it was the right thing to do. You have been telling me this for years and I'm just slow to catch on sometimes, what can I say. I was starting to believe that maybe information architecture was somehow a done thing. My own mental model was forged in the Web era. I wrote two books on information architecture, one was about new websites and one was about bloated websites, but they were both about websites. I was myopic in how I was framing information architecture. It took me years to realize that everything I do is actually information architecture because I work with information all the time.

I work with my authors and they're brilliant and they can write, but they are terrible at structuring books, they're absolutely awful, and I have to do that for them. Same thing with presentations and conference programs and their narrative structures, with structuring a business, with figuring out how people interact with virtual conference content. I don't honestly know why it took me so long to figure all this out. I might just be a creature of habit, but I think that's what you Roundtable people have probably been getting at for a long time: we can apply information architecture *everywhere*, not just to the Web.

Q: I would most certainly not call you slow. I would also posit we're all creatures of habit and that people with baggage, metaphorical or not, will move slower, and that's not necessarily a bad thing. But what you said about your own "mental model"

---

[3]The fourth edition was published September 2015.

resonates with my reflections at the time of the first Roundtable in 2013. My argument[4]
was that any reflection on the history of information architecture needed to take into
account that the Web was Argus' niche of opportunity. It makes perfect sense that
you, Peter, and the others who were there in the early days centered your expertise
on the Web and made it the object of design. In hindsight, though, it is possible to
go back, observe the larger picture, reflect, and discern slower patterns, both good
and bad. The big bad one was clearly the absolute identification of information
architecture with "solving websites" that took hold in the early 2000s, which to me
sounds as reasonable as identifying carpentry with making chairs by hand. Chairs,
and websites, are incidental. Carpentry would still exist even if we could snap our
fingers and magically erase chairs from human history. What I can say is that we now
have a very different environment from that of the mid 1990s when you started Argus:
digital information has become a pervasive, integral part of the fabric of reality in a
way that was not even imaginable back then. The obvious next statement would be
that the role of information architecture is even more crucial today than it was ten
or twenty years ago.

I may come off as I'm self-flagellating about this, but what I am is just happy. I'm
happy to be late to the game, as well as happy there's a game.

Q: If this seems like such an obvious statement for you and me, and for others at
the Roundtable, why is it not obvious for everyone? What is the problem then? Is it
semantics, or is it something deeper than that?

The word we use to name what we do is important, but I think there's an argument
to be made against staying too still. I wrote an article last year on moment prisons,[5]
probably a bad term itself, arguing that we get way too locked into our own terminology and the metaphors that the terminology is good for. I've always felt like what
we call something, for example, "information architecture," is not really important.
That's a problem I've had with our community, that people get so wrapped up in
the terminology. And I know we're supposed to be thinking language and controlled
vocabularies and so forth, but this seems to turn too often into the incapacity to accept
that our work is, by definition, constantly degrading and will get stale and will have
to be revisited. Information therapy as a way to explain what I do that resonates with
me, but I'm in no way suggesting the rest of the world uses that term.

Q: I certainly do agree with the fact that sometimes we tend to be too protective
of our own private little gardens, or that we try to figure out ways to split something
that is already small into even smaller parts so that we can call it our own (or profit
from owning it). But there is an interesting tension here: on the one hand, the labels
we use for our practice and what we call ourselves have to be refreshed now and
then to be useful to the profession. After all, you want to stay relevant to your clients
in a constantly shifting market, as you say; on the other hand, the more formal sides

---

[4]Resmini, A. (2013). Les architectures d'information. Études de communication [Online]. Vol. 41.
http://edc.revues.org/5380. Also available at https://andrearesmini.com/blog/the-architecture-of-inf
ormation/.

[5]Rosenfeld, L. (2019). *Moment prisons, and how to escape them.* Medium. https://medium.com/
rosenfeld-media/moment-prisons-and-how-to-escape-them-b391100b2d43

*of the field, related to education and research, benefit from us being able to claim
a history, an uninterrupted path, and that relies also on a continuity of language.
That's what fields such as interaction design have done much more successfully than
information architecture.*

That's true, and I can make two educated guesses as to why they were more
successful. First of all, the timing was really good. It was perfect, just on the tail of a
major shake-up in the market after the dotcom bust. Second, many of those folks came
out of the information architecture community. They left because they were frustrated
with us, and for good reasons, but they learned a lot from that frustrating experience.
As a result, they were far better at creating a model for organizing professionally
than we were. They deserve a lot of credit for that.

*Q: What good reasons do you think they had to be frustrated with the information
architecture community?*

I think a lot of it had to do with scoping. The scope we had outlined in the
polar bear book, which was the most influential scoping at the time, did not include
interaction design, or a lot of what was considered interaction design back then.
Here you have a community where we all share a lot of common history and where
we're all collectively shaping a conversation centered on new and often intangible
artifacts. Why would you care for a taxonomy or a pull-down menu if you're a
business person? It seems entirely mundane, or pointless. We all share this misery
of nobody understanding what we're really trying to say or do. But then, at a certain
point, some, those who eventually left to call themselves interaction designers, felt
like they weren't even being understood in their own home. That there was no room
in the community for the practices that they cared about.

*Q: I should thank you and confess right away that you just made a part of the
conversation I've always had a hard time with much clearer: scope and specialization as reasons for that momentous separation make a lot of sense in the context of
maturing practices. It also explains why I would miss it entirely, as I grew up, professionally, in a very different environment. Even my training as an architect wasn't
really concerned with specialization and was still by and large following Rogers'
idea of design as a practice encompassing everything "from the spoon to the city"[6].*

I bet you a lot of architect s are out of work now because they weren't trained that
way. This said, disagreements in scope and specialization often result in people
leaving, be it a company or a community. And interesting things happen when
someone decides they had enough and goes off to start something else. We have
so many examples of frustrated Young Turks packing up and leaving an established

---

[6]The original formulation we owe to German architect Hermann Muthesius who coined it circa
1916 when he was chairman of the Deutscher Werkbund. See Cecchetti, M., & Baker, S. (2011).
For sensitive skin: On the transformation of architecture into design. *Annali D'Italianistica* (29),
237–252. http://www.jstor.org/stable/24016425. Rogers supposedly re-introduced the concept at
the 1953 Congrès internationaux d'architecture moderne (CIAM) in Aix-en-Provence, France, that
marked the definitive rejection of the "modified Functionalism" of the Charter of Athens and its
understanding of the city through the categories of dwelling, work, recreation, and transportation.
See Frampton, K. (1980). *Modern architecture.* Thames & Hudson, p. 269 onwards.

profession or discipline to go found another. Really, those new territories are where the most interesting stuff is happening.

What I feel bad about with that particular schism is that the interaction design folks were emotional. They felt unincluded, unheard. Information architecture folks felt emotional as well. They argued the other side was not really being fair, and was taking it too personal. They felt attacked. Thinking about it now, it was too much about personality. You can take different paths but that shouldn't mean you end up being enemies. Which is what happened, at least for a while.[7] Or maybe that's just the way I lived it and now remember it.

Q: I do remember some of the conversation on the mailing lists around 2003– 2005, and for what it is worth I think you are giving an accurate representation of what that whole moment looked like. At least from the perspective of someone who at the time didn't know any of the people involved in person. Everyone was bitter and a few specific exchanges carried a "going through a bad divorce" vibe you wouldn't expect in such conversations. This was clearly a relatively small group of people that knew each other well, had been sharing something for some time, had maybe become friends with one another, and now suddenly and unexpectedly felt betrayed, whatever the reason. Are you saying you would try to avoid that schism now, regardless of the fact that splits can be beneficial?

In hindsight, yes, I probably would. But I'm not sure I'd be successful. Part of the issue has always been an issue of timing. Sometimes the conditions in the market are just about right. And part of the issue is linked to us being human beings and reacting to the tangible and concrete before to the intangible and systemic. You have the cosmetic aspects of the product, and you have the technological aspects of the product: those are tangible and immediately visible, and their tangibility is augmented by huge investments in marketing that play to our psychologies, press our buttons. Short term and immediate gratification is a big chunk of the larger picture and I don't think that's ever going to change.

Q: We're back to information architecture being the invisible infrastructure, aren't we? The piping of your beautiful new house. You don't really care for the pipes until you need a tap in a place where there's none, or they spring a leak and you have water everywhere.

Exactly, you care for the faucet, and how it looks and feels. Who wants to even think about the pipes? Until you don't have water or you have it all over the place and then it's a huge deal because you will have to spend ten times more than what you would have if you had dealt with replacing or repairing it five years earlier. That's the history of America's infrastructure right there.

Q: I would argue that the pipes we are discussing are really broken all over. They're not just leaking: most of the network is structurally unsound. It was built for a different world and for different people. Everything that can be connected is being connected, even though we don't or can't really understand the consequences, and the resulting, sprawling pipework impacts all sorts of activities and social structures,

---

[7] See also Jesse James Garrett's "Memphis Plenary" chapter.

including our politics. We have faucets that don't work and water flooding the living room, to keep with the analogy. We might not even have the full set of tools we'd need to address some of the problems we're facing. Does information architecture have a role in there?

It's obviously a very challenging and difficult task for anyone. I think people who are comfortable with intangibles and systems are a little better off in terms of addressing challenges like the ones we are mentioning. We're all bad at it but maybe the people that are reading this are a little better than most. What we really need are better frameworks and better terminology, to have conversations that are interdisciplinary, and to get the blind men to see the elephant. This has been my experience with the polar bear book: I don't know if it was a very good book, but it was a very useful book. And I say that because at the time we wrote it there were many people from different disciplines, graphic design, usability, programming, business, who were struggling with information challenges that they did not have a framework or the language for. They couldn't have the powerful interdisciplinary conversations that were needed to solve information problems.

The way you solve new, difficult, intractable problems is by getting different and diverse brains to work on them together. In order to do that, those brains must have a Rosetta Stone. With the polar bear book, I feel like we came up with an imperfect but useful translation system that allowed us to make progress.

Now we have a similar but even larger issue, so get the behavioral economists in the room with the architects, the AI people and the humanists to solve these problems, because we still have the same siloes we had back then and people arguing their one toolkit is the right toolkit. How can anyone's individual perspective be the right perspective? I just don't know where that new Rosetta Stone is going to come from. Maybe it's here already.

Q: Aren't you basically saying that we need an information architecture for the process? The need to structure a common vocabulary, to figure out differences and align definitions and concepts across different disciplines, isn't that an information architecture blueprint for collaboration?

You and I probably would approach it that way because that's the toolkit we come with. I don't have a problem with that, but I would have a problem with saying that's the only way. That would strike me as particularly arrogant. I know I don't know enough to say that. Would a philosophy-based approach be better? I don't know.

Q: I couldn't agree more.

I know you know and you know what I'm saying. And I agree, information architecture is everywhere. Let me give you an example: we're setting up Salesforce for Rosenfeld Media, and we're just trying to do some most basic elementary stuff, what I thought Salesforce would do out of the box. Salesforce comes with a whole bunch of default nouns to describe content objects: what is a prospect, what is an opportunity, what is a contact. But these objects are all oddly named, there's a murky relationship between them, we can't understand the transition path from one object to another or which one is the parent element, which one is the children, and which ones are siblings. I have personally sold tens of millions of dollars in consulting, books, training, conferences: still, I couldn't tell you what Salesforce's content model is and, because of that, we can't figure out how to use it. I end up throwing my hands up in the air and saying we have a huge information architecture problem there. And this is not a just Salesforce problem: these are common old problems we still haven't solved.

Q: Yes, they are. That's why continuity and consolidation have been such important parts of the whole discourse on reframing information architecture at the Roundtable from day one. The library and information science foundations of the polar bear book were needed then to help wrangle the Web into order, and are still needed now. They are not being thrown away, they are being supplemented by contributions, theories, methods, tools, drawn from disciplines that deal with complexity and human space in a way that does not belong to library science. Cognitive science, architecture, systems thinking, behavioral economics. When you say "bring the economists into the room," when you insist on the importance of systemic collaboration and interdisciplinarity, I nod emphatically. That is the way to enrich the purview of information architecture and prevent it from being shrunk. I'm not saying we solved the Salesforce of the world and that they do not matter anymore. We clearly didn't and they clearly do. I'm saying that information architecture plays an important role in problem spaces that were not a concern, and rightly so, twenty-five years ago.

We should not shrink. We should be ambitious, as a community. But the right question is not how can we solve the world's problems, but rather how can we *help* solve the world's problems. "Plays a role," as you say, is different from "is the one thing that matters."

Q: I'm still nodding emphatically in agreement. Let's get back to what you said earlier on, that you feel that information architecture and your upbringing are more related than you thought and that you often feel that what you really do is a form of information therapy. You tiptoed your way around that idea in your remarks during your closing keynote at the 2017 ASIS&T European Information Architecture Summit in Stockholm. Can you elaborate a little?

I've been thinking about it a lot. As I said, I'm in therapy and this is the type of conversation you start with your therapist. I grew up in a very loving but very dysfunctional home. Chaos in a nutshell: I was the youngest of five boys and I was the one who was trying to get everyone to get along. I was the resident peacemaker from when I was five or six, and that's probably not a healthy thing for anyone that age to be tasked with. I think subduing chaos and harmonizing points of view was my way to cope, and I continue to do that as of this day. I don't know how related they are, I think they're related. I have always been more interested in harmonizing people than information. Maybe I should have become a conflict resolution professional or something like that. Therapy has also brought clarity to how my efforts are bound with time, something that information architecture hasn't discussed as nearly enough as we should have.

Did you ever see "The Commitments?" Out circa 1991, set in Dublin and based on Roddy Doyle's novel by the same name?

Q: I haven't read the novel but I saw the movie. It was lovely.

Then you'll remember that the protagonist assembles a band with these very talented but frankly often unpleasant people. He gets them together, and they fight all the time. He gets them to play a few historically great concerts and then they completely implode. And he shows us we should be counting our blessings. This is restorative. Things were great for a moment. For one moment in time, he managed to get the egos, the weirdness, the fights out of the picture and gifted us with great music. Harmony.

To expect anything beyond that one moment is to expect too much, I suppose. Things will spin out of control, like they did this early spring with the pandemic, and it's just the way things are. If I think about what I learned from that movie is that maybe my role as an information architect is to be that bandleader. Get people together, create a sum that's greater than the parts, but be perfectly aware that it's for that moment and that moment only.

Creating long-lasting order out of chaos, or trying to make other people be orderly when they can't, is an impossible task. Expectations have to be adjusted to the objective reality of the world. That's what we do as adults. If we accept these limitations, we can do something good and healthy, like organize an event, a wonderful little space for people to come and share their expertise or learn, but also only a moment in time. It is restorative, but then you're immediately confronted with the inertia of the system or the entropy of things spinning out of control.

Q: You use the word "restored." Does that mean you believe there was some kind of preexisting order that needs to be reinstated?

Not in the traditional conservative sense of some external status quo that we want in place of today's supposed chaos, no. "Restorative" does not imply we want the good old days or their social and political implications back. Restorative is the way we feel about these moments of harmony good design can create, like in the movie: they bring back feelings we have felt in the past against a different backdrop. Which also means that what restores us in 2020 may be a very different alignment or harmonizing than what restored us in 1990.

Q: Is transient harmony then one of the traits you would say define your vision of information architecture? We've long come to terms with the idea that it's actually multiple orders we always deal with, but could it be that it's actually moment-sized, temporary ones? Orders that do not necessarily concern themselves with the world all the time, since, remember Rogers, we work from the spoon to the city, from the app to the ecosystem. You make a book that works. But on top of the book you create a successful company that makes books that work, and then the company becomes a network structure for dissemination, teaching, consulting. Are you harmonizing?

I think I am. Constantly. Right now, we're facing the consequences of the pandemic and we're looking at dismantling some of the team for purely economic reasons. Those economic reasons are also going to push the company in a different direction. When we bounce back, assuming we'll have the opportunity, it won't be the same team and it won't be the same company. It seems that information therapy could actually be information harmonics. Musicians, let's do this.

Q: Loss of control is one of the major consequences of a connected world: maintaining well-guarded borders gets complicated when everybody can share or remediate everything. Could we extend this to information architecture? Could we frame the discourse on information architecture as a field as one of moving from an idea of control, designing a finite artifact, the website, to one of transient, unfinished harmony? Facebook, Instagram, Snapchat, are scaffoldings meant to influence someone's behavior, empty containers, and they are sure very different epistemologically from what we used to design in the 1990s. I'm purposefully painting it more black and white than it actually is, of course.

To be fair, maybe we didn't have the right language at the time but while we were working on the second edition of the polar bear book, I was trying very hard, maybe not even realizing it, to write about information architecture for platforms, specifically in the chapter about Evolt. So sure, in the 1990s we were mainly reacting to absolute chaos by saying we had ways to control it and create value for users, especially, but I don't know that we were ever just working toward "finite artifacts." There's always a social aspect to information systems, no matter what: they have to be used by different people with different needs and so there has to be some flexibility. Anytime you have flexibility, you're basically acknowledging some degree of transiency.

Q: Fair enough. One final question: you happened to drop by a couple of times while we were wrapping up this or that Roundtable, but were never directly involved, which is intriguing considering you have some responsibility in its creation. After a 2010 impromptu session Keith Instone and I ran at the Summit on bridging academia and the industry, I had a conversation with you, probably in 2011. You had the idea that it'd be great to bring in "a bunch of professors" at the Summit and have them work side-by-side with practitioners on some interesting real-world problem. I remember you commenting "it's a brilliant idea, and it'll never happen." How aware have you been of the Roundtable, of its goals, and of its results these years? Do you have any opinion on whether or not it has contributed to the maturation of the field at all?

It would be easy for me to claim ignorance. I know of the Roundtable. And I know it's wrapped up with the academic publishing model. I have issues with that model in general, I'm sure you do as well, and I worry that less people than could potentially benefit from what we have to say will have the chance to. And I'm personally overwhelmed, all the time. I'm not reading much about information architecture these days unless it's something I'm publishing. But I thoroughly enjoyed this conversation, especially since you're so polite and let me ramble on, and while I honestly have to admit I still have no idea what the impact is expected to be, I just hope that some of this can be opened up later on, whatever the way. That it can bleed across media.

If I could make a wish, it'd be that these conversations reach the many academic communities out there that could benefit from hearing what advances are there in information architecture. It could be worthwhile, already with this book or with other initiatives, to help them a little, especially from a curricular perspective. That wouldn't be bad at all.

Andrea Resmini is associate professor of experience design and information architecture in the Department of Intelligent Systems and Digital Design at Halmstad University and the Director of Innovation and Research at the Center for Co-production, Jönköping Academy for Improvement of Health and Welfare at the School of Health and Welfare, Jönköping University. An architect turned information architect, Andrea is a two-time past president of the Information Architecture Institute, a founding member of Architecta, the Italian Society for Information Architecture, the Editor-in-chief of the Journal of Information Architecture, and the author of *Pervasive Information Architecture* (2011) and *Reframing Information Architecture* (2014).

The Academics and Practitioners Roundtable 2014–2019

Sarah A. Rice and Bernadette Irizarry

Abstract A summation of Roundtables held yearly in conjunction with major information architecture events between 2014 and 2019; details out the purpose, structure and experience of the Roundtable and describes the nature of resulting artifacts. Also presented is information about each Roundtable: 2014 Teaching Information Architecture; 2015 A Language of Critique for Information Architecture; 2016 A Discussion of Masterworks: What Makes Good Information Architecture Good; 2017 Mapping the Domain: Navigating to a Discipline; 2018 Ethics and Information Architecture; 2019 Diversity and Inclusion.

Introduction

The Academics / Practitioners Roundtable, or the *Annual Academics and Practitioners Information Architecture Roundtable* as was most recently advertised as part of the Information Architecture Conference, is a yearly event which started in 2013. The Roundtable provides an opportunity to discuss the current status of the practice, of research and of education in information architecture, and to gather with like-minded people with wildly varying viewpoints, backgrounds, and degrees of knowledge. The Roundtable is not a traditional workshop or masterclass, rather it is an open conversation where no one, or maybe everyone, is taking the lead. There are no masters, nor apprentices. Topics are chosen yearly by the organizers, also an open group, with the goal of developing a critical discourse in the field and helping the community grapple with emerging issues and concerns. Opinions are gathered, ideas are explored, and a theme is then chosen.

Every year, the Roundtable is that moment when the table is truly round, and everyone's voice is equal and listened to. Ideas, methods, perspectives are debated,

S. A. Rice (✉)
Seneb Consulting, San Jose, CA, USA
e-mail: rice@seneb.com

B. Irizarry
Velvet Hammer Design, Los Angeles, CA, USA
e-mail: bern@velvethammer.com

© The Author(s), under exclusive license to Springer Nature Switzerland AG 2021
A. Resmini et al. (eds.), *Advances in Information Architecture*,
Human–Computer Interaction Series, https://doi.org/10.1007/978-3-030-63205-2_10

Fig. 1 Group discussion at the 2014 Roundtable

agreed, and disagreed upon, usually after what can only be described as a lively but cordial discussion (Fig. 1) that spans the domains of academia and the practice.

Its success stems from a combination of factors. It is completely volunteer supported, and as such must continue to offer immediately relevant and interesting content to ensure volunteers continue engagement. It is attached to one of the biggest yearly information architecture events, making it convenient for the largest number of people to attend. A dedicated group of people who find the experience beneficial to their own professional development keep attending and adding their voices to the work of the Roundtable. Finally, leaders and decision makers within the community have provided acceptance and support of the Roundtable efforts, which have paved the way for space at the conference and ways to reach a wider audience during the planning and execution of the event.

For many who practice information architecture, the Roundtable represents an annual opportunity to meet and discuss in depth a single topic that is important in shaping the field and future of their profession. Their viewpoint is valued, and it is a key moment to bring questions, concerns, opinions, and help architect a vision of how information architecture might impact enterprises, industries, their communeties and the world.

Structure and Experience

The Roundtable began as a one-day event that mixed presentations, discussion, and hands-on activities, and has since expanded to include a second day. Most Roundtables have followed a similar format, with the last three editions offering presentations and discussion during day one, and using day two for a *Make-a-thon*, a focused full-day exploration of the conversations from day one through the realization of concrete artifacts in the form of prototypes, games, tools, and methods. Through the years, the organizing committee has fluctuated between as few as one to as many as seven volunteer members. Roundtable attendance has been thirteen at its lowest and forty-five at its highest.

A traditional welcome chat and introduction set the goals for the day, and provide a shared understanding of the activities. Day one of the Roundtable is split into two parts: the first part introduces contributions, in the form of presentations or talks, that approach critically the topic of discussion; the second part takes the form of group discussion, critique, and synthesis of the contributions. The format for the presentations of day one is that of short, five-minute "lightning" talks. Presentations are based on papers (for academics) or talks (for practitioners) that have been peer reviewed for quality and relevance of the subject matter. The lightning talk format encourages presenters to focus on summarizing key points quickly and precisely. Since the 2014 Roundtable, the M3 model[1] has been used as a basic framework for all discussions involving the relationship between the academic and the practice sides of the field.

Part two's format has varied through the years, depending on topic, number of attendees, and the goals set by the organizers. All Roundtables have engaged in some type of practical exercise to synthesize outcomes, with attendees breaking away for small group activities, and then returning to the larger group for a final debrief. The *Make-a-thons* have used a similar structure, embracing experimentation and free-flowing cross-pollination between ideas and teams. Make-a-thons have generally allowed participants to approach the problem space from the perspective they favored, using the tools they favored, from markers and paper to cardboard models to software, for the results and outcomes they thought could make for the most valuable contribution to advancing the conversation on information architecture practice and research.

Artifacts

Physical and conceptual artifacts have always been a primary outcome of the various Roundtables and physical ones have taken an even larger role with the introduction of day two and the *Make-a-thon*. These artifacts have taken the form of maps (*Mapping the experience*, 2017), mood boards (*Masterworks*, 2016), reports and presentation (*Language of critique*, 2015), storyboards and photologs (*Ethics*, 2018), games and tools (*Diversity*, 2019 *Make-a-thon*). In parallel, every Roundtable has captured the

---

[1]See "Classical to Contemporary" in this same book or Lacerda, F., and Lima-Marques, M. (2014). Information architecture as a discipline—A methodological approach. In A. Resmini (Ed.), *Reframing Information Architecture*. Springer.

flow of thoughts and conversations through videos,[2] wall boards, collective note-taking, post-it scribbling, and list-making. All of these artifacts have been gathered, documented, and preserved as raw data.

The Roundtable website[3] is an additional, important product of the Roundtable and a central hub for communication of upcoming events or call for papers, as well as the primary archive of all event-related materials and post-event reflections.

The Roundtable 2014–2019

Following is a list of the Academics and Practitioners Roundtables that took place between 2014 and 2018 as part of the pre-conference series of workshops at the ASIS&T Information Architecture Summit, and in 2019 as part of the pre-conference events at its successor IA Conference, in locations across North America. Themes, presentations, and a few selected artifacts are briefly described.

Teaching Information Architecture (2014)

The 2014 Academics and Practitioners Roundtable on *Teaching Information Architecture*, the second Roundtable,[4] took place as part of the ASIS&T Information Architecture Summit in San Diego, California, USA on March 27, 2014.

Contemporary students of information architecture will be the ones to forge the path ahead in the years to come. Karen McGrane's 2013 closing plenary[5] called for a doubling down on information architecture. This included selling and positioning our practice in the marketplace as well as how we educate our next generation of learners.

The Roundtable on teaching information architecture sought to extend the conversation by focusing on:

– What and how should we be teaching students of information architecture?
– How do we mature the practice of information architecture through education?
– How do we bridge practice, theory, and education?
– What does the field as a whole require from education? This includes businesses, agencies, academia, and the community of practice.
– What is the full breadth of information architecture education? When does it end? And how could we coordinate its development?

---

[2]IA Rountable YouTube Channel. https://www.youtube.com/channel/UCHqryKW89KgdoVRja SEilOw.

[3]IA Roundtable, http://www.iaroundtable.org.

[4]The first Academics and Practitioners Roundtable, Reframing Information Architecture, is documented in Resmini, A. (2014). *Reframing Information Architecture*. Springer.

[5]14th ASIS&T Information Architecture Summit, Baltimore, United States.

Those who attended the event benefited from deep discussion, lively debate, and co-design sessions that explored the intersection of education, practice, and theory. More specific take-aways included:

- A deeper knowledge of the current global state of information architecture education
- An understanding of contemporary theoretical positions and case studies on teaching information architecture
- An understanding of what is required to challenge and develop the field of information architecture through education
- Models for the critique of information architecture produced both for students and practitioners
- Definition of what we should be teaching from and for the field of information architecture
- Innovative approaches to teaching information architecture.

Featured Talks

- Research in Information Architecture, Andrea Resmini
- How I teach Information Architecture to design students, Abby Covert
- Information Architecture thinking, Jason Hobbs and Terence Fenn
- Teaching Information Architecture, Keith Instone
- Teaching Information Architecture by learning about architecture, Dan Klyn
- What can Information Architecture learn from Library and Information Science: Perspectives from LIS education, Craig M. MacDonald
- Designing a shared digital future: Institutionalizing UX and IA. Teaching executives the value of Information Architecture and User Experience, Simon Norris
- Teaching Information Architecture .... until I sketched it, Thomas Wendt
- Teaching Tangibly on Rodents and Religion, Christina Wodtke.

Sharing of Results and Dissemination

The Roundtable was brought into the main program of the conference by means of an impromptu 45-minute session, during which the organizers were able to summarize the Roundtable activities and share what had taken place during the day-long event. Sarah A. Rice was in the audience for the session and wrote[6] about her experience learning of the 2014 Academics and Practitioners Roundtable. Here is an excerpt from that post:

---

[6]Rice, S. A. (2014). 2014 Information Architecture Summit—Reflections. *Telling the Whole World.* https://tellingthewholeworld.blogspot.com/2014/04/2014-information-architecture-summit.html.

Until now, I thought I'd moved beyond IA. I thought my career growth would come from outside this domain and community. If I went back to school, I assumed it would have to be in another field…. Business administration. Cognitive Psychology. Computer Science. These aren't bad fields, and the knowledge they offer would be very beneficial to me. What troubles me is that… I'm an information architect. I framework. I listen. I understand. I explore. I clarify. I get overwhelmed by complexity. I doubt if things will ever become clear. I talk with others. I listen some more. I construct hypotheses. I build models. I wrangle oceans of information. I talk with users, customers, participants, members. I sketch. I ponder. I give up, but never for very long. I ask lots of questions. And I framework. Document, share, update, repeat.

What have I heard at the 2014 IA Summit that has provided me such relief? I heard that we've moved beyond the web but have kept our identity as information architects. I heard about reframing IA…we don't just build navigation, we support wayfinding. We don't draw sitemaps, we show context. We don't (just) build models, we support sense-making. And we can do this anywhere.

We started with digital environments and are expanding from there. For example, I've architected future plans for nonprofits, and revised messaging platforms for emerging startups. My current project is to create a culture of customer experience (within) a growing company…. This is the path I've taken, and until recently, I thought I was alone. I thought I needed to leave my chosen field in order to pursue the Next Step. But the 2014 IA Summit [and the Academic /Practitioners Roundtable] set me straight.

The Good, the Bad, and the Ugly: Developing a Language of Critique for Information Architecture (2015)

The Third Academics and Practitioners Roundtable on *Developing a Language of Critique* took place as part of the pre-conference workshops at the ASIS&T Information Architecture Summit in Minneapolis, MN, USA on April 22, 2015.

This Roundtable focused the discussion on how we define what is good and what is bad in information architecture, given that "the sprawling, cross-channel information spaces we design today are nothing like those we designed in the 1990s, and we have struggled to articulate a comprehensive language to describe and critique them. Is this one good? Is that one bad? Why?".

To lay the initial basis for a conversation on a language of critique for information architecture, the 2015 Roundtable intended to provide preliminary answers to questions such as:

– Is such a language really necessary or can this proposition be challenged?
– If necessary, is this language an entirely new language? Can it be derived from existing languages, such as those for new media or architecture?
– How would such a language work?
– Who should help in shaping it?
– Can practice and research share a common language of critique or are their goals different if complementary?

Summary of Interviews from Roundtable Participants

Participants were individually interviewed during the course of the Roundtable and asked about their views in relation to the questions put forward on the necessity of developing a structured language of critique. These semi-structured interviews were conducted one on one in a separate space, and collectively supported the idea that the field needs a language of critique. Points raised included the necessity of identifying what is the object of critique proper, how such a language should be first developed and then, even more critically, used, and whether or not academics and practitioners could use a shared language or not.

Interviews showed general agreement among interviewee that there is a problem within the field of information architecture: the community of practice confuses "what we do" as a field with the medium in which we do it; it conflates the field with current practice, and so muddles the distinctions between core information architecture theories, principles, methodologies, and models that guide work, and the deliverables that are created in response to a specific task or job. The result is that many practitioners have been pigeon-holed into small boxes, "wireframe jockey", "creator of web sites", and many assume that information architecture simply means executing a card sort. Such an approach keeps the community small, and makes it irrelevant. Marsha Haverty mentioned the necessity of bringing rigor into any conversation about the field, while Stacy Surla stated that being intuitive, rather than methodological, is the consequence of a lack of consolidated frameworks. Clarity is required in distinguishing problem space, the "what", from process, methodology, and tools, the "how", and from the philosophical "why". Misty Weaver maintained that broad support from the wider community is needed for change, and Simon Norris stated that a language of critique that we can agree on and disseminate is what can help that process and demonstrate the value of information architecture in a design process.

Ren Pope stated that a common language to identify good and bad information architecture will also provide a shared understanding and facilitate discussions in and out of the field. Bern Irizarry noted that this will give us rules and stories that govern what was done and provide structure to the discipline. Duane Degler commented that such structures would also help challenge assumptions, both methodological and philosophical.

Discussion

It was suggested that a language of critique could be seeded from a number of different fields and disciplines, such as traditional architecture, design in its various flavors (industrial, graphic and print, service), cinema, game design, computer science, human factors, library science, business administration, and the social sciences (psychology, sociology, anthropology). Building a body of critiqued work would be done over time, and would likely be done by multiple people or groups, in order to ensure robustness. Such individual critiques could then lend themselves to revealing patterns to further develop the coalescing framework and formulate a specific language to clearly and objectively communicate quality and value. Such developments would help give the field some of the structure and clarity it is currently lacking.

> Abby Covert—We know we need a language of critique. We need to talk about what we do, consistently. Can we pick words to use that we all agree on?
> Sarah Rice—Who does the picking?
> Abby Covert—Whoever shows up. If you are reading this, consider this to be a formal invitation into the process to develop a language of critique for information architecture. Be part of the community. Be part of the conversation.[7]

A Discussion of Masterworks: What Makes Good Information Architecture Good? (2016)

The 4th Academics and Practitioners Roundtable on *Masterworks* took place as part of the pre-conference events at the 17th ASIS&T Information Architecture Summit in Atlanta, Georgia, on May 5, 2016.

In an ideal continuation of the conversation from the previous year's Roundtable, the debate centered on what is a masterwork in information architecture. How do we recognize, identify, explain a work's value, relevance, originality, and influence? Questions included:

– What defines a masterwork of information architecture?
– What are examples of masterworks of information architecture?
– How do we determine if an architecture is "good"? What are the frameworks? What are the indicators?
– What is a masterwork in the age of post-digital artifacts and anonymous mass co-creation?
– What is the role of the information architect?
– How are individuals or studios and collectives recognized for their contributions to communal work?
– Can a masterwork be the deliberate creations of corporations? Can it arise from like-minded creative thinkers drawing inspiration from one another?
– Can it be the product of mass co-creation?
– What are the benefits of establishing a canon for information architecture practice?
– Can a solid body of knowledge and an established canon broaden discourse and become platforms for well-rounded education and research?
– Do we risk division in the field? Are ambassadors necessary to drive broader acceptance of information architecture?

---

[7]Excerpt from the 2015 Roundtable Final Report. https://is.gd/RoundtableFR2015.

Featured Talks

- Structuring the Conversation: The M3 Model and Information Architecture, Flávia Lacerda
- Learning from James Joyce's *Ulysses* and Richard Saul Wurman's *The City, Form and Intent*, Dan Klyn
- The Information Architecture of the Mundane, Michael Adcock
- A Language of Critique for Information Architecture, Stacy Surla
- CAMP: A Model for Critique of Masterworks, Christina Wodtke
- Taxonomies of Othering: Creating Systems of Oppression, David Bloxsom
- Machines for Making the Future, Marsha Haverty (Fig. 2).

Mapping the Domain: Navigating to a Discipline (2017)

The 5th Academics and Practitioners Roundtable on *Mapping the Domain* took place as part of pre-conference activities at the 18th ASIS&T Information Architecture Summit in Vancouver, Canada, on March 22, 2017.

The Roundtable reflected on how over the past several years, the information architecture community had been considering how to progress beyond the practice (what's done in the field), help establish a body of knowledge, and consolidate its disciplinary part in research and education. It brought together results and open questions from the four previous editions and resulted in the collective creation of a domain map of information architecture as a discipline.

Fig. 2 The 2016 Roundtable discussion

Featured Talks

- The Evolution of Information Architecture: A Journey in the Micro-Meso-Macro-Meta, Simon Norris
- Designing Against Humans: Lessons from Masterworks, Jeffrey Ryan Pass
- Lessons from UXPA, Carol Smith
- What is our responsibility to the information environment? Bram Wessel
- Is Information Architecture Undefinable? Stuart Maxwell
- Information Planners, Chris Chandler
- Roundtable Retrospective: 2013 to Today, Sarah A. Rice
- Agile Heuristics, Laura Federoff.

Artifacts: The Domain Map

The primary goal of the Roundtable was to map the domain of information architecture. The Domain Map, which in its "live" version consisted of a wall-to-wall board in a three-by-three grid, with the three levels of the M3, "Paradigm", "Theories and Models", and "Solutions to problems" as its horizontal rows, and "Questions", "Discoveries", and "Examples" as its vertical columns. This board was used throughout all of day one as the collective hive mind for the room to allow moment-by-moment capture of insights, comments, thoughts, and questions. Sticky notes were added, moved, edited, removed, in an exercise which was part reflections on the ongoing conversation and part an emergent systematization of the attributes and characteristics of the field at large.

Toward the end of the day, a final loose clustering activity of all content on the board was conducted in the form of a group discussion, to consolidate the concepts and relationships between them.

After the Roundtable, that map was then further synthesized and summarized in digital form for wider distribution. This digital Domain Map (Fig. 3) preserves the original structure and grid, but offers a bullet-point, focused version of the main highlights, examples, and problems as they relate to the levels of the M3.

Ethics and Information Architecture (2018)

The 6th Academics and Practitioners Roundtable took place during pre-conference at the 19th ASIS&T Information Architecture Summit in Chicago, Illinois. Day one, March 21, 2018, was presentations and discussion; day two, March 22, 2018, was the first *Make-a-thon*.

That year's Roundtable discussed how information architectures are not neutral and the ethical implications of working with information. By structuring information environments that people can inhabit, by creating organizations for discovery and

Domain Map

	Highlights	Examples	Problems
Epistemology	Some want IA as a **discipline**, not just a craft, but there has been pushback. Building our **discipline**: Thats why we have the Roundtable. Value academic discourse. Our discipline has **evolved**: moving from wireframes to strategy. More architecture than design. **Defining IA**: help practitioners define what they do; empower them to do their craft. Many fields constantly **question** their definition. IA is inherently **abstract**. Info is abstract, arch is abstract.	**Definitions** as seen in: Official IA org websites Polar Bear book Pervasive IA Wikipedia **Gap**: Computational IA missing from our epistemology We've relied on qual, but quant is out there as well.	**Defining it** - is IA: science or philosophy discipline or craft? **Not easy** If it is easy, it has little value Should we aim for discourse rather than definition? **Why should we do it?** Funding, professions **What framing are we using?** Disciplines can exist outside of economic systems, like capitalism **Professional needs** Language for critique Defining masterworks Ethics & values
Theories	**Defining: What goes into a definition?** Facilitate conversations Focus on meaning Framing problems Standards and objectives Information ecologists **Teaching IA:** How to let others know this profession exists? What classes are there in IA? Teaching information literacy **Evaluating IA works:** Lang. of critique - what is peer review for IA? Heuristics: best practices & common sense Is heuristic at model level or practice level? Language of IA is still evolving	IA as job title absorbed into other things. IA lives at the conceptual level. Output is validated when clients pay more for IA services Books about IA Books about navigation and search Design critique - finally catching up to this in 2017	What is the thing that tools live in? How do we define rigor in our field? **Heuristics** are valuable for novices and new practitioners. Standard process for an IA heuristic? How to identify **masterworks** in a changing and evolving field? What is canonical? What are the masterworks? Why are all masterworks things not designed by Its?
Practice	Businesses need IA but don't know it. IAs need jobs Students are the best bridge from academia to practice Impact of tech on environment and context (means our craft is changing) Not have a point of view with others When doers become mentors or teachers Agile structure does more harm than good some of the time. IAs become grand advocates (IA informs overall brand strategy)	Still focus on web sites, but now with user. How much more of the bridge. Lots of **challenges** bridging research & practice	Who are students of IA? What are pedagogical priorities? Formal teaching vs apprenticeship or journeymen IA? Is certification important or meaningful? Diverse continuums How do we identify and preserve IA masterworks?

Fig. 3 Synthetic version of the Information Architecture Domain Map (S. A. Rice, 2017)

use, information architecture not only makes information accessible but also provides the lens through which people will experience it. It encodes power relations and imposes value choices, and presents the research and the practice fundamental ethical questions. The information architecture community has considered ethics at the micro level, that of the specific interaction, but has somewhat failed to consider it in its larger context. When designing an information architecture, do practitioners surrender their moral authority to someone else? Are they aware or unaware of this happening? Do they follow a code, a series of best practices, or do they improvise when facing ethical questions as part of their work? Does education and research consider ethics a part of the teaching and investigation of information architecture as a discipline?

Featured Talks

- Ontological and Epistemological Notion of Being, Arturo Perez
- Wicked Ethics in Design, Jason Hobbes
- Toward a Feminist IA, Stacy Surla
- Personal Ethics and Ethical Codes, Kat King
- Boundaries and Relationships in IA Practice, Dan Zollman
- Everything that Rises must Converge, Jeff Pass
- Your Ableism is Showing, Anne Gibson
- Information Architecture's Moral Imperative: Protecting Difference, Dan Klyn.

Applying Ethics to Practical Information Architecture Scenarios

Attendees were split into teams, given a number of scenarios, and tasked with providing a solution while applying ethical principles. At the end of the exercise, each team had produced a storyboard-like deliverable describing an experience and its ethical implications from the point of view of the information architecture, and highlighting a principle or key insight. Each team gave a ten-minute presentation of their scenario and proposed solution (Fig. 4).[8]

---

[8]S. Cook, K. Instone, and S. Surla: *A Sex Offender Registry that Maximizes Good and Minimizes Harm.* https://www.youtube.com/watch?v=jsuepJhleGM; A. Perez, A. Rosenthal, C. Smith, T. Whalen, and A. Gibson: *Facebook and Fake News.* https://www.youtube.com/watch?v=kfrUV6 yIA2c; D. Zollman, J. Pass, J. Hobbs, and A. Resmini: *Kill 'Em Right—Building a system to carry out the death sentence in Texas.* https://www.youtube.com/watch?v=wIFpwj4idR4.

Fig. 4 Group presentations at the 2018 Roundtable

Make-a-Thon Artifacts

During the day two Make-a-thon, attendees divided into teams and created both conceptual and physical artifacts that engaged with the ethical dimensions discussed during day one and that affect the domain of information architecture. Artifacts included a scenario-creation tool and an ethics game (Fig. 5).

Fig. 5 Explaining the mechanics of the ethics game at the 2018 Make-a-thon. Photo: S. Surla

Dissemination During the Conference

Roundtable results were also disseminated during the main program of the conference by means of synthetic deliverables from day two at Poster Night, as well as during a forty-five-minute session in which Roundtable organizers presented a readout[9] of the main practical and conceptual take-aways from both day one and day two of the Roundtable.

Dissemination at Other Venues

Outcomes of the Roundtable were further discussed at other venues following the conclusion of the conference. Stacy Surla presented *A Scenario Creation Tool for Ethical Design* at a Washington DC[10] industry event. Sarah Rice and Bernadette Irizarry developed an *Ethics Canvas*[11] based on the scenario-creation tool which was presented at a number of events, including Code4Lib, Content Strategy Applied, and the Information Architecture Conference.

Diversity and Inclusion (2019)

The 7th Academics and Practitioners Roundtable on *Diversity and Inclusion* took place as part of the pre-conference activities at the Information Architecture Conference in Orlando, Florida. Day one, March 13, 2019, was presentations and discussion. Day two, March 14, 2019, hosted the second Make-a-thon. Additionally, a forty-five-minute session was held on March 16, 2019 as part of the main conference to disseminate the results of the two days of Roundtable activities.

The 2019 Roundtable followed-up in the steps of the previous year's event, broadening and deepening the conversation on the ethical side of information architecture.

Information architectures give structure to the world we live in: they provide boundaries, enact constraints, categorize, and label the opportunities for action, and allow comparison. They carry with them implicit value judgments and impact everyone in ways which can have far-reaching social implications. Working and living

---

[9]Rice, S. A. (2018). Summary Presentation on Ethics and Information Architecture. 19th ASIS&T Information Architecture Summit. https://www.slideshare.net/seneb/privacy-settings-analytics-free-ethics-and-information-architecture-the-6th-academics-and-practitioners-Roundtable-at-the-information-architecture-summit-2018.

[10]Surla, S. (2018). *Ethics and Information Architecture: A Scenario Creation Tool for Ethical Design.* https://www.slideshare.net/stacysurla/ethics-and-ia-a-scenario-creation-tool-for-ethical-design.

[11]Rice, S., Irizarry, B. (2018). *The Ethics Canvas.* http://bit.ly/ethics-canvas.

in a post-digital age means that many of the structures that support placemaking and sensemaking are embedded into digital as software, apps, or shared platforms, and are therefore invisible. Examples include Facebook's content guidelines, Google's search algorithms, and Twitter's rules governing user behavior. Additionally, new generations that have no direct experience of a world without computers approach categories and labeling in a fundamentally different way.

Invisible, disempowering structures do not serve society well. Homogeneity, subordination, and group thinking do not serve society well: everyone, regardless of age, culture, gender, politics, ability, beliefs, takes part, and participates in the pervasive information architectures that make up today's world. It is therefore of the utmost importance that the architectures we build to make sense of the world around us and of the information we must navigate are planned, architected, and designed by people who understand the implications of their work and who bring with them an open, diverse, and inclusive mindsets.

Featured Talks

- Racial Identity Development Theory; What's Our Role in Supporting Diversity, Veronica Erb
- Architecting Information Architecture Industry Events for Diversity & Inclusion, Jeff Pass
- Diversity of Thought; How We Can Foster Responsibility to Mindfully Shift Culture, Amy Espinosa
- Trust and Inclusion in Vulnerable Populations, Noreen Whysel
- Just Being Your/Self, Evgeni Minchev
- Do's and Don'ts for Diversity: Yes, They DO Exist!, Ylce Irizarry.

Artifacts: Diversity and Inclusion Meditation Activities Cards (DIMA)

The group prototyped a series of mindfulness exercises and scenario cards to support individual, peer-to-peer, or team discussions on diversity and inclusion. Titled "Diversity and Inclusion Meditation Activities Cards (DIMA)", the cards contained exercises and practices designed to encourage teams to evaluate products and services they craft on three spectrums: safety, intersectionality, and visibility. The safety spectrum challenged creators to examine the impact of their services on underrepresented communities while probing the creators' potential implicit biases. The intersectionality spectrum drew inspiration from the work of Kimberlé Crenshaw and asked creators to consider how overlaps in identity can contribute and compound the inequalities experienced by vulnerable groups. The visibility spectrum probed how open and transparent teams made the process and methodologies used for product and service development.

Sarah A. Rice is founder and CEO of Seneb Consulting and is an information architect with over two decades of strategy and consulting experience, architecting complex information experiences for companies such as Google, Sony, PayPal, Microsoft, eBay, Princess Cruises, and NetApp. She has also taught information architecture to interaction design students at California College of the Arts. She holds a Master's degree in Library and Information Science with continuing interest in data science and visualization. She is a past Information Architecture Institute board member, ran the Institute's premier conference on Information, Design, Experience and Architecture (IDEA) three years running, and has organized the Academic / Practitioner Roundtable since 2015. She has a passion for ethics in information environments, leading her to create and speak about the Ethics Canvas for Information Professionals regularly at industry conferences.

Bernadette Irizarry a creative leader with roots in graphic design and sculpture, Bern is the founder and CEO of the Los Angeles-based design consultancy, Velvet Hammer. Bern has built and led cross-disciplinary teams for over 20 years, holds two patents in color selection and served as an organizer for the Academics and Practitioners Roundtable from 2016–2019. Dedicated to growing diversity in technology and design, she currently sits on the Board of Advisors for AIGA Los Angeles, and co-founded the Los Angeles Chapter of Ladies that UX.

Architectures

She Persists: In Conversation with Abby Covert

Bernadette Irizarry

Abby Covert is an information architect, writer, and community organizer. Abby served as President of the Information Architecture Institute, Co-chair of the ASIS&T Information Architecture Summit, and Executive Producer of the IDEA conference. She is a founding faculty member of the School of Visual Arts' Products of Design program, Design Operations Summit, and Advancing Research Conference. She invented World IA Day and wrote "How to Make Sense of Any Mess", a book teaching information architecture to everybody.

B. Irizarry (✉)
Velvet Hammer Design, Los Angeles, CA, USA
e-mail: bern@velvethammer.com

© The Author(s), under exclusive license to Springer Nature Switzerland AG 2021
A. Resmini et al. (eds.), *Advances in Information Architecture*,
Human–Computer Interaction Series, https://doi.org/10.1007/978-3-030-63205-2_11

Q: What is your history with information architecture and how did your interest in the field develop?

I've been practicing information architecture since I could talk or move things around. In terms of education, I went to school at Northeastern University in Boston, Massachusetts for graphic design with minors in multimedia and typography. This was during the transition between print design and digital design. I was one of those lucky designers that was given a heads up on the way out of school that digital was the thing I should be looking toward. My first foray into doing information architecture professionally was in the world of Microsoft Consulting. I was brought in as a freelancer to design a set of icons for some banking software and through the process of designing these icons, I realized that icons were probably not what the client actually needed. I learned my first information architecture lesson: I should have asked what they were going to do with the icons before jumping into designing them. I started to dip my toes into navigation schemas, understanding how people navigate through software—much of which was very different from print design fundamentals I was taught. I was interested in the idea that information architecture was something that I had learned about in the print design world, but it was being practiced in this new capacity. I was lucky enough to fall into a junior information architect position back when things like that existed working at that same consultancy.

After several years of finding my way through the professional information architecture landscape, of getting a paycheck enough to not ask my parents for money, I finally got to a place where I wanted to meet other information architects. First as a lurker on email lists and blogs, then eventually through conferences I became a member of the larger information architecture community and connected with folks at the Information Architecture Summit and the Information Architecture Institute.

I was at the midpoint of my professional career, and had started to dip a toe into the user experience world trying to decide if I was going to manage teams or continue to be a practitioner. Eventually, I realized that management was not for me, and that the world was not really set up for information architecture specialists inside organizations, so I went out on my own for a few years and established a private information architecture practice, as an information architecture specialist working for brands like Nike, IHOP, and Microsoft.

I started to think of information architecture as my super power about a decade ago and haven't looked back since. After establishing my own process and information architecture practice, I became really interested in teaching. I started teaching weekend workshops and evening classes as continuing ed places and co-working spaces started to invade New York City. Finally, I moved on to accepting an adjunct teaching spot at Parsons. I then went on to become a founding member of the SVA Products of Design Master's program, which is where I conducted most of the research and iterative design on my book, *How to Make Sense of Any Mess*, which is now used to teach information architecture to students all over the world.

Q: You have been a leader in the information architecture community for many years, what is your relationship with the Roundtable?

I was the executive producer for the ASIS&T Information Architecture Summit for a few years and I was the last executive producer for the IDEA conference and subsequently the person who recommended that the Information Architecture Institute replace the IDEA conference with something more equitable and global—which we ended up calling World IA Day.

In 2009 our community reached a turning point. There was a big statement made at the Information Architecture Summit that year by Jesse James Garrett about the job title of information architect, and about the words "user experience" and the role of user experience designers—and how those two things were going to impact one another. There was a group of us that were honestly shocked and heartbroken at the idea that information architecture as a specialty might be lost to the generalization of the user experience field. Many of us saw the warning flags flying for what it might mean long term if played out over decades and we didn't like what we saw in those projections. So, after 2009 and Jesse James Garrett's speech, it was super easy for us to all find each other, we were in pain and needed camaraderie as we sifted through it.[1]

---

[1] In the late spring of 2012, Andrea Resmini, then president of the Information Architecture Institute, proposed that an "academic pow-wow" be part of the 2013 conference to 2013 Information Architecture Summit chair Kevin Hoffman. This came as a result of conversations Resmini had at Interaction 2012 and at the 2012 Information Architecture Summit with then ASIS&T president Dick Hill, who also wanted to try and bring academics back to the conference, and with this group of "heartbroken" people Covert hints at in the text: Covert herself, Jorge Arango, Jason Hobbs,

Q: Were you working on your book at that time?

Yes. That was an interesting starting place for me. I forced my poor students to read a book as I was writing it—which was very good for me and probably not so fun for them. From a teaching perspective, I could do whatever I wanted because it was an elective. It was an evening class and it included undergraduates coming from different programs. It was open to anyone, and I ended up with this real ragtag bunch of people from all sorts of backgrounds—I had architecture students, I had fashion students, I had digital design students. They came from these different places, which I found fascinating, as a cross section of what a designer looks like in modern times.

It was interesting to think about information architecture as a skill set that might equally serve each of those designers from the same basis, tenets, and principles. I went to a traditional design school, so I didn't identify as a digital designer until my third year of undergrad. But information architecture was a part of that education–all the way through it.

I wanted to revisit information architecture through a modern lens, and look at these kids and their trajectory through the design world as varied as those trajectories might be. Were there similar tools I could give them? My hypothesis was that there were. I found the same concepts could be applied across the different mediums that they were working in.

As a teacher looking to explore, it was great. It was the first time I taught in a university setting, not an evening workshop or a conference workshop. It was structuring my first long-form, and an evening elective was lower stakes and had no prerequisites. I put the class through some weird stuff with the things I asked them to do—while I was writing a textbook in public, I was also making them make floor plans of the building.

I'm not sure that the elective evening class sets you up for success in something as deep as information architecture, but it set me up for having fun exploring the space with fifteen willing participants.

Q: Do you think there is an ideal point when students should be introduced to information architecture?

I question that all the time. I want to know what's the right grade level. When I was writing my book, I made the decision, and it was insulting to some in our field, to write that book to a sixth-grade reading level. I was specific with it, because it opened up the opportunity to get it into the hands of younger folks. The idea that you would teach information architecture in high school is something that has not been explored. The earliest you're going to hear about it is college. Consider how set your mind is, by the time you get to college, in terms of the way you think about things.

I can only speak for the American school system, but we have obliterated critical thinking, as a skill set. It's about test taking, it's about there being a right answer. And that knowing the right answer makes you better than people that don't know the right answer. This exceptionalism that we have seems a weird space to introduce

---

Andrew Hinton, Lis Hubert, Dan Klyn, Keith Instone, and Dan Willis. The proposal was approved in late 2012 and would go on to become the first Academics and Practitioners Roundtable.

information architecture. It does make sense for that age group, but it doesn't fit into the current curriculum.

In 2011, I had an opportunity to teach in an afterschool program for a school in Brooklyn. It was for girls aged twelve to fourteen. It was fascinating. I watched them making a sitemap for a website about their program, working at the whiteboard, talking about what to call things and different ways that they might arrange the space—just as if they worked at any design agency or tech shop. They thought about users and how they might move through things. With little guidance, they got it.

I did a career day for third and fourth graders at a school in Queens, and we had an exercise where we were talking about Facebook. This was before emoji reactions on Facebook, so it was just the Like button at that time. I had an exercise where they had to improve Facebook, and they came up with the *dislike* button. And then, they proceeded to have this fascinating discussion about how the dislike button was a really slippery slope to go down. These were third and fourth graders—having detailed conversations about mental models, perception information, ethical responsibility—all of it.

I feel like in many cases we're not introducing information architecture early enough. I worry that we've missed the boat with the older generation. I'm including myself in that, the people who are currently working. You might catch them in a continuing education class, where you might break their brain about a project that they're on or one they just came off of. They might say "it would be better if we had that." To get people to change their process, to get them to fundamentally change how they're doing work—it may happen for some—but I think it really is about going younger. I want to write a children's book about information architecture. I want there to be videos of information architecture like the ones my son watches to learn about math, shapes, and colors. I want that for information architecture. Who's going to do that, I don't know, but I have hope.

Q: Early on, the Roundtable set a goal to bring education and practice together. Do you see a difference in how we practice, talk or teach information architecture today—has the Roundtable been successful?

I think that it's tough, it's so much bigger than just the Roundtable in my mind. I'd like to take the question to a higher level than that, to the field of information architecture.

I see a lot of stagnancy right now. If I look over the last ten years of what has happened in the field of information architecture, I feel really good about the movement in terms of what we accomplished in the first half of those ten years. There was a scheme that was lost, around five years ago. Honestly, I don't know that that has anything to do with the people that have been involved with the Roundtable as much as the industry sorting itself out.

One of the questions that I have had around the Roundtable is whether or not it is the right mechanism to get the work done. Or if it's the only mechanism—because sometimes it feels like the only mechanism—which may be the problem in itself. It's a really hard question.

I see very few job titles with information architecture represented in them. Perhaps even more important, very few jobs where information architecture is represented as a skill. That's a more valid metric in the more modern, generalized user experience world. This alarms me because the rate at which people are reaching out to me, either young in their career or career changers, midway through their career wanting to get into information architecture—that number hasn't gone down. I see a consistent rising level of people asking for advice. More and more each year, and I feel sad that I am unable to give them advice on how to get to the place where information architecture is their sole job and focus, like it is mine. My best advice for them right now is to get a generalist job and fight like hell for ten years to focus, and hope that they can do information architecture over time without express permission.

That advice is very different from the path I'm hoping to outline for people five years from now. But I look at the way the user experience field has met that same advice seekers, and the rise of fifteen-week, twelve-week, ten-week programs where you get in and out and you get a label and permission to market yourself as a user experience practitioner. When I see the relative low quality of students that are coming from those services, I struggle with that being a path for these advice seekers either. If we hope to get at the problem, we need to tackle it academically and from the practitioner standpoint, and it needs to be tackled years in advance.

My generation is already through. We are still young but we have already decided to generalize because that's where the stability, clear value, and paychecks are. I'm a standout from that crowd, and I would be lying if I said that information architecture gives me tons of opportunity. It doesn't. It gives me very few opportunities in reality. I've been very lucky. But I think that the privilege that I've had is something that I'm unable to shift to others—and that doesn't seem right. The fact is that I probably won't be replaced by another information architect at Etsy, and that many companies will have the one information architect they have now and then not replace them when they decide to leave, feeling lonely and undervalued. That's what I see right now and it's not a happy, optimistic place. I'm a very optimistic person, so for me to have this outlook is saying that it's pretty dark out there.

Q: What do you think is driving this change in the profession? Why this loss of relevance?

I think humans have an allergy to long-term systematic thinking. That's it. Period. We're fighting an uphill battle. There's a very small group of people that like doing things like that.

It has taken me a really long time to realize that. I went through a period in my career where I thought I was fighting other people for the ability to do those things. That's not true. I was never fighting for the ability to do those things. They were fighting me because they did not want to do those things alongside me. They didn't want me to go do it, because they knew that that would mean that they would need to do it too.

They never said, "Oh I want to do all the juicy problem solving. You don't get to do that." Instead it was, "No, no, no. Don't open that box. There are worms in that box. We don't want the worms to spill out all over the place. We've put that in the closet and we've locked it away. And we've given it a fine label for now. Don't go mess with it." And that's what it comes down to. We're fighting an uphill battle where humans don't want to make sense of things.

Q: Having problems to solve every two years is a very good way to structure a business. You don't really solve the issues, and go through cycles where you put in a temporary fix.

Exactly. So, take the allergy to systematic thinking and long-term problem solving and add to it, business people who have been taught that you can get two things for the price of one when it comes to generalist designers. You can both get the "implementer" and the "strategic thinker." People are not willing to admit that there might be people who are more aligned to the strategic part or more aligned to the tactical part, and quite happy doing their share.

Q: Years ago, the information architecture community was trying to make a point of saying there is a distinction between the tactical work and the strategic work; between designing a thing to the pixel and thinking about the big box in which it goes in, but that doesn't mean that one is more valuable than the other. They are simply two different ways of doing things, that need to come together in different moments—to collaborate.

Strategic designers don't want to say they're not tactical enough, because they don't want to cut themselves off from job opportunities. Tactical designers don't want to say they're not strategic, because that's become an insult in the world that we live in. That's wrong too.

Not every person has to walk around spouting strategy all the time. There is a place in this world, for people that want to do deep tactical work to get things done. I've worked with some brilliant people over the years that have just been completely overlooked, because "all they are is tactical," and that's just really wrong. We information architects can get a bad rap, making it feel like everyone should be in their head up in the clouds strategizing all the time. I don't want to live in that world.

Q: It seems that many have taken that to mean that their work is less valuable.

That's a myth that happens all the time—that the information architect is going to hand the designer a coloring book. I think that does happen at times. I had that happen a couple weeks ago. I'm a product manager on a project and I was working with a product designer. She was late getting on-boarded to the project, so I had to make some wireframes.

It was the first time I ever made wireframes at Etsy. And so, I said "hey I'm really sorry, I made you a coloring book, but like that's where the project is right now." She responded, "That's fine. It happens." It was not a tense moment because there was an understanding that my role was not to do what I was doing, to set an interface guidance. That is her role, but that we have to blend sometimes to get stuff done.

In the beginning, the conversations we had were defined by wanting to put some sort of a line between architecture and design. I remember several years of painstakingly trying to make that definition—that divide—happen. Where we have landed

Fig. 1 The Why, What, How
Möbius strip. Illustration,
from Covert, A. (2014) *How
to Make Sense of Any Mess*

was sort of more of a Mobius strip, where architecture and design are so connected
to one another (Fig. 1). The problem is that conceptually, we have this Mobius strip,
but when it comes to roles, we don't have this mobius strip all of the time. It's not
always the same person's responsibility, and it's not always the same person's strong
suit to do both the strategy and the design. The fact that the concepts don't line up
with the role has become an unfortunate thing that we've had to work through.

*Q: What are you seeing in large organizations around information architecture
maturity today? What are the implications for practitioners and the field?*

One of the cornerstones of my thoughts on information architecture is that it is a
skill set that can apply to anybody's job. With that, you understand that as a specialist
in information architecture, you have to be practicing it at a level where people who
are doing it at the everyday level may not be able to comprehend and jump right into.

Now, in order to get to that level of specialty in the space of information architecture, you have to have a tremendous amount of project experience. We currently
don't have great educational experiences to give to information architects from that
path. So as a practitioner, you have to come in early in your career and spend the first
decade, just racking up lots and lots of different project experience. You develop a
language that you can use to associate problems to other problems that you might
have seen. Over time you get to the place where you start to see the repetitive part
of that.

Now the problem with organizations is that we went from a world where, when
I started practicing as an information architect sixteen years ago, I had information
architect as a title. There were other people who had that as a title. There were
thousands of people in the world that had that as a title. We had similar salaries.
We had conferences we went to; we had a professional institution that got together
online and in-person. We had a sense, a touchstone of a field, and it was a *thing*. That
broke apart with the introduction of user experience.

This all comes from a really interesting place, right? Because information architecture is the thing that broke user experience into the mix. Jesse James Garrett, who
is at our conferences, having conversations with information architects, progressing
the field of information architecture, was trying desperately to figure out how to

wrangle this problem in his head—which was information architecture is only one of the things. And for years we had been billing information architecture as all of the things.

When I first got trained into my first information architecture job, I was running user tests. I was doing CSS style sheets. I was doing technical specs. I was doing the work of a business analyst. I was the QA engineer for damn sake! I did a soup-to-nuts, full stack designer job plus the work of a product manager. That's what we would say now, but I was called an information architect. At the time, I honestly couldn't architect my way out of anything. Something more than three levels of hierarchy was really going to screw up my day. I didn't understand anything about metadata. I didn't understand anything about back end systems. I had no concept of those things. During that time period, there were a lot of information architects that were full stack designers that had picked the title of information architect because it was new, it was shiny, and it was something where they could do the type of work that they wanted to do. Basically, they were saying "I want to be a webmaster, but bigger than that and for companies now—not just for little things."

That's my very naive, coming-into-the-field, right-out-of-college interpretation of what was going on. But if you fast forward to just five years later, when I'm working in an agency, I'm about to take my first director of user experience position, and everything has now changed. Now there are arguments about whether or not we should even be wireframing. Now, you should just be going right into the interface, you should just be drawing pretty pictures of the thing. There was a period where I felt pretty convinced that information architects were the people that made others think about what they were doing before deciding what they were going to actually do. Back in that period, a lot of my work was convincing design teams to slow down and actually do sitemaps. Convincing design teams to slow down and actually look at the idea of a mental model for a user, and talk to people—outside of usability tests.

Fast forward five more years, and you have organizations that are entirely devoid of information architecture by title, by skill, or by deliverable. They don't have sitemaps anymore; they don't do wireframes anymore. I'm not saying that they should, I'm just describing the history of what's happened. What we're left with are organizations that when they do hit a bigger information architecture challenge—which they do, they all do—call outside to get help.

So that's the first stage in the maturity model of bringing the modern sense of information architecture into an organization. That's where Etsy was in the very last year of my consulting time with them, where they had finally stumbled into territory they realized "Eek, we need somebody who understands this at that higher level than a product designer is going to." So that's the first entry point on the maturity scale. Step one, you have some information architecture work that is bigger than the skill set of your team, so you bring in an outsider.

The next step is, you have received information architecture guidance and you've realized that it differs from the guidance you're getting from your design team. You realize there's a gap on the team. So, you hire that person from outside. Generally, it's going to be a very senior level person. They're going to come in as an internal consultant like I did at Etsy. My very first year, I basically was just a consultant inside. I went from project to project, helping where I could on bigger things. So, stage two is "Somebody works here that does that thing". But at the point of stage two you're also starting to make decisions about a lot of things. The organization realizes that information architecture is important. You realize it touches everything—*everything*—your other designers do. Now is when you start to have conversations about what's the effect of autonomy on our information architecture over time? If we have all of these teams making decisions about what to call things, and how to structure things, what's the actual impact of that?

And so, I think that stage three of the maturity matrix of information architecture is, how can we put structures in place that take the skill of information architecture and democratize it? Democratize it to a place that it's not only understood by more people that are having to practice it, but it's also governed by a body of folks whose job it is to make sure that quality is upheld over time, and over the many people that might be touching it in the project work.

What I'm coming to is that we have to look at this new information architecture model, because this is what's happening. I'm not just describing my experience at Etsy. About a year and a half ago, when I came back from leave after having my son, I reached out to other people who are in product companies who have information architect as a title. Officially—or maybe not officially, as some of their HR systems won't allow it—on Twitter, they might have information architect as a title.

I went to all of them I could find and I started to ask for their stories: how did it happen? Where are you in the organization? These were the common things that I was seeing. There are more organizations in phase one, but we're also seeing a lot of organizations start to gobble up the contractor network in this space and bring people in-house. I feel many organizations are going to be facing phase three. Phase three being, we have a single person that does this but we have an entire organization that this skill set would benefit. How do we bridge that gap? How do we ensure that one person does not become a bottleneck?

Q: Is there a stage four?

Oh, I hope there's a stage four. I don't know what it is. Maybe everything is so crystal clear that we get to start thinking about more innovative things to do with our skills. That would be wonderful.

Q: If we look at the panorama of today's information landscape, digital is everywhere. We've moved from building single products or websites, to companies that control things that directly impact the lives of billions of people, and connect people to each other in ways we couldn't have imagined before. Yet, suddenly, nobody cares for the piping that supports that? It feels like we found out that we can build cities as opposed to our own cabin in the woods. But nobody cares about the sewers, or even the electricity, or the power grid, everything. This seems kind of counterintuitive.

Oh my gosh it's so counterintuitive! If you think about it, it's going to lead to a massive need for renovation. When people move into those cities, they realize there's no toilet, so it's going to be a problem. That's what's happening right now. Everyone is moving into those walled gardens and realizing this through using them over the course of years. It is too long to have to take to have a communal recognition of what's going on here, but it's what's happening. They're moving in and they're realizing—"Oh wait. A very small group of not diverse people made some very specific decisions about life as we now know it." Decisions based on the way they structure these products, based on the business logic that they're inflicting, and based on the connections that they're making with other people around the data that they're collecting—impacting our lives.

It's downright terrifying, and honestly, it's interesting because organizations make all of those things happen over time. As a result of people not being around long enough to see it happening, the small decision that you're making on a project doesn't feel like the big decision that's being made. I was listening to an interview with one of the algorithm engineers that was on the original team for the YouTube algorithm. That thing wreaked havoc on humanity. He was very humble and said something to the effect of, "you have to understand, when we built that we were making recommendations for kitten videos and "Charlie bit my finger." So, we could not have understood the magnitude of the decisions we were making." I appreciate that sentiment, but I disagree.

You could have recognized the magnitude of the decision that you're making. You didn't. It's not his fault that he didn't. He doesn't own YouTube. But he was not incentivized to think about the long-term situation that he was creating. I think that's something that information architects are going to play a part in. I hope that everyone practicing information architecture in modern times is asking very difficult questions about ethics within their organization. I know I am. That's a bigger job than just us. I think that we can be the clarity bringers in some of these murkier territories. Ultimately, we're going to have to partner up with everyone.

Q: The 2015 and 2016 Roundtables explored how we might communicate good work in information architecture—are there masterworks in the field and could we develop a language of critique as we have seen in architecture and design? In product design you might show and discuss a lamp, a chair, a table, or a radio. That hasn't happened for information architecture so far. Why?

I think that it's incredibly hard to share information architecture work. It is important for us to admit it, because we need to figure that out. For example, let's say there are two deliverables in the project that I'm a part of: a final deliverable of a map that I made representing an intense business process, and then a controlled vocabulary that I wrote. The amount of context that I need to explain how those things came into being, to represent them as anything but a moment. People might say "Oh, she made a diagram. Is your whole job is just making that diagram and that spreadsheet? How is that your whole job?" I'd respond "You come over here, and take forty hours a week and you tell me how quickly you could get that diagram agreed to by thirty people." Get the definitions agreed to, understood, and conversational with thirty people. Show me you can do all that. But if I write it up—it's a paragraph. That is problem number one. Problem number two: I've been doing this for sixteen years. How many things have I information-architected that still exist?

Q: True.

No, no, take a guess. I will tell you exactly how many. Three. I have a sixteen-year career and I've got three case studies where I can point anybody to the actual modern result of what I did. I'll give you an example I've been working on relaunching my website and gave me a goal of discussing five case studies from my sixteen-year career. I could not do it because the minute that I write up something that I did ten years ago that's no longer the direction of that company, or a good modern standard, I have to ask myself what would people understand and why am I talking about this work?

It's too easy to be confused and to ask the question of how good was it—it didn't last very long. The expectation that our work is supposed to last is an important question. Look at the rate at which interaction design examples become stale. People are not showing interfaces examples at design conferences as much because they immediately age out. Yes, we need to figure out a way to represent the work. I've had this happen to me, where I prepared to point out something on a social platform, and by the time I get to talk, they've redesigned it and it's gone.

Q: Yet, there are books that examine products that don't exist anymore, or architecture books composed of blueprints of buildings that have been demolished. Could we not point to work from 2005, say it looks dated, and that some of the problems it solved don't exist anymore or are different today? Couldn't we argue that there's a difference between what Argus was doing in 1995, and today where many teams don't even consider "search" for run-of-the-mill websites? Is longevity the only lens for what is worthy of discussion?

First, it's twenty years later, and we're still terrible at "search." It's still a thing, it's still broken, and we're still dealing with the exact same things that Argus was dealing with back then but using a slightly different shade of technology.

Let's talk about TikTok—it is a very interesting information architecture. The idea of attaching to a sound clip as your organizing principle—fascinating—we haven't seen anybody do that. That's a new interaction pattern that no one's ever thought of before.

Q: Agreed, that is worth discussing. Like Snapchat and the idea of making posts "die", these posts are living things, right? We do not have many people looking at these things. Why don't we see the same level of reflection that we see in other disciplines?

Who has time? Everybody's doing three jobs. Everybody's being pushed on a project that's been put in scope at half the time that it was supposed to be. What is the role of education in this? When I went to design school, I was at the tail end of the group that got taught critical thinking. Everything since then is deliverables. The industry wants deliverables, and we're back to the earlier point about what happens when information architecture is no longer called information architecture and nobody has a name for it. That's what happens when it becomes fully deliverableitized. What may happen is that we will no longer have information architecture and people coming out of all those twelve-week and ten-week programs will know what a sitemap is. They will know what a flow diagram is. But they won't know what information architecture is.

Q: This year you were a keynote speaker at the IA Conference. You spoke about resilience and values. Do you think information architects are up to today's challenges?

In my keynote this year, I went to a real squishy place inside. That was something that really took a lot of courage to do for me. Being asked to give that talk was a really big honor, and I knew that it was a moment that would mean a lot to me and also a lot to the people that look up to me. I wanted to make sure that I left them with a message that was authentic. We were in a really weird place at the time. I'll be totally honest with you, there was a moment where I got close to canceling because I was thinking, no one should be talking about information architecture right now, it's not important enough. There are bigger things like being with your family right now, getting through your damn day.

And then, I had a seriously life-changing moment with Jorge Arango. I asked for time because I was legitimately losing it, he gave it to me readily. We talked through pros and cons of doing the talk—about how persistence was a really interesting concept to think about in this time when everything feels so dark and it is about just getting through every day. I had started to write about the idea of bravery and the concept of persistence. Talking to Jorge about it, I realized I needed to take my own medicine on this one. I needed to be brave, and I needed to persist, and then it became meta. We have to show up and be persistent for the people that we're working with and working through problems with. We have to realize our own personal place in things, and represent that authentically.

I hope people understood that I was not only bringing tools and a perspective for tackling projects at work, but also a perspective of bravery and kindness, and thinking about your effect on other people, which will serve you well no matter what's going on in the world—or what you're trying to accomplish.

Bernadette Irizarry a creative leader with roots in graphic design and sculpture, Bern is the founder and CEO of the Los Angeles-based design consultancy, Velvet Hammer. Bern has built and led cross-disciplinary teams for over 20 years, holds two patents in color selection and served as an organizer for the Academics and Practitioners Roundtable from 2016–2019. Dedicated to growing diversity in technology and design, she currently sits on the Board of Advisors for AIGA Los Angeles, and co-founded the Los Angeles Chapter of Ladies that UX.

Information Architecture for Industry Events: Intention, Diversity, and Inclusion

Jeffrey R. Pass and Asha R. Singh

Abstract Industry events should reflect the diversity of their body of practitioners, but diverse, inclusive, and safe events don't happen by accident; like the information-based structures that Information Architects create in the digital space, the information-sharing structure of a conference, workshop, or other events must be designed with intent and purpose. This case study outlines efforts undertaken by several Washington, DC-area events as well as the Information Architecture Conference during 2018 and 2019 to better architect Diversity and Inclusion within industry events. The purpose of these activities was to help event organizers to plan and execute better, more diverse, and more inclusive industry events. It describes the 2019 Diversity & Inclusion Workshop series that was undertaken at three of these events to inform diversity and inclusion efforts by the IA Conference, for which one of the authors served as 2019 diversity and inclusion co-chair, and shares the diversity, inclusion, safety, and accessibility topics identified by workshop participants. The chapter concludes with actionable steps that can be taken to improve industry events and their organizational bodies. The goal of this case study is to encourage and support conscious efforts to engineer better events, by leveraging information architecture (IA) and user experience (UX) techniques applied in larger contexts and information spaces.

Background and Introduction

At the time of this writing, the notion of diversity and inclusion (D&I) is top-of-mind for many industry event organizers due, in no small part, to social unrest and cultural shifts related to issues of race, equality, representation, and justice sparked by police violence toward people of color in the United States, and the resulting Black Lives Matter and associated movements.

J. R. Pass (✉)
Booz Allen Hamilton, McLean, VA, USA

A. R. Singh
UXPA DC, Washington, DC, USA

© The Author(s), under exclusive license to Springer Nature Switzerland AG 2021
A. Resmini et al. (eds.), *Advances in Information Architecture*,
Human–Computer Interaction Series, https://doi.org/10.1007/978-3-030-63205-2_12

But these are scarcely new issues and event organizers have been working to address them for decades. As early as the 1990s, the American Institute of Graphic Arts (AIGA) had identified the importance of D&I in design and design-related fields (Vernon-Chesley, 1990).

The need for D&I efforts, especially in programming and curation, became a growing concern at events, leading to the creation of D&I positions or expectations explicitly stated in organizer roles. Simultaneously, the need for a proper deep dive into what D&I means to participants became apparent when a series of high-profile events each had different issues that exposed weaknesses in D&I, safety, accessibility, and enforcement of codes of conduct (COC) at events. The environment of expanded audience voices, prior event faux pas, and lack of previous exploration led to a workshop series designed and conducted across information architecture (IA) and user experience (UX) events in 2018 and 2019, culminating in a lightning talk at the 7th annual Academics and Practitioners Roundtable. This chapter is an extension of the workshops and lightning talk.

The talk summarized the D&I efforts undertaken by the Roundtable's host event, the 2019 Information Architecture Conference (IAC19), as well as the findings from D&I workshops facilitated at three industry events in 2019: UXCamp DC, World Information Architecture Day DC (WIAD-DC), and IAC19. The workshops were organized and facilitated by Jeffrey Pass to help inform and prioritize D&I efforts by the IAC in his role as IAC19 D&I co-chair.

To expand the reach of that original lightning talk, the authors worked with the organizers of IAC, WIAD-DC, UXCamp DC, as well as other Washington, DC-area events and professional association chapters to better understand their D&I (as well as safety, D&I+S) efforts and to identify actionable steps that can be taken to improve industry events as well as the organizations that run them. The contribution to this publication is meant to showcase the process, experience, and present realities for organizers to be able to architect D&I into their events, using the authors' experience during the 2019 event year as an anchor.

The authors have worked organizing industry events going back more than a decade. They have also independently organized and facilitated industry and non-industry events that focused on diversity, inclusion, and safety, as well as initiatives for their respective employers. Information presented here is meant to offer insight into the thought process for those who organize and participate in events. The authors would also like to note the following: While this chapter and the work that preceded it is born out of information architecture- and user experience-related events, its substance is broadly applicable to event organizing regardless of industry or domain; The authors are practitioners and not strictly information architects. They, like the majority of individuals that contributed to this chapter, either through event or workshop participation or through discussions with the authors about industry event organization/facilitation, fall into the larger domain of user experience design as articulated by Jesse James Garrett at the 10th annual Information Architecture Summit.

Limitations

This case study is based on work that largely focused on a single geography, the larger Washington, DC area, and a single international event, the IA Conference, during a limited period of time. The authors also acknowledge other significant limitations of this study:

- Workshop findings and resulting findings and recommendations have not yet been socialized with or validated by workshop participants or host event organizers
- The workshop organization and structure varied from host event to host event; the workshop methodology remained consistent, but size and circumstances of individual workshop sessions necessarily resulted in different information collection environments
- While the attendance at individual workshops was relatively diverse, the combination of geography and event focus (IA or UX and IA) necessarily limited the diversity of participants
- While workshop participation at individual events was significant, the combined data sample is very small
- Like websites, events are transient (here today, then gone, or gone for a month or year, etc.) and ever evolving; repeating the workshops today would likely provide similar outcomes, but there would certainly be notable differences reflecting evolving expectations, new event D&I+S exemplars, recent scholarship on the topic, etc.

Additionally, the case is built on the reflective practice of longtime industry event organizers rather than on a purposeful preexisting research question. While the authors believe that the observations and recommendations offered here are valuable and actionable, they acknowledge that they are not necessarily repeatable and that the topic of organizing events fostering diversity, inclusion, and safety warrants more formal, academic studies, perhaps informed by the work accounted in this chapter.

Definitions

It is important to acknowledge the meanings of the terms used here (diversity, inclusion, safety, and accessibility) vary across events and have evolved over the years. This is all the more important viewed through the lens of information architecture (IA), wherein labeling is at the very heart of information architecture practice and critical to context and understanding. To clarify what is intended for this chapter, we offer the following definitions (and framing) for our use of these terms:

Diversity. Diversity refers to "a range of many people or things that are very different from each other" (Oxford Learner's Dictionary, n.d.). Applied to workplace and professional environments, traditional definitions of diversity used by

Baby Boomers (born 1946–1964) and Generation X (born 1965–1980), generally focus on gender, race, ethnicity, religion, sexual orientation (Smith & Turner, 2015, p. 7). Importantly, this focus has been expanded by the entry of Millennials (born 1981–1996) and Generation Z (born 1997–2012) into the workforce. They have expanded the definition to include cognitive diversity, diversity of thoughts, ideas, and philosophies; i.e., diverse, inclusive perspectives (Smith & Turner, 2015, p. 7). The notion of "diversity of thoughts" is sometimes understood as the inclusion of alternative perspectives, but it is important that it also be understood to mean not only the visible inclusion of minorities, but also inclusion of their perspectives and insights.

Inclusion. Inclusion refers to "the practice or policy of providing equal access to opportunities and resources for people who might otherwise be excluded or marginalized" (Lexico, n.d.). Applied to workplace and professional environments, "diversity refers to the traits and characteristics that make people unique while inclusion refers to the behaviors and social norms that ensure people feel welcome" (Musser, 2019).

Safety. Safety is the "condition of being protected from or unlikely to cause danger, risk, or injury" (Lexico, n.d.). At events, it is the trust those attending have that harms have been mitigated and that infractions will be enforced, especially when there is a code of conduct, or an established guidance all participants have agreed to follow.

Safety is somewhat problematic in that legal considerations and liability come into play (or at least potentially do). For this reason, safety is often not included with D&I when discussing event facilitation. The authors include it here because of their core belief that safety is integral to both diverse event participation and broad adoption of inclusive behaviors and norms.

Accessibility. Many different definitions of accessibility exist ranging from academic to legal (e.g., the Americans with Disabilities ACT [ADA] or the European Accessibility Act [EAA]).

For the purposes of this chapter, the authors posit that accessibility is a measure of how simply a person can participate (or engage) in an activity. For events, it relates to how comfortable or difficult participation in any capacity is, and for organizers, the breadth to what kinds of accommodations for which types of abilities or disabilities have been accounted for.

As we learn more about neurodivergence, individuals whose neurological development and state are atypical (Disabled World, 2020), different ability levels, and better strategies to adapt to these differences, notions of "accessibility" are likely to expand or become more nuanced.

D&I+S Efforts and Activities

The work and events that informed this chapter all occurred before 2020 and the global coronavirus (COVID-19) epidemic. Virtual/remote event facilitation was not a consideration for the authors at that time and the following does not consider changes to the event organizing landscape as a result of COVID-19 (however, the Coda for this chapter does consider COVID-19 and makes broad recommendations for post-COVID-19 event organizing and facilitation).

Planning Considerations

D&I+S efforts should be viewed as occurring along a continuum, beginning with pre-event planning and preparation efforts (the majority of effort), continuing on to "day-of" efforts (what is actually done during the event itself), and concluding with post-event follow-up and documentation efforts (all of which then inform pre-event planning for the next event).

Important considerations that help identify what sorts of D&I+S efforts should be undertaken include:

Event scope and location. Events that are associated with a single organization (e.g., a college or employer), are typically easier to manage and have fewer variables to control for. Open events, at public venues such as a hotel or convention center, have more variables to control for. These variables include audience uniformity; for example, a departmental event at an academic institution draws from an insular and well-defined audience as where an open event at a public forum may draw a broad audience, potentially including passers-by.

Event size and duration. One-day (or shorter) events have fewer considerations compared to multi-day events, especially those involving event hotels or multiple locations, complicating logistics, and creating situations where event participants may be: gathered at the event location outside of event hours, moving between event locations, or offsite for unofficial programming (such as networking dinners or happy hours).

Event audience and affiliation. Association-based events may have existing CoC and D&I policies in place as well as structures for lodging and processing complaints as well as administering rulings (e.g., expulsion from the association, fines, legal action). For open events, in which anyone can attend, the only binding expectations and rules are set by the event itself.

Event cost and cost-related expectations. While all events should be diverse, inclusive, and safe, free, or volunteer events may not have resources to devote to D&I+S efforts whereas there is an expectation that high-cost events include such efforts within the price tag.

Accessibility requirements and accommodations. Beyond meeting basic, legal accessibility requirements (e.g., ADA or EAA), including additional services or accommodations (e.g., live captioning services, sign language interpreters, or transportation services for multi-location events) necessarily increases event budgets (unless they are provided gratis or underwritten by sponsors). Costs inevitably rise for each accommodation, forcing many organizers to weigh costs against values to the largest possible number of participants.

Safety measures, staffing, and liability. Safety considerations potentially increase in more diverse and inclusive gatherings, and with them possible event liability. Some events provide their own safety officers, but these roles are typically volunteer and do not carry any authority (or if they do, they also carry liability).

Additionally, based on the authors' experience and discussions with other industry event organizers, most event organizers are not trained in, qualified to, or legally empowered to enforce safety. Options for incorporating official safety staff include using venue-based security (may incur additional costs), contract security (requires contracting and budget), or local law enforcement (for larger, public events; may require licensing/permitting as well as fees). If working with official safety staff, important considerations include having a CoC, and a clear, documented escalation plan including when and under what circumstances to involve official safety representatives.

Event-Specific Efforts, Activities, & Underpinnings

The following table identifies notable D&I+S efforts and activities that were taken by events the authors helped organize, as well as the foundational codes and documentation that supported them.

All of the items listed in Table 1 were found to be successful and impactful based on event participant feedback and event organizer postmortems.

Table 1 Event-specific efforts, activities, & underpinnings

Item	IAC19	IAS18	WIAD DC 17-19	DCUX19	UXDC17
Leadership roles/duties	D&I co-chairs	D&I chair	Executive team (ET)	ET + curators	ET + curators
D&I Goals	Internal	--	Internal (18, 19)	Internal	--
CoC	Yes	Yes	Yes	Yes	Yes
CoC hotline	Yes	--	Yes	Yes	--
D&I statement	Vision & Values	CoC	Driving Principles	CoC	CoC
D&I+S info included in/on/with	Welcome packet, badge, web, blog, emails	Welcome packet, web, blog, emails	Welcome packet, web, emails	Welcome packet, badge, web, emails	Welcome packet, webs, emails
D&I survey/poll	Pre-, Post-event	Pre-event	Post-event	Post-event	Via event survey
Must accept CoC	Yes	Yes	Yes	Yes	Yes

(continued)

Table 1 (continued)

Item	IAC19	IAS18	WIAD DC 17-19	DCUX19	UXDC17
Participant D&I self-ID	Optional in registration	Optional in registration	--	Optional in registration	--
Accommodations	Accessibility, dietary	Accessibility, dietary	Dietary (18, 19)	Accessibility, dietary	Accessibility, dietary
Speaker D&I self-ID	Optional in registration	Optional in registration	Optional in registration	Optional in registration	--
D&I workshop	Yes	--	Yes (19)	Yes	--
D&I event	Roundtable	--	Panel (19)	Talk	--
Financial assistance	Scholarships, discounts	Scholarships, discounts	Discounts	Discounts	Discounts
Quiet, nursing, and prayer rooms*	Quiet room, multi-purpose rooms	Quiet room; event office if needed	Multi-purpose (17, 19); designated (18)	Quiet room; event office if needed	Event office if needed
Gender-neutral bathrooms*	"Family" bathroom (in lobby)	--	Designated gender-neutral bathroom (19	"Family" bathroom (in lobby)	"Family" bathroom (in lobby)

Notes (1) *subject to venue accommodations and event budget; (2) "--" indicates explicit data on this category was not captured for that event

While it is not possible to make any causal statements, the IAC, WIAD DC, and UXPA DC (parent of both DCUX and UXDC) organizers feel that the above efforts, activities, and underpinnings contributed to the success of their events, not just in terms of D&I+S, but also more generally.

D&I+S Workshops

The D&I+S workshop series was initiated by Jeffrey Pass, in his capacity as IAC19 D&I co-chair, to inform and help prioritize D&I+S efforts at IAC19 as well as the larger IAC. The workshops not only occurred during events focused on information architecture and user experience, they leveraged traditional methods and tools (labeling, affinity mapping, categorization, etc.) long employed by information architecture and user experience practitioners. They were open to all event attendees (with certain space limitations) with the goals of:

- Learning about D&I+S efforts for that particular event
- Improving future instances of the event
- Informing and improving event planning and facilitation work for IAC and across the larger domain.

The workshop outputs provided a useful tool for identifying the depth and breadth of possible D&I+S efforts that can be undertaken as well as validation for efforts already underway by the participating events.

Workshop Facilitation

2019 workshops were conducted at Washington, DC-area events and at IAC19.

- January 12: UXCamp DC—D&I+S@UX-events
- February 2: WIAD DC celebration event—Architecting IA Industry Events For Diversity & Inclusion
- March 16: IAC—IAC19 Diversity & Inclusion Roundtable.

All workshops began with the setting of expectations and establishment of definitions and parameters (not unlike the preceding sections of this chapter). Additionally, the WIAD DC workshop was immediately preceded by a D&I panel. Additionally, the IAC19 workshop was preceded by a presentation on the work undertaken by the Conference Co-Chairs, Diversity & Inclusion Co-Chairs, and event volunteers and staff.

Following this background and framing, workshop attendees broke up into informal groups organized around stations with a variety of sticky notes, pens, and other supplies alongside large posters boards, horizontally or vertically oriented depending on the space, broken out into four categories (Fig. 1).

- **Experiences:** what happened to you
- **Observations:** what you witnessed
- **Lessons Learned:** personal, professional, insights
- **Recommendations:** constructive, realistic, actionable feedback.

Participants were encouraged to create sticky notes and to place them on the board within the appropriate category. Additional exercise instructions and encouragement (projected on-screen during the exercise with printed versions at each station) included:

- Be honest, no accusations please
- Focus on industry conference-related D&I+S topics
- Work as a group; affinity map (group topics)
- "Dot" to indicate shared topics
- Discuss, share, and synthesize.

Understanding that some workshop participants might feel overwhelmed by this approach or have (physical) accessibility issues, instructions also included prompts for anyone that wished to post their stickies from afar to identify themselves to the workshop facilitators and volunteers (or any other surrogate) who, in turn, worked with those individuals to ensure their comfortable participation in the exercise.

Fig. 1 Representation of the matrix used to capture workshop participant inputs

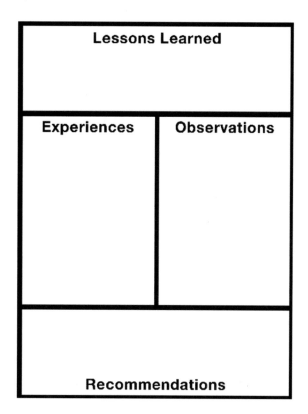

Workshop Participation

Workshop participation varied based on the event-based format. At UXCamp and IAC the workshop occurred during normal conference sessions, when event participants could choose among sessions; for both events, the workshops filled their rooms beyond capacity. For WIAD it occurred as part of a D&I plenary session (Table 2).

Participant feedback from all three events indicated a deep appreciation for the workshops and excitement (and in some cases relief) that D&I+S were being discussed in such an open and "democratic" forum.

Table 2 Workshop participation

Metric*	UXCamp DC	WIADDC	IAC
Event Attendees	120	135	255
Workshop Participants	12	100	42
% of Attendees	10%	74%	16%

*All numbers approximate. Attendees based on event registration, participants based on room counts during workshops. Percentage based on those estimates

The authors interpret workshop participation and participant feedback as evidence of a larger trend toward professional awareness of and commitment to D&I+S both as concepts and as an endeavor. Anecdotally, in the authors' experience, events that make a point to undertake explicit D&I efforts, and especially those that involve event participants in those efforts, are lauded for their efforts.

Data Collection and Tagging

Following each workshop, boards were photographed, as-is (to preserve groupings) then individual sticky note topics were recorded as well as the number of "plus one" dots. All data was plugged into a spreadsheet then tagged by theme, with themes emerging from the data itself.

- Categorization (theme-based tagging) was performed by the workshop facilitator (and co-facilitators when involved) in the days immediately following the event
- Some topics appeared in multiple categories (Experiences, Observations, Lessons Learned, Recommendations) and were recorded accordingly
- Topics were frequently tagged with multiple themes
- For a given event topics were de-duplicated; duplicates were recorded as part of the "Plus" column; however, topics were not de-duplicated across events, though they were consolidated when generating the list of key, actionable items by theme.

The initial workshop at UXCamp DC 2019 informed the creation of the original theme tag set; however, additional themes were added when identified at subsequent workshops. When this occurred, the facilitator revisited preceding workshops and, if the new topic was in evidence from the past workshop tagging, notes, or recordings, the tag would be retroactively applied.

A total of 249 topics were recorded that consolidated down to 185 unique topics. Key, actionable D&I+S topics were identified from select themes and are listed below, followed by a complete listing of themes.

Key, Actionable D&I+S Topics by Theme

Accessibility

- Control noise (ambient as well as attendee); ensure participants can hear proceedings and presenters
- Require that all presentations (or other materials) meet accessibility guidelines, especially related to color, contrast, type size, strobe effects, etc.
- Provide subtitles or sign language interpretation for all sessions
- Record all sessions and make them available in an accessible format

- Select venues with accessibility in mind and clearly identify accessibility limitations and accommodations
- Plan and facilitate with accessibility in mind (including understanding your audience and their needs)
- Provide portable microphones for Q&A sessions and discussions (static microphones on a mic stand pose accessibility concerns).

Culture

- Understand all groups you are designing (events) for (design for everyone)
- Promote a culture in which all participants stand up for themselves and others
- Convey interest in and appreciation for all participants regardless of their role, skill, or experience
- Define and promote D&I together; it is the responsibility of all event participants, not just organizers
- Commit to respectful, honest, and transparent communication; create structures supporting constructive dialogue as well as promoting feedback aimed at improving future events
- Create a safe space to challenge/grow self and community
- No one should dominate the proceedings; everyone should make space for others to engage and participate
- Promote honestly.

Curation and Programming

- Provide outreach and support for new, underrepresented, and marginalized voices
- Avoid tokenization; don't simply have D&I speakers addressing D&I topics
- Incorporate the event audience in the curation process where appropriate and feasible (e.g., via input on theme/topic, speaker recommendations, or even community curation)
- Provide presenter resources and support; help prepare and elevate new or disadvantaged presenters
- Make no excuse for majoritarian programming.

Diversity and Inclusion

- Ensure that the D&I focus includes all event participants (participants + organizers, presenters, sponsors, volunteers, etc.) as well as the event venue and surroundings
- Involve the larger event community in planning as much as possible

- Program in a variety of formats to facilitate different types of speakers and topics as well as different attendees
- Proactively engage underrepresented groups mindfully (taking care to avoid superficial representation or tokenism)
- Don't just seek demographics (arbitrary goals and "safe" KPIs do not a D&I+S event make)
- Provide, or at least fight for, non-gendered bathrooms (potentially including "family" restrooms) as well as labeling and directions to help participants find/utilize them
- Provide accommodations for participants with special needs such as designated lactation, prayer, and quiet rooms
- Provide scholarships or discounts for students and individuals with limited financial resources
- Provide pronoun stickers and promote (or require) their use (note: from a safety standpoint, optional pronoun sticker use can make a target of individuals that chose to use them)
- Offer resources, coaching, and periodic outreach designed to address Imposter syndrome, especially for emerging leaders and new talent
- Facilitate inclusive participation, including addressing systemic power politics, issues relating to accessibility and introversion, etc.
- Mitigate against individuals dominating discussions, Q&A, etc.; normalize inclusion strategies, such as "Move Up, Move Back" (a technique for creating space for marginalized participants to speak).

Introversion and Social Anxiety

- Heavy-handed facilitated participation can backfire or reduce participation; ensure that mechanisms to encourage/facilitate introvert participation leave room for non-participation (listening/observing only)
- Provide safe/quiet rooms; monitor or manage rooms to ensure their proper use
- Provide clear info about event, activities, accommodations (set reasonable expectations); alternatively, include flexible, open-ended activities that participants can shape in real-time
- Provide mechanisms for introverts to engage comfortably (e.g., having volunteers provide feedback on behalf of attendees, or including feedback received digitally (via text, tweet, etc.)
- Include social/networking activities that do not involve alcohol (e.g., happy hours) or loud, crowded environments (e.g., karaoke).

Safety

- Provide/promote a clear mechanism for reporting, escalating, resolving, and learning from issues
- Acknowledge relevant safety concerns as well as relevant movements related to safety (as well as D&I such as #BlackLivesMatter and #MeToo)
- Make safety an explicit part of event planning, marketing, and facilitation
- Limit activities (e.g., banquets, happy hours) involving alcohol and for those that do, guard against drunken, aggressive behavior
- Clearly identify and promote safe spaces (e.g., lactation, prayer, and quiet rooms)
- Make any D&I data collection entirely optional.

All Identified Topic Themes

Data tagging was based on a distillation of themes identified during the sticky note exercise. Identified topic themes included:

- Actionable Solutions: use in combination with any other topic theme where a clear action is identified
- **Accessibility** *(see Key, Actionable D+S Topics by Theme)*
- Communications & Promotions: the full life cycle of event-related messaging, marketing, and other content
- Cost (event): primarily the cost associated with event attendance/participation (inclusive of travel and accommodations), but also related to the cost of running the event
- **Culture** (event, industry, society) *(see Key, Actionable D+S Topics by Theme)*
- **Curation & Programming** *(see Key, Actionable D+S Topics by Theme)*
- Dispute Resolution: clear mechanisms for reporting, investigating, resolving or remediating, and learning form issues and complaints
- **Diversity & Inclusion** *(see Key, Actionable D+S Topics by Theme)*
- Gender-Related: including gender representation, gender identification, gender-based services or accommodations (e.g., restrooms), etc.
- Hospitality (event): vegetarian and vegan options, affordances for dietary restrictions, non-caffeinated and non-alcoholic beverage options, etc.
- **Introversion & Social Anxiety** *(see Key, Actionable D+S Topics by Theme)*
- Logistics & Location: issues relating to event site access (both in terms of distance as well as accessibility), setup, scheduling, etc.
- **Move Up, Move Bac**k (culture and inclusion) *(see Key, Actionable D+S Topics by Theme)*
- Outreach: event marketing and communications as well as targeted outreach to communities of practice, institutions (associations, educational, etc.), and D&I target audiences
- Planning: all aspects of event planning and the team(s) that undertake it

- **Safety** *(see Key, Actionable D+S Topics by Theme)*
- Social Events (associated, outside): both official events, such as event-sponsored banquets or sponsored activities such as a karaoke night, as well as ad hoc events such as informal happy hours or outings into the event host city
- Support (for attendees, presenters, etc.): overlapping with Accessibility and Cost, including accommodations, communications, facilities, logistics, etc.
- Training (all parties): including training for organizers, volunteers, presenters, and sponsors, as well as resources for attendees.

Concrete Guidance for Architecting Diverse, Inclusive Events

Organizing an event, especially for D&I+S, is a kind of information architecture endeavor employing both IA theory and practice in order to:

- Identify and understand the event audience (inclusive of organizers, presenters, vendors, and attendees)
- Define and categorize participants based on both observable and hidden characteristics
- Frame the event via policies, procedures, and guidelines (information and relationships)
- Facilitate attendance and involvement based on physical, social, psychological, economic, and other criteria.

All of these, and indeed all of the D&I+S topics identified in this chapter, are contributing factors to creating the underlying information architecture of what an event is; or perhaps put another way, an event's IA of inclusion.

In their years of experience organizing industry events with an eye to D&I+S, the authors have employed all of these points into their efforts helping to define and adopt many practices and approaches that are now D&I+S best practices. The D&I+S workshops not only validated this work, they informed and expanded it.

Taken together, along with insights gained during the COVID-19 global pandemic, the authors offer the following guidance that, their experience indicates, will help industry event organizers (and event organizers in general) meet their diversity, inclusion, and safety goals, and help empower event attendees to hold the events to a higher standard.

Lead by Example

Organizing a diverse, inclusive event is easier when the event itself has diverse and inclusive leadership, organizers, curators, and volunteers. Often, this requires both active recruitment and mentorship of individuals who have little to no active experience organizing events and for existing event organizing leaders to make room for new individuals. If the goal is not merely to incorporate but center D&I+S, these individuals should be spread across the leadership team, not just in a single "D&I" position that may or may not have tangible impact on the larger event, (e.g., curation of the program or selection of the safety enforcement policies).

Plan, Prepare, Document, and Share

Diverse, inclusive, and safe events don't happen by accident or coincidence. Organizers must frame, define, create, architect, label, document, promote, and evolve underlying structures to support D&I+S goals, including:

- A strong Code of Conduct (CoC) with enforcement provisions
- An articulated stance or statement on diversity and inclusion (ideally also safety), including any articulated goals or key performance indicators (KPIs)
- Promotion and diligent enforcement of the CoC and D&I+S stance, including prominent inclusion in the event website(s), registration and confirmation materials, communications (be they via mail, email, blog, or social media), and event welcome materials
- Resources and/or training for leadership, organizers, curators, and volunteers, as well as speakers/presenters, vendors, and attendees
- Communicate what D&I+S efforts have been undertaken and what accommodations are being provided at the event (e.g., gender-neutral restrooms, sign language interpreters, or prayer rooms).

The authors would recommend that event organizers meet together to review the Event-Specific D&I+S Efforts & Activities and Key, Actionable D&I+S Topics by Theme sections. These sections can serve as a starting point for events that are just beginning to focus on D&I+S or to validate efforts already underway. Not all efforts, activities, and topics will apply to every event, but you would do well to consider those that do.

Remain Vigilant and Engage Your Audience

The event landscape is ever-changing and social norms are ever-evolving. At the time of this writing, the Black Lives Matter, racial equality, and anti-racism movements are driving important discussions and actions related to equity and safety. It is impossible to organize perfectly diverse, inclusive, and safe events, but you can make the process easier (and likely more successful) by:

- Setting realistic and attainable D&I+S goals and revisiting them with some frequency

- Polling, surveying, or otherwise communicating with the event's audience well in advance of the event
- Socializing any CoC, D&I+S policies, as well as reporting and escalation procedures as part of the event welcome and materials/documentation
- Follow-up communications, surveys, or polls to evaluate the success of D&I+S efforts and to identify any failures, gaps, or future goals.

For recurring events, It is prudent to revisit your goals, targets, KPIs, and general definition of Diversity on at least an annual basis. As diversity is, by definition, a resulting difference between the majority and minority, organizers should be prepared to adjust their D&I targets, categories, and KPIs to reflect the community's changes over time in order to continue elevating voices that are less represented.

Coda: Learning from COVID-19

The D&I+S workshops all occurred prior to the COVID-19 pandemic, as did most of the work that laid the groundwork for this chapter. The pandemic has forced the cancellation of many industry events, but others, like the Information Architecture Conference 2020 (IAC20) shifted to an all-virtual format. The broad adoption of remote work and all-virtual events like IAC20 will likely create higher expectations relating to D&I.

These practices have allowed many individuals with accessibility issues, financial limitations, and social traits such as introverts and individuals with social anxiety disorders, to engage and participate in ways that may not have previously been possible/practical.

In a post-COVID-19 world, industry event organizers would do well to consider hybrid (in-person and virtual) events or, at the very least, virtual participation options for those with a personal preference for or a demonstrable impediment to in-person participation. Early observations seem to suggest that hybrid events may allow for broad participation: the 8th Academics and Practitioners Roundtable—part of the IA Conference 2020—was entirely virtual and benefited from increased participation from Asia and Europe, owing largely to the format that freed many from the necessity to travel.

Acknowledgements The authors wish to acknowledge and thank the editors of this volume, the organizers, past and present, of DCUX, IAC, IAS, UXCamp DC, UXDC, and WIAD-DC, the leadership, past and present, of GoodGovUx, the Information Architecture Institute, the Information Architecture Foundation, UXPA, and UXPA DC. They also wish to thank their peer reviewers, Brittnee S. Alford and Raffaella Isidori.

References

Disabled World. (2020). *What is: Neurodiversity, neurodivergent, neurotypical.* https://www.disabled-world.com/disability/awareness/neurodiversity/.

Lexico. (n.d.). *Inclusion.* https://www.lexico.com/en/definition/inclusion.

Lexico. (n.d.). *Safety.* https://www.lexico.com/en/definition/safety.

Musser, H. (2019). *Diversity and inclusion: What it is and why it matters.* Agile alliance. https://www.agilealliance.org/diversity-and-inclusion-what-it-is-and-why-it-matters.

Oxford Learner's Dictionaries. (n.d.). *Diversity.* https://www.oxfordlearnersdictionaries.com/us/definition/american_english/diversity.

Smith, C., & Turner, S. (2015). *The radical transformation of diversity and inclusion: The millennial influence.* Deloitte University Leadership Center. http://www.bjkli.org/wp-content/uploads/2015/05/report.pdf.

Vernon-Chelsey, M. (1990). Equal opportunities: Minorities in graphic design. *AIGA Journal of Graphic Design, 8*(1).

Teaching Information Architecture in South Africa: In Conversation with Terence Fenn

Sarah A. Rice

Terence Fenn is a senior lecturer in interaction design in the Department of Multi-media at the University of Johannesburg's Faculty of Art, Design and Architecture. He holds a bachelors in fine arts, master's degrees in art & design education and information technology, and he's currently pursuing a PhD in design. He has written extensively on the intersection of information architecture and design thinking and co-chaired the 2nd Academics and Practitioners Roundtable on Teaching Information Architecture with Jason Hobbs.

S. A. Rice (✉)
Seneb Consulting, San Jose, CA, USA
e-mail: rice@seneb.com

© The Author(s), under exclusive license to Springer Nature Switzerland AG 2021
A. Resmini et al. (eds.), *Advances in Information Architecture*,
Human–Computer Interaction Series, https://doi.org/10.1007/978-3-030-63205-2_13

Q: I understand that you were lecturing at university when you first encountered what you now know to be information architecture. Why did it interest you and how has that interest developed over the years?

My original qualification and experience was in fine art, and when I began working in the Multimedia Department, typically we were designing digital products on platforms such as Adobe Flash and Macromedia Director. Our approach tended to emphasise visual creativity, and very much a continuation of graphic design tradition towards design. Around 2006, I realised that creative digital design can and should be more than a tool for online marketing and game-play and I started moving out of that world. Thus, I started to look more closely at the traditional design fields of architecture, industrial design/product design that focus on the how people interact with the world, through the artificial.

So, my approach to digital and design has always emphasised the creative role of technology design, and how it alters, enhances and occasionally disrupts people's lives. In this sense, I think of design as a separate tradition to engineering approaches to technology development, one that emphasises integrative creativity over techno-centricism. So, in a shift away from advertising-orientated design, I started to view interaction design as an opportunity to practice and teach design in a more innovative manner. I don't think I was particularly alone in this view, and this general move aligned with the emerging fields of user experience design and subsequently service design.

This move towards a consideration of the design of digital technology from an innately human-centred perspective, really changed my whole approach to thinking about how design should be taught. At the time a whole range of new dynamics were emerging in creative design. Central to this was the emergence of design thinking, both in the practice-world sense, through companies such as IDEO, as well as in the recognition of a lot of important work done in the previous decade on design cognition and philosophy by authors such as Nigel Cross, Klaus Krippendorff, Richard Buchanan (among many others).

In 2009, I began collaborating with Jason Hobbs in both design teaching as well as academic design research. Jason had recently returned to South Africa from working abroad in the UK digital design and was more familiar with the global emerging practices in digital design, in comparison to what was going on in Johannesburg, at the time. I had a more traditional design and design education background. We both shared a vision that design should be applied to engage with problems faced by society, should have a social impact, and should work towards making a better country for all, particularly from our context in the Global South. While we were perhaps a little more radical or political in our views than mainstream digital design, we recognised a major 'turn' towards societal factors. Through our academic and professional work, Jason and I realised that in design, practices such as user-experience design that were incorporating human-centred, design thinking methodologies was going to be really important.

We began to realise that one of the core results of this human-centred design thinking turn, was the escalation of conceptual and cognitive workload faced by designers, and that a traditional design education that was largely centred on aesthetics and persuasion wasn't sufficient for the task.

Both Jason and I felt, and still do, that information architecture provided an approach to both generate and organise creative thinking in response to complexity. We started to see the potential of information architecture, to address complexity, and related approaches to resolution not from a universal design pattern angle but particularly in terms of the situated and uniqueness of individual problem framing and solution pairings. We viewed design as capable of engaging with the real-life complexities of everyday, and, information architecture as the principal design tool for achieving this.

As researchers, and (self-appointed) advocates, we also realised that in our local design community (professional and academic) there was a lot of misunderstanding and land grabbing around terms such as information architecture, interaction design, user experience, etc. Suddenly, everyone was a user experience designer, or an information architect or an ethnographer. But there was very little theoretical and conceptual knowledge to what those practices or terms actually meant. While we were never particularly interested in prescribing to people how they could self-identify, we strongly believed that design, and its corresponding fields (including information architecture) should be respected enough as fields of expertise to have certain competencies and knowledge explicitly associated with them. Hence, we seek to clarify or at least raise discourse on many of these issues through our writing, but in addition, we have done much advocacy work through such local and international conferences and public speaking opportunities, as well as hosting World IA Day in Johannesburg since its global inception.

Q: What unique perspective do you have to offer as a South African educator and designer?

A very important aspect to teaching design here in South Africa is that the majority of our students are black Africans, and the history of design is largely built on the Western tradition. It's really important and in line with human-centred design to use information architecture to break down many of the tacit constructs of [western] design, and focus on assisting students to construct their own understanding of the world and creative action. In my view, instead of design being some kind of magical act that a person was born to or inherited special abilities for (which was very much how I was taught design 20 years ago), information architecture thinking abilities allows one to be able to develop and communicate design thinking all the way through the creative process. In this way, students are able to learn how to organise and articulate their own construction of design contexts and designerly responses. By making the tacit visual, through information architecture modeling, allows for abstract concepts and understandings to be made visible, and as such open for discussion, critique and confirmation. This way, information architecture directly helps the 'hidden mastery of practice' to become a developmental process, rather than a cultural inheritance. Information architecture allows us to unpack design decision-making in the space between the problem and the final product.

Information architecture is also a great tool to address social problems. South Africa can be considered both a first- and a developing-world country and is characterised by extreme inequality. It's quite easy to see a lot of social problems brought on by Apartheid, and in more recent times apathy, mismanagement and corruption. A lot of the urban areas suffer from the lack of infrastructure and service delivery, poverty abounds, there is a very high alcohol consumption rate, and it is a very violent society in general. When I went to university, in the mid-1990's, the student body was about 90% white European. When I began to teach, the dynamic had shifted at the university as naturally many more Black students had the opportunity to attend. Johannesburg has been described as one of the most diverse places in the world and the sheer range of ethnicities and languages of our student body makes working in education a very interesting place to be in.

As I stated earlier, I became interested in information architecture and digital media as I was particularly interested in human and societal centred design. I also realised that design is completely cultural. Right now, even in a place like South Africa, that design culture and capabilities are often equated with an exposure to Western culture. The ability to excel in the field was built around certain dispositions that were often expected but never explicitly taught. These dispositions were often a result of your social class and home culture. It was more about how many books you grew up within your home, what sort of movies you were exposed to, did your parents take you to art galleries, etc. Many of the students we taught didn't have access to any of those Western cultural moments that would allow them to arrive at university with a full-fledged 'design mind'. Looking back on it now it seems ridiculous, the degree of embedded privilege that was expected to gain access and thrive as a student of design. Unfortunately, I still routinely see examples of this mono-cultural approach to design.

Avoiding this top-down approach to design knowledge drove us to apply information architecture thinking and technique in our programme. We extended the pragmatic uses of information architecture in, say, navigation design or site content organisation, and applied information architecture as an approach to meaning-making or 'structure thinking'. We focused on the ability to articulate the designer's thinking process throughout the entire design process. While fully aware that design is also about imagination, pushing the levels of the possible and bringing beauty to the world, we felt that information architecture as a language for meaning-making should be a fundamental skill for both design educators and students seeking to create alternative ways of being, thinking and engaging with the world, through design.

Q: What is your approach to teaching design and how does information architecture fit with that?

I work in an interaction design programme housed within a larger department focused on digital media design. In the interaction focus, we emphasise a human-centred creative approach to digital product design. The other focus of our department is digital content design such as animation, format, video editing, compositing, narrative design, etc. However, all our students do primary modules in both foci, so there is a large degree of overlap. Our student work focuses on what Floridi describes as the 'outer- loop' of technological design and as such is concerned more with how technology is created to enable human needs as well as cultural and environmental sustainability. I would not consider us a traditional 'engineering-orientated' human computer interaction (HCI) programme, although of course, we have inherited many aspects from HCI.

In my view, it's impossible to do interaction design without information architecture. You can't have a product without structure, and you can't have structure without some sort of intentionality. In an analogy to language, the meaning of words are conditioned in terms of how they are contextualised in sentences. Jason and I argue all the time whether interaction design is the bigger field or information architecture is the bigger field, with the other being a subset underneath. Ultimately, when people ask us what we do, we respond with 'user experience design', because we know they will understand what that means.

I think overall, our tendency is to consider clear conceptual lines between the various approaches in our writing and teaching but in application, I feel any specific design activity would integrate information architecture and interaction design, with other approaches, in novel and holistic ways, and we shouldn't get too hung up on classification. That's why I tend to prefer to describe what I do and teach as 'design' and think of information architecture and interaction design as approaches to thinking about and taking designerly action in the world.

Early in the digital media programme, first and second year, students are taught by a variety of people on a variety of topics. We also do a lot of information design. Information architecture is packed within information design projects. They are first introduced to Richard Wurman, and they start thinking about typologies and topologies and hierarchies. That is offered through the lens of information design. They are visual students, not science students. So that approach hooks them into those ideas.

Q: Is information architecture called out explicitly in your courses?

Early on, students are taught a range of basic information architecture principles explicitly as a core aspect of information design. Content is centred around organising information and focuses predominantly on classification systems. A lot of this foundational work is informed by Richard Wurman's approaches to information organisation. At the same time, the students learn front-end programming basics like HTML, CSS, JavaScript. As much of our course requires practical outcomes, these early stage projects tend to also incorporate the more pragmatic aspects of information architecture, such as user-journeys, site navigation, wireframes, etc. Much of this is packaged as interaction design rather than explicitly information architecture.

I also teach design research at various levels of our undergraduate, where I bring in a lot of the organisational principles and practices of information architecture, particularly towards framing of design problems and strategic opportunities. In the third year in the programme, in our 'interaction design' focus, information architecture is taught in a much more explicit sense, from both a conceptual and practice focus. Here, various informational, technological and research-orientated approaches, learned earlier, are taught in more depth and framed as information architecture. So, all our students recognise the information architecture character of their broader interaction design practice.

We get quite formal about how we approach these things so that our students are clear about what they are being taught. Many design/development practitioners, in my experience, are often inclined to treat these disciplines such as information architecture, interaction design and experience design, often as they lack formal qualifications, as design approaches that you can absorb via YouTube, or pretend to know by simply stating so on your business card. I believe my students need to understand there is a strong tradition of knowledge for each of these fields. They've got to be able to defend their qualification and their knowledge. When they go out into the world and state that they are an interaction designer or an information architect or an experience designer, they need to know and be able to state clearly what that means.

In our postgraduate courses students often develop 'research through design' projects that explore specifically information architecture concerns.

Q: How else is information architecture helpful?

I encourage students to develop a visual language that communicates their information architecture thinking. This 'thinking as drawing', is an embodied activity of capturing thoughts, organising principles and decisions on paper by hand. Joining circles to create affinities, testing visual arrangements through diagramming, structuring content in spatial and temporal arrangements, etc. These are very tangible skills. This type of sketching, helps the design student figure out what works and what doesn't work. Not just in their thoughts, but in more concrete and editable forms. This type of embodied thinking becomes such a natural and important process, particularly when responding to complex 'wicked' problems. In my mind this may well be the most important contribution of information architecture within design language.

Q: What is your philosophy of design and information architecture?

Firstly, as a country with an ongoing struggle with employment, poverty and ineffective (but very rigid top-down) governance, I believe design can play a strong role in helping individuals and communities to focus their agency. Thus, there is a need to restore the role of creative innovation as a way of life. Everybody can design, as all people have the potential to design, it is a human ability. But in a country like South Africa, generations of cultural and societal repression has led to a crisis in creative action. Design as a social activity that can drive positive change needs to be better understood, then taught to others, so that everyone can build a better country.

However, while everybody has the potential to design, I also strongly believe that design expertise must be highly regarded and nourished in order to support, and in many ways enhance the potential of both communities and industry. And that perhaps these shouldn't be seen as separate agendas, as fundamentally all design should seek to improve the human and planetary conditions.

Focusing on human-issues raises a number of questions, some of which cannot be unanswered without paradox. As designers, on what terms should we engage with people and communities? Are we leaders, facilitators or neo-colonialists? How do we understand people's problems? Can we? Who asked us to? But, also, recognising that change and disruption can also lead to emancipation. As designers, we need to also reflect on what is the most important contribution we can make. We can't solve everything. Are we social workers or cultural theorists, or artists or technologists? Do we have to choose? In our research and teaching these are the type of the questions we have tried to answer.

My personal response is to understand that the world is overwhelmed with conditions that could be better (as well as things that must be preserved and cared for as they are). As a designer, it is not enough to 'problematise', we need to work towards achieving the world we want to live in. Our fundamental intention should be to create and articulate human meaning through design action. Information architecture is essential to this goal as it provides the means to engage with human meaning in a transparent and traceable manner. Information architecture bridges the abstraction and the concrete, the theoretical and the pragmatic, and finally helps to ensure that final designed outcomes can be reconciled with human contexts from which they gain their original cause. That's the interesting part of design for me. Not so much the crafting of design products but the integration of the real, the true and the ideal through the abstract to the artificial.

In my teaching, I view the type of thinking imbued in information architecture in its 'turn' towards meaning-making as critical in terms of my personal philosophy towards education and design. While my own art and design education was in a time when design craft was perhaps at its peak, for the reasons stated earlier, I felt this was a particularly unhelpful approach for my students. I wanted my students to think of design as a form of intellectual curiosity—a way of building their own knowledge and creative intentions through an informed engagement with the world. I felt that the then emerging design thinking methodologies provided a high-level structure but that information architecture had the potential to provide a greater degree of conceptual structuring within the various phases of a design thinking process.

For example, while design thinking would suggest a 'Discover' phase, information architecture can help frame and communicate at a useful level of detail the intricacies of a wicked problem. In this manner, information architecture becomes a core ability for all designers, in any situation to both manage and communicate decisions and intended action.

Q: How has your approach to teaching design changed over the years?

Initially we were concerned with helping our students to structure their thinking through all the phases of the design thinking process. This may now sound a bit run of the mill, but at the time there was an absence of serious scholarship and educational know-how in this area. So up until about three-four years ago, we were focused on establishing how information architecture could be effective, or on new techniques for the various phases of a design thinking process. We had very good success with this approach, we really managed to ramp-up the quality of our student's work and gained a very good reputation for teaching 'serious' user experience in our local industry. Graduating students have excelled in placements overseas and generally there is a high level of competency in terms of the commercial world of design that we've managed to instill in our students.

In addition to notions of industry 'readiness' we focused on pushing our students beyond commercial competencies to engage with the role of the designer in the social world. In South Africa, the role of design for social upliftment is fairly mature. Many people here tend to focus on providing a service to the greater community and to society. In South Africa, this is very much the ethos of most design faculties. So, a lot of our teaching for the first six or seven years that we collaborated was about trying to build those structures into course work. A lot of the concepts emerged out of our research practice, so we published quite a lot and wrote quite a lot about it.

All that was helpful because it gave us a structure of good design education and (in our opinion) a really solid course.

In the last three years, I've become more interested in the traditional role of design in terms of the role of artefacts as vessels of human desires and values. Intellectually for me this is a shift away from the more pragmatic range of mainstream user experience design. Principally, as I have become really jaded with commodification of design particularly in relation to fintech and the 'silliconvillification' of digital design, I am more interested in terms of how we add something of value to the world. And, I don't consider a billion-dollar market value estimation, value. I consider preserving the planet, sustaining and adding to culture, equality and social emancipation as value. Thus, I am concerned with design as more than just a response to the problems of the world, but rather as a creative mode of consideration and taking action in the world that suggest alternative ways of being. This approach shares many similarities with speculative or discursive design, however, in my mind the current failures of these approaches as their inability to move beyond highly personal interpretations of discourse.

I believe the role that information architecture can bring to this approach is to aid the designer to organise, structure and communicate their suggested alternative futures in a mode that engages with qualitative research aimed at the intersubjective rather than the personal. Thus, moving beyond the current 'design as an imitation of art' approaches to speculative design to be capable of interrogating the ideas behind them more transparently and consequently testing them in the world of people. I call this design speculation. This approach takes information architecture as a structuring tool and scaffolds conceptual design on top of, and utilising, many of techniques and concepts that have emerged as a result of human-centric design approaches. So, in summary, I feel we should avoid being overly responsive to current problems and rather design more for the future we want.

Q: How do you build a focus on social impact into students' design education?

At a general level across our faculty all students are exposed to critical theory as well as a high proportion of societally oriented practical projects. For example, in our fourth-year programme in digital media studies, students must do three projects.

This year, in the first project assignment, the students had to imagine they were back in Apartheid South Africa and then design using contemporary today's technology in order to resist Apartheid. Students alike were required to interview somebody in their community that has actually experienced life in South Africa in the 1980's. The experience of these interviews was a strong learning curve for most of them as they began to understand what went on during that time in our country's history as many of them had very superficial views on the realities of that time. Thus, and based on their explorations, they had to envision a speculative product that could inform their peer generation of about what life was like for people in South Africa during Apartheid (Fig. 1).

The second project titled *Smart Services in the Democratic City* involved interaction and industrial designers collaborating in groups. Each group first had to investigate the notion of a democratic city. With that knowledge, they were tasked with

Fig. 1 Where's Thabo? during apartheid many young people were involved in either defending or resisting the state. Using the narrative device of a *Where's Waldo?* this work comments on how the fate of many of these people is unknown, their bodies lying in unmarked graves across South Africa. Appropriately, the character 'Thabo' is not present anywhere in the illustration (Student K. Hulley 2020)

going out into the city to find a way to make an identified 'place' more democratic and more accessible for citizens using technology associated with the fourth industrial revolution. We thought the theme of the project was pretty cool as in many ways in people's minds democracy and smart [cities] are oxymorons. So, while this project typically concluded with a conceptual or 'blue sky thinking' design intervention, these concepts emerged from a fairly sophisticated design research process involving site visits, secondary research, interviews in order to engage with the complexities of Johannesburg in addition to the implications of emerging technologies (Fig. 2).

The final project is the student's own independent design project. It can vary depending on the student but our general expectation is that the students must identify a need evident in the world and respond to this need through their own practice that can be normative design thinking focused, speculative design or design speculation.

Q: What is important to you to say to the information architecture community right now?

Together with Jason Hobbs, I chaired the 2014 Roundtable on education and information architecture in San Diego. It was amazing to gather such a group of people to articulate things in a different kind of space in a different kind of place. While attending the corresponding IA Summit, what (didn't) surprise me was that while a lot of conversation was geared towards global issues, there was little awareness or representation of the information architecture community outside of North America,

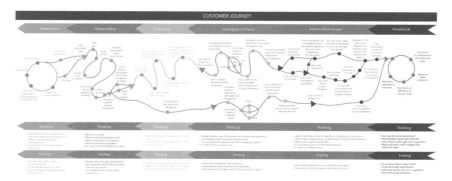

Fig. 2 A customer journey for a smart service for the Democratic City. It describes the concept for a drone delivered rentable smart glasses navigation device for visitors to the inner city. The glasses which project holograms, would help with wayfinding, provide narration, and warn off tourists from entering unsafe areas (Students K. Hulley and M. Shushan 2020)

with maybe one or two people from Europe. The reverse seemed true when I attended EuroIA. For us to have a global conversation, it can't be kept in one place. There are a lot more interesting and diverse voices that need to be heard. A lot of what information architecture is about is about culture. We want to recognise the world is full of multiple diverse and interesting cultures, and we've got to let them all into the conversation.

Sarah A. Rice is founder and CEO of Seneb Consulting and is an information architect with over two decades of strategy and consulting experience, architecting complex information experiences for companies such as Google, Sony, PayPal, Microsoft, eBay, Princess Cruises, and NetApp. She has also taught information architecture to interaction design students at California College of the Arts. She holds a Master's degree in Library and Information Science with continuing interest in data science and visualization. She is a past Information Architecture Institute board member, ran the Institute's premier conference on Information, Design, Experience and Architecture (IDEA) three years running, and has organized the Academic /Practitioner Roundtable since 2015. She has a passion for ethics in information environments, leading her to create and speak about the Ethics Canvas for Information Professionals regularly at industry conferences.

Inversion Within Information Architecture: A Journey into the Micro–Meso–Macro–Meta

Simon Norris

Abstract The chapter discusses the impact of increasing amounts of information; the limitations of micro- and macro-models; the benefits of the levels of analysis framework introducing additional levels to manage information complexity; inversion as a mechanism to leverage complexity.

Introduction

The digital world has changed dramatically since the introduction of the World Wide Web in 1991. What was originally conceived as a hypertext information sharing system for CERN researchers 30 years ago, today touches every part of our lives with over 59% of the world's population, 4.57 billion people, being online (Statista, 2020b).

The number of people and the amount of time they spend online also increased exponentially, and with them the amount of information being created, consumed, and shared (Bulao, 2020). When the Web was launched there were 2,600,000 internet users, representing 0.05% of the world's population. Compare that percentage with 59% of people online as of July 2020. Today the Web represents a fundamental part of the online experience and has achieved adoption on an exceptional scale, providing a platform for other digital technologies to emerge (Krippendorff, 2005; Statista, 2020a) and grow through equally rapid adoption life cycles, including the smartphone, tablet, social media, and voice-operated technologies. These have in turn created increasingly more complex information environments people traverse during their day-to-day experiences (Lucas et al., 2012).

S. Norris (✉)
Nomensa, London, UK
e-mail: simon@nomensa.com

© The Author(s), under exclusive license to Springer Nature Switzerland AG 2021   151
A. Resmini et al. (eds.), *Advances in Information Architecture*,
Human–Computer Interaction Series, https://doi.org/10.1007/978-3-030-63205-2_14

The Impact of Increasing Information

In the early days of the Web, designers, and especially information architects, were concerned with the categorisation of information to support how people searched and navigated individual websites.

The pace and scale at which information is being generated and made available to everyone is still increasing, as are the means through which people can access and manipulate it. This very real "tsunami of data" (Wurman, 1997), flowing through innumerable devices to permeate society (Mitchell, 2003), has meant an exponential increase in the complexity of our information environments.

The field of information architecture has undergone successive waves of transformations in response to these socio-technical changes (Resmini & Rosati, 2012), with the latest wave emerging in the early 2010's and being largely driven by machine learning (ML) technologies used to comb through the constantly growing amount of information available. ML has allowed for the mass processing of data, the consequent automation of processes, and the implementation of real-time responses and interactions within dynamic digital environments. Engaging with the largest amounts of data available, rather than just acting on the information available requires a change in design perspective and, for information architects, creates a tension that can be considered contradictory. It introduces complexities that prompt the information architect to explore alternative ways of reducing the amount of information with which they are providing end users. It is a tension that exists between maintaining meaning and managing feelings of being overwhelmed and that was already identified by Wurman when he stated that "the creative organisation of information creates new information" (1989).

Increasing amounts of information creatively rearranged for a purpose can result in almost infinite information relationships and consequently potentially infinite patterns. Inversion is a way to approach this problem by means of an analytical evaluation of the data structures that make up those information relationships at different levels of analysis (Marr, 1982): in information architecture, inversion results in an approach that relies on the data generated from all interactions to shape the design of all and subsequent interactions.

This contribution adopts the micro–meso–macro model developed in evolutionary economics by Dopfer et al. (2004), applies it to information architecture practice to investigate inversion, and extends it to include Sheng and Geng (2012) additional meta layer to provide a fourth, more abstract view of an information environment. This extended model is the micro–meso–macro–meta model.

The Limitations of Micro–Macro Models

Micro–macro models have their roots in economics, in the work of Adam Smith in the eighteenth century and of John Maynard Keynes in the 1930's.

The advantage of a micro–macro model is that it has scale factored into it, so we can understand individual behaviour and how that manifests into market behaviour and vice versa. This understanding between micro and macro represents a relationship that can be studied and used to explain certain behaviours at different scales, either at a micro or macro scale. However, there are limitations with the model because of the implicit granularity at each end of the scale: whilst "the simplicity and elegance of the micro and macro models make them useful in explaining the price mechanism and the balance or imbalance of key aggregate economic variables (...) both models are unable to describe or analyse the actual behaviour of key market participants" (Sheng & Geng, 2012).

In the social sciences, this shortcoming has led to models that include intermediate steps of analysis to better understand existing relationships, provide greater levels of detail, and combat the "black box" approximations that naturally accompany a binary micro–macro mindset when describing human behaviour from an economic perspective (Bocong, 2012). Waltz's level of analysis framework is one of the most used frameworks (Waltz, 1959).

Level of Analysis

Waltz's level of analysis framework draws upon the field of international relations theory to explain conflicts from a micro, a meso, and a macro level. The micro-level represents the smallest unit of analysis (for example, a person); the macro level represents the largest (for example, a population); and the meso level sits between the micro and the macro (for example, a community).

The framework can be applied to explore integrated sets of relationships that can influence the location, size, or scale of a target event. It provides a foundation on which a picture can be built of how any relationship or set of interrelationships can increase in complexity because of a change in scale that in turn can represent differences in behaviour or feature. Specifically, we may observe behaviours or features at one end of the scale that does not exist at the other end of the scale.

Applying a level of analysis approach allows the exploration of those relationships that may exist between the big and the small, the part and the whole. It also introduces changes in the way information is understood and represented: the meso layer allows for the creation of three-way interrelationships where the micro–macro model only identifies simpler two-way interrelationships, providing more detail in support of understanding behaviour.

If we apply the levels of analysis approach to information architecture, we can abstract and represent information as a hierarchy that starts with data. The data can be abstracted to information; further abstracted into an information architecture; then abstracted again and shaped into an automation process that can, for example, be managed through machine learning algorithms. This ternary representation of abstraction can help us to understand the similarities and differences between data and information structures when we analyse them at different scales, for example helping

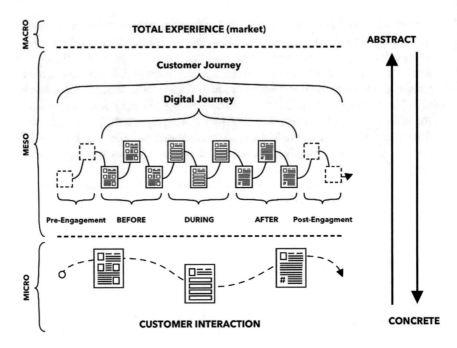

Fig. 1 From user interface to customer experience via the micro–meso–macro layers

with the design of user interfaces. A fundamental component of any information system, by providing a formal way to anchor it to a customer journey and to anchor the journey to the overall experience (Fig. 1).

At the customer interaction level, the micro level, we have the most concrete form of interactions, typically happening between a person and the user interface. One level up, at the meso level, we can characterise the various customer interactions in the form of a single customer journey. A customer journey is a more abstract construct than the individual interactions we have at the micro level, but presents a unified vision that is missing there.

The customer journey is part of an individual's broader experience: at the macro level, that scales to the market, presenting an even greater level of abstraction. In this sense, the customer journey represents the meso elements that sit between the micro (user interface) and the macro (experience).

In a more formalised way, we could represent the different tiers as a hierarchical information model that can be considered analogous to the model of biological organisation and that is based on a series of transformations (Fig. 2).

Data (lowest tier) goes through a first-order level of abstraction and is transformed into information. Information then undergoes a second-order level of abstraction to become information architecture. Finally, a third-order level of abstraction occurs which transforms information architecture into autonomous processes. Each order of abstraction increases the overall abstraction within the system.

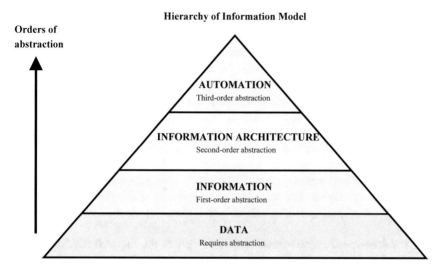

Fig. 2 Hierarchy of information showing increasing orders of abstraction bottom to top

In this model, the customer journey represented in Fig. 1 constitutes a second-order level of abstraction that bridges the customer interaction with the customer experience.

The increase in abstraction that we can observe moving from the bottom to the top of Fig. 2 can also be represented differently by using the micro–meso–macro–meta model (Fig. 3) and a more system-oriented visual approach. In itself,

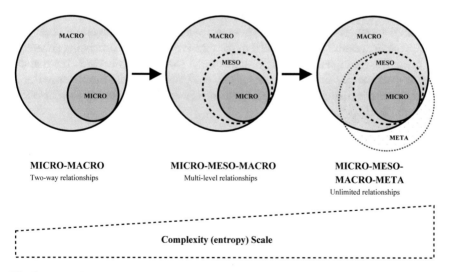

Fig. 3 From micro-macro to micro-meso-macro-meta

the micro–meso–macro–meta model adds one more level of abstraction and therefore increases the potential complexity of the system. Abstraction, and specifically abstract thinking, becomes a mechanism for considering the interrelationships that may exist within a system considered as an information ecology.

Just as the order of abstraction applied to each layer of the hierarchy of information model in Fig. 2 increases in abstraction as we move up, not only does abstraction increase from left to right in Fig. 3, but the total number of interrelationships increases.

The micro–meso–macro–meta model allows the incorporation of data as a layer in its own right, similar to what the hierarchy of information model does (Fig. 2), but it also provides a meta layer that intersects and overlaps with each of the micro, meso, and macro layers. The meta layer increases the total information within the system and consequently also increases the total meta information within the system as well.

The micro–meso–macro–meta model, as well as the hierarchy of information model, relies on the level of analysis framework to examine the interrelationships that can exist within a system by considering them as different levels or orders of abstraction.

Information represents first order of abstraction that provides a bridge for understanding the relationship between data (micro) and information architecture (macro). Furthermore, we can consider information representing a meso layer that allows exploration of the interrelationships that exist as we move from information to data, and, from information to information architecture. Essentially, this means we can observe new interrelationships that exist within an information ecology to better understand the relationships between information structures, enabling better designs that fit with behaviour in more abstract, more generalisable ways than can be considered from a micro–macro approach.

The meta aspect of the micro–meso–macro–meta model is important because it allows the integration into the model of the massive amount of data being generated by the pervasive digital practices of today in "a world which is much more about peer-to-peer sharing and user-generated content", a world in real-time "where traffic directions are instantly provided and groceries are delivered directly to your door" (Schwab, 2016).

Inversion

Inversion started as an in-house conversation at Nomensa in 2013.[1] Changes could be observed in the way we were designing for cross-channel experiences that blended digital technologies with more traditional physical channels.[2] The increased usage

---

[1] Jason Hobbs, then working at Nomensa, was instrumental in starting and developing the concept.
[2] Cross-channel experiences were first defined in information architecture and user experience in Resmini, A., & Rosati, L. (2011). Pervasive Information Architecture. Morgan Kaufmann. For a

of digital technologies and the proliferation of devices also resulted in increasing channel interactions that produced even greater amounts of data: this data could in turn be used as a feedback mechanism to shape the design experience and the practice of information architecture. What was required was an acknowledgement of the importance of algorithms and algorithmic design, necessary to make sense of massive amounts of data, in the practice of information architecture, and a more precise approach than the micro–macro model could offer.

The micro–meso–macro–meta takes care of handling both the increase in data and the increase in data points because of the multiplication of devices and touchpoints. Combined together, these two create a new design scaling problem which can be addressed by means of inversion, essentially producing a data view of design that can be abstracted into different layers representing the different interrelationships that could (and may) occur.

Where contemporary information architecture as described by Resmini and Rosati (2011) is primarily interested in shifting the focus away from website-only practices and in how digital transformation processes are blurring the boundaries between the physical and the digital environment, wide-scale adoption of digital technologies is also opening up data-based possibilities of intervention that were not there before: for example, we are able to measure how people move around a physical space, whether it is a building or a city, similar to how we measure how people navigate within digital spaces. As such, the primary difference between pervasive information architecture research and practice and inversion as described here is in the type and amount of data they consider and in the change of scale made possible by ML-driven design: an "inverted" view is a data-orientated view.

Inversion suggests that designers should consider this emerging anthropological space (Levy, 1999), in which digital and physical coexist to create new interrelationships that generate massive amounts of data, as being primarily made of data. Rather than taking a top-down approach, designers should take an "inverted" view and think of this space as a space of data flows, exploring and discovering patterns that can shape and influence what is being designed. This also means data and data visualisation become a more explicit method for providing additional and novel feedback.

Inversion is not a new approach: the German mathematician Carl Jacobi[3] introduced inversion as a method for problem-solving over two hundred years ago. In simple terms, inversion requires reversing the classic approach of observing and understanding the effects to determine the cause and starting with the cause to determine the effects. This lack of novelty is a strength rather than a weakness, and such an approach is especially familiar to anyone exploring the application of data visualisation. Specialists in this field amongst other things are examining the data that sits behind the customer interaction (Fig. 2) with the aim of generating new meaning,

more mature conversation on the blending and systemic aspects, Benyon, D., & Resmini, A. (2017). User experience in cross-channel ecosystems. *Proceedings of the British HCI Conference* 2017.

[3]https://en.wikipedia.org/wiki/Carl_Gustav_Jacob_Jacobi.

understanding, and insight, that in turn provides feedback to improve the design of customer interactions.

In its application to information architecture, inversion is proposed as an approach to understanding and applying the massive amounts of data generated to observe existing and new patterns of behaviour. Data visualisation is one of the tools that allow designers to uncover the relationships supporting these patterns and to access the meta layer of the micro–meso–macro–meta model: it therefore becomes a fundamental lens and a key component of the inversion approach to information architecture.

Understanding scale is important, as designers now approach this issue across platforms, screens or interfaces, or even as components of an interface; abstraction increases as the information available is progressively generalised and undergoes order of magnitude changes (Fig. 2). Understanding the relationship between the smaller parts of the design and how that design scales up requires abstract, conceptual, and representational thinking. The levels of analysis framework support the conceptual thinking required to architect systems at scale, whilst the micro–meso–macro–meta model allows designers to identify and understand the system-wide relationships that can be used to create meaning for those interacting with the system.

Conclusions

Whilst we can consider classical approaches to information architecture as primarily top-down, such as a taxonomy providing a structure that allows people to navigate an information environment, inversion is neither top-down or bottom-up. The sheer amount of information available increases complexity and renders both approaches inadequate.

Inversion introduces an entirely different angle based on the application of the levels of analysis framework, that takes into account that what works at a certain scale will not necessarily work at all scales. The micro–meso–macro–meta framework then provides a conceptual methodology to identify and understand the relationships existing in the data at different levels of abstraction, completing the model.

References

Benyon, D., & Resmini, A. (2017). User experience in cross-channel ecosystems. In *Proceedings of the British HCI Conference 2017*.

Bocong, L. (2012). *Engineering, development and philosophy: American, Chinese and European perspectives from a micro–macro framework to a micro–meso–macro framework* (pp. 23–36). Springer.

Bulao, J. (2020). *How much data is created every day in 2020?* Techjury. https://techjury.net/blog/how-much-data-is-created-every-day/.

Dopfer, K., Foster, J., & Potts, J. (2004). Micro-meso-macro. *Journal of Evolutionary Economics, 14*, 263–279. https://doi.org/10.1007/s00191-004-0193-0.

Krippendorff, K. (2005). *The semantic turn*. CRC Press.

Levy, P. (1999). *Collective intelligence* (R. Bononno, Trans.). Perseus Books.

Lucas, P., Ballay, J., & McManus, M. (2012). *Trillions: Thriving in the emerging information ecology*.

Marr, D. (1982). *Vision: A computational investigation into the human representation and processing of visual information*. The MIT Press.

Mitchell, W. J. (2003). *Me++*. The MIT Press.

Resmini, A., & Rosati, L. (2011). *Pervasive information architecture*. Morgan Kaufmann.

Resmini, A., & Rosati, L. (2012). A brief history of information architecture. *Journal of Information Architecture*. http://journalofia.org/volume3/issue2/03-resmini/.

Schwab, K. (2016). *The fourth industrial revolution*. Currency.

Sheng, A., & Geng, X. (2012). *The new economics: Meso and meta. world economic forum.* https://www.weforum.org/agenda/2012/10/the-new-economics-meso-and-meta.

Statista. (2020a). *Daily time spent online by device.* https://www.statista.com/statistics/319732/daily-time-spent-online-device/.

Statista. (2020b). *Global digital population as of July 2020.* https://www.statista.com/statistics/617136/digital-population-worldwide/.

Waltz, K. (1959). *Man, the state, and war: A theoretical analysis*. Columbia University Press.

Wurman, R. S. (1989). Hats (*Design quarterly* no. 145). The MIT Press.

Wurman, R. S. (1997). *Information architects*. Graphis.

Simon Norris, Nomensa is the founder and CEO of Nomensa, an international experience design agency. He is an experience strategist with over twenty-five years' commercial experience working with high-profile private and public sector organisations.

Information Architecture Do (道)

Atsushi Hasegawa

Abstract In this chapter, I discuss the state of information architecture as a professional occupation in Japan from the perspective of Edward Hall's distinction between high- and low-context cultures. I describe the Japanese cultural practices and the attitude toward the division of labor based on Hall's and use these to situate the professional development of information architecture as a practice in Japan. I then present the traditional Japanese educational method of learning skills called "do (道)," discuss Seigow Matsuoka's editorial engineering as a "do" form of information architecture, and introduce a possible "IA-do" approach to information architecture and information architecture education.

Japan's High-Context Culture

In his "Beyond Culture," anthropologist Edward T. Hall situated the world's cultures along a spectrum from high-context culture to low-context culture (Hall, 1976). Hall argued that, among others, China (at that time), Japan, the Arab countries, Greece, and Spain were highly context-dependent, while German–Switzerland, Germany, the Scandinavian countries, the United States, and France were less context-dependent.

In high-context cultures, the content of the communication is richer in unspoken content than in actual verbalized content. Hall cites the Japanese language as an extreme example of this. On the other hand, in low-context culture communication, only the content expressed in words has meaning as information, and unspoken content is usually either not conveyed or devoid of meaning. Hall mentions German as the most extreme example of a low-context language (Table 1).

For example, in everyday speech, characteristics such as not saying the subject or not explicitly saying what can be inferred from the situation are common in Japan. In English, when you call someone on the phone, you usually ask "May I speak to Mr. (or Ms.) A?" On the other hand, in Japanese, you ask "Is Mr. (or Ms.) A there?" In Japanese, the goal is not to confirm his or her presence. The unspoken message

A. Hasegawa (✉)
Concent, Inc., Tokyo, Japan
e-mail: hase@concentinc.jp

© The Author(s), under exclusive license to Springer Nature Switzerland AG 2021
A. Resmini et al. (eds.), *Advances in Information Architecture*,
Human–Computer Interaction Series, https://doi.org/10.1007/978-3-030-63205-2_15

Table 1 High-context vs low-context cultures

High-context	Low-context
Long-lasting relationship	Shorter relationship
Exploiting context	Less dependent on context
Spoken agreements	Written agreements
Insiders and outsiders distinguished	Insiders and outsiders less distinguished
Cultural patterns ingrained, slow change	Cultural patterns change faster

is that "since I have called Mr. or Ms. A, it is clear that I want to talk to Mr. or Ms. A," so you do not say the "may I speak" part. You only need to ask if Mr. or Ms. A is there.

This phenomenon can be seen in business, as well. In Japan, individuals tend to give more importance to their direct trust and experience and to disregard formalized contracts and frameworks.

It is also common in Japan to avoid explicitly stating things in the form of contracts. This can be seen in the use of the court system. As of 2009, the number of court cases per capita in Japan was one-eighth that of the United States, one-fifth of the United Kingdom and France, and one-third of Germany and South Korea (Japan Federation of Bar Association, 2011). This is because Japan values trust between individuals: if there is a problem, the parties will try to resolve it through discussion instead of directly take it to court.

High-context is also correlated to another characteristic Japanese workplace trait, in that people tend not to specify their work duties and do not like the division of labor (Nishimura, 2014). In many cases, company employees perform work under the title of "generalist" without separating into specialized positions. Knowledge of the company's unique culture is prioritized over specialization in marketing or management.

In the next section, we will look at how this high-context culture has led to the rise of Japan's information architecture and has shaped its development.

Information Architecture in Japan

The concept and the term "information architecture" was first introduced in Japan with Richard Saul Wurman's book "Information Anxiety" (Wurman, 1989) which was translated into Japanese in 1990 (Wurman, 1990). Translation has its importance, since in Japan untranslated books have a slimmer chance of being read, and because, in this specific case, of the identity of the translator. While Wurman's work acquainted the Japanese with the terms "information architecture" and "information architect," at this stage they were understood to be concepts in a book rather than a field and a job title. The translator was editorial engineer Seigow Matsuoka, who went on to promote "editorial engineer" as a concept very similar to that of an information architect. We will discuss Matsuoka and editorial engineering in more detail further on.

Around the year 2000, Internet use in Japan exceeded 16% of the population and entered what Rogers (1962) calls a period of diffusion. Website design and development became a popular activity with a professional side which was primarily the purview of advertising companies or system development companies. This led to initial business requirements that focused either on visual designers or system developers' roles only.

Around the same time global interactive agencies such as Razorfish, marchFirst, and Sapient began to expand into Japan. Better connected to the international developments that were happening in the United States and in Europe, these agencies had already internally created job positions for information architects. When they entered the Japanese market, the agencies did not localize their job titles, including that of information architect, or their methods: they brought these into the Japanese web design industry as they were. That meant that an increasingly large cohort of information architects was responsible for designing the site structure, was in charge of user research, and generically cared for all those aspects of design that fell outside of the visual designer's realm.

Books also played a significant role in popularizing this new understanding of information architecture in relation to web design. Rosenfeld and Morville's (1998) and Garrett's (2002) books were translated and published in Japan in 1998 and 2005, respectively, and greatly contributed to that early promotion of information architecture in the country. Garrett's "elements of user experience" diagram, created in 2002, was translated into Japanese in that same year, prior to the book's translation. The diagram framed how practitioners situated information architecture in web design.

In 2003, "Web Creators," one of the leading magazines in the Japanese web design industry, published a special issue on information architecture, leading to the general recognition of the field in the Japanese design industry: by 2005, "information architecture" was an established term. On the other hand, the job title of "information architect" did not spread far in the industry. As mentioned earlier on, this can be attributed to a cultural disposition that does not value specialization and the division of labor: if a client company felt such compartmentalization was unnecessary, and this was the norm because of the way web development started in Japan, it was common business practice for domestic agencies to accommodate the request to the extent it was possible. As a result of this tension between imported job roles and local preferences, it became common for a "web director" to be in charge of multiple structural tasks, including project management, production management, content direction, and information architecture. Thus, in Japanese web design, information architecture education has come to be recognized as something a web director should have. There are both pros and cons to this.

One of the cons is that the number of people who specialize in information architecture has not increased, and even today there are fewer opportunities to discuss information architecture in Japan. Another one is that a mature conversation has not coalesced on how to structure and carry out information architecture education in

Japan, which in turn means that very little consideration has been given to those issues that specifically relate information architecture and Japanese language and culture. However, the creation of the web director role also resulted in a positive outcome, since, as the person primarily responsible for developing the website, they were put in charge of the site structure and were able to accurately connect site design to project goals, potentially resolving or minimizing a major point of friction and misalignment in large projects.

This corresponds to the point made by architect Joshua Prince-Ramus in his keynote at the 2007 ASIS&T Information Architecture Summit that architects must become project architects (Prince-Ramus, 2007).

This contribution argues that now that digital products have become common-place, we are even past the idea of the information architect as a project architect: information architecture is no longer a job title, but rather a fundamental skill. Not only can the Japanese case be used as a precedent, but Japan also offers a very specific, "do"[1] approach to learning skills in a high-context situation.

"Do" Culture

In Japan, many fields exist whose name includes the word "do (道)," such as sa-do (茶道), ka-do (華道), kyu-do (弓道), ju-do (柔道), and so on, all in such areas as art and technique. The word "do" means "way," so "sa-do" means "the way of tea" and refers to the Japanese tea ceremony, "ka-do" means "the way of flowers" and refers to the art of flower arrangement, "kyu-do" means "the way of the bow" and refers to archery, and "ju-do" means "the way of the yawara" (柔: soft). This "do" culture is known to be characteristic of Japanese high-context culture (Suzuki, 2011.)

"Do" is the process of training for the development of skills and also the process of training instructors. In any "do," the learner is initiated into a school and trains daily with one teacher to achieve certification. In "do," when someone masters a technique they become "Shihan" (the master), and as "Shihan" they can have a disciple. In general, though, the purpose of practice in "do" is not to improve one's skill, but rather to grow as a person. While a very common approach to learning in pre-modern Japan, "do" is today found only in the traditional arts. It has been criticized for its inefficiency when compared to modern education, and also from a human rights perspective, because of the inherent imbalance and often intimidating character that the master–student relationship assumes.

One of the primary characteristics of "do" is that it "enters from the kata (form)," meaning that, as German philosopher Eugen Herrigel explains, it is a method aiming at an unconditional mastery of the form where the master does not teach or reason, but only instructs (Herrigel, 1848.)

Typically, when a beginner is introduced to the "do," he or she is tasked with repeatedly practicing the basic kata (form) until they master the movement and their

---

[1]To be read "doh" and not to be confused with the verb "to do."

body learns the technique. If a student were to ask how they should do it, the master does not teach them but only corrects their mistakes. This was the author's personal experience when learning sa-do (茶道): the tea master never taught me how to do it and forbade me to practice at home where he could not correct me.

Japanese linguist Shigehiko Toyama compares the relationship between modern education and "do" education to the one existing between a glider and an airplane (Toyama, 1983): the glider-type flies with the lead, while the airplane type flies by itself. According to Toyama, modern education is glider-type, in that the teacher leads and guides the students. Students can gain a wide range of knowledge, but they are mostly passive. Educators understand that this is not how learning is supposed to be but, in today's society, the method has proven to be valuable in terms of scale and investment.

In comparison, in the Japanese "do" style of education, students are frustrated because the master does not teach them. Toyama says the "do" masters knew from experience that such a situation would eventually benefit the students by fuelling the student's motivation to learn and their desire to "steal" the master's know-how and techniques from the daily practice of the "kata." This "do" system is why the traditional arts still show individuality despite being built on strong old traditions.

What can we learn from the "do," from starting from the form? Is "道" always inefficient? What does being expected to understand the meaning and reason for doing something ourselves do to our understanding of the meaning of what we are learning?

Editorial Engineering

In his seminal "Information Architects," Wurman defined the information architect as:

1. The individual who organizes the patterns inherent in data, making the complex clear.
2. A person who creates the structure or map of information which allows others to find their personal paths to knowledge.
3. The emerging twenty-first century professional occupation addressing the needs of the age focused upon clarity, human understanding, and the science of the organization of information (Wurman, 1997).

Wurman was one of the closing keynote speakers at the 2010 ASIS&T Information Architecture Summit. During his plenary he stated that "what makes an information architect is an attitude. A desire, a passion to communicate systemically with rules and systems, and transfer information to another human being" (Wurman, 2010). When we consider these definitions, Seigow Matsuoka and his editorial engineering really can be recast as a local, Japanese variation of information architecture.

After working for an advertising company, Matsuoka founded his own publishing company and launched the magazine "Yu" (遊: play) in 1971. He called it an "object magazine" and as the editor he carefully crafted it to transcend genres, something that resulted in "Yu" having had a significant influence on Japanese art, philosophy, media, and design.

In the 1980s, Matsuoka proposed his concept of "editorial engineering" and established his own company, the Editorial Engineering Laboratory. Through the company, Matsuoka produces cultural projects and provides training for companies. He calls himself an "editorial engineer" and works on cross-cutting projects on culture, science, and information in Japan and internationally. Matsuoka's editorial engineering is a comprehensive methodology that integrates human thinking, social communication systems, and creativity.

Editing as Handling

In editorial engineering, "editing" is not a specific occupational skill, but rather broadly refers to the handling of information. The activities that lie between receiving information and providing information, such as memory and recall, choice and action, recognition and expression, are all considered "editing." It is a creative act that can be said to be the engine that runs behind the scenes of all types of communication. While there are clear parallels with Wurman's centering on "understanding" as the central moment of information architecture, there is a significant difference between Matsuoka's "editorial engineering" and the more information science-based roots of information architecture in the handling of "meaning."

Matsuoka's idea of "meaning" centers on human consciousness and emotions: he created editorial engineering to handle what he called "living information systems," systems that generate and exchange information, emphasizing a dynamic, emergent side that was in direct opposition to the more formalist approaches based on symbolic data processing that could be found in information science at the time.

Matsuoka's approach identifies "data" as having two distinct meanings: pure data, and the semantic information attached to the data itself. It then introduces a set of basic techniques for handling these data that are divided into five patterns: collection, selection, classification, school, and lineage, which are labeled "compile." The techniques for dealing with the semantic part only are further patterned into fifty-nine categories: summary, model, order, and exchange, labeled as "edit." These sixty-four "editing techniques" were derived from Matsuoka's own experience.

The Editorial Engineering Laboratory offers an educational program centered on Matsuoka's approach as "the School of ISIS Editing" (Interactive System of Inter Scores). The school teaches a way of thinking rather than techniques that focus on specific technologies like the web, and is by and large attended by the general public rather than by designers, editors, or media professionals. Thirty thousand people have attended the basic program to date.

The program is offered as a training course for individuals and companies, and many Japanese companies in the manufacturing, financial, and trading industries have adopted it for management training. A unique feature of the program to this day is that, together with more traditional lectures and workshops, the advanced course incorporates a "do" type of teaching based on unexplained experience. For example, students would practice the traditional Japanese art of "Noh" (能) under a "Noh master," and experience the actual training of a monk at Koya-san, the headquarters of Japan's Shingon Esoteric Buddhism.

For Matsuoka, these experiences are necessary for students to obtain an "editorial" perspective for themselves, and constitute a "do" approach.

Information Architecture "Do"

Matsuoka's "do" approach to education could not only be cast as a type of information architecture in itself, but illuminates two important and complementary facets of the current conversations dealing with the field, in Japan and internationally: that of education, and that of the outcomes. In these terms, we could say we have both an experiential type of information architecture education, and an experiential information architecture.

An experiential approach to education in information architecture could follow Matsuoka's "do" approach and recast its processes and methods so that students become the ones responsible for shaping up their own perspective through experience.

An experiential approach to information architecture would suggest that when designing specific information architecture, the primary goal should be to allow users to find their own answers in the experience, rather than presenting them with answers.

Both of these aspects resonate strongly with the Japanese high-context cultural landscape. Information architecture has already been conceptualized and integrated into the Japanese industry not as a profession, as a job role, but rather as an outlook that is needed by everyone. Practitioners, entrepreneurs, and researchers need information architecture as an attitude, not as a technique. To master such an attitude of structure and order, a "do" type of education could benefit the global community and the maturation of the field. Instead of providing predetermined paths through content to facilitate understanding, a design approach anchored to a less complex and less connected information landscape, and information architecture do approach would radically rebalance the relationship between designers and users. Ultimately, it would lead to designing information architectures that support self-determined, self-driven comprehension in a world of information that has no boundaries of device, place, amount, space, or time.

References

Editorial Engineering. https://www.eel.co.jp/philosophy/meme/.
Garrett, J. J. (2002). *The elements of user experience: User-centered design for the web.* New Riders.

Hall, E. T. (1976). *Beyond culture*. Anchor Books/ Doubleday.
Hasegawa, A. (2003). *Information architecture as the new foundation* (Japanese). Web creators (18), 34–137. https://www.mdn.co.jp/webcre/Volume/Vol18/.
Herrigel, E. (1848). *Zen in der Kunst des Bogenschießens* (Konstanz Weller). Konstanz Weller.
Japan Federation of Bar Association. (2011). *Basic statistics about lawyers.* https://www.nichib enren.or.jp/document/statistics/fundamental_statistics_2011.html.
Nishimura, Y. (2014). *Hinomaru semiconductor. The truth behind the decline in labor division.* The Nikkei. https://www.nikkei.com/article/DGXMZO75359980X00C14A8000000/.
Prince-Ramus, J. (2007). *The lost art of productively losing control.* ASIS&T Information Architecture Summit. Opening keynote.
Rogers, E. (1962). *Diffusion of innovation.* Free Press.
Rosenfeld, L., & Morville, P. (1998). *Information architecture for the world wide web: Designing large-scale web sites.* O'Reilly.
Suzuki, E. (2011). Japanese culture through Ikebana: The history of flowers revealed (in Japanese). Shibunkaku Publishing.
Toyama, S. (1983). *Organizing of thoughts* (Shiko no Seirigaku). Chikuma Publishing.
Wurman, R. S. (2010). 11th ASIS&T information architecture summit. Closing keynote. https://boxesandarrows.com/ia-summit-10-richard-saul-wurman-keynote/.
Wurman, R. S. (1989). *Information anxiety.* Doubleday.
Wurman, R. S. (1990). *Information anxiety* (S. Matsuoka, Trans.). Nippon Jitsugyo Publishing.
Wurman, R. S. (1997). *Information architects.* Graphis Inc.

Atsushi Hasegawa is the founder and president of Concent, a Tokyo-based design firm and has been a professor at Musashino Art University since 2019. He started his career as an information architect in 2000 and founded Information Architecture Association Japan (IAAJ). He is a co-representative of Service Design Network Japan Chapter and vice president of Human Centered Design Organization Japan, and the author of IA100—Information Architecture for User Experience Design (2009).

In Search Of: Masterworks of Information Architecture

Dan Klyn

Abstract In order to identify and enumerate some of the normative criteria for critique (or appreciation) of a given info-architectural structure, system, or solution, two candidate "masterworks" of information architecture are provided for evaluation and discussion: the 1st edition of James Joyce's first novel, *Ulysses*, and the only edition of Richard Saul Wurman's second book, *The City: Form and Intent*.

Introduction

> Comparison is the thief of joy—Theodore Roosevelt

Information architecture theory is anchored in apperception: a term I have borrowed from cognitive science and that encompasses the various processes using which people come to understand new things in comparison with things they already understand (Klyn, 2013).

During my time as an undergraduate English Literature major at the University of Michigan in Ann Arbor, I split my time between two seemingly incomparable activities: studying the works of James Joyce, and working at a bike shop. I was keen to develop expertise with both, and was surprised, after asking the shop owner how he got into the business, to learn that he had no particular interest in bicycles. He said he had decided to buy a bike shop because his training in the US Army equipped him to perform an exacting inspection of anything, so long as there were at least two of the things to inspect. The "bi" in "bicycle" ensured his success in that business, because even while he did not personally possess the expert knowledge of how to adjust a brake, or true a wheel, he'd learned that careful comparison of "sames" makes it possible to discern something about the quality of both entities under inspection. He routinely found flaws in the work of technical experts solely on

D. Klyn (✉)
The Understanding Group (TUG), Ann Arbor, MI, USA
e-mail: dan@understandinggroup.com

University of Michigan School of Information, Ann Arbor, MI, USA

© The Author(s), under exclusive license to Springer Nature Switzerland AG 2021
A. Resmini et al. (eds.), *Advances in Information Architecture*,
Human–Computer Interaction Series, https://doi.org/10.1007/978-3-030-63205-2_16

169

the basis of comparing the configuration of what they were working on to an adjacent instance of what was supposed to be the same configuration.

Thankfully, comparison is not the only way to understand. Because very few non-expert humans on planet earth in the twenty-first century know anything about James Joyce's first novel, "*Ulysses*" (Devlin-Glass, 2004). And far fewer, by perhaps two orders of magnitude, are the contemporary humans of any stripe who know about Richard Saul Wurman's second book, "The City, Form and Intent" (Wurman, 1963). Which makes me, for most of my readers, the thief of comparison, as I am contending that these two now-rare books—separated in time by a half century or so of innovations in printing, paper, and ink technologies—exhibit some of the most finely crafted architectures of information in the Western tradition (and in Joyce's case, in the so-called canon of English Literature) since the Enlightenment. And further: that comparison of specific masterworks such as these can help crystalize a shared set of characteristics for evaluating and appreciating information architectures, generally.

Content, Context, and Users

How might we go about identifying the most info-architecturally relevant features of the admittedly obscure examples being put forward as exhibits in this discussion? The three core dimensions of info-architectural concern presented in the four successive editions of Rosenfeld and Morville's "Information Architecture for The World Wide Web" (Rosenfeld et al. 2015) provide gaze direction; content, context, and users.

Content

Architectures of information are often invisible. Detecting the boundary conditions between "the content" and everything else that belongs to and is part of a given environment becomes a less ambiguous operation when the product or service being examined exists in multiple formats, and across channels. Teasing-out and then evaluating information architectures through the lens of content thus begins with identifying instances of words and images whose morphological expressions vary in the given environment, even while the meaning of the content isn't meant to be variable.

Context

In today's inherently cross- and multi-channel products and services, the fitness or desirability of the aspects of a given experience that are caused by and through decisions about information architecture is best evaluated through an analysis of the choreographies enacted by end-users (Benyon & Resmini, 2017). Recognizing that "everything takes place some place" (Wurman 2017), it follows that the more context-driven characteristics of a given work of information architecture would begin lending themselves to analysis through something akin to Bachelardian topo-analysis (Bachelard & Jolas, 1994)—working backward from what people do and how they feel in an environment, as a function of and in relation to a given structure.

Users

Human beings are not only placelings (Benyon & Resmini, 2017), we are also earth-lings: with bodies that are festooned with sensors, and coordinated by a sensorium that assigns meanings based on natural forces such as gravity, and based on cultur-ally encoded spatial conventions of up-ness, and down-ness: left- and right-ness (Bloomer & Moore, 1979). Normative evaluation of a given info-architectural struc-ture, system, or artifact through the lens of the user begins with the embodiment of human beings, and their subjective experiences with things in places.

Ideally, the candidate masterworks of information architecture would be coporo-rally, physically available to (if not directly experienced by) anybody and everybody, for their own scrutiny and analysis. With the continuing expiration of international copyrights, advances in digital imaging, and the multiplication of open-access digital libraries, most humans who're connected to the internet today can access digital repre-sentations of the candidate works under scrutiny in the present discussion without having to make a purchase, or travel to an archive. The inadequacy of facsimiles for certain kinds of literary and bibliographic analysis, in the case of the 1922 1st edition of *Ulysses*, has been well established in the work of John Kidd (Rossman, 1988). Whether or not contemporary people's experiences with facsimiles of Wurman's 1963 *tour de force* will prove adequate for assessing it as a masterwork is anyone's guess. However, based on what we have observed thus far, and will continue to insist, about the importance of embodiment and proprioception in the processes of under-standing, any conclusions one might want to draw about Wurman's 1963 project without having used both hands in the exploration of its various contents, and spent time physically arranging and rearranging the plates on a table top must be viewed with some skepticism. The rareness of the items in question and relative fragility as physical objects underlines the importance of archives, where would be architects of information can explore and handle primary source materials that testify to the evolution of the thinking in our field.

Considerable Similarities

It was in 2012 that I first began considering similarities between the makers of what I'm proposing as two masterworks of information architecture—subsequent to Wurman being feted by University College, Dublin with the James Joyce Award. Until then, it had not occurred to me that their lives or works might connect.

At face value, Wurman seems to have more in common with Leopold Bloom, the heroic "everyman" avatar for Odysseus in Joyce's send-up of Homer's epic, than with the alternately "jejune," "fearful," and "cursed Jesuit" who penned it, and who appears in the story in the character Stephen Dedalus. Yet the similarities between these two author-architects, and between these works of theirs, are considerable.

Joyce and Wurman each received the best schooling available at the time in their respective communities. Both were noteworthy among their peers and teachers for having immense potential and a certain precociousness in the early expressions of their talent. Prior to beginning undergraduate work in their respective fields, both men thought they might pursue fine art as vocation: Joyce was a celebrated tenor; Wurman was (and still is) a marvelous painter.

Wurman and Joyce alike had difficulty submitting as schoolboys to their respective schoolmasters. In the case of the former, Dr. Lloyd W. Ashby, principal at Cheltenham High School in Elkins Park, Pennsylvania, refused to shake hands with Wurman at his graduation in 1953.

The list goes on, but one crucial similarity stands out when comparing the stories of how these men came to produce the extraordinary works in question: they were both very close to the means of production, and were able to rely on the resources of close friends and collaborators who were involved in avant-garde publishing.

Were it not for radical American expatriate Sylvia Beach's willingness to start her own publishing imprint, risk imprisonment for obscenity, and pay for the typesetting and printing of the now-storied first edition of *Ulysses* (Fig. 1), it may not have come out as a book at all. And even so, most copies of that first edition were intercepted and burned as pornography on the pier at Folkestone in Kent, England.

For his part, Richard Saul Wurman (whose first job in England, coincidentally, was in Dartford, Kent) relied on close collaboration in manufacturing with a pioneering offset lithographer by the name of Eugene Feldman. When I asked him, Wurman remarked that Feldman:

> was well known as an experimental printer. He was my collaborator on the first-ever Lou Kahn book: I designed it, but I gave Gene co-credit, and he paid for the whole printing. If you see how beautifully that was printed and how he matched that yellow "trash" color (of Kahn's tracing paper originals) and the feeling of Kahn's charcoal of the drawings, that was Falcon Press. Gene taught me about printing (Klyn, 2015).[1]

Masterworks in Terms of Content

Published when he was just twenty-six years old, *The City: Form and Intent* was actually Wurman's second mature foray into the architecture, design, and manufacture of a print publication, and his second collaboration with Eugene Feldman. Even so, I consider it to be Wurman's (and the world's) first self-consciously info-architectural

---

[1] A facsimile of Wurman's first book, originally printed by Eugene Feldman, is slated to be launched as a Kickstarter in Spring 2021. Kroeter, S., Kahn, N., & Wurman, R. S. (2020). *The Louis I. Kahn Facsimile Project.* https://www.louisikahn.com/.

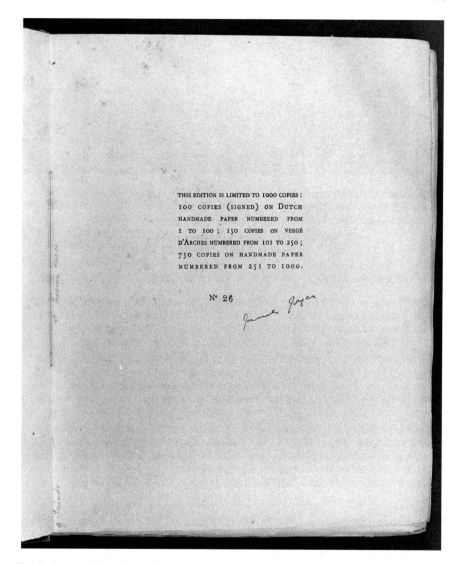

Fig. 1 Edition information and author signature from limited edition of James Joyce's *Ulysses* (Photo by Shane Davis)

work: built by many hands, with most of the discrete choices about the ways that information would be situated circumscribed by an over-arching structural order that, when followed like a set of good instructions, enhances the "information carrying capacity" of the total work.

The City, Form and Intent: being a collection of the plans of fifty significant towns and cities all to the scale 1:14400 (Fig. 2) was created by Wurman in response to the library at the University of North Carolina in Raleigh not being able to provide

Fig. 2 Covers of R.S. Wurman's 1963 book, *The City, Form, and Intent: being a collection of the plans of fifty significant towns and cities all to the scale 1:14400* (Photo by David Rumsey Map Collection, David Rumsey Map Center, Stanford Libraries)

the maps and city plans he required for teaching second-year architecture. When you ask him about it today, Wurman refers to this project as his "Sand Models" book:

> I got some money to buy plasticine from the school, you know… $100 bucks or whatever it was. I got the light green plasticine blocks you use in kindergarten. You could press down into the clay with balsa wood and pick it up, and that was a road. And we got a couple widths for big roads and smaller roads. It was shitty, but okay, right? They looked fine.
>
> I constructed that book in my head, and that's why I made [each model] 17 inches on a side: because I knew I could do every model and reduce it in half and have it 8.5 inches on a side, which was the size of the student publication. And I wanted to do it so I could build them sloppy: it's much quicker to build something large and sloppy than very neat and small. So, it was much faster to build it big: like how it takes longer to do a short speech.
>
> I sent the negatives up to Gene [in Philadelphia] and he said, "I think I should make my own half-tone screen." And so he did his own half-tone screen of enlarged paper fibers – not a real screen – but the large paper fibers is what you see as a screen; that's what we used, and it had the additional benefit of obscuring imperfections, like fingerprints, and it makes it look more like sand models: more like it was hand done. And that's how I did the book. (Klyn, 2015)

The resulting publication manifested the fractal core of Wurman's signature conceptualization of the architecture of information (Fig. 3). It is the first appearance in print and remains one of the most powerful artifacts from his oeuvre exemplifying what he would later coin as Wurman's First Law: you only understand something new relative to something you already understand (Amoroso, 2010).

Wurman involved his entire second-year architecture class for four weeks in the production of the plans of 50 towns and cities in kindergarten clay, all at the same scale. In so doing, professor Wurman ensured each one of his students' ability to understand any one particular city or town by way of a calibrated comparison with the other forty-nine. If any of the students in Raleigh, North Carolina, had been to Savannah, Georgia, they would now be able to understand something about Amsterdam. Or Ankor. Or Assisi. Or Athens.

The content strategy for the project produced by Wurman and his students in North Carolina in 1963 is isomorphic to the specific content, context, and users

Fig. 3 Loose plate of Amsterdam city from R.S. Wurman's 1963 book, The City, Form, and Intent: being a collection of the plans of fifty significant towns and cities all to the scale 1:14400 (Photo by David Rumsey Map Collection, David Rumsey Map Center, Stanford Libraries)

for the project, even while its physical realization is polymorphic, and functions on the basis of a loose coupling of words and pictures, with an imagined end-user choreography that entails the use of both hands, and consideration of multiple entities (and even media-types) in ad hoc configurations. The plates are numbered, but their sequencing is largely determined by whoever last handled the physical artifact: with loose-leaf pages that afford being put together (or back together) in a near-infinite number of ways. The numbering scheme for the plates depicting cities and towns is keyed only to the book's index (as opposed to some external source of meaning, such as degrees of latitude or longitude), and is merely a reflection of the alphabetical ordering of the names of the cities and towns selected for inclusion in the project. Wurman's decision to render the plate numbers in Roman numerals (as opposed to Arabic) helps to ensure that this arbitrary numbering scheme won't be used as the primary method for accessing the information, and relieves the book's reader of the obligation to re-assemble its components in any particular sequence.

Part of what gives me the confidence to propose the 1963 edition as a masterwork of information architecture is comparison (talk about being the thief of joy!) with an edition of the work that Wurman printed subsequently in 1974 under his own Joshua Press imprint (Fig. 4).

The 1974 version, titled *Cities: Comparisons of Form and Scale* provides readers with access to the "same" content that Wurman's students created in 1963, only in an inexpensive, perfect-bound codex. It comprises all of the pictures and words from 1963, and one could argue that it is a more "user friendly" version of the project. It was certainly a more commercially viable way to make the project understandable and accessible in cases where access to one of the 1963 original versions is not possible. The Joshua Press edition is also, in my view, a manifestly inferior object, whose architectures and end-user choreographies are at odds with the purpose that generated the original work in 1963 (Fig. 5).

Comparison here proves that a given quantity of pictures and words, when presented within a different information architecture—where the spatial and semantic relationships are re-keyed to a wholly different geometric configuration, around an entirely different end-user choreography—simply doesn't mean the same thing, and doesn't operate in the same way.

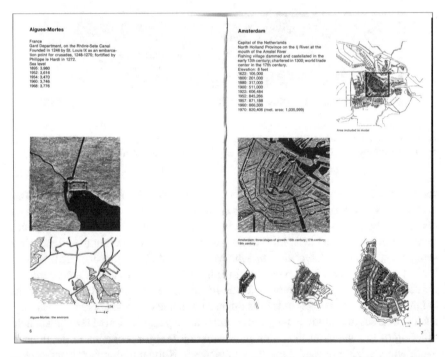

Fig. 4 Two pages, Aigues-Mortes and Amsterdam, from R.S. Wurman's 1974 book, *Cities: Comparisons of Form and Scale*. (Photo by Dan Klyn)

Fig. 5 Side-by-side comparison of Amsterdam page from 1973 version (left) and loose-leaf page from 1963 version (right) of R.S. Wurman's works (Photo by Dan Klyn)

The Scandal of *Ulysses*

How to introduce, especially to those who have not yet read or examined it, what is widely esteemed as the twentieth century's ultimate work of fiction in the English language? How might one better equip people who understand information architecture, but who have not yet read the novel, to adequately appreciate the experience of reading it? I like what Vicki Mahaffey says:

> *Ulysses* is an ebullient, compassionate, raucous, radically democratic, searingly honest yet full-of-blarney anti-narrative. It is far longer than you would like until you've read it once; then, suddenly, it seems way too short. It can seem daunting, even ponderous if you approach it with awe tinged with resentment, but if you hear it as a repeated injunction to "choose life" as it is, as it was, as it can be, it turns into a verbal and emotional thrill-ride where the only thing to do is to let go and enjoy the journey. And it is about journeys, or Homeric odysseys, here compressed into a single day (Mahaffey, 1988).

Joyce's use of Homer's "Odyssey" as a structuring device for the actors and actions in his story is widely known and used by today's readers, many of whom would have been assigned interpretive aids in tandem with the text of the novel in a college course in English Literature or Modern Novels. The Odyssean scaffolding is likely to have been quite less tangible to readers in the ranks of Joyce's original audiences, for whom the eighteen numbered-but-not-named episodes that comprise the work would have seemed non sequitur in relation to the canonical 24 episodes of Homer's epic. That is, if they could get their hands on a copy of the book, which was suppressed in England, France, and the United States under contemporary obscenity laws.

In the same way that the loose-leaf "book" Wurman brought out in 1963 was and is capable of meaning differently, and in more complex and extraordinary ways, than what is possible and available for people from 1974 forward who have interacted with the subsequent codex version, the meaning that Joyce was able to create in the work we all refer to as "*Ulysses*" is very much a function of its original configuration in 1922, and the process of its realization as a made object under conditions of capitalism and censorship. To such a significant degree, that the physical realizations of the work must be addressed as spaces for and of meaning that are covalent with the "text." In both "*Ulysses*" and in "The City, Form and Intent," as with many great works of architecture in the built environment, the structure itself is authored and architected to be legible, and to be read as text (Kidd, 1989).

To put it another way: had either author realized the work in question as a letter that you or I would receive in the post, the envelope, and the paper stock, and the geometries of how the paper is folded (Fig. 6), and the orientation the postage stamp; even the smell of the paper would be considered instrumental to the meaning that has been made. These elements are not subsequent or a side-show to the delivery of some other "actual content;" they are actually content.

An example of just one of many bibliographic/architectonic codes available for readers in 1922 to interpret as part of the meaning of the *Ulysses*: the blue of the cover (Fig. 7). Basic historical research finds abundant witnesses to the fact of its having been selected by Joyce to evoke the hue of the Greek flag. Understanding this particular aspect of the realization of the work as codex in 1922 enriches the reader's experience with the other versions and editions, irrespective of the choices made

Fig. 6 Photograph of limited edition 1922 printing of *ULYSSES* by James Joyce with folded paper

Fig. 7 Photograph of blue cover of James Joyce's *Ulysses* (Photo by Shane Davis)

around the design of the cover in other versions and editions. It may even embolden the reader to interpret other color choices for cover stock and binding cloth in the six or seven different editions Joyce is known to have been involved in the manufacture of as authorial.

Contrarily, one example of a particular artifact of the realization of the work as codex in 1922 that those same readers might have found less helpful in interpreting the work: a word that looks more like the name of a bird (Kildere) than the name of a place in Ireland (Kildare). Much like the infamous error in the text of Moby Dick that caused critics to do gymnastics in their analyses to come to grips with Melville's supposed "soiled fish of the sea," only to have later editorial scholars identify the authorial reading as "coiled" (Shillingsburg, 2006), the 1922 typist's error Kildere can be corrected to Kildare through collation across other versions and editions.

Basic editorial scrutiny of this sort, sometimes referred to as "copy-text editing," reveals a plentitude of other features inherent in the first edition of "*Ulysses*" existing as they do primarily or solely on account of the work having been assembled and printed in Paris under conditions of censorship, and under conditions that were embraced willfully by the author and his co-conspirators as generators of textual instability.

Richard Ellmann's biography has Joyce saying: "I've put in so many enigmas and puzzles that it will keep the professors busy for centuries arguing over what I meant."

Masterworks in Terms of Context

There were six distinct editions of "*Ulysses*" printed during Joyce's lifetime, none of which were based on a single, intact manuscript source. Prior to its publication in Paris in 1922, several but not all of its episodes were published serially in magazines in the USA and in the UK (Gaipa et al. 2015).

As patrons of the literary arts became aware of Joyce's quickening trajectory toward being esteemed as the finest writer of his generation, Joyce's colleague Ezra Pound arranged for the constantly impoverished Irishman to create a composite "manuscript" of "*Ulysses*" specifically for the purpose of selling it as a fetish object (as opposed to its use being the generation of a printed artifact) in America.

The net result of Joyce and Beach and Pound's myriad decisions and actions around matters of composition and publication for the first edition of "*Ulysses*" and its progenitor drafts and variants is a structural design to the total work that permits and even generates ambiguity around what Joyce might have meant. And to the extent that the consequences of these decisions and actions depend on a blending of diegetic and nondiegetic space and place for their effects, the lens of information architecture is (arguably) essential to any attempt to describe the nature of the order of the work.

As such, I do not believe it is too much of a stretch to assert that the context within which Joyce composed, edited, published, corrected, and re-published "*Ulysses*" was inherently cross-channel. And yet, the structural integrity of its meaning inheres, even as creative and commercial forces push that meaning into, through, between, and across channels and touchpoints.

There is no one touchpoint, in fact, where the diegetic universe of the work exists intact. "*Ulysses*" may be the first work in English in the twentieth century whose information architectures can be said to cohere across channels but not within any particular one. And to the degree that these aspects of the work occur in at least two kinds of space (diegetic and nondiegetic), and can be described on the basis of a whole field of geometric and semantic interrelations, the verb which encompasses so many crucial acts of making both works—for Joyce and Wurman alike—is architecting.

Joyce's style of architecting *Ulysses* looks more like judo than karate: anticipating and incorporating the ebb and flow of artifacts in and out of the diegetic space where the work's meaning undulates. He accommodates. The way that Wurman architects information is more muscular, perhaps on account of having developed those muscles quite specifically through five years of architecture school at the University of Pennsylvania, and two years working in the practice of Louis Kahn.

Kicked Out of the Nest?

Louis Kahn is known to have placed extraordinary responsibility in the hands of very young practitioners in his office (Kahn, 2013). He entrusted the entirety of a complex project in England to 23-year-old Richard Saul Wurman, and Wurman told me that he was working on the Fisher House during the second year of his stint in Kahn's office when his boss and mentor suggested a change.

> Lou asked me to come join him in his office, and he said Henry Kamphoefner was in from North Carolina State University in Raleigh and was looking for somebody to teach first and second year down there, and he thinks I should do it. He recommends that I do it, [and says] that Stanislawa (Siasia) thinks I should do it and Bob Geddes thinks I should do it.
>
> I said, "You know, I feel like you're rejecting me." I didn't want to go. I didn't want to leave. So he pushed that aside and said, "I think it'd be good for you." He said, "Why don't you go over there and talk to him."
>
> Siasia was known by Henry Kamphoefner because Matthew Nowicki's one masterpiece before he died very young in an airplane crash is in Raleigh,[2] and he taught at the school. And they both [Nowicki and Geddes] had recommended me. So… I mean: I felt strange. I didn't want to. I just bought a little house in Philadelphia. I had one child, Joshua, who was a little over a year old, and one on the way. But Lou… basically Lou said he thought I should do it, so I did it.
>
> I mean it was that relationship. And I was young, and I hadn't taught. I was 25, I guess, and it wasn't just a walk-on: they were making me Assistant Professor of Architecture. And I taught first and second year. Two classes. They had maybe three sections. (Klyn, 2015)

It is clear that, for himself at a minimum, Kahn placed an extraordinarily high value on teaching. He taught unceasingly, even during times of great need for his presence at the office, saying "yes" to every invitation to give a speech, while also holding down a full-time professorship at Penn, and guesting intermittently at Princeton and Yale (Kahn, 2013). Did that range of classroom experience allow Louis Kahn to foresee the specific ways that teaching would affect young Richard Wurman's future practice?

Wurman told me that he now understands what his mentor was suggesting. Kahn knew it would be good for Richard to hear his own voice in the classroom, and to work through his ideas in front of the students. I cannot help but see what Kahn did there in 1961 as "kicking the chick out of the nest," and the near-immediate result was Wurman seizing what would turn out to be a marvelous opportunity for flexing his info-architectural muscles, and for stretching his wings. The opposite of the Icarus myth:

> When I went down there, I wheedled my way into be the advisor to the student publication of the School of Design. The fame of the school was really based on that student publication,

---

[2] Dorton Arena was noteworthy for incorporating an unusual elliptical design by Matthew Nowicki, of the North Carolina State University Department of Architecture. It was listed in the National Register of Historic Places on April 11, 1973. Originally named the "State Fair Arena", it was dedicated to Dr. J. S. Dorton, former North Carolina State Fair manager, in 1961. From Wikipedia. Nowicki was chief architect of the new Indian city of Chandigarh at the time of his death in a plane crash in August of 1950, and was replaced by Le Corbusier.

and they had done some very good ones in the past; notable ones. I mean: remarkable publications (Klyn, 2015).

In his 1989 best seller "Information Anxiety," Wurman extols the virtues of constraints, calling them "happy limitations." Surely the pre-existence of an already-successful student publication, with its predetermined set of requirements, presented Wurman with specific constraints for structuring information and for rendering carto-graphic comparisons that would not have manifested up in Philadelphia, in the comfortably architectural nest of Kahn's office.

As Wurman would go on to say at the age Kahn was when he kicked a young Wurman out of the nest: "comfort is the enemy" (Klyn, 2013).

Masterworks in Terms of Users

How many people have had their ability to be an actor in the interplay between works of art, their makers, and the means of production totally blown up and re-constituted by an experience with "*Ulysses*"? Far fewer, I suspect, than those who have read or have attempted to read Joyce's novel in just one codex edition, without regard to the cross-channel ecosystem of meaning that pulses through and around the one touchpoint they hold in their hands—this one discrete version/edition coupling from among hundreds of thousands of possible combinations of version and edition.

I count myself among the former, but have had little success finding reliable figures to speak to the latter. What is the total number of copies of the book printed and/or sold since its first edition in Paris in 1922? Millions, it would seem. And unlike a radical work of art that exerts an outsized influence on the next several generations of artists, but realizes little or no commercial success during its day (I am thinking about that first Velvet Underground album), the esteem accorded to "*Ulysses*" once it broke free from obscenity constraints on its commercial availability drove and still drives a more-than-just-a-cottage industry in products and services.

In contrast, Wurman's "Sand Models" book was printed in an edition of 1500, and that was it. As would become the pattern with all but a handful of the 100+ books Wurman did forward from 1963: there's only one edition, in just one printing.

> We sent it to a couple hundred people who were on our student publication list and then all of a sudden, we had a thousand copies I think, and they were gone.

> Then we started getting things back: a Norwegian architectural magazine put some of them on the cover. L'Architecture d'Aujourd'hui, the fancy architecture magazine in Paris, made it the frontispiece. Yale School of Architecture mounted (the plates from the 1963 edition) into an exhibit, and it was up for 25 years.

The near-mythic status "The City, Form, and Intent" would go on to attain among cartographers and urban planners may have had something to do with its scarcity as a physical artifact: it is impossible to know for sure. Wurman's subsequent projects in cartography would take on even more fabulous modalities, 1966's "Urban Atlas" being the most fabulous of all (Passonneau & Wurman, 1966), earning a recommendation from Denise Scott Brown that it be acquired as a highly valuable piece of Op Art (Scott Brown, 1969).

Wurman as THE User

Any other candidate proofs for establishing that "The City, Form and Intent" is a masterwork of information architecture in the dimension of use and users show up as incidental compared with the impact of the work on its maker.

> It (the 1963 Sand Models book) just got to be known. And I said, "What is this?" I thought this must have been done a hundred times before. And the revelatory thing was that nobody had ever done it. And I said, "Holy Moly! You know, I backed into, you know, dog poop here…in some terrific way." That uh…here's my life laid ahead of me. I could just do this! If this hasn't been done, man; there's a lot of things that hadn't been done comparatively.[3] And I thought that was all I was going to do for the rest of my life. And indeed it seemed that way because for the first few things, that's all I did. Then I didn't. And now I'm doing it again (Klyn, 2015).

What Wurman meant by "doing it again" in the passage above is a project called "The Urban Observatory," an idea he first described as a concept in 1967, and then published in Design Quarterly in 1971. It was realized 47 years later by the engineers and designers at Esri in 2013 as a web-based application (Dangermond and Keegan 2013). And as had been the case with all but a handful of the books and conferences he had designed previously, the "user" of the product in question, whose needs and preferences would drive key decisions about the architecture, was Richard Saul Wurman.

In ways that are profoundly opposite to Joyce's provisional architectures of cross-channel information, where ambiguity, evanescence, and multiple readings of the "same" contents are brought about on purpose, as a function of the information architecture, Urban Observatory uses equalized cartographic scales and demographic datasets across disparate information layers to provide unambiguous, user-driven comparisons among "vertical" seams in info-architectural space (Benyon & Resmini, 2017), through the touchpoint of a website.[4]

What It Takes to Architect a Masterwork

For information professionals who are primarily working on screens and digital interfaces, what strategies might we apply to what we are doing, and how we are

---

[3]Wurman would go on to publish several more books based in comparative cartography, including The Urban Atlas (1966), Man Made Philadelphia (1972), US Atlas (1990, 1991), and MAP (2017).
[4]Urban observatory. http://urbanobservatory.org.

doing it, knowing (as we now do) at least a handful of the shared characteristics of fine examples of information architecture from the twentieth century?

It depends. And here's what it depended on, for Joyce and Wurman alike: the constant involvement of the architect in practically every aspect of the production and marketing. Neither of the information architecture development processes that resulted in the manifestation of these two works under consideration in the present discussion is characterized by "the architecture part" happening first, and being deemed complete, before design and production got underway. Rather, the information architecture was under development at every step, from inception to manufacture. In both cases, in fact, the work continued to be architected even after initial publication in a first edition.

So, if the necessary prerequisite to the realization of an information architecture masterwork is complete involvement by those doing the architecting, from start to finish, and even beyond the finish, and before the beginning (Wurman, 1989), the likelihood of such works emerging in the present screen-based milieu seems low given that specialists in information architecture are most often involved in audits, and blueprints, and plans; as contrasted with engineering, construction, and production. As long as information architects are practically unknown in the development teams that build software, and who operate in the so-called 2nd diamond (Wearing and Cruickshank 2013) of contemporary design process, the most fruitful direction for seeking out additional candidate masterworks of information architecture might continue to be backward. As the prophet said:

> We look at the present through a rear-view mirror. We march backwards into the future. (McLuhan, 1964)

References

Amoroso, N. (2010). *The exposed city: Mapping the urban invisibles*. Oxon, UK: Routledge.

Bachelard, G., & Jolas, M. (1994). *The poetics of space: The classic look at how we experience intimate places*. Boston: Beacon Press.

Benyon, D., & Resmini, A. (2017). *User experience in cross-channel ecosystems*. Proceedings of the British HCI Conference 2017.

Bloomer, K. C., & Moore, C. W. (1979). *Body, memory, and architecture*. New Haven: Yale University Press.

Dangermond, J., & Keegan, H. (2013, Fall). Urban observatory opens lens into comparative understanding. *Esri*. https://www.esri.com/about/newsroom/arcnews/urban-observatory-opens-lens-into-comparative-understanding/.

Devlin-Glass, F. (2004). Who "curls up" with "*Ulysses*"? A study of non-conscripted readers of Joyce. *James Joyce Quarterly, 41*(3), 363–380. http://www.jstor.org/stable/25478065.

Ellmann, R. (1983). *James Joyce*. New York: Oxford University Press.

Kahn, N., HBO/Cinemax Documentary Films. (2013). *My architect: A son's journey*.

Kidd, J. (1989). *An inquiry into ulysses—The corrected text*. Boston: James Joyce Research Center, Boston University.

Klyn, D. (2013, August 20). Dumb: 5 patterns from the life and work Of Richard Saul Wurman. *UX Week*. https://vimeo.com/74401319.

Klyn, D. (2016). A comparison in pursuit of "The masterworks of information architecture": Learning from James Joyce's *Ulysses* and Richard Saul Wurman's the city, form and intent. *Bulletin of the American Society for Information Science and Technology, 42.*(5). https://doi.org/10.1002/bul2.2016.1720420508.

Klyn, D. (2015). *Previously unpublished interviews with Richard Saul Wurman.*

Mahaffey, V. (1988). *Reauthorizing Joyce.* Cambridge University. Press.

Mcluhan, M. (1964). *Understanding media.* MIT Press.

Passonneau, J., & Wurman, R. S. (1966). *Urban Atlas: 20 American cities: A communication study notating selected urban data at a scale of 1:48,000.* MIT Press.

Resmini, A., & Rosati, L. (2011a). A brief history of information architecture. *Journal of Information Architecture, 3*(2). http://journalofia.org/volume3/issue2/03-resmini/.

Resmini, A., & Rosati, L. (2011b). *Pervasive information architecture.* Morgan Kaufmann.

Rosenfeld, L., Morville, P., & Arango, J. (2015). *Information architecture: For the web and beyond.* O'Reilly.

Rossman, C. (1988). The new '*Ulysses*': The hidden controversy. *New York Review of Books, 35*(19). https://www.nybooks.com/articles/1988/12/08/the-new-Ulysses-the-hidden-controversy/.

Scott Brown, D (1969). On pop art, permissiveness and planning. *Journal of the American Institute of Planners, 35,* 184–186. Reprinted in Scott Brown, D. (2009). *Having words.* Architectural Association (pp. 55–59).

Shillingsburg, P. (2006). On being textually aware. *Studies in American Naturalism, 1*(1–2), 170–195. http://www.jstor.org/stable/23431282.

Wareing, L., & Cruickshank, L. (2013). *New design processes for knowledge exchange tools for the new IDEAS project.*

Wurman, R. S. (1974). *Cities: Comparisons of form and scale: Models of 50 significant towns and cities to the scale of 1:43,200 or 1" = 3,600'.* Joshua Press.

Wurman, R. S. (1963). *The city, form and intent: Being a collection of the plans of fifty significant towns and cities all to the scale 1:14400.* North Carolina State University.

Wurman, R. S. (1990). *Information anxiety.* Bantam Books.

Wurman, R. S. (1971). Making the city observable. *Design Quarterly.* No. 80. MIT Press.

Wurman, R. S. (1972). Invisible city. *Design Quarterly.* Nos. 86–87. MIT Press.

Wurman, R. S. (1989). Hats. *Design Quarterly.* No. 145. The MIT Press.

Wurman, R. S. (1997). *Information architects.* Graphis.

Wurman, R. S. (2017). *UnderstandingUnderstanding.* Oro.

Dan Klyn works as an information architecture and business management consultant at The Understanding Group (TUG), teaches information architecture at the University of Michigan School of Information, is a member of the core faculty in the architecture program at Building Beauty, and is writing the biography of Richard Saul Wurman. His research is focused on the spatiality of meaning, with an emphasis on the interplay of ontology, topology, and choreography in the built environment.

Institutions Are People and Leadership Is Key: In Conversation with Flávia Lacerda

Sarah A. Rice

Flávia Lacerda is a specialist in public policies evaluation and in information technology management, and serves as Director of Institutional Relations, Postgraduate Studies and Research at the Serzedello Corrêa Institute in Brasilia, Brazil. In 2015 she earned a PhD in information architecture from the University of Brasilia, Brazil.

S. A. Rice (✉)
Seneb Consulting, San Jose, CA, USA
e-mail: rice@seneb.com

© The Author(s), under exclusive license to Springer Nature Switzerland AG 2021
A. Resmini et al. (eds.), *Advances in Information Architecture*,
Human–Computer Interaction Series, https://doi.org/10.1007/978-3-030-63205-2_17

Q: I understand that you were studying information architecture before the term became popular. Tell me more about that.

I started studying information architecture in the late 1990s, at the time the first edition of the polar bear book[1] came out, which feels vintage now. I have a background in information science and information technology. In 2005 I completed a master's in Information Architecture at the University of Brasilia, Brazil, and ten years later I finished the PhD, both oriented by professor Mamede Lima-Marques. Andrea Resmini was my supervisor in the doctorate too. My last academic adventure was a specialization in public policy evaluations concluded this year, where I investigated the impacts of the governmental agenda on the internet of things for smart cities, focusing on issues related to citizens' privacy and data protection.

Since 2005, after my master's, I've been working at the Brazilian Federal Court of Accounts (TCU). For the first nine years I worked in their information technology division. I was responsible for the corporate portal, what you could say is the result of my very first project for the Court. I was tasked with the redesign of the information architecture of the existing web solutions, converting them to a portal concept. It was a huge, yearlong project during which we transformed the many independent TCU' websites around the country into a coherent and cooperative platform. The Court has offices in every capital of Brazil, and when we started in the job, they were still all managing their own platforms independently, resulting in a very disorganized, confusing landscape. Identifying larger patterns, standardizing structures and language, that alone involved plenty of taxonomy and visual identity work.

For the last seven years, since 2014, I've been focusing on the continuing education for public servants, mostly auditors, at the Capacity Building Institute of the Court. We run quite a lot of extension and specialization courses, now, as everyone else, with this challenge to convert them into an online format. I mostly manage, but I do participate in the day-to-day conversations discussing the students and teachers' experiences and journeys. So, I still do a lot of information architecture work, whether it is in my job title or not.

Q: What sort of teams and people are you working with these days?

The teams that I work with vary in composition, but it's fair to say that the majority of the people have a legal background. Others come from the information technology and education sectors. I'm personally in charge of the postgraduate and research department, and institutional relations.

The core mission of the Institute is to promote personal and professional development for TCU's auditors and employees, public servants from other institutions and citizens. The main subjects we focus on are public sector audit, financial audit, government accountability, data science, public policy evaluation, regulation and legal issues. We offer education and research programs, disseminate and apply knowledge management and innovation methods to improve the public administration, supporting the work of audit courts from Brazil, Latin America and Caribbean.

---

[1] Morville, P., & Rosenfeld, L. (1998). *Information architecture for the world wide web* (1st ed). O'Reilly Media.

The Institute has an innovation lab that spreads and implements design thinking methods and co-creates solutions together with the public managers from other agencies. In the last few months, the lab team has been running a project focused on government procurement of spatial technology, to investigate with the actors involved ways to deal with the challenges and limitations of current legislation and other constraints in this kind of project.

Q: It sounds like you are doing more strategic work now than you were at the beginning of your career. You are setting up a vision for how people need to be interacting with information that you think is important, and figuring out how to get important ideas across. You work with people to set strategy, and you implement that strategy by working with auditors on how courses will be built and what they will look like. Do you feel like you are still doing information architecture work?

I sure feel like there is continuity in my work from the beginning until now. Information architecture is my lens to the world, so it's easy to see it everywhere, in every project. When I'm trying to make public policies better, am I not following in Wurman's footsteps, "making the complex clear"? Public policies are information after all, information people need to understand and interact with. Brazil passed its own General Data Protection Law (LGPD), based on the European GDPR,[2] in 2018. If people have to be aware of their rights when it comes to their online sharing of data, policies such as the LGPD have to be explained and clarified in ways that a layperson can understand them, not just the lawyers. This is information architecture, and it's necessary. The government is giving in under the push of tech companies that promise all sorts of free services in exchange for access to our data. While we don't need a dystopic posture or to reject technology advances, we sure need widespread awareness of the long-term pros and cons of any such behavior.

I have a graphic above my desk that illustrates how the lawmaking process is slower in Brazil than in the average of other countries when it comes to adaptability of the legal framework to the impact of technological innovations. This has remarkable effects on people's lives, especially in the context of smart cities and pervasive technologies like IoT. If I can help a little by making things clear and simpler to understand, I'm part of the solution.

Q: Van Gigch and Pipino's Meta-Modeling Methodology, the M3,[3] which you discussed in your PhD research and that became a chapter of "Reframing Information Architecture",[4] has been used as the basis for all subsequent yearly conversations at the roundtable. It helps facilitators clarify the relationships that exist between practice, theory, and epistemology, something of the utmost importance given we have

---

[2] An English translation of the Brazilian LGPD is available on the website of the International Association of Privacy Professionals (IAPP). https://iapp.org/resources/article/brazils-general-data-protection-law-english-translation/. The text of the EU General Data Protection Regulation (GDPR) is available at https://eur-lex.europa.eu/eli/reg/2016/679/oj.

[3] Van Gigch, J. P., and Pipino, L. L. (1986). In search of a paradigm for the discipline of information systems. *Future Computer System, 1*(1), 71–97.

[4] Lacerda, F. and Lima-Marques, M. (2014). Information architecture as a discipline—A methodological approach. In A. Resmini (Ed.), *Reframing information architecture*. Springer.

both academics and practitioners in the room. We always introduce it at the begin-
ning of the day, and we make sure that everybody has access to the model so they can
situate the current conversation in its rightful place. What's the story behind your
adoption and adaptation of it?

I should share whatever little merit there might be here with Andrea (Resmini), who was my advisor at Jönköping University in 2013. We used to have weekly conversations in which we would discuss my research in information architecture from any number of different perspectives, including how to critically approach a possible systematization of the field: the practice, education, research. I remembered using the M3 in my master's dissertation in 2005. I discovered it when a colleague from my research group showed me an article citing it. It was not easy to find the original paper at the time. I got it from an online service in a Kansas City library.

I was planning to use it again in the PhD thesis, but just as a methodological piece. I thought there was something interesting there that we could apply in a broader approach, but I wasn't sure. So I brought it up in one of the conversations with Andrea, discussed it as a possible way to help me frame the discourse, and asked for his opinion. He thought I had something important there, some piece we were missing, and insisted that I work on it.

The M3 is a high-level framework that can be used to discuss any field of knowl-edge: going back to it, I was struck by its immediate applicability. I guess we had rediscovered the M3. So many articles, talks, presentations flatten everything to the level of the practice, paying little to no consideration to reflection or to separating practical dos and don'ts from theory: the M3 helps explain how these two are different. I ended up drafting an article with Mamede (Lima-Marques). Andrea thought it was really good, and that it was key to so many of the conversations we were having. The results are in *Reframing Information Architecture*, in my thesis, in a couple of other articles we wrote together, and at the Roundtable.

I must confess that when I attended the Roundtable in 2015, I was so amazed to see we'd get to discuss information architecture from a philosophical standpoint at the Information Architecture Summit. That is a rare opportunity in our community. Our events have been extremely practice-led so far.

Q: Tell me about information architecture in Brazil.

We are facing dark times for sciences in Brazil, even before the pandemic.[5] Scholarships and research funding are being cut, and higher education programs are suffering as well. My own academic home, the Research Center for Informa-tion Architecture at the University of Brasilia, led by professor Mamede, has been a victim. We were a strong united idealistic group there, but when he retired in 2018, the center closed down. Institutions are people, and leadership is key. We still have information architecture courses in the information sciences, at the undergraduate and graduate levels. Technology-oriented programs also run courses in information architecture.

But this is nothing like the golden times we had before: programs on user expe-rience have taken center stage, and this, at least to me, is problematic. My personal

---

[5]Global coronavirus pandemic of 2019–2020.

take is that user experience is an aspect of information architecture, not the opposite. Information and the way it's structured is the foundation, it's the raw material we work with, in all of its forms—visual, tactile, audible. We can aim to create experiences, but each experience is unique, individual, subjective. In some ways, it feels like we're reducing the field of architecture to the "resident experience" and building higher education curricula only concerned with that specific angle.

Brazil has been for a long time very active in information architecture research and education. But the practice of information architecture has seen a shift, with user experience becoming the anchoring identity and covering everything from user research to information architecture to interaction design. We have seen changes in the academic background of this new generation of practitioners: while some still come from information science or technology, a large part of them comes from design. Advertising agencies dominate the market of information architecture and user experience in São Paulo and Rio de Janeiro, the biggest capitals. Brasilia, where I live and work, has mostly government and public institutions, so, expresses a different market, but it is also dominated now by user experience practitioners. Anyway, regardless of the title, if the job is being done with the appropriate methods and techniques, great!

Q: What would you consider to be the most important part of your education? Also, if you had a chance to go back and do something differently, knowing what you know now, is there anything you would change?

I think the most important thing I have today is that part of my education which gave me a systemic view. That is what gives me the capacity to deal with wicked problems, with complexity. I think this is independent of the area of study or background from which someone might come. I'm very grateful for this lens I was given. If I could do it all over again, I guess I would take an undergraduate course in architecture. That is the only thing I would change: I would do the same master's and PhD, but I would want to have an architecture background. Anyway, during these years, I have learned, working with others who have studied architecture, that what we do is architecture, just made of information instead of bricks. The more I learn, the more I agree with that statement.

About my original academic formation, I would like universities today to be more focused on information sciences, regardless of specific support or service, such as books or libraries. At least here in Brazil, it seems to me the field is too attached to its past, with market reserves and methods that are no longer justified at the present time.

In these last years, the role of digital information in everyone's life has increased immensely. We have many important things to work on, many important conversations to have that deal with huge problems, those that live at the upper levels of the M3, and people are still discussing information architecture as a website-only practice. How many pixels to the right, what color, what font? It's not like those are not important details, but if we obsess over them, we'll completely miss the picture. Websites are one of the many outlets of what has become a really pervasive information layer: mobile devices, the Internet of Things, smart objects, smart cities. If we don't care for the picture, we risk seriously damaging our societies. Everything requires a thoughtful information architecture today: our politics, our healthcare, our education systems. I don't know if it is the same in other countries as in Brazil, but just see a few information science courses concentrating on the foundations of information architecture, even considering such problems.

When I was doing the PhD, the information science faculty had an information architecture research line. But not all the professors recognized the work we were doing on the research group. Unfortunately, some of them simply didn't consider it to be information science. We certainly have a lot to contribute to the field and everyone would benefit from more multidisciplinary views.

Q: If we are dealing with environments in which information is becoming pervasive—people are constantly immersed in a flow of information—how do we structure the way in which people receive the information they need?

Like I said before, information is what we work with: information is the material we use, it's a thing, as Buckland famously wrote[6] in the 1990s. Information architecture is what makes this thing available to people. You can't really design the experience, since it depends on what actors, users, bring to the situation themselves. We can give them scaffolding, structure, architecture, but creating the actual experience requires the presence and action of the person.

This is a phenomenological perspective that distinguishes between subject, object and experience in terms of relation. We must understand the subject, so that we can act on the object meaningfully, for example improving its affordances. But we can't guarantee an experience: we are architects, we model information. This is the reason why transdisciplinarity is so important, what justifies bringing in theories and methods from the cognitive sciences or architecture, for example: we have to understand the subject as a system and its interactions with other systems—actors, objects.

What we decide is whether we are presenting these people with this information at this time, if we allow them to act upon it or if we need to keep them away from it. All of this comes before deciding how they will interact with the "thing", what kind of feedback they might receive from it, in what fashion, and how that will change their experience. As Andrea often says, the structures we create might in the end be implemented as digital touchpoints, as physical artifacts or environments, or any mixture of these, but these are not concerns we should be considering in the early stages. He thinks of this process as being very close to the way a city planner would structure the plan of a city: they figure out where the streets will be in relation to buildings, where there'll be green spaces, what density, how people will move

---

[6] According to Buckland, the term "information" had traditionally three meanings, one of them "used attributively for objects, such as data and documents, that are referred to as 'information' because they are regarded as being informative", and that this specific meaning "appears to be becoming commoner" in "the practice of referring to communications, databases, books, and the like, as 'information'". Information as a thing is what any field dealing with information systems deals with. Buckland, M. K. (1991). Information as thing. *Journal of the American Society for Information Science, 42*(5), 351–360. https://doi.org/10.1002/(sici)1097-4571(199106)42:5%3c351::aid-asi5%3e3.0.co;2-3.

around. This plan comes way before we start deciding whether a certain building will be in red bricks of glass and metal and whether the shop on the corner will be a café or a grocery.

Q: Jorge Arango makes a similar interesting observation in his book "Living in Information". He also brings in an architectural perspective, but compares the way we work more to the way we would seed and tend a garden: we nudge, but we're not entirely in control, and we're never really sure of the outcomes. I'm not sure I entirely agree, but it's certainly an interesting reflection, and one that reminds me of your work with Andrea Resmini,[7] when you discuss the difference between designing "within" the ecosystem and designing "the" ecosystem. The point you make is that it seems unreasonable to claim we can design something we have a hard time modeling and that we don't really control.

Exactly. It's a systemic principle. We affect the ecosystem, but predicting its behavior and outcomes is beyond our possibilities. These ideas are related to the ongoing global conversation on reframing information architecture that was the spark behind the first Roundtable. Jorge (Arango) has always been a part of that, so I'm not surprised that a common way of interpreting things emerges from our individual discussions. That's why we spoke of designing in the ecosystem: we're not creating ecosystems from scratch, far from it. We're adding, changing, moving around elements to promote experiences. So, for sure there is a lot of nudging. In behavioral economics, nudges[8] are a way to influence automatic, irreflective behavior. It has been used to influence people's actions in public policy design. For example, with respect to COVID-19, we can look at what Singapore is doing compared to China: China tracks everyone, Singapore instead created a system that nudges people into being cooperative. In information architecture, that speaks to what we'd call bottom-up approaches.

It's clear for me that the system thinking frame of reference is one of the greatest contributions of transdisciplinarity to information architecture studies. In the moment we shift the paradigm from information pieces—websites, nodes—to entire ecosystems and the relationships they contain, we inject one more necessary element into the debate going on at the epistemological level of the discipline. That way, we reframe the debate to another baseline, to a broader perspective that considers people, objects and places as connected elements that communicate with each other as a system. This is the transformative dimension of information architecture I'm interested in.

---

[7]Resmini, A., & Lacerda, F. (2016). The Architecture of Cross-channel Ecosystems. Proceedings of the 8th International ACM Conference on Management of Emergent Digital EcoSystems (MEDES'16); Lacerda, F., Lima-Marques, M., & Resmini, A. (2018). An information architecture framework for the Internet of Things. Philosophy & Technology (pp. 1–18). https://doi.org/10.1007/s13347-018-0332-4.

[8]Thaler, R. H., & Sunstein, C. R. (2008). *Nudge: Improving decisions about health, wealth, and happiness.* Yale University Press.

Sarah A. Rice is founder and CEO of Seneb Consulting and is an information architect with over two decades of strategy and consulting experience, architecting complex information experiences for companies such as Google, Sony, PayPal, Microsoft, eBay, Princess Cruises, and NetApp. She has also taught information architecture to interaction design students at California College of the Arts. She holds a Master's degree in Library and Information Science with continuing interest in data science and visualization. She is a past Information Architecture Institute board member, ran the Institute's premier conference on Information, Design, Experience and Architecture (IDEA) three years running, and has organized the Academic / Practitioner Roundtable since 2015. She has a passion for ethics in information environments, leading her to create and speak about the Ethics Canvas for Information Professionals regularly at industry conferences

The Organization and Exploration of Space as Narrative: Information Architecture in Video Games

Andrea Resmini

Abstract The chapter analyzes the organization of space and narrative in video games as an instance of the information architecture of digital environments and of the structural role it plays in shaping experience. It does so by adopting two different ways to analyze the space/narrative relationship: Lynch's spatial primitives for cognitive mapping, and McGregor's taxonomy of spatial patterns. These are then applied to read three different action/adventure video games: *Prince of Persia: The Sands of Time, Shadow of the Colossus,* and *Middle-earth: Shadow of Mordor.* The reason is threefold: to illuminate the individual information architectures of games that might, on the surface, be regarded as providing very similar experiences; to contribute to the ongoing conversation on embodiment and spatiality in information architecture; and to provide an example of how contemporary information architecture can be employed to critique different types of information environments.

Introduction

This chapter investigates the organization of space and narrative in video games as an instance of the information architecture of digital environments and of the structural role it plays in shaping experience.

The reason is threefold: to illuminate the individual information architectures of games that might, on the surface, be regarded as providing very similar experiences; to contribute to the ongoing conversation on embodiment and spatiality in information architecture; and to provide an example of how contemporary information architecture can be employed to critique of different types of information environments.

A. Resmini (✉)
Department of Intelligent Systems and Digital Design, Halmstad University, Halmstad, Sweden
e-mail: andrea.resmini@hh.se

Jönköping Academy for Improvement of Health and Welfare, Jönköping University, Jönköping, Sweden

© The Author(s), under exclusive license to Springer Nature Switzerland AG 2021   195
A. Resmini et al. (eds.), *Advances in Information Architecture,*
Human–Computer Interaction Series, https://doi.org/10.1007/978-3-030-63205-2_18

Architectural theory plays a role in the expansive view the chapter adopts in relation to contemporary information architecture as much as it does in its analysis of video game spatiality, and for the same reason: to help explain how an information-based environment, be it a game world or a digital/physical ecosystem (Resmini & Lacerda, 2016), can "gain significance and a quality of 'place'" (Nitsche 2008, p. 159).

A number of scholars posit that spatiality is a foundational element of video games and a valuable aproach to understanding them (Manovich, 2000; Aarseth, 2001; Adams, 2003; Schell, 2008; McGregor, 2007; Nitsche, 2008). In *The Language of New Media* (2000), media scholar Lev Manovich considers navigation through game space "an essential, if not the key component, of the gameplay". Games present players "with a space to be traversed, to be mapped out by moving through it", in direct contrast with contemporary narratives in literature and cinema, "built around the psychological tensions between the characters and the movement in psychological space" (Manovich, 2000, p. 214). From this perspective, video games signal a return to "ancient forms of narrative where the plot is driven by the spatial movement of the main hero, traveling through distant lands to save the princess, to find the treasure, to defeat the dragon" (ibidem.).

Since "the organization of space and its use to represent or visualize something else have always been a fundamental part of human culture" (Manovich, 2000, p. 218), from memory palaces to maps, understanding game space and the way it is built, the way it works, and what relationship it entertains with narrative, can provide interesting insights into how to structure our experiences in other information-based environments, including digital/physical ecosystems.

In tying space with narrative, it is useful to consider the concept of a "quest". A quest is "a journey across a symbolic, fantastic landscape in which a protagonist or player collects objects and talks to characters in order to overcome challenges and achieve a meaningful goal" (Howard, 2008, p. xi). It is an old storytelling construct: a typical example of a quest-type narrative is that of Homer's *Odyssey*, or of the medieval Arthurian stories written by Chrétien de Troyes (1991). More recently, novels such as Tolkien's *The Hobbit* (1937). Manovich (2000) emphasizes how quest narratives were traditionally used to connect what often were disconnected pieces of information into cohesive storytelling with the purpose of transmitting culturally and socially useful information.

Embodiment and Cognitive Mapping

While not offering "the concreteness and inexhaustible detail of indexical cinematic images", the game world is "a space that can be roamed like the physical one and thus is experienced as an inter-enactment as well as an embodiment" (Crick, 2011, p. 261). Allowing players to create "an ergodically embodied sense of self", video games offer a more radical way to exploit spatial memory "over traditional non-ergodic forms of entertainment such as adventure books with survey maps, or traditional cinematic media" (Champion, 2005). For this reason, games "are phenomenologically experienced in (a) way that is as spatio-temporal, embodied, immersive, interpellative, visceral, mobile, and animate" (Crick, 2011, p. 261) and do not, in this sense, conceptually differ from the perceptual space of action centered on immediate orientation that identifies experiential space (Norberg-Schulz, 1971).

More pragmatically, as progress in understanding the nature of the brain functions and the role played by the embodied interplay of brain and body in our own understanding of the world continues (Mallgrave, 2013), research strongly hints at a fundamental equivalence between experiences happening in physical and digital space: they affect the same areas of the brain and are both fundamentally comprehended spatially (Benn et al., 2015; Aronov and Tank, 2014).

This "reading" of a space happens through the mediation of cognitive maps. Cognitive mapping is the process through which "an individual acquires, codes, stores, recalls, and decodes information about the relative locations and attributes of phenomena in his everyday spatial environment" (Downs & Stea, 1973, pp. 9–10, quoted in Soini, 2001; Bellmund et al., 2018): a cognitive map is then the product of this process and represents a dynamic mental image of a real or imaginary environment. This process is eminently embodied (Jacobs, 2003; Williams Goldhagen, 2017, pp. 52–62) and relying on schemas, "dynamic, recurring pattern(s) of organism-environment interactions" (Johnson, 2007, p. 136). In the creation of a cognitive map, people draw on schemas derived from past experiences, which also means that unfamiliar environments will have people return to more primary schemas, some of which were "internalized as children. 'Important is big.' 'Substantial is weighty'" (Williams Goldhagen, 2017, p. 77), or "dark is scary".

Cognitive maps are eminently personal artifacts, and different individuals will map the same environment differently based on a vast array of variables that include past experiences, emotional state, and purpose: for example, a member of staff and a patron would develop completely different maps of the same restaurant, reflecting their different subjective experiences. One important role cognitive maps play in someone's experience of a certain environment is that of mediators, since "(s)ome types of spatial behavior are uniquely tied to characteristics of the environment" by means of the representations encoded in cognitive maps (Lloyd, 1999, p. 1).

Game design scholars have argued that just like the built environment, game space is both a designed space and a human space, in that it necessarily relies on a human understanding of spatial relationships and embodiment, and as such also acts as a primary constraint that can allow and support "certain patterns of events and make others less likely to occur" (Nitsche 2008, p. 160) and as an enabler whose "specific structures can help particular patterns evolve" (ibidem., p. 159).

Kevin Lynch and the Image of the City

Kevin Lynch's work on spatial primitives in the 1960s offers an experiential entry point to the process through which a cognitive map of the city is created. Lynch identified five basic spatial building blocks used to create a cognitive map of the environment: paths, such as streets or bridges; edges, such as a curtain of walls or a river; nodes, such as intersections and crossings; districts, such as downtown or the suburbs; and landmarks, such as a tall building, or a monument (Lynch, 1960, p. 47).

As someone proceeds with the exploration of an environment, their cognitive map is updated and rearranged as any space is experienced "in relation to its surroundings, the sequences of events leading up to it, the memory of past experiences" (Lynch, 1960, p. 1). This dynamic process is rendered more robust and flexible by the poly-morphous nature of the five constitutive elements, which can connotate differently depending on one's position and perspective. A castle's walls could be an edge for someone outside and on the ground, a path for someone walking the rampart, or a landmark for someone who sees it in the distance. Lynch also considers purpose as an additional, important element in the construction of a cognitive map, one that "ties spaces together in a meaningful way, assembles events in a spatial order, and positions the human in relationship to them" (Nitsche, 2008, p. 161).

Space in Games

All games happen in some type of space (Schell, 2008). It might be the rigidly bounded space of a football game, the procedural space of a game of hide and seek, the allegorical space of a board game (Aarseth, 2001) or the immersive space of a virtual reality game (Manovich, 2000). Even games that at first may not seem to present spatial elements, such as for example a game of charades, require a play space: players need to be in visual and aural contact, either because they share the same physical space or because they can operate similarly through the mediation of technology. In this sense, the game itself structures its space and imposes constraints. For example, while charades could be played over Google Meet, it would be difficult to do the same across the full extent of a football field without some type of technological help.

Ultimately, game space possesses a dual nature: it is both mathematical, made up of areas, cells and lines, or algorithms, and experiential, directly related to our engagement and our understanding of the game world.

It is from this perspective that McGregor (2007) argues it is useful to investigate game space as architecture. McGregor recalls how Adams (2003) maintains that as "imaginary space", game space "is necessarily constructed by human beings and therefore may be thought of as the product of architectural design processes" and then concludes that game space, being "an artificial construct designed by human-ity", is "a built environment" that includes "both representations of urban settings and natural landscapes" (McGregor, 2007). Adams considers that while game space architecture is ultimately a subordinate of gameplay, it shares with real-word coun-terpart "a profound aesthetic instinct: the urge to create dramatic and meaningful spaces" (Adams, 2003).

Three Games

The three games described and analyzed hereafter are all action/adventure games, and situate the player in what is meant to be a living, breathing world. They have been chosen as they can be used to illustrate how the information architecture that structures the relationship between space and narrative varies from being extremely prescriptive and predicated on identity (in *Prince of Persia: The Sands of Time*) to being emergent and partially decoupled (in *Middle-earth: Shadow of Mordor*), while still creating a believable game world and an engaging experience.

All three game examples can be considered variations of the narrative structure of the "quest" (Howard, 2008) and of the "monomyth" as described by Campbell (2004).[1] In spatial terms, not only are the main storylines of all of the three games structured through episodes that are spatially anchored to specific locations, but the end of the narratives themselves coincides with the end of game space. Exploring the world, "uncovering its geometry and its topology (Manovich, 2000, p. 214) means exploring and uncovering the story and thus giving meaning to the actions that the player carries out in game space".

The games all also present a spatio-temporal structure built around a "mission" structure, even though this structure is not explicitly stated in both *Prince of Persia: The Sands of Time* and *Shadow of the Colossus*. A mission structure works by dividing the narrative in individual episodes centering around a specific challenge, such as finding the key that unlocks a certain door, that the player has to complete one at a time. Progress to later missions is usually tied to successful completion of earlier missions.

Rhythm and Flow: Prince of Persia

Prince of Persia: Sands of Time is a 2003 video game developed by French company Ubisoft and a re-imagining of the original *Prince of Persia* developed in 1989 by Jordan Mechner. The player takes control of the titular character from a third-person, over-the-shoulder perspective as he parkours and fights his way through a palace brimming with sand monsters created by the imprudent release of the "sands of time" from a magical hourglass. While not apparent at the beginning, the goal of the game is for the prince to reach the Tower of Dawn, the tallest tower, and seal the sands back inside the hourglass.

---

[1] All three games betray the template in different ways. In the prototypical monomyth, the hero goes on an adventure, is victorious in a moment of crisis, and returns home transformed. In *Prince of Persia: The Sands of Time*, the game resolves folding back on its beginning, with the narrative loop restarting anew; in *Shadow of the Colossus* there is no return, and players realize they might have been the villain all along; in *Middle-earth: Shadow of Mordor* there is no closure, no real resolution, and the suggestion of an upcoming fall into darkness.

Fig. 1 In-game acrobatics in *Prince of Persia: Sands of Time*

Prince of Persia: The Sands of Time is a primary example of a game where space and narrative coincide. The palace where almost all of the game is set, presented as a realistic if fantastic environment, is experienced by the player as a succession of separate areas, clearly identifiable as individual "districts" (Lynch, 1960), and through camera movements that liken it to a filmic mise-en-scène and contribute to the game's distinctive cinematic quality (Fig. 1).

While McGregor correctly argues that "(v)ideogames are spatial constructs and the environments of videogames architectural" (2007), the palace is not an architecturally sound artifact: its verisimilitude is subordinated to the narrative. It is a "topologically illogical or physically impossible ludic space" (Adams, 2003) whose role is to create a stimulating, surprising, and challenging environment in the same way a movie would use different locations, cuts and the camera position to present viewers with a cohesive and engaging space.

Most interestingly, for all its emphasis on exploration, the game is also not a sandbox[2] game the way for example *Minecraft* is. In sandbox games, players are allowed plenty of freedom of action and especially, from the perspective of this chapter, freedom to roam. In *Prince of Persia: The Sands of Time*, the player has very limited spatial choices that usually consist in figuring out the right path across pits, high walls, columns, traps, or bodies of water, to move from one area, again a district in the Lynchian sense, to the next one and thus progress through the story.

Space is the only metric for advancement in the game and, with the notable exception of a series of timed palace defense traps starting and stopping after triggers are activated, nothing will ever happen if the player does not move forward through game space. To advance the narrative, the player has to explore the palace: "narrative

---

[2]A sandbox game is a game in which we have "automated responsiveness to player behavior" and where game design "facilitates and encourages a sense of player freedom, while providing a framework for play and a rich and detailed world for interaction" with the ultimate goal of supporting exploration and emergent, meaningful, rewarded use of game space (Breslin, 2009).

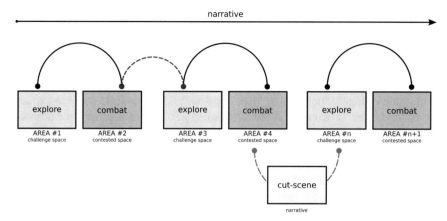

Fig. 2 Repeated use of the same binary spatial patterns gives *Prince of Persia: The Sands of Time* its characteristic rhythm and flow

and time itself are equated with the movement through 3D space, the progression through rooms, levels, or worlds" (Manovich, 2000, p. 214). In this sense, *Prince of Persia: The Sands of Time* is as far removed from a sandbox game as *Pac-Man*. It is a glorified, and spectacular at times, game of the goose: while it provides an experiential three-dimensional space for action, it is conceptually a mono-dimensional, linear structure (Schell, 2008, p. 132) with no way to turn back.

Prince of Persia: The Sands of Time is defined by a rigid information architecture that structures a rhythmic succession of alternate spaces: an area identifying a challenge space, a space "where the environment directly challenges the player", is always followed by an area identifying a contested space, a space "where the game environment is the setting for conflict between entities" (McGregor, 2007, p. 539). Occasionally interspersed with a plot-forwarding or explanatory cut-scene, this binary pairing constitutes the core building block of game space and generates the rhythm of the game. The prince explores an area, using the environment to reach a designated point, avoiding traps, jumping across columns, vaulting from flagpoles (challenge space): from there he enters an area where he has to defeat increasing numbers of tougher foes (contested space) in order to proceed to the next challenge space. The two narrative elements, exploring and fighting, never spatially overlap (Fig. 2).

Enterprising players might encounter a third type of space: magical, out-of-time areas in which the prince can drink from enchanted fountains which will make him stronger and increase his capability to sustain injuries. These areas configure what McGregor calls codified space, or space "where elements of game space represent other non-spatial game components"[3] (2007). In this case, a permanent power-up. It is noteworthy that finding and entering these secret areas is entirely optional and

---

[3]It could be argued that, in McGregor's taxonomy, these areas could be also read as nodal space, space "where social patterns of spatial usage are imposed on the game environment to add structure and readability to the game". Since both the magical fountains found here and the shrines found

completely unnecessary to conclude the game,[4] and hence completely disconnected from the binary pulse created by the repeated sequence of challenge and contested spaces.

In terms of Lynch's mapping language, the two area elements that give the game its characteristic rhythm present an interesting difference: challenge spaces are primarily built around "edge", "path", and "node" spatial primitives, while contested spaces are construed as "districts".[5] These structural constants are kept in place across a diversity of environments as the prince moves across the palace and traverses zoos, baths, mess halls, underground caves, observatories, and ramparts: while different architectural elements might be used to provide a path or an edge, challenge spaces are always composed primarily of these. Once again, the magic fountains areas are an exception to this rule, as they are structured as paths and nodes and always represented in the form of identical networks of rope bridges suspended over a foggy abyss.[6]

This differentiation directly responds to the needs of gameplay: edges, paths, and nodes make for an interesting, challenging space to figure out and traverse; districts, which the player "mentally enters 'inside of' and which are recognizable as having some common, identifying character" (Lynch, 1960, p. 47), provide on the other hand the necessary room for the player to engage in combat while constraining but not hindering play.

The game keeps pushing the player forward relentlessly, and the explore—combat sequence gives the game its characteristic rhythm (Fig. 2), one that is quite distinctive and different from that of both *Shadow of the Colossus and Middle-earth: Shadow of Mordor*. As this pairing of different spaces is iterated throughout the game, players come to expect what awaits them as they enter a new area as they would during a movie, experiencing a constant emotional ebbing and flowing between tension and anticipation before a battle, and release and respite after it.

Loss and Pause: Shadow of the Colossus

If *Prince of Persia: The Sands of Time* can be compared to a well-oiled filmic or theatrical machine, hiding a tightly written script behind its pyrotechnical action, Fumito Ueda's *Shadow of the Colossus* is a game of loss and pause. A cornerstone game published in 2005 and part of a trilogy[7] that has been critically applauded (Ciccoricco, 2007) but has somewhat underperformed commercially, *Shadow of the*

---

in *Shadow of the Colossus*, discussed next, represent an unrealistic practice, drinking or praying to increase one's "life force", I have decided to frame them as codified space.

[4] Additionally, restoring the prince's health also happens as an in-game action performed in codified space, through the drinking of water at fountains, basins, and pools.

[5] There is arguably one real landmark in the game, the Tower of Dawn, that is nonetheless never experienced in-play but rather shown in cut-scenes as the prince progresses through the narrative.

[6] To the point that they could be the same place.

[7] The other two games being *Ico* (2001) and *The Last Guardian* (2016).

Fig. 3 Riding through the empty landscape of *Shadow of the Colossus*

Colossus presents players with an apparent sandbox world of very limited choices. Ueda himself has often described his approach to the game in terms that could only be described as "minimalist", mentioning how he is inspired by the subtractive nature of Japanese haiku poetry (Batchelor, 2017), and the game clearly embodies this aesthetic in both its narrative and its use of game space (Fig. 3).

Taking the role of a young man who enters a ruined temple in a forbidden realm in a desperate quest to resurrect a young woman, the player is told by an entity which calls itself Dormín that it will grant his wish if he will defeat the sixteen gigantic colossi that inhabit that land. The player is then off to roam a vast, lush but deserted expanse in search of the aforementioned colossi, his sole help being the only other character in the game, the young man's horse and ally Agro. Riding the horse, exploring the landscape in search of the colossi, and fighting them one after the other in one on one battles is all that the player will do in *Shadow of the Colossus*. There are no other enemies in the game, and no other tasks to perform outside of collecting apples and killing lizards to increase the young man's health and stamina, again an unnecessary requirement for reaching the end of the story.

As in *Prince of Persia: The Sands of Time*, progression in the game's narrative is tied to events that are only triggered by visiting a specific location and accomplishing a specific task, that of defeating the resident colossus.

The structure is rigid, since the colossi are to be fought in a preordained sequence that cannot be altered: each time one is vanquished, the player is returned to the temple structure where the young woman lies waiting, ready to ride out in search of the next one. This creates what spatially can only be described as a "hub and spoke" structure throughout the free-flow space of the game: a ternary rhythm of venturing out, finding a colossus, fighting it, being returned to the temple, and venturing out again.

Despite its low-key sense of urgency and its impressive fight moments, *Shadow of the Colossus* is a reflective game, and a morally ambiguous one at that (Zoss, 2010). But most importantly, it is a game that intentionally leaves the player plenty of time to

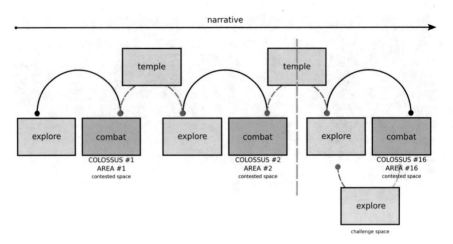

Fig. 4 Ternary space and narrative patterns in *Shadow of the Colossus*

take in its environment, its desolate beauty, and to think. There is no clear indication of where the next colossus can be found: the player's only aid in finding his way is the young man's sword, which shines in the light to indicate an approximate course. And there is no way to shorten one's way there: it's a horse ride, or a walk, or both, all the way, with the most remote colossus area requiring roughly eight minutes of uninterrupted travel without losing direction or committing any gameplay mistakes.

Figure 4 illustrates the information architecture of game space in respect to narrative and the "hub and spoke" nature of progression. Players can spend as much time as they want in the exploration stages of the game, with very little to do except ride to a cliff and perhaps enjoy the extremely atmospheric soundscape, but the narrative will not move forward unless the combat stage is triggered and the player fights and defeats a colossus. At the end of the fight, the player's character passes out and wakes up in the temple, where they can start the next iteration. As the game progresses, combat phases are often introduced by climbing and jumping phases that are reminiscent of *Prince of Persia: The Sands of Time*. There is a ternary rhythm to *Shadow of the Colossus* that emphasizes even more the dream-like nature of the quest by introducing yet another pause, forcing the player to ride out again and, by contrast, heightens the urgency and brutality of the fights.

The game world depicts a peninsula, with rolling hills, steep rocky peaks, and meadows encircled by the sea except for the side the player only experiences during the cinematic introduction, where an impossibly long stone bridge[8] crossing a deserted stretch of land connects it to what we can only surmise to be the "normal" world. There is no human settlement in this land.

Using Lynch's grammar, we can observe two distinct ways for the player to operate in game space, that coincide once again with its dual ergodic nature (Aarseth, 1997): on one side, exploration, relying on districts, the most recognizable ones being the

---

[8]Clearly indebted to Gerard Trignac's work and especially to his "Station Broubourg" etching.

area of the temple and the lairs of the colossi, and on a vast array of landmarks that guide the player in their wanderings: shrines, ruins, solitary trees, natural bridges over spans of water, waterfalls, rock formations; on the other, combat, during which edges and paths also come to the forefront.

In terms of McGregor's taxonomy of game spaces, combat areas are once more tied to a precise location and clearly identify contested space. The occasional shrines where praying increases the player's health and stamina encode codified space. But much of the sprawling game world can be hardly said to fit in any of the types of space identified by McGregor, including "backdrops" (McGregor, 2007, p. 543), defined as being "non-interactive – not part of gameplay" spaces. Challenge space, while forming "the core of gameplay", is defined as a space where "architecture is an adversary and the landscape an opponent" (McGregor, 2007, p. 540), which is a description that does not apply to the contemplative, non-threatening nature of much of the game world. In keeping with Ueda's stated goal of giving players a reflective game experience, this forbidden land can only be represented as an instance of what Adams calls "exploration space", a space that "require(s) the player to understand the shape of the space he is moving through, to learn which areas leads to which other areas" (Adams, 2003).

A Taxonomy of the Orcanization: Shadow of Mordor

Middle-earth: Shadow of Mordor, developed by American studio Monolith, was one of the commercial and critical surprises of 2014. Heavily influenced by Ubisoft's *Assassin's Creed* and Rocksteady's *Batman: Arkham* game series, the game is set in a non-canonical version of Tolkien's legendarium in the years between the events of *The Hobbit* and those of *The Lord of the Rings*. Weaving a grim story of death and revenge, *Middle-earth: Shadow of Mordor* places the player over the shoulder of Talion, a Ranger commanding the Gondorian outpost guarding the Black Gate. Orcs attack under the guide of the Black Hand of Sauron, kill everybody including Talion's wife and son, and intend to kill Talion as part of a ritual. Things do not go according to plan and Talion becomes one with an Elven wraith, incapable of dying and in possession of supernatural powers, and bent on stopping the orcs from preparing the return of the dark lord Sauron (Fig. 5).

Middle-earth: Shadow of Mordor also presents the player with a fantastic but realistically imagined landscape to explore, this time in the wastelands of Mordor where ruins, orc camps and orc strongholds are the primary elements of the built environment. While working from a very similar template, one providing the player with well-known game mechanics and all of the expected adventure tropes, the game offers players freedom to roam and a mostly non-linear narrative that make it a strikingly different experience from both *Prince of Persia: The Sands of Time* and *Shadow of the Colossus*.

Different in that it partially decouples spatial progression from narrative progression: Mordor is a place where things are constantly in motion, regardless of what the

Fig. 5 The player character observing an orc camp from above in *Middle-earth: Shadow of Mordor*

player decides to do. The non-constraining game space comes with a non-constrained narrative: the information architecture of the game allows game play, and up to a point progression, to be unhindered by progression in the main storyline. This is a decision that rebalances the relationship between space and narrative in a direction that was not possible in *Prince of Persia: The Sands of Time*, where the tight spatial structure pushes the prince and the narrative onward, nor in *Shadow of the Colossus*, where the relative freedom to explore the game space is decoupled from the passage of time and is still narratively meaningless.

Players are free to ignore Talion's story entirely and concentrate their attention on undermining the orcs' efforts in Mordor, and factually shaping their society, for as long as they want, engaging in battles, raids, and side missions that are constantly generated by the game. While doing so would limit a player's game world to roughly half of the total game space and prevent concluding the game, since overall progression ties opening up the second part of the game world to completing a series of missions in the main narrative, *Middle-earth: Shadow of Mordor* feels anything but empty, pointless, or purposeless.

This happens thanks to *Middle-earth: Shadow of Mordor*'s most interesting feature, the Nemesis System, and also marks an important difference with the two games here previously analyzed. The Nemesis System is an orc-creation and orc society managing engine internal to the game: apart from a few selected scripted events featuring primary non-playing characters, both human and orcs, every foe encountered during play is generated by the Nemesis System from a taxonomy vocabulary of orc names and features, characteristics, and attributes, and placed within a hierarchical structure of ranks that the player influences directly, by actively pursuing enemies or disrupting activities such as recruiting or hunting, and indirectly, by dying or by eliminating a rival.

This invisible information architecture can generate millions of individual orcs and produce, through subsequent interactions with the player and well-crafted logical

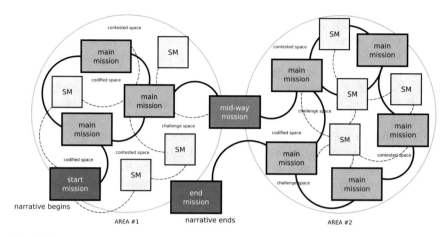

Fig. 6 Space and narrative structures in *Middle-earth: Shadow of Mordor*

branches, entirely emergent narratives in which enemies left for dead come back to haunt (and taunt) the player, sometimes more than once; in which no-name orcs manage to momentarily dispatch the player, thus climbing the ladders of orc society, gaining a nickname (such as "the Ranger-killer"), and becoming more powerful; or in which the combination of attributes of individual procedural orcs, such as their strengths and weaknesses, the environmental conditions, and the skills acquired, open up possibilities for the player to improvise a previously impractical strategy.[9]

Figure 6 illustrates the information architecture of the game in relation to game space and narrative. The dark gray "start mission", "mid-way mission", and "end mission" boxes represent, respectively, the beginning of the game in Area#1, the mission that leads to gaining access to Area #2, and the mission that concludes the game, which brings the player back to the Area #1. In between these three missions, other "main missions" (twenty-one in total, with only seven represented here) advance the primary narrative, sometimes branching off so that the player can decide which story thread to follow. Eventually, all of the main missions in Area #1 will have to be completed to access the "mid-way mission", and all of the main missions in Area #2 will have to be completed to access the "end mission". All main missions tie specific narrative events with specific locations in Mordor. Lighter "SM" boxes represent "side missions": these are randomly generated by the Nemesis System and will appear regardless of progression in the main storyline. The continuous thick black lines between missions represent the primary storyline: the dotted thin black lines represent how the player can move in and out of it to play side missions.

---

[9]This has led to a deluge of videos, walkthroughs, and guides that illustrate infinite variations in approach, combat, strategy, and ways to spend one's time in the company of orcs for both *Middle-earth: Shadow of Mordor* and its sequel, *Middle-earth: Shadow of War*, which features an improved version of the Nemesis System and gives the player a larger game world and a longer and more structured narrative.

The two circles "Area #1" and "Area #2" represent the two subdivision of the game world: Udûn, where the player starts, and the Sea of Núrnen, which only becomes accessible after playing the mid-way mission. Both these areas comprise vast landscapes in which all of Lynch spatial primitives can be identified: a specific mention should be made of orc encampments and orc strongholds as clearly identifiable and named districts, and of forge towers as nodal spaces/codified spaces. What really separated *Middle-earth: Shadow of Mordor* from the two games already described is the dynamic nature of the game space. The player is brought to visit and revisit specific places at different times and for different purposes: locations that present no threat one-time can be reconfigured to contested space by the appearance of foes, by choosing to play a specific mission, by changes in atmospheric weather or by the alternation of day and night. The game world becomes an ever-changing, emergent, and immersive landscape in which the game's scripted narrative is often pushed into the background.

Figure 6 clearly shows how the game presents the player with a much more complex world. The Nemesis system, in itself a conceptually simple if extensive information architecture, creates the illusion of a living, breathing orc world inhabited by an orc society that lives its autonomous life of scheming, hunting, searching, fighting, and gives the player agency in it. In doing so, it also creates an entirely new relationship between game space and game narrative, a more free-form one.

It is worthwhile to note that while both *Prince of Persia: The Sands of Time* and *Shadow of the Colossus* perfectly fit Manovich's consideration that the end of exploration coincides with the end of narrative and thus with the end of the game, *Middle-earth: Shadow of Mordor*'s endgame concludes the story but leaves the player free to wander around Mordor and engage in side missions and orc warfare ad libitum.

Conclusions

Space is a primary component of video games. The relationship between space and narrative in games is predicated on the model of the quest, in which progression between locations also advances the story. That is to say that space is organized to be narratively meaningful and to support the play experience.

By introducing ways to read this relationship structurally, for example by using Lynch's spatial primitives for cognitive mapping or McGregor's taxonomy of spatial patterns, it is possible to describe the information architecture of a video game as a spatio-temporal construct and clarify the differences between similar games, such as those described in the article, in information architecture terms, without having to delegate to game design theory. Insights derived this way could be applied to the design and critique of other types of digital/physical information architectures where spatial elements and narrative, in the form of storytelling, can be used to sustain, support, and improve experience.

Acknowledgements This chapter follows and expands on a series of lectures and talks on game design and the relationship between new media phenomena, including video games, and contemporary information architecture going all the way back to 2012. More specifically, on my lectures in the course on Game Design at the University of Borås, Sweden, and on the following talks: *Groundhogs in the Source Code* at the 14th ASIS&T Information Architecture Summit and UX Australia 2013; *It's Pitch Black. You're Likely to Be Eaten by a Grue* at World IA Day 2014 Bristol; *Notes on games, place, narrative, and information architecture* at World IA Day 2018 Genova; and *A Taxonomy of the Orcanization* at the 2019 ASIS&T European Information Architecture Summit.

References

Aarseth, E. (1997). Cybertext—Perspectives on ergodic literature. Johns Hopkins University Press.

Aarseth, E. (2001). Allegories of space: The question of spatiality in computer games. In M. Eskelinen & R. Koskimaa (eds.), *Cybertext yearbook* 2000. University of Jyväskylä.

Adams, E. (2003). *The Construction of Ludic Space*. DiGRA '03—Proceedings of the 2003 DiGRA International Conference: Level Up. http://www.digra.org/digital-library/publications/the-construction-of-ludic-space/.

Aronov, D., & Tank, D. W. (2014). Engagement of neural circuits underlying 2D spatial navigation in a rodent virtual reality system. *Neuron, 84*(2), 442–456. https://doi.org/10.1016/j.neuron.2014.08.042.

Batchelor, J. (2017). Fumito Ueda: "For me, it's not important to tell the details of the story". GamesIndustry.biz. https://www.gamesindustry.biz/articles/2017-05-18-fumito-ueda-for-me-its-not-important-to-tell-the-details-of-the-story.

Bellmund, J. L. S., Gärdenfors, P., Moser, E. I., & Doeller, C. F. (2018). Navigating cognition: Spatial codes for human thinking. Science. No. 362. https://doi.org/10.1126/science.aat6766.

Benn, Y., Bergman, O., Glazer, L., Arent, P., Wilkinson, I. D., Varley, R., et al. (2015). Navigating through digital folders uses the same brain structures as in real world navigation. *Scientific Reports, 5*, 14719. https://doi.org/10.1038/srep14719.

Breslin, S. (2009). *The history and theory of sandbox gameplay*. https://www.gamasutra.com/view/feature/132470/the_history_and_theory_of_sandbox_.php.

Campbell, J. (2004). *The hero with a thousand faces* (commemorative edition). Princeton University Press.

Champion, E. (2005). Place space & monkey brains: Cognitive mapping in games & other media. Proceedings of the 2005 DiGRA International Conference: Changing Views: Worlds in Play.

Ciccoricco, D. (2007). *"Play, memory": Shadow of the colossus and cognitive workouts*. Dichtung Digital. http://www.dichtung-digital.org/2007/Ciccoricco/ciccoricco.htm.

Chretién, de Troyes, active 12th century. (1991*). The complete romances of Chretién de Troyes*. Indiana University Press.

Crick, T. (2011). The game body: Toward a phenomenology of contemporary video gaming. *Games and Culture, 6*(3), 259–269. https://doi.org/10.1177/1555412010364980.

Downs, R. M., & Stea, D. (1973). *Image and environment: Cognitive mapping and spatial behaviour*. Aldine.

Howard, J. (2008). *Quests: Design, theory, and history in games and narratives*. CRC Press.

Jacobs, L. F. (2003). The evolution of the cognitive map. *Brain, Behavior and Evolution, 62*(2), 128–139. https://doi.org/10.1159/000072443.

Johnson, M. (2007). *The meaning of the body*. The University of Chicago Press.

Loyd, R. (1999). *Spatial cognition: Geographic environments*. Kluwer Academic Publishers.

Lynch, K. (1960). *The image of the city*. The MIT Press.

Mallgrave, H. F. (2013). *Architecture and embodiment the implications of the new sciences and humanities for design*. Routledge.

Manovich, L. (2000). *The language of new media*. The MIT Press.
McGregor, G. L. (2007). *Situations of play: patterns of spatial use in videogames*. Proceedings of DiGRA 2007 Conference.
Nitsche, M. (2008). *Video Game Spaces*. The MIT Press.
Norberg-Schulz, C. (1971). *Existence, space and architecture*. Praeger.
Resmini, A., & Lacerda, F. (2016). *The architecture of cross-channel ecosystems*. Proceedings of the 8th International ACM Conference on Management of Emergent Digital EcoSystems (MEDES'16).
Schell, J. (2008). *The art of game design*. Morgan Kaufmann.
Soini, K. (2001). Exploring human dimensions of multifunctional landscapes through mapping and map-making. *Landscape and Urban Planning, 57*(3–4), 225–239. https://doi.org/10.1016/s0169-2046(01)00206-7.
Tolkien, J. R. R. (1937). *The Hobbit*. George Allen & Unwin.
Williams Goldhagen, S. (2017). *Welcome to your world: How the built environment shapes our lives*. HarperCollins.
Zoss, J. M. (2010). *Ethics 101: Designing Morality in Games*. https://www.gamasutra.com/view/feature/133712/ethics_101_designing_morality_in_.php.

Andrea Resmini is associate professor of experience design and information architecture in the Department of Intelligent Systems and Digital Design at Halmstad University and the Director of Innovation and Research at the Center for Co-production, Jönköping Academy for Improvement of Health and Welfare at the School of Health and Welfare, Jönköping University. An architect turned information architect, Andrea is a two-time past president of the Information Architecture Institute, a founding member of Architecta, the Italian Society for Information Architecture, the Editor-in-chief of the Journal of Information Architecture, and the author of *Pervasive Information Architecture* (2011) and *Reframing Information Architecture* (2014).

Keepers of Structure: In Conversation with Nathaniel Davis

Sarah A. Rice

Nathaniel is the founder of Methodbrain, an information architecture consultancy specializing in user interface structural engineering and advocates for the advancement of information architecture. He established the DSIA Research Initiative to investigate information theory and how it translates to methods to improve human interaction in complex information environments. Nathaniel has over twenty five years of experience working in web design and technology with Fortune 100 companies and with startups. He is a regular contributor to industry journals and conferences.

S. A. Rice (✉)
Seneb Consulting, San Jose, CA, USA
e-mail: rice@seneb.com

© The Author(s), under exclusive license to Springer Nature Switzerland AG 2021
A. Resmini et al. (eds.), *Advances in Information Architecture*,
Human–Computer Interaction Series, https://doi.org/10.1007/978-3-030-63205-2_19

Q: How did you first become interested in information architecture?
I come from the marketing and communications field and was introduced to the web in the mid-1990s when it was called "new media." After a few years of trial and error, I became interested in understanding how to transfer print-based visual communication and language strategies into this more highly interactive medium offered by the web. At the time, it was a new landscape that had a few best practices. There were many disciplines coming together quickly and everyone was trying to figure things out.

Computing user interfaces had been around for decades. But the web was brand new. It made computing available to literally everyone. Masses of people. Computing was no longer reserved for geeky computer folks, large businesses, researchers, or other types of subject matter experts. Coding, designing, and interacting with user interfaces became accessible to practically anyone. It was a whole new game.

I did everything in the beginning, from strategy and design to coding to client relations. As the project-level challenges grew, the systemic responsibility of keeping track of assumptions that impacted the interface increased. I saw this as the biggest risk to success, so it became my new obsession.

When looking for a new job, during the dotcom bust, I eventually came across the term "information architect" on a job board. An information architect was someone who wore many different hats in order to figure out the complex aspect of making sense of an interface for those who wanted to use it. I embraced this general description at the time because it was a label that fit what I was doing.

I worked as a team of one for several years and as I sought deeper insights into what I was doing, I eventually came across books by Rosenfeld and Morville and

Richard Saul Wurman, as well as a community of others who were doing similar work.

Q: You attended the first Roundtable. What role would you say that the Roundtable plays in the field of information architecture?

That's correct. I participated in the first one. The intent of the Roundtable is very important. Cross-pollination between academics and practitioners helps to build and sustain a connection that we need. The connection provides a more rigorous and thoughtful approach and line of thinking. Nothing is off-limits. The Roundtable approaches challenging questions and posits big ideas that have an impact on our domain. Participants then get to think about moving from theory and hypotheses to practice. Many of us realize that practice is an essential path to validating hypotheses. The Roundtable, as well as the Journal of Information Architecture, has played an important role in promoting formal discourse and maturity in our field.

The biggest challenge has been to keep people interested in attending over the years. Each side, academics, and practitioners, have different perspectives. What are their incentives to attend? Academics need to publish. In my opinion, practitioners need to publish a lot more than they are today, but I feel there are fewer incentives for them to do so. Right now, the Roundtable does the heavy lifting to engage practitioners in sharing their insights and interests. I'm sure it's a thankless task, and I'm encouraged that it has survived over the years.

I remember now, that the theme of the first Roundtable, "Reframing Information Architecture," was a motivating factor in a poster that I presented at ASIS&T Information Architecture Summit 2014 called "Information Architecture Schools of Thought" (Fig. 1). It was based on a few articles and posters on "IA Schools of Thought" and framing for a couple of years prior to the poster.

The outcome from the first academic Roundtable effort helped to expose a range of ideas that were of intellectual interest to the field. My research poster segmented these and other insights into areas of specialization (using an approach that I developed). A key observation of the poster was that any framing of information architecture should be inclusive of multiple problem spaces as opposed to articulating a single and potentially restrictive frame.

While early reframing efforts and the first Roundtable did not influence my practice or approach, they did heavily influence how I positioned my practice in relation to others.

For example, when referring to the model shown in the poster (Fig. 1), I can now express how I spend my energy on the left side of the continuum (classic), while we could demonstrate how Andrea Resmini, Dan Klyn, and Jorge Arango have made valuable contributions to the right side of the continuum (contemporary).

The classic and contemporary schools of thought presented in the poster are like the dichotomy of classic and quantum mechanics found in physics. They are ways of understanding the same thing (physics) at different scales and with different lenses. Classic and quantum mechanics are equally important to the field and their application in practice.

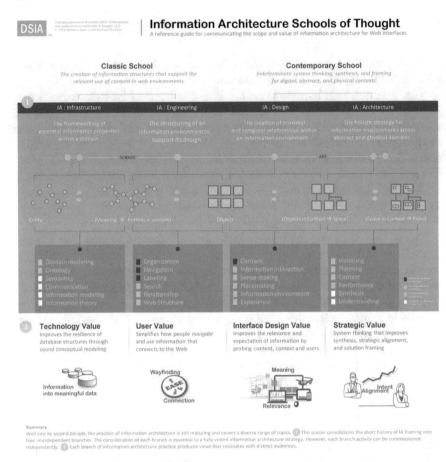

Fig. 1 Information Architecture Schools of Thought (2013), showing both a classical and contemporary view of IA and the value they produce for varying audiences

I would argue that the activities around how information architecture practice was being framed over the years reached a level of maturity by 2014. This growth was heavily influenced by reframing efforts and the first academic Roundtable. My own first major synthesis of information architecture framing as a practice was titled "IA Schools of Thought - Beta" and was published in 2013.

Q: What does information architecture as a field need to be asking right now?

People interact with a spectrum of various devices, physical space, and time. Where is the information? Where are the information environments? How do we scope the environmental context so that we can clarify the edges for anyone working on a project? When we recognize that a set of targeted information behaviors take place within a larger ecology, how should that be used to impact strategy and design?

For me, this line of questioning comes from the desire for an epistemic basis for the nature of information—meaning a way to be specific about what we think we know about information. This would, for example, allow us to posit the properties and attributes of information and then correlate such understanding to the projects we work on to add a degree of confidence and even predictability to our recommendations. This kind of thinking is clearly within the realm of information science and the philosophy of information and is an area where I tend to focus.

The complimentary side of informational behavior is its relationship to human behavior. This is when we consider the impact that human and ecological systems have on the design of a user interface and is where information architecture expresses its affinity with the user experience discipline. I make this delineation to suggest how information architecture connects with user interface- and user experience-based disciplines.

By the end of the 1990s, information architects were today's user experience designers and the "land" that information architecture was grabbing was a recurring debate. In the early 2000's Boersma's T-model argued how information architecture was just one of many disciplines that contributed to the creation of effective user interfaces and proposed the scope of the budding user experience design practice. In 2011, I derived the user experience design practice verticals model that enumerates the areas of interest for each discipline. In this way, I was able to clearly show information architecture's contribution in the context of other disciplines. Since the rise of user experience practice, information architecture has had to come to terms with its purpose.

I have noticed that how I think about information architecture tends to be similar to how others are talking about it, even if we are using different language. I've seen others write about ecologies, information environments, and context. In particular, I follow the work from Resmini and Klyn. We may have different lenses and approaches; we may study different patterns and phenomena, and use different labels. However, we share a similar appreciation for systemic thinking and, at the conceptual level, there is a lot of similarity in our work.

As we continue to evolve our approaches, it will be important to ask, "How do we position information architecture as a *best practice* (leveraged by anyone) and *professional practice* (performed by specialists with deep subject matter expertise)?" We've had less success with the latter. However, despite our challenge to get companies to invest in information architecture-related matters, the underlying issues that birthed this field have only increased. I'm convinced that market interest will come full circle and when it does, we'll need better arguments and evidence as to why information architecture is good for business, digital teams, and even society.

Q: Would you agree if I say that the information architecture community has not been able to consistently explain its value to business in a way to remain viable over the years? And if you do, have you found ways to handle this issue?

I agree. I feel that this is complicated by the fact that the natural topic of information architecture is quite abstract in nature compared to more tangible subjects like interaction and visual design. Over the years, our critical discourse has been mostly esoteric with theoretical and philosophical overtones. So, it's important that we find ways to transition our intellectual insights to practice. I try to remain mindful of this by asking myself, "How do I move my ideas forward?" When I come across an interesting hypothesis and a conclusion that seems sound, I will think, "How does this extend what I already know and how is it relevant in practice?" This line of questioning has been central to my practice over the years and has grounded my efforts to build new insights and discipline through a form of practice-led research.

I'm busy making observations, building a technical vocabulary, and maturing my practice. But, finding ways to effectively communicate the essential nature of my skills is equally daunting. Over my career, I've had to constantly work in parallel to understand the language and mental model I needed to communicate the value of IA practice, in less technical terms, to others or even my next manager. I've learned to be cautiously optimistic because value can be subjective.

Q: What basic concepts have you focused on that are foundational for information architecture?

For me, structure is the central value proposition of my practice as an information architecture analyst. I've written about the importance of structure over the years and there are many reasons why I've stuck with that. For one, it's a familiar concept for people to grasp.

Information architects often rely heavily on correlations to architecture for the built environment. This connection has been a great way to get people to understand the work that we are doing. Structure, as a basic concept, offers a tangible mental image and implied function. For example, if we were in a building together, we could strip away the first couple of layers of the wall to see a structural column. An engineer could point and say, "this is the beam that's holding the load of the floors above. If you remove this load-bearing beam, your building will collapse." Information architects have a comparable skill in the digital space: to engineer and consult on-site structure to mitigate collapse.

People will often ask, "What is the deliverable?" What's the artifact? What's the tangible thing that comes from the work that I do? In the past, there were sitemaps and wireframes. Others might say the artifact is the act of "making the complex clear," "consensus building," "facilitation," and it goes on and on. However, facilitation, nurturing alignment and making the complex clear are achieved in other fields as well. They are not exclusive to information architecture.

The answer that I give, that seems clear to me, is that we deliver comprehensive models. If you read "How to Make Sense of Any Mess," you'll notice how the book is all about types of models and visual representations, of things, that could be classified as models. Yes, we're inadvertently making the complex clear through the models that we use to express the interrelationships between things. The model *is* the deliverable. Clarity is a by-product.

Q: Why is it important to use models to express structure? And why is that unique to information architecture?

I gave a presentation in Boston a few years ago to explain how information archi-tects use models as their primary tool to express site structure. I then expressed how "structure supports the design and sustainable use of an environment by providing resilience to informational forces." Hence, models are important because they are the embodiment of structure.

What information architects practice, at least in my practice, because I can speak for myself, is the wrangling of concepts with conceptual modeling. We don't just pull concepts out of people, out of business stakeholders, out of customers, and out of users for the sake of capturing them. We capture them so that we can document the formal relationships between things—like intent, people, content, etc.

Now, modeling is not unique to information architecture. We simply have a different use for it. User interface and user experience designers, content strategists, program managers, product managers, and business analysts are all very comfortable modeling. They can effectively use models to articulate site structure to a certain level of complexity. It's like saying, I want to go outside and build a doghouse. It can be pretty straightforward to model a doghouse. You don't need a trained engineer. However, many teams don't realize until late in the process that instead of a doghouse, they are creating a user interface that's equivalent to a one-hundred-story skyscraper.

There is a different level of structural integrity and expertise that's needed to engineer the structure for a dog house versus a skyscraper. You have to ask different questions: Unlike a dog house, designing a skyscraper requires asking different questions like, "How will the local environmental conditions affect the structure? How should you engineer load-bearing columns to support 100 floors? What predictions can be made about the performance of the structure and the impact of continued use over time?

Similar to buildings, user interfaces and their respective human engagement have structure. As a result, information architects (or the individual responsible for user interface's structural integrity) should investigate questions, like: What factors of information load introduce risk to the performance of the user interface? What contextual and situational factors should we take into account as structure-based constraints? These and many other questions are ultimately meant to ensure the user interface performs as intended by removing the risks associated with structural failure.

With this lens, we can talk about the structure of a shopping cart as it relates to its respective ecosystem of potentially thousands of products and various user types. The structure of a user interface must counter environmental constraints and factors of direct user interaction that produce *load* (e.g. volume, volatility, information literacy, etc.) and exert *force* (e.g. infrastructure, context of use, culture, etc.). Anyone taking ownership of site structure should be considering this line of thinking.

Q: If this is how you approach a problem with clients, how did you first come up with this way of approaching a problem? What was your methodology?

I view information architecture as an information science. I am most interested in developing a theory of information that explores the qualitative (as in semantics, intent, behavior) nature of information that Shannon views as being "irrelevant to the engineering problem" of communication. As a result, I fall into the *philosophy of information* (PI) "camp" which is concerned with a wide array of questions concerning the nature of information.

In my research, I deduced a set of informational patterns that are essential to sustainable domain behavior. When a function is applied to this set, the outcome reveals a pattern of behavior that appears to offer a degree of invariable support, whereby if it were compromised, the domain would collapse. This behavior conceptually aligns with our idea of structure. Subsequently, if you correlate this theoretical outcome to the creation of application user interfaces, you'll notice how human concepts and their interrelationships are critically supportive of how we create application interfaces. Hence, based on my early epistemic stance on structure and a clear understanding of the other contributing disciplines, I'm confident that the structure of a user interface is instantiated through the modeling of its respective system of concepts.

I refer to the organizational function of creating and managing the system of conceptual models as UI structural engineering. The objective is to tend to the site structure and operationalize any related activities as it scales.

Q: If information architecture is all about structure, what does that mean for the practice?

Information architecture is not all about structure per se. For me, information architecture is about information theory and how I apply theory to solve information-based problems that benefit humanity and improve human–computer interaction. I'm confident that this also involves framing a professional practice with tangible artifacts. I think others have a similar use for their lens of information architecture.

With that said, information architects have an opportunity to position themselves as the "keepers of structure." We can assume ownership of this complexity to provide value to teams that seek user interface structural integrity by validating how everything connects and the implication of each connection to user interface behavior and user experience.

Back in the 1990s and early 2000s things were simpler. You could map out the pages and content relationships of a site with simple software. When we needed to see how things connected, process flows, sitemaps, and wireframes would suffice. That was then.

Today, we live in an already highly interactive and dynamic world that is teetering on the aspirations of the internet of things, personalization, and machine learning. However, there's anecdotal evidence that the structure of complex environments is simply not being addressed; far too many products and services do not meet our expectations and countless digital teams struggle with not having adequate structural inputs that would support digital design activities. And no matter how much data science, artificial intelligence, and deep learning you throw in, a general lack of structural knowledge in the industry is leading to unnecessary failure that has both human and financial consequences.

More of us need to be asking, "How do we create, assess, and manage user interface structure at scale with confidence?" What structural factors should be monitored?

What structural insight do we offer digital teams, to business, and in some cases to society? The good thing is that we have an opportunity to meet this future need.

Q: Are we, as information architects, in a position to be able to ask some of the right questions?

While I think information architects are great at asking relevant questions, as a field, we have some important milestones to reach in order to get a chance to contribute in a meaningful way.

First, we need more depth in our approach to say, "Hey, digital and product teams out there, hire more information architects." They're going to ask, "What do you bring to the table? What is your process? What is your approach? What is your legacy? How can you quantify your value to us?" There's a great deal of market education that is needed, but I'm not convinced that we have a platform (pitch) upon which we can educate.

Secondly, our message can be drowned out by anything with "design" in the name. So, we have to convince an influential group of project gatekeepers that an information architect is necessary and what may appear to be a design problem, could actually be a structural issue built on poor conceptual assertions. Design can't fix a lot of the problems that we have with software. I deal with designers all the time. Designers want to solve problems. They don't have the natural desire or training to resolve systemic conceptual structures even though they are inadvertently expected to do so due to the expectation that they operate as master generalists of the user interface. It's an unfair and sometimes unrealistic burden to place on designers.

While information architects are in a position to ask the right questions, there is a line of other disciplines (product owners, designers, design thinkers, business stakeholders, technologists, etc.) waiting to give their input and we're in the back of that line! Getting to the front will likely be a matter of timing, readiness, and opportunity.

Q: What does our field need in order to advance?

It helps to have an advocate. We had the Information Architecture Institute (IAI) from 2002 to 2019. While the IAI had several programs that promoted knowledge sharing, apprenticeship, and community building, it never established a voice in the tech industry. The loss of the IAI creates a strategic communications gap for our field.

In essence, we need to reach a critical mass of consensus for expressing the benefits of information architecture as a work product and as a specialized area of practice. This could be facilitated by either establishing a new professional association, consortium, or open group of contributors who work together to promote guidelines, standards, and even ethics. I know, this is easier said than done and if there isn't enough interest in the industry, then an advocate is a moot point and all this remains academic.

I recognize that many in this field have become fatigued by defending the practice and how the approach to creating application interfaces are in constant flux. It seems like the kind of thinking that relates to information architecture gets relegated, pushed off, or is highly undervalued in environments of software and product agility.

The market understands software functionality. It understands the need for good interaction design and it's recently come to accept the importance of good user experience. But, the market has yet to appreciate how our system of concepts can be used to generate structure and ultimately improve software functionality, interaction design, user experience, and business outcomes.

We've lost many potentially great practitioners in this field because they couldn't find a solid professional footing with a viable career path. I think our time has yet to arrive. Until then, we need to continue to build a perspective on information architecture, mature our collective knowledge, and continue to bridge theory to practice.

We don't have to have all the answers and that's okay. I think getting companies to say, "I'm going to give this practice a shot because I think it will have an impact" is the opportunity we need to be ready for. And you know the saying: "practice makes perfect."

Sarah A. Rice is founder and CEO of Seneb Consulting and is an information architect with over two decades of strategy and consulting experience, architecting complex information experiences for companies such as Google, Sony, PayPal, Microsoft, eBay, Princess Cruises, and NetApp. She has also taught information architecture to interaction design students at California College of the Arts. She holds a Master's degree in Library and Information Science with continuing interest in data science and visualization. She is a past Information Architecture Institute board member, ran the Institute's premier conference on Information, Design, Experience and Architecture (IDEA) three years running, and has organized the Academic / Practitioner Roundtable since 2015. She has a passion for ethics in information environments, leading her to create and speak about the Ethics Canvas for Information Professionals regularly at industry conferences.

Futures

There Is No AI Without IA: In Conversation with Carol Smith

Sarah A. Rice and Andrea Resmini

Carol Smith is a Senior Research Scientist in Human-Machine Interaction at Carnegie Mellon University's Software Engineering Institute where she conducts research for AI and emerging technologies and teaches for CMU's Human-Computer Interaction Institute (HCII). Smith has a nearly twenty-year career as a user experience researcher and is an active community organizer. In 2018, she presented her work on the intersection of information architecture and artificial intelligence[1] at the 19th ASIS&T Information Architecture Summit in Chicago, USA.

---

[1] Smith, C. (2018). IA in the Age of AI. 19th ASIS&T Information Architecture, Chicago, USA. https://www.slideshare.net/carologic/ia-in-the-age-of-ai-embracing-abstraction-and-change-at-ia-summit-2018.

S. A. Rice (✉)
Seneb Consulting, San Jose, CA, USA
e-mail: rice@seneb.com

A. Resmini (✉)
Department of Intelligent Systems and Digital Design, Halmstad University, Halmstad, Sweden
e-mail: andrea.resmini@hh.se

Jönköping Academy for Improvement of Health and Welfare, Jönköping University, Jönköping, Sweden

© The Author(s), under exclusive license to Springer Nature Switzerland AG 2021
A. Resmini et al. (eds.), *Advances in Information Architecture*,
Human–Computer Interaction Series, https://doi.org/10.1007/978-3-030-63205-2_20

Q: How do you practice information architecture in your work at Carnegie Mellon University's Software Engineering Institute?

Sensemaking is an important part of information architecture, but there's an additional step we have to consider: now that we understand this content, this topic, or this body of knowledge, what are we going to do with it? Ideally, the answer to that question is 'make it into something that really is helpful to other people'. Applying it to a specific problem. Those particular individuals. Making sure that it not only makes sense but is also pragmatically useful, something that can be implemented.

This means organizing information and taking disparate data or what may be already semi organized and doing something with it. This part has an interaction side to it: how do we turn this information we have into something that supports someone's experience? How are we going to take this and really apply it to that particular problem?

In this sense, and in my specific professional environment, information architecture is different from design. Design here is intended to be leaning more towards the visual rendering of the information we work with. Design is the part that brings it to life. It's that necessary activity of really making something work for people and be beautiful or be functional or be whatever it needs to be at the end. I think of information architecture as that part of the work that really makes information first make sense, then be usable and then functional, all of which are necessary preliminary steps before you can get to design.

Q: How do you decide what is going to be the next problem you and the emerging technologies group work on? And what is the added value your participation brings to these projects?

Sometimes we get specific requests from customers such as the xView 2 Challenge.[2] The Challenge was to explore how to assess disaster damage by using computer vision algorithms to analyze satellite imagery. In some cases, we can propose work that we're interested in. For example, this past year I worked on a framework to guide AI development and created a Checklist and Agreement[3] to help teams implement ethics in their work. A project I'm working on is helping a customer figure out a better way to work with robotics and ways that they could be explored more fully. We are figuring out the human teaming aspect of working with robots and figuring out how we can communicate with them. How can we make sure that we understand what a robot is doing, and when a machine or a robot needs help? How do we address that situation?

With another customer, and with a larger team, we are figuring out how to work with multiple robots, multiple people and more complex systems. We are figuring out a lot of the sticky environment-related problems: for example, how do I know that that particular robot sees the other robot, and who's dealing with that robot? That's more about the sense of place and about making sense, and how information flows relate to their physicality. The relationship with human beings in that space is another element we have to consider: lots and lots of information can be gathered from a robot, but what's really important if we want to help people to understand what's going on or what the robot will do next? Conversely, how do we get machines to focus on whatever the most important thing is at that particular moment?

When working on a particular project I'll usually start from the big picture so that I can figure out what aspects need to be worked on from that specific, pre-design, structural point of view of information architecture I mentioned earlier. Then I'll take a particular topic area or work with an existing interface and try to improve it. I'll take it step by step and try to understand what I have to work with, what information I think is relevant and how I could make this even more helpful or how can I implement some new functionality that we've been asked for when looking into this situation as part of the project objective.

If the project is more of an open space, one where we're not really even sure what we're going to end up with, more time is spent early on researching the problem space, understanding how people are thinking about it, and building up from there

---

[2] xView 2 Challenge. Software Engineering Institute. Carnegie Mellon University. https://www.sei. cmu.edu/research-capabilities/all-work/display.cfm?customel_datapageid_4050=295280.

[3] *Designing ethical AI experiences: Checklist and agreement.* Software Engineering Institute. Carnegie Mellon University. https://resources.sei.cmu.edu/library/asset-view.cfm?assetid=636620.

what the information architecture might be and what the space needs to solve the problems I'm seeing.

Another side of my job is to figure out how to explain AI engineering to people who are either new to AI in general or thinking about starting projects with AI. I work on answering questions like 'what is the practice?' It's still early enough in artificial intelligence as a practice that people are really grasping at straws and have very different approaches, despite some agreed upon best practices. Trying to help think through and organize these processes is a big challenge, mentally. How do you even talk about it when there's just so many different types of technologies that encompass the area?

Q: Why is it important to focus on information, and the structure of information that information architecture provides, when doing artificial intelligence work?

Something is missing in the teaching of artificial intelligence development right now. People don't understand how important the organization of information itself is when we have to teach a new system how to understand that information. That's unfortunate. As a result, these systems are often not created in a way that is smart and that makes sense: the unspoken assumption is that it will all work out somehow. That the language will work itself out: 'it's a computer. It'll get figured out'. That's how people think, but that's not how it works.

There's a big knowledge gap. Unfortunately, it will be a while yet before people really realize that to make a smart system we have to do the hard work necessary to understand 'smart' first. Right now, that's not happening in a systematic, intentional, routine way. Not that I can see.

Q: There is so much complexity around human expectations, communication, and the context in which we operate. What is important to make a system truly 'smart'?

While some of these systems, the more specialized ones, can claim a measure of success, in a lot of cases there's a lot of work that needs to be done before we can even claim they work according to expectations. This is a really important point when we want to broaden them to more complex fields, such as law enforcement, or healthcare.

If we consider healthcare, for example, an information architecture approach has an immediate and very visible positive impact. With such disparate systems in healthcare, it is common to find that people use the same words to mean different things, or different words to mean the same things. Human communication is in itself a very complex system, and trying to break it down for software to understand, particularly words that mean the same thing, or words that mean different things but read the same, it's just really hard. The human side of things doesn't make it a simpler task. Education, or practical knowledge derived from previous encounters, has some weight: in describing symptoms or some past ailment, someone may not know the 'right' word, the one used by a medical professional, for example. They may say 'I have a bruise', but medically that's a contusion. How do you help the individual figure out what information they need to provide or look up? And how do you know the difference? When they say 'bruise', do they actually mean a cut maybe, which is a very different thing?

These are relatively simple concepts: the overall complexity only keeps increasing if we consider, say, diagnosis. Imagine you have or are treating a particular illness: will the treatment be very aggressive or very conservative? Think about the differences there. One person may choose to do something very aggressive to treat cancer, for example, while someone else may choose to wait and see. How do you train an AI system to understand the difference between the patient's point of view and the physicians' points of view? Contextual sensemaking, that information architecture perspective, cannot be avoided. There's a lot of nuances that need to be properly understood for us to be able to teach them to a system so that in turn it can be able to present the right information or the right suggestions at the right time in the right way.

Contextualization and context-switching is what people are very good at. We find it fairly easy to switch between topics and we can actually have two different conversations going on at the same time and still keep track of them. You can be on the phone with somebody and watching a webinar and not necessarily lose contexts of either. At least for brief periods of time, anyway. We can recognize separate types of information (e.g. dinner options vs. results of a card sort), know what the differences are, and when these contexts are appropriate. We know when and why to switch between them. We understand the context: AI systems can't yet do that. And here you have one of those systemic issues we face constantly in the field. This is both an information architecture problem, centering on meaning, context, and the relationships between concepts and the environment; and a technological problem, because computing power is a finite quantity and scalability a partial answer.

Q: One thing that information architecture has focused on in the past fifteen years is bottom-up categorization, recommendation systems, and filtering. Could filtering be part of the solution for these systems?

I believe that helping artificially intelligent systems filter the content is definitely an interesting approach, especially since discriminating, finding patterns in data, is something that machines can do really well when they're properly trained. Once they have an understanding of deep-sea biology, for example, we can give them a thousand papers and ask them to single out the ones that discuss a specific topic of interest that is appropriate, such as articles on deep-sea worms. Figuring out what matches means also figuring out what doesn't match. So outliers, such as a paper on archeology, could be recognized as not fitting with the context. However, the system will not know what to do about the situation without being trained in that regard. AI systems only know what they are taught and, if left to determine their own meaning, will rarely do what a human would do because they do not have general intelligence.

Q: You touched on this briefly when you discussed the human angle of dealing with an AI system managing a healthcare service and the complex problems posed by language and context, but what's your position when it comes to the social and cultural implications of moving towards real artificial intelligence? In 2018, CNN Business ran Samantha Murphy Kelly's story of how "(t)he first four words (her) toddler understood were 'mom', 'dad', 'cat' and 'Alexa'.[4] *Kelly mentioned in her piece how there's both a dark side to this, after all what Amazon wants is to sell you goods and services, as much as a bright side: while the research is not really there, preliminary studies seem to indicate that children exposed to voice assistants are more autonomous and develop more structured and clear speech patterns earlier. Should we be worried then or should we not?*

I see this as a big problem and one we've already seen in many different systems that have been developed. For whatever reason, teams weren't speculative enough about the potential implications and unintended, or unwanted, consequences, or the danger that they're exposing people to. Data collection is an important aspect of this problem that we often discuss: how we are collecting it, what data we are collecting, what data we are not collecting. But there's a prior step, one we don't take often-thinking through how ethics should be discussed and implemented when any problem with technology is being approached.

We should take time to think through the worst-case scenarios: for systems that accumulate data and self-improve, those are often scenarios where humans misbehave. Assuming not everybody is going to be nice should be the default. When we're making a system that we're going to release to the public, or even within an organization, we really need to think about the potential misuse and abuse, and how we're going to prevent them, ideally, or at least mitigate those issues when they arise. Thinking it through ahead of time and not after the fact is key. It's not enough to claim 'Oh, we didn't know'. Figuring out those types of situations ahead of time and doing a little bit of extra homework can go a long way to protect people.

Q. How can information architecture help artificial intelligence research and implementation become more focused on the ethical side of the process? Is there an ethical benefit to combining information architecture with artificial intelligence?

There are signs these are becoming more important questions. We're seeing a lot more people and organizations develop sets of technical ethics which identify values to be upheld. That's very positive. We're also starting to discuss the original sources of harm, why we have racism, why sexism, and what we need to do to address these problems. These have organizational consequences in the way we recruit and reach out, in the way we assemble diverse teams.

In a podcast[5] aired earlier this year, Ayana Howard, a professor at Georgia Tech and the Chair of the School of Interactive Computing, mentioned how it is possible to gamify ethical challenges by providing benefits to team members who find ethical bugs, similar to what we already do with software.

And then I think we just need to have those difficult conversations, those where we ask each of us to take a hard look at our own biases. Being aware of bias is really the first step. Acknowledging that anyone can be racist, for example, and how we can

---

[4]Murphy Kelly, S. (2018). *Growing up with Alexa: A child's relationship with Amazon's voice assistant*. CNN Business. https://edition.cnn.com/2018/10/16/tech/alexa-child-development/index.html.

[5]Fridman, L. (2020). *Ayanna Howard: Human-robot interaction and ethics of safety-critical systems*. Lex Fridman Podcast on Artificial Intelligence. https://lexfridman.com/ayanna-howard/.

work on being anti-racist, address the problem and move forward without bringing that stigma into the systems that we're building. Rather we are protecting people and creating a more equitable and fair landscape.

In a way, this is still about the human angle we mentioned at the beginning of this conversation. Humans bring in complexity in many different ways and mathematics and AI alone cannot solve all of the problems we encounter. There isn't an easy, algorithmic solution for a lot of this: it's messy problems with messy people.

Sarah A. Rice is founder and CEO of Seneb Consulting and is an information architect with over two decades of strategy and consulting experience, architecting complex information experiences for companies such as Google, Sony, PayPal, Microsoft, eBay, Princess Cruises, and NetApp. She has also taught information architecture to interaction design students at California College of the Arts. She holds a Master's degree in Library and Information Science with continuing interest in data science and visualization. She is a past Information Architecture Institute board member, ran the Institute's premier conference on Information, Design, Experience and Architecture (IDEA) three years running, and has organized the Academic / Practitioner Roundtable since 2015. She has a passion for ethics in information environments, leading her to create and speak about the Ethics Canvas for Information Professionals regularly at industry conferences.

Andrea Resmini is associate professor of experience design and information architecture in the Department of Intelligent Systems and Digital Design at Halmstad University and the Director of Innovation and Research at the Center for Co-production, Jönköping Academy for Improvement of Health and Welfare at the School of Health and Welfare, Jönköping University. An architect turned information architect, Andrea is a two-time past president of the Information Architecture Institute, a founding member of Architecta, the Italian Society for Information Architecture, the Editor-in-chief of the Journal of Information Architecture, and the author of *Pervasive Information Architecture* (2011) and *Reframing Information Architecture* (2014).

Toward a Feminist Information Architecture

Stacy Merrill Surla

Abstract The need to focus on feminism in information architecture; the importance of defining "the user"; defining feminism in social and academic contexts; feminist studies and practices within information architecture and related disciplines such as HCI, information science, and interaction design; a feminist agenda for information architecture.

Introduction

A feminist information architecture is concerned with informing and strengthening the design of information systems by including feminist perspectives, theories, and practices. To move toward a feminist information architecture we need to better understand the current paradigms—the social, cultural, and technological shifts that are making a feminist information architecture something that can now be part of the discourse; engage in a robust academic debate on feminisms in information architecture, to include research projects, publications, and discussions; and develop, test, and employ tools and methods that can integrate considerations of gender into the processes by which the artifacts of information architecture are generated.

Misogyny in technology manifests as a lack of women in roles as producers and in leadership positions, and in designs and approaches that favor male perspectives and needs and are blind to those of females and other non-archetypal groups. Equity in information architecture would show up, for instance, as inclusion of women in the production of information architectures, the propagation of feminine approaches in addressing information architecture problems, solutions that address needs of female audiences, and an opening to consider the ethics of design in information architecture more broadly, with feminism as both a focus and as a way to open doors to inclusivity of other sorts.

S. M. Surla (✉)
University of Maryland, College Park, MD, USA
e-mail: ssurla@umd.edu

MetaMetrics Inc., Durham, NC, USA

© The Author(s), under exclusive license to Springer Nature Switzerland AG 2021
A. Resmini et al. (eds.), *Advances in Information Architecture*,
Human–Computer Interaction Series, https://doi.org/10.1007/978-3-030-63205-2_21

Pervasive Over Space and Time

Several years ago, at the UXDC user experience conference in Washington, D.C., I eagerly awaited a talk by Karen Holtzblatt, a headline speaker and co-author of the seminal guide to user-centered observation, "Contextual Design." Holtzblatt's presentation was scheduled for the main ballroom in order to accommodate the huge crowd that was expected to attend. The title of her session was "Women in Technology" (2017). A dozen people came to that talk. Two of them were volunteers for the room. And all of them were women.

It was, nonetheless, an excellent presentation, which Holtzblatt accommodated to the circumstances by gathering everyone around one table. Among other insights, I learned that the problem of women in technology isn't one of getting women into technological fields. Rather, it's that women leave tech at twice the rate men do, and at a much higher rate than do women in other high-paying fields including banking, law, and medicine. An understanding of these drivers is necessary to address the flight of women from careers in technology.

Earlier that day Christina Wodtke, also a woman, gave a compelling presentation on designing successful teams, and she gave it to a capacity crowd in the same room. But Holtzblatt, an academic and consultant known to the DC metropolitan user experience community, had only a tiny group willing to engage on the topic of how to build successful teams *that include women*. For myself, as a practitioner and teacher, the incongruity brought into focus several questions I had been exploring casually for more than a year.[1] In conversations with colleagues it appeared that gender issues in information architecture have barely begun to be raised in our field. I now wondered: Do women face barriers in the context of information systems production or use? Is the topic of women and technology being engaged within academia and practice, or is it absent? What would a feminist information architecture entail?

Looking for "Who"

Judging by the outcomes that surround us and the standards employed to achieve them, the user of information systems is someone who is white, male, cisgender, able-bodied, and young. The concept of Reference Man (Snyder et al., 1975) was introduced to research the effects of radiation exposure. This archetype, a Caucasian male between 25 and 30 years of age weighing 154 lb, standing 5 feet 6 inches tall, and living a Western European or North American lifestyle, has gone on to be used in research into nutrition, pharmacology, population, and toxicology, and can be found "in every corner of the designed world" (Tapia et al., 2020).

---

[1] For instance, in discussions with Karl Fast in March 2017 and Jeff Pass in June 2018.

A study into gender inclusivity in the European Union uncovered a persistent gender gap in ownership, access, and use of information and communication technology products, and revealed that "essentialist and binary understandings of femininity and masculinity are remarkably pervasive and tenacious," impacting how women and girls are approached even by projects that have an explicit goal to engage females in IT (Faulkner & Lie, 2007). As design critic Philippa Goodall (1983) states, "(i)t is not for nothing that the expression 'man-made' refers to a vast range of objects that have been fashioned from physical materials," and that these objects are meant to support men in carrying out work that is largely owned by men. A gender data gap—a female-shaped "absent presence"—is described by Criado-Perez (2019) as a silence that pervades art, science, and technology, and is both the cause and consequence of an unexamined conception of humanity as being almost exclusively male.

Likewise, at this moment in time, information architecture, as practice and discipline, prioritizes and privileges the members of the unexamined male archetype, as both producers and consumers of information environments. To the extent this is true, information architecture is overlooking the needs of half the world.

A feminist information architecture is therefore concerned with informing and strengthening the design of information systems by including feminist perspectives. A key component of moving toward a feminist information architecture is to investigate what is currently present and what is absent from speaking about and framing the discipline and in carrying out the practice of information architecture.

Feminism Defined

Within the context of improving information system design, feminism must be understood as both a social movement and an academic discipline.

As a social movement, feminism advocates for "equality of the sexes and the establishment of the political, social, and economic rights of the female sex" ("Feminism", 2020). In the social context, feminism seeks to define "the problem that has no name" (Friedan, 1963) in order to achieve goals such as equity. Putting a name to the female-shaped absence in the discourse and then advocating for change is akin to feminism finding the bootstraps and then pulling itself up by them.

Generally stated, academic feminism seeks to recognize and understand the realities of women's situations within the social construct (which is a descriptive view), and/or to define what the situation of women ought to be, perhaps with an agenda for getting there (a normative view). This binary normative/descriptive epistemology is not all-encompassing (Wise & Stanley, 2006), but it parallels that of activist feminism and is a solid foundation for pursuing a feminist information architecture.

Taking academics and practice together in the context of information system design, Kotamraju provides a strong practical definition of feminism as "a focus on gender and an acknowledgment of its role in relationships of power" (2011).

In the more general area connected to new media, Bardzell (2010) identifies two general ways feminism can advance interaction design in particular. The first is by critique-based contributions, which use feminist approaches to analyze existing designs and processes to reveal their consequences. The second is through generative contributions, which apply feminist approaches to impact design decisions and processes themselves.

Feminist Studies and Practice Within Information Architecture and Related Disciplines

In the academy, feminism operates as a theoretical framework in numerous fields. These include such disparate disciplines as feminist criticism, which looks at "the ways in which literature reinforces or undermines the economic, political, social, and psychological oppression of women" (Tyson, 2006) and urban planning, for instance in examining feminist and decolonial contributions to knowledge systems for urban resilience (Wijsman & Feagan, 2019).

Noteably for the project of developing a feminist information architecture, library science and human–computer interaction (HCI), two academic disciplines with which information architecture has close affinities, can boast active voices in feminist studies. For example, Hope Olson (2007) has used feminist critique as a tool for the organization of information. From the perspective as a producer (of knowledge, teaching, and built information structures), Marcia Bates (2005) speaks about being a woman in the academic world in which she has spent her career:

> (M)ine was the first generation large enough to be perceived as a serious threat to the comfortable boys' club. And the boys were not happy (…) I had naively thought that men would be embarrassed to realize how much women had been discriminated against and would quickly act to correct things once the unfair rules of the game came to the light of day in the 1960's. Au contraire.

The most relevant literature to the development of a feminist information architecture comes from human–computer interaction, a research-oriented field that has contributed significantly to building the body of knowledge informing effective user experience design, interaction design, and other user-centric digital practices. In the proceedings of CHI 2010, Bardzell draws the connections between interaction design and feminism, describing the state of feminism within human–computer interaction, and outlining a feminist HCI agenda. She observes that

> (f)eminism is a natural ally to interaction design, due to its central commitments to issues such as agency, fulfillment, identity, equity, empowerment, and social justice (…) By making visible the manifold ways that gender is constructed in everyday life, contemporary feminism seeks to generate opportunities for intervention. (Bardzell, 2010)

Bardzell and Churchill co-edited a 2011 special issue of "Interacting with computers" on "Feminism and HCI: New Perspectives" containing eighteen ground-breaking articles covering theory, critique, and practice. Muller (2011) observes that "feminism asks the 'who' questions in HCI" to find the identity of the user, the organizational actors, and the researcher. Rode (2011) outlines an agenda for feminist HCI, stating that "(a)s researchers we need to stop attempting to answer the question 'do women and men display different aptitudes for technological tasks?' but rather, 'how are beliefs and use of technology embedded in the production and ongoing management of gender in the world?'".

More recently, Sano-Fronchini (2017) discusses "where feminist rhetoric and interaction design can, and should, intersect" in order to conceptualize and create robust, compelling, human-centered, and complex experiences across digital and physical spaces. She states that

> feminisms and interaction design have much to offer one another, considering interaction design's concerns for social justice and engaging wicked problems, in tandem with feminist rhetorical approaches that suggest that we engage in critical imagination, strategic contemplation, and imagining radical futures.

Practical case studies include work in incorporating multilingual user experience in supporting technology innovation within marginalized communities through a community-driven, technofeminist mentorship (Shivers-McNair et al., 2019).

The conversation around feminism and information architecture is currently thin, and has been confined to isolated conference presentations, such as Jessica Ivins' "What Everyone Needs to Know About Designing for Women" presented at the 2011 ASIS&T Information Architecture Summit, and discussions and lightning talks at the Academics and Practitioners Roundtable on Information Architecture (Surla, 2018).

A Feminist Agenda for Information Architecture

Information architecture as a field must take actions that incorporate feminist perspectives into theory, research, and practice, in both the academy and the workplace.

The Meta-Modeling Methodology or M3,[2] as described by Lacerda and Lima-Marques (2014) as a means to develop a language of critique for information architecture, is a useful framework for brainstorming an agenda for a feminist information architecture. At each of three levels—that of applied work, theories and models, and paradigms—it is possible to uncover areas of discrimination, areas of blindness, and opportunities. The following questions are preliminary probes which are meant to help initiate a thorough exploration of the problem space.

At the Applied Work Level of the M3

How can considerations of gender be integrated into the processes by which information architecture artifacts are generated?

---

[2] See also "Classical to Contemporary" in this same volume.

Practices such as persona development, contextual research, prototyping, and usability studies, and the notion of the "user" itself, are governed by unexamined assumptions concerning gender. These practices are key points of engagement and mediation between users, designers, and the designed object, and getting feminist perspectives into place within the discovery and design of systems and services will result in artifacts (e.g., wireframes, prototypes, taxonomies, and recommendations) that better support the production of accessible and equitable information environments.

To improve gender-awareness in existing practices, and to engage teams and clients in valuing gender equity in system design, we need new, concrete tools and methods. These can include lists, talking points, exercises, and processes. One suggestion is to develop a tool similar in approach to the Scenario Creation Tool for Ethical Design (Pass et al., 2018). This is a framework and a process which seeks to help teams see and solve ethical problems when designing information architectures.

At the Theories and Models Levels of the M3

What insights do different feminist theories provide for information architecture research? What metaphors are currently in place, and what do they make possible or prevent?

A robust academic discourse on feminism in information architecture is a foundational step which is nascent at this time. Research projects and publications are needed to kickstart the conversation. Within a male-centric paradigm, the pervasive subjugation of women has been all but invisible to our perception. This makes distinguishing and defining feminist/non-feminist/anti-feminist theories and metaphors difficult to articulate and argue about.

Consideration of gender and feminism involves critiquing core concepts, assumptions, and epistemologies in a discipline. Feminist HCI literature suggests, for instance, that

> Universality, a value traditionally associated with masculinity, continues to dominate usability evaluation (e.g., mental models, Fitts' and Hicks' laws, usability lab protocols) and design methods (e.g., design process models such as waterfall and agile, design principles). (Bardzell, 2010)

There are, presumably, values associated with femininity and gender non-conformity in information architecture. The extent to which these are recognized and embodied in information architecture theories, and the consequences of incorporating those values, are as yet unknown. Identifying feminist and non-feminist theories and metaphors, and examining their impact on the development of information systems, is a green field open for exploration.

At the Paradigm Level of the M3

What social, cultural, and technological shifts are making a feminist information architecture something that can now be part of the discourse?

The paradigms within which we live and work are the containers that give shape to everything we can perceive, think, and do (Foucault, 1966). Our current paradigm, with respect to equity in gender and race, is often called "the patriarchy." Being immersed in a paradigm makes it difficult to see its lines of force and boundaries. Feminism has a history that reaches back to Christine de Pizan (1405) and before, and we still do not live in an equitable society. However, our present age has given rise to new paradigms, bounded within new geographies, values, modes of perception, and technologies, and these are enabling feminist concerns to be thought of in particular ways and to have particular impacts.

The #MeToo movement has raised awareness for survivors of sexual assault, increased the numbers of female candidates seeking and gaining political office, and uprooted male perpetrators of assault from positions of power (Stone & Vogelstein, 2019). It also reflects a fundamental shift in how women's rights are perceived and acted upon in society and legislation. This shift in the paradigm can support the development of a feminist information architecture.

The Black Lives Matter movement is another epoch-making shift whose inter-sections with feminism have important implications for gender and racial equity in information systems design. It's important to take into account the ongoing disso-nances between a feminism of white women with the imperative to create a just and equitable society for all (Watters, 2017). Nonetheless, feminism is important in racial justice movements and has the potential to transform both practice and theory. Cohen and Jackson (2015) suggests that

> (p)articularly for women of color, there is an understanding that you may never be fully embraced in the academy, (which) gives you a kind of freedom to pursue the work that will transform institutions of oppression, including the academy.

Conclusions

By grappling with feminism and information architecture we should be able to design better information environments. Therefore, it is imperative that we do so grapple. Pursuit of a feminist information architecture requires engagement by and among individual academics and designers of systems. Specifically, we can:

- Include feminist considerations in determining our own behaviors as teachers and practitioners, and modeling our behaviors for others
- Create tools and methods that integrate gender considerations into the processes by which the artifacts of information architecture are generated
- Develop a research agenda for feminism in information architecture

- Participate in an academic discussion on feminisms within information architecture
- Take part in a practical conversation about what a feminist information architecture can be

By identifying gaps, blind spots, and inequities, a feminist information architecture can turn injuries into opportunities, and shape information architecture into a discipline that better enables the production of information environments that work for everyone.

References

Bardzell, S. (2010). *Feminist HCI: Taking stock and outlining an agenda for design*. Proceedings of CHI 2010: HCI For All. Association for computing machinery, p. 1308.

Bardzell, S., & Churchill, E. F. (Eds.). (2011). Feminism and HCI: New perspectives. *Interacting with Computers, 23*, iii–xi.

Bates, M. J. (2005). *Acceptance speech for the American Society for Information Science and Technology Award of Merit*. Annual conference of the American Society for Information Science and Technology, Charlotte.

Cohen, C., & Jackson, S. (2015). Ask a feminist: A conversation with Cathy Cohen on Black Lives Matter, feminism, and contemporary activism. *Signs*. University of Chicago Press. http://signsjournal.org/ask-a-feminist-cohen-jackson/.

Criado-Perez, C. (2019). The deadly truth about a world built for men – From stab vests to car crashes. An edited extract from Invisible women: Exposing data bias in a world designed for men. *The Guardian*.

de Pizan, C. (1999). *The book of the city of ladies* (R. Brown-Grant, Trans.). Penguin Books (original work published 1405).

Faulkner, W., & Lie, M. (2007). Gender in the information society: Strategies of inclusion. *Gender, Technology and Development, 11*(2), 157–177.

Feminism. (2020). *Oxford english dictionary online*. https://www.oed.com/view/Entry/69192. Accessed September 11, 2020.

Foucault, M. (1966). *Les mots et les choses; une archéologie des sciences humaines*. Gallimard.

Friedan, B. (1963). *The feminine mystique*. Norton.

Goodall, P. (1983). Design and gender. In G. Robertson (Ed.), *The block reader in visual culture*. Routledge.

Holtzblatt, K. (2017). *Women in technology*. Paper presented at UXDC 2017, Washington.

Ivins, J. (2011). *What everyone needs to know about designing for women*. Paper presented at the 12th ASIS&T Information Architecture Summit, Denver.

Kotamraju, N. (2011). Playing stupid, caring for users, and putting on a good show: Feminist acts in usability study work. In S. Bardzell & E. F. Churchill (Eds.), Feminism and HCI: New perspectives. *Interacting with Computers, 23*(5), 439–446.

Lacerda, F., & Lima-Marques, M. (2014). Information architecture as a discipline — A methodological approach. In A. Resmini (Ed.), *Reframing information architecture*. Springer.

Muller, M. (2011). Feminism asks the "Who" questions in HCI. In S. Bardzell & E. F. Churchill (Eds.), Feminism and HCI: New perspectives. *Interacting with Computers, 23*(5), 447–449.

Olson, H. (2007). How we construct subjects: A feminist analysis. In C. Ingold & S. E. Searing (Eds.), *Library Trends: Gender Issues in Information Needs and Services, 56*(2). Johns Hopkins University Press.

Pass, J., Surla, S., Perez, A., Instone, K., & Cook, S. (2018). *A scenario creation tool for ethical design*. Poster presented at the 19th ASIS&T Information Architecture Summit, Chicago.

Rode, J. (2011). A theoretical agenda for feminist HCI. In S. Bardzell & E. F. Churchill (Eds.), Feminism and HCI: New perspectives. *Interacting with Computers, 23*(5), 393–400.

Sano-Fronchini, J. (2017). Feminist rhetorics and interaction design: Facilitating socially responsible design. In L. Potts & M. J. Salvo (Eds.), *Rhetoric and experience architecture*. Parlor Press.

Shivers-McNair, A., Gonzales, L., & Zhyvotovska, T. (2019). An Intersectional technofeminist framework for community-driven technology innovation. In D. DeVoss, A. Haas, & J. Rhodes (Eds.), *Computers and Composition, 51*.

Snyder, W. S., Cook, M. J., Nasset, E. Es, Karhausen, L. R. Howells, G. P, & Tipton, I. H. (1975). *Report of the task group on reference man*. International Commission on Radiological Protection. Pergamon Press.

Stone, M., & Vogelstein, R. (2019). *Celebrating #MeToo's global impact*. Foreign Policy. https://foreignpolicy.com/2019/03/07/metooglobalimpactinternationalwomens-day.

Surla, S. (2018). *Towards a feminist information architecture*. Paper presented at the Academics/Practitioners Roundtable on Information Architecture, 19th ASIS&T Information Architecture Summit, Chicago.

Tapia, A., Kirtzman, F., Polonskaia, A., & Gisbert, G. (2020). *The "Reference Man" rules*. Korn Ferry.

Tyson, L. (2006). *Critical theory today: A user friendly guide*. Routledge.

Watters, J. (2017). Pink Hats and Black Fists: The role of women in the Black lives matter movement. *William & Mary Journal of Race, Gender, and Social Justice, 24*(1). William & Mary Law School.

Wijsman, K., & Feagan, M. (2019). Rethinking knowledge systems for urban resilience: Feminist and decolonial contributions to just transformations. *Environmental Science and Policy, 98*. Elsevier.

Wise, S., & Stanley, L. (2006). Having it all: Feminist fractured foundationalism. In K. Davis, M. Evans, & J. Lorber (Eds.), *Handbook of gender and women's studies*. Sage.

Stacy Surla teaches information architecture and user-centered design as an adjunct professor at the University of Maryland iSchool. As a practicing consultant and the Vice President of Meta-Metrics Inc., she works with clients, teams, and students to design products and services that work well for their intended users. Ms. Surla's career spans more than thirty years, with a concentration on human-centered transformation in not-for-profit and government settings. She received her M.A. in Literature from the American University.

Information Architecture in the Anthropocene

Dan Zollman

Abstract Today's information architecture (IA) practitioners work in a morally and politically challenging climate where pervasive, systemic problems demand that we consider the consequences of our work for social justice and sustainability. Using "Information Architecture in the Anthropocene" as a framing device, and drawing from critical perspectives in design scholarship, this chapter explores what these systemic problems mean for everyday information architecture practice, and it asks what methodological, theoretical, and paradigmatic qualities would enable information architecture to respond adequately to social and environmental challenges. Both design and information architecture practitioners are deeply involved in ongoing sociopolitical problems, which highlights the need for awareness of their limitations and their situatedness within the systems that are traditionally treated as objects for detached research and design. Reflexivity, informed by a systemic epistemology, is identified as a critical attribute for information architecture in the Anthropocene. Three proposals are offered as ways to achieve this: information architecture as a developmental process, information architecture as ethical practice, and information architecture as a network. These approaches apply processual and relational interpretations, along with biological theory, to the practice of information architecture, challenging our field to include ourselves in the systems we study and to rethink information architecture as a responsible practice.

Introduction

Today's information architecture practitioners work in a morally and politically challenging climate. Digital technology and design professionals, among others, have been named as enablers of harmful phenomena including addictive and manipulative software, products driven by biased algorithms, surveillance capitalism, and misinformation spread through online advertising and social media. At the same time, ongoing social movements such as those focusing on racial and gender justice

D. Zollman (✉)
Dialogue for Design LLC, Cambridge, MA, USA

© The Author(s), under exclusive license to Springer Nature Switzerland AG 2021
A. Resmini et al. (eds.), *Advances in Information Architecture*,
Human–Computer Interaction Series, https://doi.org/10.1007/978-3-030-63205-2_22

in the United States have asserted a shared responsibility for all to act in light of systemic injustices that pervade our cultural and economic institutions. All of this stands against the backdrop of the Anthropocene: a period in history marked by the large-scale human impacts on Earth's geology, climate, and ecology, which present existential threats such as anthropogenic global warming. The involvement of design and technology in these wicked social and ecological problems makes them a central concern for practitioners. Like the climatic markers of the Anthropocene, the ethical ramifications of information architecture are everywhere. Practitioners must consider the broader consequences of their work and the systems that their work supports.

The field of design has wrestled with these issues. Critical scholarship in design (Costanza-Chock, 2020; Fry, 2011) have addressed design's contribution to, and responsibility within, ongoing systems of injustice and unsustainability. While the design professions have had more than a century of movements espousing design as a vehicle for social change, more recent critiques have departed from conventional idealism and celebration of design by acknowledging its *fallibility*. They show how social change-oriented design has often had negative outcomes. For example, it may generate undesirable second-order consequences, support colonial or imperialistic dynamics (Tunstall, 2013), or produce anti-social and anti-political effects (von Busch & Palmås, 2017). From this standpoint, a theory of design as an agent of social good is incomplete unless it can account for the complexity of social context, the likelihood of negative consequences, and the unequal power relationships that condition the act of design.

The same critiques apply to information architecture, as well as fields like user experience design (UX) as the settings where information architecture practice takes place. Information architecture has been framed as a kind of design that focuses on the structure of information environments for their inhabitants (Wodtke & Govella, 2009; Resmini & Rosati, 2011; Hinton, 2014; Arango, 2019). Information architecture is concerned with the human experience of information, the nature of information structures in the world (whether intentionally designed or not), and the process of modeling and planning those structures. Philosophically and methodologically, information architecture operates in ways similar to design (Fenn & Hobbs, 2014), but it has a distinct history, body of knowledge, culture, and communities of practice.

Like design, the field of information architecture features *origin myths* (Malazita, 2018) and narratives about the role that information architecture can, will, or should have in creating a better world; the unique strengths it offers; and why it is necessary in the world. It also includes narratives about the threat posed by a lack of information architecture done well. However, information architecture as a field does not yet have a mature set of theories and approaches that support information architecture as a practice that holds responsibility for its own consequences as it seeks better social conditions (Hobbs et al., 2010). If information architecture practitioners aim to improve the wellbeing of human beings who are "living in information" (Arango, 2019), how will information architecture rise to the ethical, political, and systemic challenges of that work?

This chapter explores what it means to practice information architecture under *Anthropocene* conditions. The narrative of the Anthropocene is used here as a framing for information architecture and user experience practice to bring the ecologies of complex social and environmental problems into the area of concern for practitioners. The proposition of *information architecture in the Anthropocene* asks what configurations of values, practices, theories, and frameworks—what paradigms—might enable the field to operate responsibly in light of its complex interrelationships with these problems. To explore this challenge, this chapter applies a dual lens of *reflexivity* informed by a *systemic* epistemology. This approach draws from recent critiques in design and complements a range of discourses in science and technology studies (STS), human–computer interaction (HCI), and anthropology that emphasize the situatedness of the practitioner in a social, cultural, and political context, problematizing the traditional, Cartesian divisions between subject and object; process and outcome; designer and user and system (Suchman, 2002; Kimbell, 2012; Ingold, 2000; Escobar, 2018). The design or information architecture practitioner is not an outsider who intervenes in a system they wish to change, but an active participant whose behavior is shaped by personal, social, cultural, and political factors. To reconcile practice with broader systemic problems, practitioners and theorists must reflect upon how they are personally entangled with the objects of their work and the complex systems in which practice occurs. By bringing these ideas together with information architecture, I hope to broaden the conversation about what it might look like for information architecture and its practitioners to operate in a responsible, reflexive, and systemically aware way.

Limitations

Before continuing, I must acknowledge my own position and limitations as an author. As a Northeast US-based practitioner of information architecture and user experience design, my foundations are in mainstream, Western approaches to design thinking, design methods, interaction design, usability, and user experience. Although I have sought out alternative perspectives in Science and Technology Studies and other fields, I work from an epistemically and socioeconomically privileged position from which many, though not all, of the "problems" discussed here are observed rather than lived. These problems hinge on power relationships, and their solutions must begin with approaches that center marginalized perspectives in understanding the world and its future—including feminist, indigenous, and other critical design scholarship that has already been exploring these issues for a long time. One version of this argument, along with a review of many such voices, is presented effectively in *Design Justice* by Sasha Costanza-Chock (2020). I cannot personally speak from marginalized perspectives in this chapter. Instead, I draw from critical approaches as much as possible while offering my own, situated interpretation of the challenges faced by information architecture practitioners.

Anthropocene Conditions

The original use of "Anthropocene" describes a new period in geological history characterized by extensive human influence on the Earth's atmosphere, geology, and ecosystems (Crutzen & Stoermer, 2000). Various markers for the Anthropocene have been proposed, including anthropogenic global warming and the testing and use of atomic weapons, which has left traces of radioactive material virtually everywhere on Earth (Zalasiewicz et al., 2015). While the formal scientific status and timeframe of the Anthropocene is under active debate, the Anthropocene functions as a "semantically and symbolically rich cognitive cultural model" that has been appropriated by theorists, environmentalists, journalists, and others (including me) across multiple fields and has acquired multiple meanings in framing feelings and ideas about the relationships between humans and nature (Strydom, 2016; Delanty & Mota, 2017). As it relates to design, a key theme in accounts of the Anthropocene is the role of designed technology and sociotechnical systems in ongoing ecological crises that threaten the stability of human civilization.

Design and Plastic Pollution

One such crisis—to begin with an example from the domain of tangible products—is the accumulation of *microplastics* and *nanoplastics* throughout the biosphere. Micro- and nanoplastics are small plastic particles which are the ultimate fate of any plastic material that breaks down due to use, erosion, or degradation. Between 1950 and 2015, an estimated 8300 million metric tons (Mt) of plastic were manufactured, 6300 Mt of plastic waste were generated, and 4900 Mt accumulated in landfills and the natural environment (Geyer et al., 2017). As of 2016, approximately 11% of all new plastic waste enters aquatic ecosystems (Borelle et al., 2020) leading to hundreds of millions of tons of accumulated microplastics and nanoplastics in the oceans (the true amount is unknown and seems to increase with each partial estimate, e.g. Pabortsava & Lampitt, 2020). This plastic pollution—plastic fragments, films, and filaments—has now been shown to be present at virtually every location and depth in the ocean (Jamieson et al., 2019); falling from the atmosphere onto remote mountaintops (Allen et al., 2019); displacing food in the stomachs of large and small marine creatures and seabirds (Cole et al., 2016); flowing from washing machines into wastewater treatment plants and natural water systems (Browne et al., 2011); and finally, in humans' own food, digestive systems, and lungs (Wright & Kelly, 2017).

Research on the consequences of this pollution is still emerging, with physical, chemical, and microbial hazards presented by chronic exposure to plastic particles in the lungs and digestive tract (Wright & Kelly, 2017), and hypothesized impacts on marine organism populations across ecosystems (Worm et al., 2017). The effects are more difficult to study as the particles get smaller, while the quantity is bound to increase as the production and disposal of new plastic accelerates each year (Borelle et al., 2020).

Plastic pollution is the product of complex social, material, biological, and technical arrangements: industrialized lifestyles that are organized around habitual use of plastic products; the availability and affordability of plastic for both manufacturers and consumers; a lack of alternatives to existing products, materials, supply chains, manufacturing systems, and waste management infrastructure; policies that affect those industries; and economic relationships that enable the largest consumers of plastic (e.g. the United States) to externalize the environmental and social impacts of manufacturing, disposal, and recycling to others (e.g. China). Among the actors who produce these systemic behaviors, such as consumers, engineers, business owners, and policymakers, designers must be considered. Throughout the decades after plastics emerged as usable materials for consumer products in the 1920s, industrial designers helped to make plastic acceptable and desirable to American consumers, sought new applications for it, and promoted it to manufacturers as a material of choice (Meikle, 1995). Today, industrial designers make choices about how to use plastic and what products to make with it.

Today's designers may seek to create sustainable products with fewer environmental impacts, but this comes with practical and moral challenges. Consider the oft-repeated story about an IDEO designer who was walking on a beach and found an Oral-B toothbrush he had designed lying in the sand, washed up from the water, months after the product had launched (Brown, 2009, p. 194). A designer in this position might feel that structural forces—their inability to influence their employer or client, the lack of feasible technological alternatives, or the medical necessity of toothbrushes—preclude any possibility for intervention in such an assignment. The designer has inherited a complex of social and economic arrangements that demand a plastic toothbrush which will ultimately become plastic pollution. Yet the designer may feel responsible for participating and facilitating this perverse systemic outcome—not only toothbrushes on beaches, but the microplastics that we are all eating and breathing in. This exposes a "crisis of agency" for design:

> The Anthropocene is a critical time in terms of our understandings of human agency– or lack of it. What are the possibilities for 'rational or concerted action'? Just at the moment when we recognise our 'gargantuan agency' we also become aware of our limited capacity to do anything at all. (Tyszczuk, 2014)

Problems like plastic pollution are frequently characterized in design literature as *wicked problems* that are so complex and dynamic that they cannot clearly be defined, understood, or solved (Rittel & Webber, 1973). The concept of wicked problems has been used extensively in theory on design thinking, which has positioned design as a pragmatic response to the *indeterminacy* of such problems (Buchanan, 1992). It is not only large-scale social problems, but also everyday design problems, that carry this indeterminacy and share the characteristics of wicked problems (Coyne, 2004). Of particular relevance to the framing of the Anthropocene in this chapter, Levin, Cashore, Bernstein, and Auld extend the idea of wicked problems to *super wicked problems*, adding four characteristic features:

time is running out; those who cause the problem also seek to provide a solution; the central authority needed to address it is weak or non-existent; and, partly as a result, policy responses discount the future irrationally. (Levin et al., 2012)

Although the authors were commenting on policy interventions in climate change, these challenges are shared by design, which is often situated in an organizational context that limits project scope to items of immediate concern to the organization (Resmini & Lindenfalk, 2021); is placed in service of narrow, short-term goals that may disregard or perpetuate the status quo (Jones, 2008); and continues to contribute to the same problems it seeks to address.

Systemic Problems for Information Architecture

The tangible problem of plastic pollution is analogous to intangible problems for information architecture. In a society where digital information systems play a vast role in the organization of political and economic power, information architecture has social and environmental consequences. A product as simple as online billing for a power company might affect how much electricity customers consume by changing what feedback they receive about that usage via their bill, or whether they receive feedback at all.

Information architecture and user experience practitioners may find themselves working on products or services that contribute to unchecked consumerism by influencing purchasing behavior (Crocker, 2016); toxic pollution and human abuses resulting from production of materials needed to manufacture increasingly networked consumer products (Frankel, 2016); enormous amounts of electricity consumption and greenhouse gas emissions due to wireless network usage (Andrae & Edler, 2015); and gig economy platforms that benefit from economic disparities while reinforcing segregation of customers from the workers who experience the consequences (Campbell, 2019). Information systems enable the acceleration and scaling of these outcomes while introducing their own sphere of sociopolitical concerns, ranging from the "automation of inequality" (Eubanks, 2018; O'Neil, 2016) to challenges to the quality of civic discourse (Tucker et al., 2018).

As the influence of digital information systems becomes deeper and more pervasive, Resmini and Lindenfalk contextualize the practice of information architecture within a set of "distinct cultural and socio-technical shifts" that they call the "postdigital condition" (Resmini & Lindenfalk, 2021):

William J. Mitchell observed that "once there was a time and a place for everything; today, things are increasingly smeared across multiple sites and moments in complex and often indeterminate ways" (Mitchell 2004, p. 14)…[U]biquitous data access, smartphones, tablets, sensors, ambient appliances, smart environments and wearables have made computing a dominant part of the cultural and social zeitgeist (Kirby 2009; Floridi 2014). Phenomena such as convergence (Jenkins 2008) and digital transformation (Skog 2019) have blurred the distinction between products and services (Norman 2009; Resmini and Rosati 2009) and between producers and consumers (Tapscott and Williams 2010); the rise of an online read/write culture (Lessig 2008, p. 28; Cramer 2015) and the generational shift (Prensky 2001; Swingle 2016) have challenged the centrality of authorship and ownership (Sterling 2005); linearity is losing its sway to the rhizome (Deleuze & Guattari 1987).

The "smearing" of information resembles the proliferation of microplastics, chemical pollution, and nuclear traces that "blur the distinction" between producers and consumers, the technological and the social. Social problems in this interconnected, rhizomatic information society are Anthropocenic: They extend across large, entrenched sociopolitical/sociotechnical systems, and they carry a moral weight and crisis of agency for practitioners who are entangled with these preexisting systems. To find a way forward, we must identify forms of agency within these complex processes that simultaneously give information architecture so much power and limit our ability as individuals to intervene in the consequences.

Ontological Design as a Link Between Information Architecture and Social Systems

Fry argues that "structural unsustainability is an ontology, which means that causally and essentially the unsustainable has become elemental to existing and extending modernized human beings" (Fry, 2011, p. 23). While Fry links these ontological conditions—conditions of *being*—to design, thinkers in information architecture have argued that information architecture, too, operates at an ontological level. Hobbs and Fenn (2019) characterize "the semantic, structural logics present in IA ... as efforts of meaning-making [that create] contrived ontologies which are encoded into the artificial, human-made world as subjective, constructs of reality" (p. 746). They warn that our engagement with artificial information ecologies

> will be so immersive that it will in all likelihood radically transform [humanity's] social ontological understanding of the world... [W]e are likely to see certain sets of cultural norms (as contrived ontological ecologies) imposed upon other cultures...preferring one way of 'being' in the world over others. (p. 763)

They conclude that information architecture "can and will make its most significant contribution to ensuring socially sustainable ontological ecosystems" (p. 747).

Such assertions that acts of design (re)produce social reality, which can then be extended to information architecture, are best elaborated in the literature on ontological design(ing). Anne-Marie Willis (2006) summarizes the basic claims of the theory of ontological designing,

> that designing is fundamental to being human – we design, that is to say, we deliberate, plan and scheme in ways which prefigure our actions and makings – in turn we are designed by our designing and by that which we have designed (i.e., through our interactions with the structural and material specificities of our environments); that this adds up to a double movement – **we design our world, while our world acts back on us and designs us** [emphasis added]. (p. 70)

By way of Heidegger, Willis explains this double movement as a process of inter-pretation, or a hermeneutic circle, "in which knowledge comes to be inscribed" in a relationship with a tool, "modifying (designing) the being of the tool-user," who then "acts back upon the tool or the material being worked on" in a third act of inter-pretation (p. 73). She illustrates this with the example of the "familiar brick-shaped, tetrapak fruit juice box" and how it structures the activity of humans around it:

> A single serve juice box gathers fruit juices and packaging materials from different parts of the world; it also gathers a distribution and marketing infrastructure and a product image (which could be thought of as its designated, and crudely, inauthentic essence). It quenches thirst and nourishes … its design inclines against sharing – you can't outpour from a single-serve juice box. It is designed for, and it designs individual consumption on the move. Its handy size, its built-in straw which ingeniously doubles as a piercing instrument, its spill-proof design, all make it possible to have a drink away from the gathering places of eating and drinking – at your desk or walking along the street. The juice box (along with other kinds of packaged take-away food) designs eating and drinking as an individualised, rather than communal activity…

> The juice box on the office worker's desk sits within a totally desacralised, instrumentalised culture of convenience where a worker's productivity has nothing to do with soil, rain and the bounty of the gods, and everything to do with de-materialised output of electronic work and production, which has no place for the gathering of eating, only for the sustenance of working bodies which can be conveniently met by products like single-serve juice boxes…. [The juice box] designs activities and 'the use of time', allowing its users to do several things simultaneously – keep working at the desk, answer the phone, have lunch… [It] designs its casting aside without thought or concern and its temporal destination and semiotic fate as 'garbage'. The juice box designs modes of eating, sociality, work, and even of disposition. (pp. 79–80)

It is important to note that ontological designing does not mean that a professional designer predetermines the world of users. Many approaches in the philosophy of design and technology have demonstrated that function and meaning emerge in the context of use (Vardouli, 2015); users are engaged in ontological designing as well as designers. Nor does this mean that designers can singlehandedly overturn the structural unsustainability of our built world, only that understanding the ontological character of design may inform one's approach to design (Willis, 2006, p. 82).

To extend this to information architecture, let us consider another consumer product which embodies an ontologically designing *information* structure that leads us back to the macro-level social issues discussed in the previous section—in this case, systemic racism, white supremacy, and photographic film in the twentieth century.

For much of the history of photographic film in the United States and beyond, film was engineered to capture the skin tones of white people. As shown by Lorna Roth, film and camera manufacturers gave little attention to the sensitivity of film to darker skin tones until the late twentieth century, when cultural and market pressures led to slow, incremental changes to photographic technologies. Illustrative of this history, "Shirley cards"—the color reference cards used in the photo printing process—exclusively showed photos of white women, reflecting gendered and racialized beauty standards in conjunction with the exclusion of dark skin (Roth, 2009). As a result, a photo of a Black person taken in this period might only show their teeth and the whites of their eyes against a dark, undifferentiated face. Syreeta McFadden writes a powerful account of her experience growing up as a Black child in a community where these photographic representations of Black people were commonplace. Linking these images to Western racial stereotypes, she describes the visual properties of these photos that play into a broader, ongoing system of prejudice:

> Our skin blown out in contrast from film technologies that overemphasize white skin and denigrate black skin. Our teeth and our eyes shimmer through the image, which in its turn become appropriated to imply this is how black people are, mimicked to fit some racialized nightmare that erases our humanity. (McFadden, 2014)

This is a persuasive example of a designed information structure shaping social reality, with destructive consequences: The informational properties of camera film inscribed a racial distinction that deeply shaped McFadden's lived experiences as a child and, more broadly, reinforced cultural perceptions within a long history of Black exclusion in American film and media. What made this possible was the intentional engineering of this film for a presumed white subject—conditioned by, then conditioning, race relations in American society (Roth, 2009).

Information Architecture and Power

A wide body of research has examined how material and information technologies both embody social and political relations, whether these pertain to race, gender, (dis)ability, ethnicity, class, political and cultural hegemony, or colonialism. This is apparent in the multifarious history of encoded racism in photography. For example, Polaroid's ID photo system, the Polaroid ID-2, had a "boost button" that would increase the brightness of the flash; artist Adam Broomberg suggests this was designed precisely to compensate for light absorption by black skin (Smith, 2013). Notoriously, this camera was used during Apartheid in South Africa by government officials to take ID photos for the passbooks that the government used to limit the movement of black people around the country (Morgan, 2006). What might pass as an attempt at inclusive design was appropriated as a tool for control by an oppressive regime.

Encoded discrimination has been, for many years and still today, an ongoing problem with digital photography and facial recognition technology, from consumer products to surveillance used by law enforcement (Ogbonnaya-Ogburu et al., 2020). Like the biased algorithm and machine learning applications that have received much publicity in domains from human resources to law enforcement (O'Neil, 2016), facial recognition technologies have typically been less tested and are less accurate for non-white populations (Simonite, 2019), with serious consequences for marginalized and vulnerable populations who experience disproportionate surveillance, policing, and law enforcement violence (American Public Health Association, 2018). These examples echo McFadden's account in which photographic technology establishes who is seen and valued in a white-dominated society. But Julia Powles and Helen Nissenbaum remind us again that this is a problem of power, not just inclusion. In an article on bias in algorithms, they write: "Alleviating this problem by seeking to 'equalize' representation merely co-opts designers in perfecting vast instruments of surveillance and classification" (Powles & Nissenbaum, 2018). Technologies of control and automation buttress existing power structures, and the consequences cannot be neutralized simply by encoding different information architecture structures in the product. Likewise, systems of categorization

> have been used historically as devices of control by some and resistance by others. That is, struggles over who defines agendas, interests, identities, and the like are expressed in part as contests over what systems of categorization will prevail. (Suchman, 1995, pp. 85–86; see also Suchman, 1993)

Nieusma sums it up: "Without direct intervention to the contrary, existing power relations usually, but not always, are reinforced by design decision making" (Nieusma, 2004). This occurs through several mechanisms. In the examples of photographic technology above, the outcomes were jointly determined by the creators of the technology (e.g. their assumptions and tacit racism [Roth, 2009]; Polaroid's choices about doing business in South Africa [Morgan, 2006]) and emergent processes in the context of use (e.g. South African passbooks; choices about how to use facial recognition technology). In any case, these information technologies are both shaped within, and come to reinforce, preexisting systems of power, segregation, and oppression. For a practitioner looking ahead to a new information architecture or design engagement, this raises questions about what power relations condition the current situation, who gets to make decisions, who is impacted, and what problems that may introduce or perpetuate.

We could think of this process of "reinforcing" or "intervention" as an area of ethical responsibility for practitioners, as well as a point of leverage that gives practitioners agency with respect to social issues. Our collective awareness of vast inequality, oppression, and unsustainability challenges us to consider our own role as individuals in reinforcing or intervening. Those who have the privilege of practicing design or information architecture professionally are in positions of power, however circumscribed, to establish "contrived ontologies" that will structure the lived experiences of others, sometimes in unexpected ways, at a large scale, over long periods of time, and in faraway places—which, in the Anthropocene, are never so far away. Yet we must also find the humility to know that we cannot overturn system-wide power structures singlehandedly. Contrary to popular narratives that design can "change the world," technology professionals cannot achieve sweeping cultural and institutional changes through design alone. An intermediate view is that practitioners participate, to varying degrees, in processes of change. The transformation of design and technology is an insufficient but necessary component of broader transformation toward sustainable society (Fry, 2011).

Moving Toward a Reflexive and Systemic Practice

Let us return to the framing of information architecture in response to Anthropocene-like challenges. The preceding case studies show how the primary focus of information architecture—the design of information environments—is both implicated in and shaped by social and ecological conditions. Meanwhile, information architecture practitioners are situated as active participants in those conditions as they persist or change. This differs from dominant constructions of technology design as a process in which a solution is created *for* certain users and a context of use, or as an *intervention* in a system from the outside (albeit with user research, empathy-building, or participatory design activities that add perspectives but usually do not challenge the practitioners' objectivity). On the contrary, the outcomes of design are shaped by sociopolitical relations that cross the boundaries between the *context of design* and the context of use. Here, the systems targeted for intervention *include* practitioners—their actions, values, and beliefs; the design/IA processes and methods used; and the institutional context where the work takes place. This entire ecology is part of the "information architecture" that structures human experiences.

This redrawn problem space demands reflexivity on the part of practitioners. To be reflexive means one is aware of the specificity of the perceptions, values, beliefs, practices, and philosophies that one brings to one's work, and how they shape, legitimate, and constrain one's work, with consequences for users and stakeholders. For information architecture practice, it also involves an awareness of the ways in which one's tacit perceptions, values, worldviews, etc, become inscribed in the "contrived ontologies" and artifacts one produces. This process, viewed through a systemic lens, intersects with multiple levels of personal, social, institutional, societal, and environmental systems that matter to the work we do and the products we create. To be reflexive and systems-aware in this way means realizing that, as human beings, virtually all of us have grown up, learned, and become ourselves within environments structured by systems of unsustainability, exclusion, and oppression. We embody these ontologies and bring them to our work until we gradually develop the capacity to change them.

I propose *reflexivity*, informed by a *systemic epistemology*, as an explicit theme in the research and practice agenda for information architecture, and a core attribute of the discipline that should be acknowledged, deepened, or introduced where it is missing. Although these orientations have extensive roots in the social sciences and systems sciences, they are not often embodied by mainstream design and information architecture practice apart from approaches that are academically driven or otherwise sit outside the dominant paradigms in industry. For example, industry interpretations of design thinking have been critiqued for a lack of reflexivity (Kimbell, 2011). In contrast, reflexivity is exhibited in less widely adopted approaches to values, ethics, and equity in design (e.g. Friedman & Hendry, 2019; Creative Reaction Lab, 2018; Castillo et al., 2020) that explicitly ask practitioners to identify and reflect upon the values, beliefs, politics, and personal limitations they bring to their work. Similarly, systemics (systems thinking, theories, and practices) have been adopted in limited contexts within mainstream design, albeit with increasing popularity. In IA, they have provided a central thread in the contemporary shift toward themes such as information ecosystems (Resmini & Rosati, 2011) and the cognitive, social, and organizational systems affecting information architecture (Morville, 2011, 2014). Exemplifying the shift to systemic approaches, Resmini and Lindenfalk articulate systemics as a paradigmatic foundation for information architecture theory: "To capture critical systemic aspects now part of the design space (…) (it is necessary to) thoroughly reconceptualize the object of design," which "is not a tangible, finished, individual artifact, but rather the volatile actor-instantiated spaces of relationships between artifacts" in an ecosystem (Resmini & Lindenfalk, 2021).

I affirm this proposal but insist that it go even further: the ecosystem and "object of design" being reconceptualized here include not only users and artifacts, but also the practitioners, practices, and organizations that produce information products and services (Kimbell, 2012). This information architecture of this ecosystem both structures and is structured by the professional activity of information architecture itself. This position is both practical and theoretical: It means that practitioners give attention to their context, selves, and their relationship to design outcomes, and theorists (while being reflexive themselves) conceptualize practitioners as part of the information architectures being considered. While it should not be construed as an egocentric version of information architecture that privileges a professional practitioner over other agents, this reflexive move enables reflection on the practitioner's situation, agency, responsibility, and limitations within the systems targeted for design intervention. It means that practitioners, and their organizations, are part of the design problem and must transform in the search for solutions. Without this move, it is impossible for the theorists and practitioners of information architecture to account for their deep involvement in the social conditions they wish to improve through their work.

Three Proposals for Information Architecture in the Anthropocene

Information architecture in the Anthropocene is a speculative framing that asks what kinds of paradigms, theories, and practices (Lacerda & Lima-Marques, 2014) might enable information architecture to respond to Anthropocene conditions, today and in the future. I have highlighted reflexive and systemic orientations as core attributes of theory and practice that acknowledge information architecture's complex involvement and responsibility within broader social and ecological processes.

To take a self-aware and systems-aware approach, with sustainability and justice as guiding values, suggests that information architecture should develop in a pluralistic and emergent way. It should encompass a wide range of perspectives—especially those that are marginalized within an unsustainable and unjust status quo (Costanza-Chock, 2020). While I cannot speak from those perspectives, I hope to use my partial view of *information architecture in the Anthropocene* to provoke dialogue within my own community of practice and open a space for imagining what alternative forms of information architecture might look like.

As prompts for further conversation, the remainder of this chapter offers three proposals about how information architecture in the Anthropocene might extend its reflexivity within a systemic epistemology, toward a more responsible practice.

Information Architecture as a Developmental Process

The idea that the information architecture discipline holds responsibility for its social outcomes sits in tension with the indeterminacy—and uncontrollability—of the sociotechnical arrangements that actually emerge in practice. How can we conceptualize a systemic "information architecture"? On one hand, information architecture has traditionally focused on the planning, creation, organization, management, and evaluation of information for human use. Information architecture uses techniques including modeling, mapping, diagramming, prototyping, and specification in order to solve information problems and design the structure of information-based products and services.

On the other hand, these structures are never truly specified by professional individuals or teams—the products or service development lifecycle is a social and political one, distributed across many actors and groups within an organization. Organizational structures, information flows, incentives, values and beliefs, points of view, personalities, and external forces all shape the decisions made about a product/service and how it is delivered. Development, marketing, sales, customer support, and other functions influence the informational experience of external actors and who those actors are. The production of "information architecture," such as the political negotiation of categories described by Suchman (1995), may play out through negotiation and revision of information architecture and design artifacts (maps, prototypes, specifications), or it may bypass the "designer" in the form of changes made directly to documents, software code, policies, operational programs, or communication channels controlled by different parts of the organization. Information architecture expertise may enjoy a degree of status and credibility in the organization, or it may be ignored entirely.

Ultimately, it is not only design or information practitioners, but the entire organization that provides the conceptual structures, knowledge, values, preferences, and actions that become inscribed in—or Bruno Latour's terms, "delegated" to—material and digital products (Latour, 1992; Willis, 2006; Friedman & Hendry, 2019). As discussed earlier, processes of design, interpretation, and negotiation then continue in future contexts outside the organization. From a systems point of view, the direct, first-order design techniques of research, modeling, prototyping, etc., are insufficient to account for information architecture as the (re)production of ontological structures across environments and levels of system scale.

We can look to process-relational approaches to help us account for information architecture as a distributed sociopolitical phenomenon without removing the agency of individual practitioners. Processual and relational approaches include a variety of philosophical, theoretical, and methodological approaches that view the world as constituted by ongoing processes and dynamic relations between things; these processes and relations are the primary units of analysis (e.g. Mesle, 2008; Emirbayer, 1997). This aligns with Kimbell's call for an approach that

> helps researchers see design as a situated, local accomplishment involving diverse and multiple actors. (…) (A)cknowledges the roles of objects in constituting practices (…) (and) de-centers the designer as the main agent in designing. (Kimbell, 2012, p. 129)

Kimbell achieves this by applying *theories of practice* to the phenomenon of design. This allows us to "switch the unit of analysis from individual actors or society and its norms, to a messy, contingent combination of minds, things, bodies, structures, processes, and agencies" (Kimbell, 2012, p. 141). Within this analysis, the capacities and effects of individual practitioners can be revisited.

While Kimbell uses theories of practice as one tool to rethink design, I suggest biological theory—in particular, *developmental systems theory*—as a key resource to rethink the *structures* that information architecture is concerned with in terms of the messy, contingent processes that produce them. In his anthropological studies of making, Tim Ingold (2000) shows us the connection between biological and technological development: "Artefacts not only grow, but they also evolve as they are reproduced repeatedly and are changed in the process of reproduction" (p. 340). He writes that artifacts are not replicated from designs or blueprints, but they *develop* in an environment:

> Where plans or blueprints exist, as they often do in the fields of architecture and engineering, they are generated within the same, environmentally situated process from which also emerge the forms they are said to specify. But they may not exist at all. (Ingold, 2000, p. 372)

An artifact grows through a process of autopoiesis,

> the self-transformation over time of the system of relations within which an organism or artefact comes into being. (…) The artefact, in short, is a crystallisation of activity within a relational field. (Ingold, 2000, p. 345)

This is an apt description of the system development lifecycle. An artifact, product, service, structure, or any other "object of design" emerges within the context of an organization, over time, bearing the cognitive and social imprints of the activities around it.

To make this relevant to information architecture in the Anthropocene, we might ask how, in a developmental process, semantic, social, and political relations are conferred by the organization to its products (and later to the environments of external actors); how day to day activities relate to macro-level societal processes; and where agency or control resides, if not with design and information architecture practitioners. These questions mirror fundamental problems in evolutionary and developmental biology: how traits are conferred between generations, how biological processes relate to cultural processes, and what controls the development of an organism. *Developmental systems theory* (DST), as articulated by Oyama et al. (2001), and its extensions to *scaffolding* articulated by Caporael et al. (2013), are part of an ongoing movement in evolutionary theory that has emerged in response to dominant, gene-centered approaches to evolution and development. Scholars associated with DST have argued that a "gene's eye view" of evolution, which treats genes as a "specification" or "blueprint" for a biological organism, has failed to account for human development, social behavior, and human culture. Meanwhile, it has been used to maintain unchallenged narratives about human nature, such as that of the rational economic individual who engages in social behavior only in their own Machiavellian self-interest, or the dichotomy between humans and the natural environment that they are seen to dominate. Instead, DST offers process-oriented frameworks to analyze inheritance, development, and evolution across multiple levels, from the molecular to the cultural, without privileging one type of causal agent. DST shows how genes, bodies, sociality, culture, and environment have co-evolved in complex, nonlinear ways, with *distributed control* by many agents across different levels of scale (Oyama et al., 2001; Caporael et al., 2013).

DST and scaffolding represent robust bodies of work across biology, environmental science, social theory, and anthropology that offer many lessons for design and information architecture, which cannot be fully explored here. As a starting place, let us consider the following themes and the questions they raise for information architecture:

Heterogeneous resources in development. Organisms inherit not only genes, but many other types of resources from generation to generation, including cellular material, nutrition, other material resources, the activities of parents and other individuals, and culture. Caporael's *repeated assembly* describes "recurrent entity-environment relations composed of hierarchically organized, heterogeneous components having different frequencies and scales of replication" (Caporael et al., 2013, p. 11). DST emphasizes "Joint determination by multiple causes—every trait is produced by the interaction of many developmental resources" (Oyama et al., 2001, p. 2). Similarly, in design, blueprints and design deliverables are only one set of resources used in the construction of products, and they themselves are constructed in the social environment of the organization. Returning to Ingold's (2000) "crystallisation of activity", many other kinds of relations—power relations, categories, information flows, value exchanges—may be inherited from the organization. *In information architecture, what kinds of semantic or ontological traits are inherited from the organization, with downstream consequences? What tools, resources, and artifacts are generated and used by the organization? How and where are "information structures" materially or behaviorally embodied as they are reproduced and transformed throughout the product development process?*

Organism–environment relations. DST challenges the traditional nature–nurture dichotomy in which organism and environment "interact" with or "shape" each other while remaining ontologically separate. For example, many animals construct their own environments in significant ways, thus shaping their own phenotypic and genetic evolution (Laland et al., 2001). Organism and environment coevolve, each constituting and forming a part of the other. For information architecture, the organization can be seen as both the environment for a developing product, and as an entity within a larger environment. *How does an organization itself change in the process of developing a product? How does the "external" environment (market, society, etc.) change? Does this offer benefits or challenges for information architecture? Could it be used strategically (Hill, 2012)?*

Scaffolding. Scaffolding is both a noun and a verb. A scaffold is a temporary structure that either falls away or becomes assimilated into the scaffolded organism or structure. By providing support that the organism does not have by itself, it *scaffolds* the development of activities and capabilities that would not otherwise be possible without the scaffold. For organisms and people, scaffolding may take the form of artifacts, infrastructure, or other agents (Caporael et al., 2013). In design and information architecture, practitioners scaffold the organization's development of products/services as well as its own capacity-building in design. The organization also scaffolds the practitioner's daily work and enculturation as an employee by providing artifacts, tools, information resources, and cultural resources. The organization scaffolds the development of products and services. Those products scaffold the activities and development of their users. *What capabilities of the organization provide scaffolding that makes certain outcomes possible or likely for information architecture? What kinds of scaffolding does information architecture need? How does information architecture provide scaffolding to the organization?*

Time and sequence. Development is not a uniform process of growth. The interactions, resources, scaffolding, and developmental changes occurring at one stage differ from those at another. Wimsatt's principle of *generative entrenchment* asserts that "items that are reproduced and repeatedly assembled can become entrenched early in a system and are thereby available to serve as scaffolding for later items, as a platform or as a constraint" (Caporael et al., 2013, p. 2). Entrenched components lead to qualities or behaviors that are more stable than others, and they "acquire downstream dependencies" (Caporael et al., 2013, p. 2) that make it more difficult for the previously integrated elements to change. Together, scaffolding and generative entrenchment describe "pathways by which features of environments *become* features of systems" (Caporael et al., 2013, p. 367). In an organization, behaviors occurring early in the product/service lifecycle may acquire dependencies, and entrenchment continues even in contradiction of overwhelming feedback from experts or customers. *What stages does "information architecture" go through over the course of development? What features of the organization— e.g. funding sources, influential stakeholders, technological platforms, data assets, sales pathways, cultural assumptions, routines—lead to entrenched information architecture relationships that are difficult to change? When is that desirable or undesirable? Could that be used strategically (Hill, 2012)?*

These themes help us interpret the distributed process of development in an organization. In contrast to an "information architecture" that is generated anew by a practitioner team, the architecture of a product or service comes from many sources, is embodied in multiple ways, and moves through multiple developmental stages as features are added, modified, incorporated, removed, or entrenched along the way.

When information architecture is viewed as a developmental process, information architecture practitioners may begin to examine this process as part of the research, sensemaking, and mapping that already characterize the discipline. This might describe a new type of information architecture practitioner that in some ways resembles a sociologist or anthropologist within the organization. Could information architecture practitioners play a role as researchers, interpreters, and storytellers of the organization's behavior and its ontological consequences? Could they identify new areas of engagement in order to affect information architecture outcomes? Could their insights be leveraged to direct the organization's activities toward more just, inclusive, and sustainable outcomes?

Information Architecture as Ethical Practice

Responsible practice means struggling with ethical questions: What should I do here? What are my obligations? What can I do that will have the best outcomes for others? In a processual mode, I characterize ethical practice not as the application of ethical rules or procedures, but a process which is ongoing, personal, social, reflective, inclusive, pluralistic, dialogic, agonistic, and contextual. Ethical problems in complex systems are never thoroughly solved. Solutions are approached through ongoing questioning, learning, rethinking, and imperfect decisions along the way. This is also a perpetual process of self-understanding, coming to recognize one's own beliefs, values, and partial perspective in a complex world.

Ethical design practice relies not on detached scientific study of users and systems, but "moral engagement" (Findeli, 1994). While the developmental systems approach breaks down the dichotomy between organization and product, ethical practice breaks down the boundary between practitioner and user. In the words of Lucy Suchman (2002), "we need to begin by problematizing the terms 'designer' and 'user' and reconstructing relevant social relations that cross the boundaries between them" (p. 94).

Suchman (2002) observes that Western approaches to technological production are commonly informed by an unchallenged "myth of the lone creator of new technology on the one hand, and the passive recipients of new technology on the other," underwritten by a "simple designer/user opposition" (p. 93). On the contrary, "recent research on the actual work involved in putting technologies into use highlights the mundane forms of inventive yet taken for granted labor, hidden in the background, that are necessary to the success of complex sociotechnical arrangements" (Suchman, 2009, p. 1). Drawing on feminist critiques of objectivity, she describes a culture of design that, "by losing track of the social mediations of technical production, supports the impossibility of specifically locating responsibility for it" (Suchman, 2002, p. 93). She writes:

> A recurring question for me as a participant in discussions on design is "Who is doing what to whom here?" Within prevailing discourses anonymous and unlocatable designers, with a license afforded by their professional training, problematise the world in such a way as to make themselves indispensable to it and then discuss their obligation to intervene, in order to deliver technological solutions to equally decontextualized and consequently unlocatable users. This stance of design from nowhere is closely tied to the goal of construing technical systems as commodities that can be stabilized and cut loose from the sites of their production long enough to be exported en masse to the sites of their use. (Suchman, 2002, p. 95)

She adds:

> On the contrary, it is precisely the fact that our vision of the world is a vision from some-where—that it is inextricably based in an embodied, and therefore partial, perspective—which makes us personally responsible for it. (…) (T)he only possibility for the creation of effective objects is through collective knowledge of the particular and multiple locations of their production and use. (Suchman, 2002, p. 96)

Suchman resolves this with "a shift from a view of objective knowledge as a single, asituated, master perspective that bases its claims to objectivity in the closure of controversy, to multiple, located, partial perspectives that find their objective character through ongoing processes of debate" (2002, p. 93). In a complementary view, Fenn and Hobbs (2015) argue that because wicked problems exist "at the intersection of many possible points of views held by a variety of potential stakeholders," *wicked ethics* involves ethical pluralism across the many (possibly conflicting) stakeholder perspectives in a system as well as perspectives from across the extended contexts and time scales of sociotechnical change. Thus, responsible practice involves recognizing one's own subjectivity and partial knowledge of complex situations, the active role of others' subjective knowledge, and pluralistic debate as a core process within design.

The designer–user relationship intersects with multiple, asymmetrical power relations that raise complex ethical questions. For example, personal, sociopolitical, economic, and institutional power relations are at play when a white, privileged, male designer is working for a profit-driven corporation that has a large market share and mass-produces a product that will be purchased by customers across many racial and socioeconomic groups. In this situation, the practitioner cannot neutralize this asymmetry, but they can interrogate its role in design.

One place in which these power relations manifest is in the way practitioners construct "the user." For example, Villamil (2020) identifies a "deficiency model of user behavior" operating in design projects that focus on behavior change, particularly those targeting people of color, low income, or other marginalized groups. In this model, users are seen as "uninformed, unskilled, distrustful, disorderly, undisciplined, irresponsible, etc." (Villamil, 2020). Perceived unhealthy behaviors are attributed to "individual and cultural failings" that must be addressed through behavioral interventions such as education, as opposed to structural inequities that create conditions where those behaviors are necessary (Villamil, 2020). Another common model in design is the notion that "users don't know what they want," therefore, users cannot speak for themselves. This meshes with user research methodologies that are seen as more or less valid ways to bring the user's point of view into technology development. A step further, Steve Woolgar's (1997) ethnographic study of the practice of usability testing observed how the design and testing process "configures the user"—defines "the user," establishes parameters for user action, and brings users into a "correct" pattern of interaction with a product. Designer–user relations such as these deserve examination as mechanisms for power relations to play out in technology production. In addition to the words *designer* and *user*, we might reflect on relational metaphors such as *helping, care, intervention, facilitation, service, contract*, or roles like *client, customer, expert, advocate, producer, storyteller*, and the advantages or disadvantages each may have in structuring equitable partnerships between the participants in a design process (Nelson & Stolterman, 2012, p. 47).

Finally, like the development process itself, ethical problems are distributed across institutions and social systems, and they cannot be solved by changing design practices alone. Practitioners must make difficult decisions about what to do and what not to do, when to choose personal sacrifices or self-care, when to engage in politics, and whether to do so through direct engagement or subversion (Wendt, 2017). These are all personal and context-specific decisions.

These are only a few considerations that result from a processual and relational approach to responsible practice. Practitioners can learn a great deal from philosophy of ethics (Bowles, 2018) and design scholarship related to gender, race, colonialism, participation, and other alternative design approaches (e.g. Nieusma, 2004; Irani et al., 2010; Tunstall, 2013; Escobar, 2018; Costanza-Chock, 2020; Ogbonnaya-Ogburu et al., 2020). These resources prompt information architecture, as a form of design, to ask *Who is doing what to whom here?* and to challenge the power relationships that are supported by information architecture practices.

Information Architecture as a Network

After this inward look at practice, let us end by looking outward at the communities and social networks of information architecture. What does responsible information architecture look like at the community level?

In relation to Anthropocene conditions, it is not through individual action, but through collective action, that lasting change occurs. Therefore, information architecture cannot be an individualistic practice, but must form collective responses to social problems. Similarly, the distributed nature of Anthropocene problems requires solutions to be reached through radical political inclusion and collaboration across areas of knowledge and expertise. To function in the Anthropocene, information architecture cannot succeed as an insular discipline, and it must participate in cross-disciplinary change.

Information architecture exists largely in the form of communities of practice (Hobbs et al., 2010). In the United States, the explicit narrative of "the information architecture community" strongly shapes the identity of events, conferences, and conference-goers. While all communities necessarily engage in discussion about what is *in* or *out* in order to establish shared identity, a lack of reflexivity in this process may undermine the success of the field. First, the narrative of "the community" precludes a pluralistic interpretation of what "communities" might exist. In other words, the North American community is not the only community of information architecture practice (IA Roundtable, 2019). Second, the way boundaries are established may either support or hinder cross-disciplinary collaboration on systemic problems that cut across the formal boundaries between fields. Third, "the community" fails to distinguish between the temporary social networks that currently exist, and what Jason Hobbs suggests we frame as a *field* that includes many types of practices and interpretations, and "should pursue an authentic agenda of global, cultural and social inclusion without fear or favour towards any majority" (Hobbs, 2019; Hobbs et al., 2010). If information architecture is framed this way, what new kinds of practices and practitioners might we have?

Cultures share origin myths that, according to Jim Malazita, "do at least the following vital kinds of cultural sensemaking work":

- Origin work: where are we from, when did we begin?
- Identity work: who are "we," and who are "other?"
- Normative work: how should we act?
- Proscriptive work: where are we meant to go? (Malazita, 2018).

Origin myths are indeed vital, but they also represent partial perspectives. By reflecting upon what myths are at work, what is left out or suppressed, and what alternatives are possible, information architecture communities might avoid the mistakes of Western design in the twentieth century.

To conclude, we might reframe the function of information architecture communities: not only to support individuals applying skills, but to scaffold collective action within and across disciplines toward the transformation of our shared cultures of technology production, and of ourselves.

Conclusion

The idea of the Anthropocene represents the knowledge that human experience in the world is inseparable from broad, interconnected ecologies of social, political, technological, biological, and meteorological processes, and the challenges to justice and sustainability that they entail. It also represents a belief that, as humans, we have powerful, albeit dangerous, collective agency within these ecologies, and therefore a moral responsibility for our relationships with them. This chapter inquires into what developments in information architecture theory and practice might enable the field to respond adequately to the complexity and breadth of systemic challenges in which information architecture already plays an active role.

This chapter explored the character of Anthropocene problems that are distributed across, and entrenched in, multiple levels of social, political, and technological structure. An analogy was drawn between ecological and social problems, both of which implicate design and information architecture in the histories and the ongoing maintenance of undesirable and unsustainable system behaviors. This presents a moral urgency and a crisis of agency for practitioners who wish to improve these conditions. The link between these issues and the practice of design and information architecture was framed in terms of the reproduction or modification of power relations through design and the *ontological designing* of modes of being and acting in the world. As a result, the central insight is that information architecture theory and practice must take a systemic and reflexive approach that includes practitioners, and their social and institutional contexts, within the systems that produce and reproduce the outcomes and experiences with which information architecture is primarily concerned.

Finally, with this reflexive orientation, three rough proposals were offered as examples of approaches that might factor into information architecture in the Anthropocene: developmental systems, ethical practice, and collective change. A developmental systems perspective views the design of information environments as a situated, relational process within and beyond an institution. Taking cues from social and biological theories that break down the dualisms of subject and object, specification and structure, organism and environment, inside and outside, and so forth, this framework approaches information architecture as a socially and materially distributed process of development and change. Similarly, an ethical practice perspective crosses the boundary between practitioner and user, prompting moral engagement and a reflective, dialogic habit that values pluralism and an interrogation of power relationships. Through the lens of social networks and collective change, information architecture communities of practice are challenged to reconsider community boundaries and focus on collective engagement as a core function of our communities.

Through these ideas, I hope to broaden the conversation about responsible information architecture, urge my colleagues to consider the limitations of the ways in which we frame information architecture, and ask what kind of *information architecture* we will embody in our changing and precarious world.

Acknowledgements The original idea for "design in the Anthropocene," the emphasis on reflexivity, the use of developmental, processual, and relational perspectives, and much else in this chapter result from studies and personal conversations with Linnda Caporal. In addition, Jason Hobbs, Alba Villamil, Cennydd Bowles, Emily Devlin, Andrea Resmini, and Sarah Rice shaped this chapter through critical dialogue and feedback. Finally, the organizers and participants of the Academics and Practitioners Roundtable, and the members of the Ethical Technology online community, have all scaffolded my thinking on this topic in numerous ways.

References

Allen, S., et al. (2019). Atmospheric transport and deposition of microplastics in a remote mountain catchment. *Nature Geoscience, 12,* 339–344.

American Public Health Association. (2018). *Addressing Law Enforcement Violence as a Public Health Issue.* American Public Health Association Policy Statement Database. https://www.apha.org/policies-and-advocacy/public-health-policy-statements/policy-database/2019/01/29/law-enforcement-violence.

Andrae, A. S. G., & Edler, T. (2015). On global electricity usage of communication technology: Trends to 2030. *Challenges, 6*(1), 117–157. https://doi.org/10.3390/challe6010117.

Arango, J. (2019). *Living in information.* Two Waves Books.

Borelle, S. B., et al. (2020). Predicted growth in plastic waste exceeds efforts to mitigate plastic pollution. *Science, 369*(6510), 1515–1518. https://doi.org/10.1126/science.aba3656.

Bowles, C. (2018). *Future ethics.* NowNext Press. https://nownext.studio/future-ethics.

Brown, T. (2009). *Change by design: How design thinking transforms organizations and inspires innovation.* HarperCollins.

Browne, M. A., et al. (2011). Accumulation of microplastic on shorelines worldwide: Sources and sinks. *Environmental Science and Technology, 45*(21), 9175–9179. https://doi.org/10.1021/es201811s.

Buchanan, R. (1992). Wicked problems in design thinking. *Design Issues, 8*(2), 5–21.

Campbell, A. F. (2019, May 28). *The recession hasn't ended for gig economy workers.* Vox. https://www.vox.com/policy-and-politics/2019/5/28/18638480/gig-economy-workers-wellbeing-survey.

Caporael, L. R., Griesemer, J. R., & Wimsatt, W. C. (2013). *Developing scaffolds in evolution, culture, and cognition.* MIT Press.

Castillo, V., Farai, S., & Villamil, A. (2020, September 27—November 1). *HmntyCntrd* [Course]. https://www.hmntycntrd.com/.

Cole, M., et al. (2016). Microplastics as contaminants in the marine environment: A review. *Marine Pollution Bulletin, 62*(12), 2588–2597. https://doi.org/10.1016/j.marpolbul.2011.09.025.

Costanza-Chock, S. (2020). *Design justice: Community-led practices to build the worlds we need.* MIT Press.

Coyne, R. (2004). Wicked problems revisited. *Design Studies, 26*(2005), 5–17. https://doi.org/10.1016/j.destud.2004.06.005.

Creative Reaction Lab. (2018). *Equity-centered community design field guide.* https://www.creativereactionlab.com/our-approach.

Crocker, R. (2016). *Somebody else's problem: Consumerism, sustainability and design.* Routledge.

Crutzen, P. J., & Stoermer, E. F. (2000). The 'Anthropocene'. *IGBP Newsletter, 41,* 17–18.

Delanty, G., & Mota, A. (2017). Governing the Anthropocene: Agency, governance, knowledge. *European Journal of Social Theory, 20*(1), 9–38. https://doi.org/10.1177/1368431016668535.

Emirbayer, M. (1997). Manifesto for a Relational Sociology. *American Journal of Sociology, 103*(2), 281–317. https://doi.org/10.1086/231209.

Escobar, A. (2018). *Designs for the pluriverse: Radical interdependence, autonomy, and the making of worlds.* Duke University Press.

Eubanks, V. (2018). *Automating inequality: How high-tech tools profile, police, and punish the poor.* St. Martin's Press.

Fenn, T., & Hobbs, J. (2014). The information architecture of meaning making. In A. Resmini (Ed.), *Reframing information architecture.* Springer. https://doi.org/10.1007/978-3-319-06492-5.

Fenn, T., & Hobbs, J. (2015). *Wicked ethics in Design.* Ethics and accountability in Design: Do they matter?—DEFSA Conference Proceedings.

Findeli, A. (1994). Ethics, aesthetics, and design. *Design Issues, 10*(2).

Frankel, T. C. (2016, September 30). The Cobalt Pipeline: Tracing the path from deadly hand-dug mines in Congo to consumers' phones and laptops. *The Washington Post.* https://www.washingtonpost.com/graphics/business/batteries/congo-cobalt-mining-for-lithium-ion-battery/.

Friedman, B., & Hendry, D. G. (2019). *Value sensitive design: Shaping technology with moral imagination*. MIT Press.

Fry, T. (2011). *Design as politics*. Berg.

Geyer, R., Jamberk, J. R., & Law, K. L. (2017). Production, use, and fate of all plastics ever made. *Science Advances, 3*(7), e1700782. https://doi.org/10.1126/sciadv.1700782.

Hill, D. (2012). *Dark matter and trojan horses: A strategic design vocabulary*. Strelka Press.

Hinton, A. (2014). *Understanding context: Environment, language, and information architecture*. O'Reilly.

Hobbs, J. (2019, September 24). Re: The Future of Information Architecture. *JH-01*. https://jh-01.com/?p=374.

Hobbs, J., & Fenn, T. (2019). The design of socially sustainable ontologies. *Philosophy & Technology, 32*, 745–767.

Hobbs, J., Fenn, T., & Resmini, A. (2010). Maturing a Practice. *Journal of Information Architecture, 1*(2). http://journalofia.org/volume2/issue1/04-hobbs/.

IA Roundtable. (2019, March 13). *Diversity & inclusion: The 7th academics and practitioners roundtable*. The First Information Architecture Conference 2019. http://iaroundtable.org.

Ingold, T. (2000). *The perception of the environment: Essays on livelihood, dwelling, and skill*. Routledge.

Irani, L., et al. (2010). Postcolonial computing: A lens on design and development. *CHI '10: Proceedings of the SIGCHI Conference on Human Factors in Computing Systems*, 1311–1320. https://doi.org/10.1145/1753326.1753522.

Jamieson, A. J., et al. (2019). Microplastics and synthetic particles ingested by deep-sea amphipods in six of the deepest marine ecosystems on Earth. *Royal Society Open Science, 6*(20), 180667. https://doi.org/10.1098/rsos.180667.

Jones, P. (2008). *We tried to warn you: Innovations in leadership for the learning organization*. Nimble Books.

Kimbell, L. (2011). Rethinking design thinking: Part I. *Design and Culture, 3*(3), 285–306. https://doi.org/10.2752/175470811X13071166525216.

Kimbell, L. (2012). Rethinking design thinking: Part II. *Design and Culture, 4*(2), 129–148. https://doi.org/10.2752/175470812X13281948975413.

Lacerda, F., & Lima-Marques, M. (2014). Information architecture as a discipline—A methodological approach. In A. Resmini (Ed.), *Reframing Information Architecture*. Springer. https://doi.org/10.1007/978-3-319-06492-5.

Laland, K. N., Odling-Smee, F. J., & Feldman, M. W. (2001). Niche construction, ecological inheritance, and cycles of contingency in evolution. In S. Oyama, P. E. Griffiths, & R. D. Gray (Eds.), *Cycles of contingency: Developmental systems and evolution*. MIT Press.

Latour, B. (1992). Where are the missing masses? The sociology of a few mundane artifacts. In W. Bijker, T. Hughes, & T. Pinch (Eds.), *The social construction of technical systems* (pp. 225–258). MIT Press.

Levin, K., Cashore, B., Bernstein, S., & Auld, G. (2012). Overcoming the tragedy of super wicked problems: Constraining our future selves to ameliorate global climate change. *Policy Sciences, 45*, 123–152. https://doi.org/10.1007/s11077-012-9151-0.

Malazita, J. W. (2018). Astrobiology's cosmopolitics and the search for an origin myth for the anthropocene. *Biological Theory, 13*(2), 111–120. https://doi.org/10.1007/s13752-017-0281-7.

McFadden, S. (2014, April 2). *Teaching the camera to see my skin*. BuzzFeed News. https://www.buzzfeednews.com/article/syreetamcfadden/teaching-the-camera-to-see-my-skin.

Meikle, J. (1995). *American plastic: A cultural history*. Rutgers University Press.

Mesle, C. R. (2008). *Process-relational philosophy: An introduction to Alfred North Whitehead*. Templeton Press.

Morgan, E. J. (2006). The world is watching: Polaroid and South Africa. *Enterprise & Society, 7*(3), 520–549. https://doi.org/10.1017/S1467222700004390.

Morville, P. (2011). Editorial: The system of information architecture. *Journal of Information Architecture, 2*(3). http://journalofia.org/volume3/issue2/01-morville/.

Morville, P. (2014). *Intertwingled: Information changes everything.* Semantic Studios.

Nelson, H. G., & Stolterman, E. (2012). *The design way: Intentional change in an unpredictable World.* MIT Press.

Nieusma, D. (2004). Alternative design scholarship: Working toward appropriate design. *Design Issues, 20*(3), 13–24.

O'Neil, C. (2016). *Weapons of math destruction: How big data increases inequality and threatens democracy.* Crown Publishers.

Ogbonnaya-Ogburu, I. F., Smith, A. D. R., To, A., & Toyama, K. (2020). Critical race theory for HCI. In *Proceedings of the 2020 CHI Conference on Human Factors in Computing Systems* (CHI '20). https://doi.org/10.1145/3313831.3376392.

Oyama, S., Griffiths, P. E., & Gray, R. D. (2001). *Cycles of contingency: Developmental systems and evolution.* MIT Press.

Pabortsava, K., & Lampitt, R. S. (2020). High concentrations of plastic hidden beneath the surface of the Atlantic Ocean. *Nature Communication, 11,* 4073. https://doi.org/10.1038/s41467-020-17932-9.

Powles, J., & Nissenbaum, H. (2018). *The Seductive Diversion of 'Solving' Bias in Artificial Intelligence.* OneZero. Retrieved August 16, 2020 from https://onezero.medium.com/the-seductive-diversion-of-solving-bias-in-artificial-intelligence-890df5e5ef53.

Resmini A., & Lindenfalk B. (2021). Mapping experience ecosystems as emergent actor-created spaces. In A. Hameurlain, A. M. Tjoa, & R. Chbeir (Eds.), *Transactions on Large-Scale Data- and Knowledge-Centered Systems XLVII* (vol. 12630). Lecture Notes in Computer Science. Springer, Berlin, Heidelberg. https://doi.org/10.1007/978-3-662-62919-2_1.

Resmini, A., & Rosati, L. (2011). *Pervasive information architecture: Designing cross-channel user experiences.* Morgan Kaufmann.

Rittel, H. W. J., & Webber, M. M. (1973). Dilemmas in a general theory of planning. *Policy Sciences, 4,* 155–169.

Roth, L. (2009). Looking at shirley, the ultimate norm: Colour balance, image technologies, and cognitive equity. *Canadian Journal of Communication, 34*(1), 111–136.

Simonite, T. (2019, July 22). *The best algorithms struggle to recognize black faces equally.* Wired. https://www.wired.com/story/best-algorithms-struggle-recognize-black-faces-equally/.

Smith, D. (2013, January 25). 'Racism' of early colour photography explored in art exhibition. *The Guardian.* https://www.theguardian.com/artanddesign/2013/jan/25/racism-colour-photography-exhibition.

Strydom, P. (2016). The sociocultural self-creation of a natural category: Social-theoretical reflections on human agency under the temporal conditions of the Anthropocene. *European Journal of Social Theory, 20*(1), 61–79. https://doi.org/10.1177/1368431016643330.

Suchman, L. (1993). Do categories have politics? The language/action perspective reconsidered. In G. De Michelis, C. Simone, & K. Schmidt (Eds.), *Proceedings of the Third European Conference on Computer-Supported Cooperative Work.*

Suchman, L. (1995). Speech acts and voices: Response to Winograd at al. *Computer Supported Cooperative Work (CSCW), 3,* 85–95.

Suchman, L. (2002). Located accountabilities in technology production. *Scandinavian Journal of Information Systems, 14*(2), 91–105.

Suchman, L. (2009). *Agencies in technology design: Feminist reconfigurations.* https://www.lancaster.ac.uk/fass/resources/sociology-online-papers/papers/suchman-agenciestechnodesign.pdf.

Tucker, J. A., et al. (2018). *Social media, political polarization, and political disinformation: A review of the scientific literature.* The Hewlett Foundation. https://hewlett.org/library/social-media-political-polarization-political-disinformation-review-scientific-literature/.

Tunstall, E. (2013). Decolonizing design innovation: Design anthropology, critical anthropology, and indigenous knowledge. In W. Gunn, T. Otto, & R. C. Smith (Eds.), *Design anthropology: Theory and practice* (pp. 232–250). Bloomsbury Academic. http://doi.org/10.5040/9781474214698.ch-013.

Tyszczuk, R. (2014). Architecture of the Anthropocene. *Scroope: The Cambridge Architecture Journal* (23), 67–73.

Vardouli, T. (2015). Making use: Attitudes to human-artifact engagements. *Design Studies, 41,* 137–161. https://doi.org/10.1016/j.destud.2015.08.002.

Villamil, A. N. (2020, August 14). *Dear designers...we need to talk about race* [Presentation]. QRCA Multicultural SIG. https://www.qrca.org/events/EventDetails.aspx?id=1388761.

von Busch, O., & Palmås, K. (2017). Social means do not justify corruptible ends: A realist perspective of social innovation and design. *She Ji: The Journal of Design, Economics, and Innovation, 2*(4), 275–287. https://doi.org/10.1016/j.sheji.2017.07.002.

Wendt, T. (2017). *Persistent fools: Cunning intelligence and the politics of design.*

Willis, A. (2006). Ontological designing. *Design Philosophy Papers, 4*(2), 69–92.

Wodtke, C., & Govella, A. (2009). *Information Architecture: Blueprints for the Web* (2nd ed.). New Riders.

Woolgar, S. (1997). Configuring the user. In K. Grint & S. Woolgar, *The machine at work: Technology, work, and organization.*

Worm, B., et al. (2017). Plastic as a Persistent Marine Pollutant. *Annual Review of Environment and Resources, 42,* 1–26. https://doi.org/10.1146/annurev-environ-102016-060700.

Wright, S. L., & Kelly, F. J. (2017). Plastic and human health: A micro issue? *Environmental Science and Technology, 51*(12), 6634–6647. https://doi.org/10.1021/acs.est.7b00423.

Zalasiewicz, J., et al. (2015). When did the Anthropocene begin? A mid-twentieth century boundary level is stratigraphically optimal. *Quaternary International, 383,* 196–203. https://doi.org/10.1016/j.quaint.2014.11.045.

Dan Zollman is an information architect, designer, and user experience strategist with long-standing professional experience working with large organizations such as Vanguard, Tufts University, and the Commonwealth of Massachusetts. He has organized the World IA Day Boston conference in 2019 and 2020, the Academics and Practitioners Roundtable in 2020, and local and online events focused on ethics in design. He is a graduate of Rensselaer Polytechnic Institute.

Acts of Architecture: In Conversation with Andrew Hinton

Andrea Resmini

Andrew Hinton is the author of "Understanding Context: Environment, Language, and Information Architecture". He has been a practicing information architect and design leader since the late 1990s, in both agencies and enterprises. He currently leads the Design Strategy & Research team at Honeywell Connected Enterprise in Atlanta, Georgia.

A. Resmini (✉)
Department of Intelligent Systems and Digital Design, Halmstad University, Halmstad, Sweden
e-mail: andrea.resmini@hh.se

Jönköping Academy for Improvement of Health and Welfare, Jönköping University, Jönköping, Sweden

© The Author(s), under exclusive license to Springer Nature Switzerland AG 2021   267
A. Resmini et al. (eds.), *Advances in Information Architecture*,
Human–Computer Interaction Series, https://doi.org/10.1007/978-3-030-63205-2_23

Q: Andrew, we've known each other for many years now. We have worked on projects together, and shared a stage more than once along the way. While I know you and your public records in the field, I realized that what I'm missing is your own backstory. Where do you come from? How did you get involved with information architecture? How did it all start?

My educational background is in the humanities. I was a philosophy major in college and I took quite a lot of religion classes. I ended up with a Master of Arts and Literature, and then did poetry as part of a Master of Fine Arts. Throughout this time, I had part-time jobs working with computers, and I had an obsession with the internet, which turned out to be the one thing that would actually pay me a wage. After grad school, in the late 1990s, I was a technical writer for a while. That job led to another one in the interactive group at an old school advertising agency in North Carolina. I was an "internet copywriter", because they were using the ad agency copywriter-plus-art-director model.

It was in that job that I encountered the information architecture community. I was active on various listservs, keeping up with the conversations happening there, but many of these focused on minutiae, measurable immediates, pixel by pixel interactions. My questions were less about the pixel and more about why is that button there to begin with, because that's what I was running into in my work. As a copywriter on the Web, you're the one in charge of the links, and it occurred to me very quickly that that wasn't just writing, it was something else, pathways to places.

I was already thinking that way because, when I was a tech writer, I spent more time than I should have running Quake[1] servers and hosting a website for the various teams. People started joining the site. It became the petri dish that shaped my mental model: my job was to connect all these things together so that people would show up. My headspace has always been one of placemaking.

I've worked both inside and outside, in big companies and in agencies, and I am super obsessed with what we're doing when we create these places out of information. What we are architecting, and how it is different from the ways we've made and shared the environments we lived in before.

When I ran across the information architecture community, I thought here's people who are having the conversations I'm interested in. I attended the second ASIS&T Information Architecture Summit and got involved with getting the dearly departed Information Architecture Institute going. And I think that catches me up pretty much.

Q: How did you end up at the retreat in Asilomar[2] that resulted in the founding of the Information Architecture Institute in the first place?

The conversation started online. Lou (Rosenfeld) and Christina (Wodtke) wanted to kickstart an online organization for information architecture, but it didn't go very far and ended up in a bit of drama. So, they decided to try again in real life with some of the people who didn't do drama, and I was fortunate enough to be invited and to have a chance to bring my point of view to the table. I remember we spent a couple of months preparing the weekend retreat in Asilomar. And if I remember correctly, I brought this idea of shared information environments into the conversation. The word "shared" was important to me at the time, now it seems almost redundant, at the time it seemed novel. We had university-wide MUDs and chats in the 1990s, but people inhabiting and creating digital space at global scale, a real-time digital construct on the public internet—that was different. I could add something to a webpage and then somebody else could add something else to that web page, or link to it. It was a whole different world and I brought this perspective to the group at Asilomar. I forget whose idea was to have a manifesto, but I remember taking our notes and summing them up in what then became the *25 Theses*.[3]

Q: Reading them now, they seem ahead of their time. Here's what theses seven to nine say: "Thesis 7: This work is an act of architecture. Thesis 8: This is a new kind of architecture that designs structures of information rather than of bricks, wood,

---

[1] Quake was a first person shooter video game developed by id Software in 1996. It was one of the games, together with its precededessor, Doom, that popularized online gameplay via multiplayer deathmatches in which players would try to gain as many kills as they could.

[2] The Asilomar Conference Grounds is a conference complex originally designed by architect Julia Morgan in Pacific Grove, California. In March 2002, Christina Wodtke and Lou Rosenfeld invited a group "large enough to represent diverse opinions yet small enough to stay focused" to a two-day retreat that resulted in the creation of the Asilomar Institute for Information Architecture, later to become the Information Architecture Institute. https://iainstitute.org/sites/default/files/annual-rep orts/iai_annual_report_2003.pdf.

[3] Hinton, A. (2003). *25 Theses of Information Architecture*. https://andrewhinton.com/2003/06/02/ information-architecture-manifesto-25-theses/.

plastic and stone. Thesis 9: People live and work in these structures". These are the conversations we are having today. I doubt they were a big thing back then. Am I wrong?

I still love that thing. It's really kind of prescient, if a little overwritten. And I was certainly trying to get across this idea that this is not just the Web or "online". It's not a "virtual" place that doesn't really matter: anything that we experience affects our lives, is real, not virtual. We need to understand what these environments mean, how they're different, because we make too many assumptions based on what kind of environments we all evolved in.

It was a manifesto, I was a big fan of the Dada manifesto, and I didn't want to make it too rigorous. I came out of a poetry background after all, so to me this was our "barbaric yawp" out of Ginsberg's *Howl*. I gathered up the thoughts from others at the retreat and crafted the *Theses* thinking it would be edited further. But we just released it as it was. Clay Shirky wrote a post about it somewhere, saying it was a dumb piece of writing but that it brought up an interesting point. One thing I said in there, about relevance, still stings. My assumption at the time was that more information relevance is good. We've now experienced firsthand how relevance has been asymmetrically weaponized by billionaires and bad actors, so that algorithms that are supposed to give us relevant content are not really considering relevance to us. Relevance has been tuned to keep us engaged for views and the various toxic incentives that have gotten baked into our internet life. So the *Theses* were definitely naive.

We're still learning just how wildly disproportionately our decisions affect the information environment. You can affect structural change in the physical world or in our linguistic world, of course: you can move a chair, build a house, or edit a novel. But restructure the semantics of a screen that is part of an environment millions of people use, and suddenly that changes what the environment even is and does while people are still behaving as if it's what they thought it was. *Understanding Context* was my tentative way to sort some of this out.

Q: "Understanding Context", your book on information architecture and its role in shaping the human environment, came out at the end of 2014. I joined you on that journey, first on the sidelines and then as a technical reviewer towards the end. It didn't seem you enjoyed "writing" the book that much, but I suppose that you enjoy "having written".

Writing it was hell. There was a lot of groundwork, and a lot of reading that I enjoyed because it really set the stage—but the writing was hard. I'm very public about having ADHD. When I was in grad school, I told myself I'd never do a PhD because I could never write a dissertation. Then the book opportunity came along, and I couldn't really let it go, could I? It felt like self-flagellation, but very rewarding. It rewired me; it changed the way I think about everything.

I started writing the book thinking it would be a two-hundred-page essay about context. In the middle of that effort, my editor told me it didn't really read like an O'Reilly book. I thought, "I don't know that this whole concept ever sounded like an O'Reilly book. I was actually shocked that you guys would even take me on".

Q: It sure doesn't fit with some of their more practical books.

I think they thought it was going to. They were hoping it was going to be their new "polar bear" book,[4] but it definitely isn't. The people at O'Reilly were very patient with me and gave me the time I needed to figure it all out, even though it was apparent I had been way too optimistic in my estimates. I remember, while writing, I got to the point where I had to ask myself "what is information". Should I write a few pages just defining what information is? It's clearly important, but how do I approach this? So I mailed you, Dan (Klyn), Karl (Fast) and some others, probably Christina (Wodtke) as well, those I could think of who had taught anything related to that question. Nobody had a totally straight answer, because that's a rather complex question in itself, but it had just never occurred to me it was.

I started digging deeper. The work of Marcia Bates is crucial for that question if you want to bring in an information science perspective, but I also unearthed unexpected treasures. I was already interested in embodied cognition. I'd been following these folks[5] on Twitter for a while, and information came up a lot in their conversations, so I asked them "what do you teach when you teach what information is" as well. "Gibson. James J. Gibson is what we teach" was their reply, and that blew up everything.

Gibson's ecological perspective and the concept of affordance were something I couldn't find anywhere in design literature, and while I've since realized that a big part of it was probably me being a very bad researcher, I still think that the book needed to explain all of that in order to get to what I was trying to write about. It ended up being a much bigger task than I anticipated. I should also mention that Gibson's wife was pivotal in all of his work, to that point it would be more fair to call it their work. It helped me grapple with what information is from an embedded rather than an abstract lens. My starting point was phenomenological: watching a body act in the environment, breaking down behavior in very basic ways, and directly observing the meaning-making processes operating through perception and action.

When I look back at how the conversation that led to the book took shape, I have a hard time discerning contributions. It was all very organic. You and I had conversations on embodiment and placemaking, we discussed architecture and the influx of the environment with Karl (Fast), Dan (Klyn) and Jorge (Arango). It was in the air.

Q: I honestly have a hard time myself remembering whether specific concepts or examples were individual contributions or the result of bouncing ideas off each other. If I were to try and pinpoint a few important moments, I'd say that your "Linkosophy" keynote in 2008[6] and the work Luca (Rosati) and I presented in Barcelona the year

---

[4] Rosenfeld and Morville's *Information Architecture for the World Wide Web.*

[5] Wilson A. D., & Golonka, S. See for example Embodied cognition is not what you think it is. https://www.frontiersin.org/articles/10.3389/fpsyg.2013.00058/full.

[6] Hinton, A. (2008). Linkosophy. Closing plenary. 9th ASIS&T Information Architecture Summit. https://andrewhinton.com/2008/04/15/linkosophy/.

before,[7] *and that you very kindly referenced in your talk, were turning points. I met Dan (Klyn) and Jorge (Arango) in 2009, Abby (Covert) in 2010, and in 2011 you, Jorge and me presented that "More than a metaphor"*[8] *three-part talk at that year's ASIS&T Information Architecture Summit. The first slide of my part was a screenshot from "Superman Returns" and I told that little story from "Pervasive Information Architecture*[9]*" as a way to introduce how embodiment shapes the way we perceive reality. Things started rolling from there.*

That was the conversation we were having. I remember pointing out during question time at our session in 2011 that embodiment was an important concept in what was shaping up to be the next step for digital.

Q: The period between 2009 and 2012 saw quite a few presentations enter that space from you, Jorge (Arango), Abby (Covert), and Dan (Klyn). I brought Gilbert Ryle and "Ghost in the Shell" to the Summit in 2013 to discuss the body and the role of spatiality in digital/physical environments. You were already investigating embodiment: was that early interest the primary reason for writing the book?

It was one of the reasons, maybe just not the only one. I was at a point where I was doing all of that research and writing because I needed to try to solve the question for myself, with the aspirations that it was going to be a starting point, part of the ongoing conversation or maybe a seed that grows into a tall tree in the discourse around design. The book was somehow a natural outcome of that process.

We had very concrete questions: if we're practicing information architecture, what's the material that we're supposed to be affecting with our work. It seemed critical to me to be able to articulate why this is architecture but of a fundamentally different kind, because of the environment, material, and rules that digital implies. Embodiment is key to this distinction: to understand how we function in a digital environment we really need to understand how our body and environment mean something to one another, how they're really inseparable and how they're fundamentally a dynamic system. Understand what bodies do in environments first, and then how language works, and then we have the basis for understanding how digital information structures affect us. I realized I couldn't take a shortcut; I had to build from those first principles and take readers along that journey to get to the digital stuff.

---

[7] Resmini, A., & Rosati, L. (2007). *Towards a cross-context information architecture.* ASIS&T European Information Architecture Summit Barcelona. https://www.slideshare.net/resmini/towards-a-crosscontext-ia-1556629.

[8] Arango, J. (2011). Architectures. *Journal of Information Architecture, 3*(1). http://journalofia. org/volume3/issue1/04-arango/; Hinton, A. (2011). *More than a metaphor: A few thoughts on IA and architecture.* https://andrewhinton.com/2011/04/07/more-than-a-metaphor-a-few-thoughts-on-ia-architecture/; Resmini, A. (2011). More than a metaphor (I). https://www.slideshare.net/resmini/more-than-a-metaphor-i.

[9] The gist of that little story is how lucky we are that Superman, while being an alien, is literally shaped as we are. Same size, same morphology, same physiology. A superpowered human being, but still a human being who can understand human frailty and empathize.

Q: If embodiment, placemaking, sensemaking are the starting points of that journey, where are you headed today? Is there more to explore in that space that "Understanding Context" opened up for you?

I've been toying with the word "radical" and this phrase, "radical information architecture", for a while. Radical as in "root". Radical embodied cognition, one of the schools of thought in embodied cognition, is what's called a "replacement hypothesis" for mainstream cognitive science. It advocates we do away with the twentieth century "the brain is a computer" model, because it's wrong. And it leads me to wonder, how do we change at the root the way we architect for humans? The way I think about my work or my practice is still centered on understanding the context. When you do an information architecture card sorting exercise, contextually you're really only finding out how someone organizes labels on cards. That's the real context you're observing. Can we better educate our guesses for structuring a website from that? Sure. But it's not the same environment, not the same behaviors. I've seen people have completely different behavior once those labels are contextualized in a real site. Our methods carry assumptions and conflations that obscure what's happening at the root of human experience of these environments we make, because we've learned it's all happening in our heads, but it's happening in the intertwined dance between our bodies and environments. When people in a workshop have some type of voting activity, my thought is immediately "that's cool, but what's informing the voting other than the arbitrary feelings of the people in the room?" What's the environment this voting happens in? What's its impact? There's a constant feedback loop between a living being and its environment. That's how it survives. That's where our practice should be grounded. Whereas in the profession we're flying by broken instruments: we don't have that immediate feedback loop with the people who are using what we produce. My gut tells me that we'll need a whole new methodology and that this emphasizing and repossessing those parts of current methodologies that fit the ecological framing is just a temporary fix. What that methodology is going to be though, that's a different question.

Q: You mentioned that the information spaces we've created have been weaponized and used against us by twisting the meaning of relevance. I do agree with that. But if we consider the larger picture, digital spaces built to provide advantage to those who control them follow in the footsteps of physical spaces, don't they? Dominant groups have always built environments that were meant to sustain whatever politics and power relations they wanted supported. With no intention to normalize it, couldn't we say that the exploitation of digital space is just an extension of preexisting practices, rather than a radical new phenomenon? Wouldn't that help solving the problem, if this were not some "virtual" problem but just another facet of the political conversation? I'm very often confused by how people who work on the built environment side of placemaking or architecture seem to often stop right before considering digital an integral part of reality. Like it could be possible to think about the city of the nineteenth century without thinking about the Industrial Revolution: Dickens' London is an embodiment of the Industrial Revolution. Pretending digital is a phone in your pocket, or a browser you use, and not world-shaping social and cultural infrastructure does not seem healthy.

That's one of the fundamental ways I got rewired: it's all environment, isn't it? In terms of the ecological experience of a creature in an environment, it is all one single environment. That is how our bodies process it.

Those of us who work with the structure of the environment need to understand the differences between the layers, just like medical science has to make a distinction between different organs in your body. But the layers, just like the organs, are sort of meaningless outside of the whole dynamical system that is you. I was reading an interesting article about how in the early twentieth century, tuberculosis had an impact on the building codes in cities such as New York, where many brownstone houses and tenements were built following sanitary regulations such as "each room has to have a window" and heating was sized up so that indoor spaces could be kept warm even if you had your windows open in the winter. Much of this is now out of common knowledge, you need to read an article to know about it, but it's another good example of how the environment is the result of often obscure systemic decisions that attempt to draw a bright red line that tells people "this way of making things is good and this way of making things is bad".

So yes, logic dictates that if it's all one environment then distinctions should be made tactically but not strategically. You know we've had people in our community who very early on were trying to warn us that we were being blindsided and that we needed to be more broad. Greenfield in the early aughts, for example.[10] Are we thinking about what these levers that we're creating architecturally in these environments are doing to people? To what degree are we just following suit and perpetuating a capitalist or neoliberal mindset, reinforcing a skewed tunnel vision?

These are important things, but we've also all been trying to figure out what it is that we're doing to begin with. How do we do it, what are the good ways and the bad. For a long time, this meant the field had little patience with the more academic or theoretical conversations. It was all "we need jobs", "we're trying to make websites here", "let's not boil oceans here". Much of the design community was not there for this side of the conversation when the Web went big boom. Conferences today at least seem to be catching up: talks discussing high-level topics such as inclusivity or critique are common, which means that the community is more consistently aware of these discourses. Consistent practical applications of these concepts, I don't know that I'm seeing these yet. I'm curious of what these might be, and if they would challenge the notion that it is even possible to stay within the limits of whatever current economic and social systems we have around.

It's an honest question, because yes, I had this Copernican revolution in my own head about what it meant to make information environments. But that doesn't mean that at every company I work for I have the power to turn things completely around. There are limits, and we have to fit the mold of the organizational mode of production, the culture, both in making things and in making money out of services and products.

---

[10]See Greenfield, A. (2006). To IA or not IA, in Part I of this same book.

At the same time, the design community should give more thought to what could go wrong, how something could be misused. It's not just a fun brainstorm activity to do on the side, but an important part of ideation. A digital environment shouldn't function like a sleight-of-hand magician's trick: here's your delightful experience, while in fact they're using your engagement for hidden, nefarious purposes. So much of what we've come up with to give people great experiences is being misused. "Here's great free services and communication and community": but the real guts of the business model is not about that value, it's about the value of manipulating you with mechanisms that are largely governed by the environment's information architecture.

I'm not so familiar with the built environment disciplines, but my impression is that over the centuries, standards have emerged that better correlate structural decisions with their social and ethical dimension. I don't think our field is there yet, but as I said I'd be curious to see what these could be for what we do.

And events such as the Roundtable have been really important for creating a space for people with an appetite and aptitude and interest in these more high-level topics to meet and discuss. They've been incubators for recognizing like minds who were thinking outside of the specifics of whatever the day-to-day practice was preoccupied with at the time. This cannot be underestimated, especially as fields such as information architecture are still being redefined and recast as explicit "things" people do.

Anytime someone's trying to make sense of more than one object or concept in relationship to each other, there's an information architecture problem to solve. Only most people aren't calling it that, and while I'm very much at peace with that, I still think that we can do a better job by calling things with their proper names as that opens up the opportunity to reach out to the knowledge and resources created by those who got there before us.

Q: We talk a lot about mapping and modeling, and these seem to be accepted foundational parts of information architecture. But slowing down to discuss the structural relationships that shape those maps and models does not seem like anything anyone is really willing to do. I think we all agree that visibility is a major problem as of now, so have you seen any emergence of new ways of making these architectures more visible? To your point: why do we care so little about who or what is behind the curtain and what are they doing?

This is where service design has been helpful. I was a latecomer to it, only really getting more exposed to it when researching and writing the book. I think it presents a huge opportunity for information architecture. Service design hits just the right mix of conceptual thinking, modeling, mapping, and very pragmatic, concrete tools and methods. It sits at an inflection point where abstract models become grounded into what people do with their bodies. The whole frontstage/backstage distinction is a powerful construction that allows us to distinguish between what people are perceiving and what they are not perceiving. It is a Trojan horse for going behind the curtains and changing those parts of an experience that are not immediately visible but that have profound repercussions on it. The frontstage experience can only be so good if the backstage isn't. And no matter how well or efficiently we structure the process, if people can't understand it or make sense of it, we'll fail. Implementing the last mile, so to speak, or the last inches, more realistically, where we execute the actual physical actions, handing over the brochure, restocking the shelves, or whatever it is that somebody is doing, becomes systemically linked to all of the invisible parts. If the links break down, all of our planning is for naught.

There's an architectural perspective to such an approach that feels like a natural home for information architecture. Suppose your company deals with customers for multiple kinds of services: you need to make sense of all of those different landscapes and bring them together in one single ecosystem. That's when you start realizing you're going to be labeling all these things you're mapping, and you're mapping similar patterns which also will need labels. Before you know, you're knee-deep in taxonomies and you need a framework to make sense of it all.

Q: Would you mind me turning that around? I would argue that information architecture is a great opportunity for service design. While I would consider its academic side differently, the practice of service design often becomes "product design for intangibles". What I mean is that because of organizational and professional constraints, designing a service often results in processes that stay company-bounded. But digital has really broken down the product-centered model: if I want to pay my taxes, I'll probably connect a number of different services and products, depending on availability, choice, resources, to achieve my goal. The way I do that, my individual path, will be somewhat different from yours, I might skip sending paper receipts while you might need an accountant, but they'll both be part of a contextualized ecosystem where the possible relationships are pragmatically limited. I can't look at that from the single perspective of a company selling tax services, even if they're my client. This systemic and emergent view of individual experiences is what contemporary information architecture centers on.

Sure, absolutely. What I'm saying is that service design is a pragmatically understandable discipline. It offers a clear pathway, one that is easy to grasp. Blueprints, flows, and scenarios. It helps when you want to answer basic questions around planning. I went from a job at a company that had almost too much architecture to a company that had almost none. And so I introduced service blueprinting as a way to think about that architecture that they didn't have yet. It's a foot in the door, a very practical, concrete way to get people into a conversation where, at some point, you're going to hit a moment when you need to ask what are we calling these things, what do they mean to one another, what do they mean to the organization versus what do they mean to the user.

It also helps with addressing value exchange questions. I worked for an insurance company: in that context, how are we defining what value a phone call has? I always brought up the example of a claim. Someone had an auto accident and they're calling to report the damage. That first call is an important moment of truth for that person. They need a certain value out of the interaction, which is different from the insurance company's value. These are complementary in a system. Once you lay the mechanism bare, you start realizing that either you need that same mechanism in all of your interactions, or that you need different mechanisms for different subsystems, workflows, interfaces, or call centers. You start to define the relationship these have with one another.

I agree that information architecture, at least in the way that some of us have practiced and conceptualized it over the years, does go outside of the strict boundaries of "a service". That's why, honestly, I'm back talking about the ecological perspective. It's one environment: we're checking the boundaries, figuring out what we should leave out, and mapping the structure of the ecosystem we're in. Are we leaving out important things that are not necessarily bound to the purview of what the company wants or is interested in but that are really important for the individual participants? This has been part of what you have helped define and clarify in the past few years.[11] It's also what I explore in the book in relation to what are the design concerns when you're putting a product out into the world. You have to think about what ecosystem it'll become a part of, what niche it is filling, and what changes this might bring. Thinking outside the boundaries of the frame of the simple transaction is also how we figure out whether it's even going to make sense to bring any additional value in or not.

Incidentally, that's another reason why I'm glad to see a lot of designers working with journey mapping asking themselves whether they're involved with the bigger picture and how, what are these people trying to achieve, and are they using their service or not, and how do they might fit in there if they don't. That's the first step to realize we're actually a rather minor player in our customers' stories and that whatever we do, we are not the sole center of their focus.

Q: My major gripe with this, and where I think an information architecture approach could help, is the fact that customer journeys are a reductionist approach that forces everyone into linear ways of thinking. Even if you branch, you'll have directionality and a hierarchy of behaviors, one of which is considered primary. You'll also fall short of capturing the space of possibility that people do enjoy today thanks to digital: your location, your environment, but also your freedom to connect objects, people, information at will. Earlier, you mentioned the need for a different mindset to accommodate for the ecological perspective: this is another example. We require different tools we don't have yet, but we can learn from how other fields, such as systems thinking for example, deal with representing complexity. Since refitting descriptive approaches to generative processes is not going to be that easy, the coming years will be interesting indeed.

That and the fact that the times are ripe for asking ourselves if we're really thinking about the problem space or simply accepting the version of it that our clients are interested in. It's a loaded question, with profound implications in terms of the relationship between information architecture and the economic and social superstructures of our society, and potentially helpful to clear the table. "There goes a person who has a

---

[11]Resmini, A., & Lacerda, F. (2016). *The architecture of cross-channel ecosystems.* Proceedings of the 8th International ACM Conference on Management of Emergent Digital EcoSystems (MEDES'16). See also Lindenfalk, B., & Resmini, A. (2016). *The Myth that is service.* Proceedings of ServDes16.

body and they're doing something" still doesn't sound like an information architecture problem to a part of the community, the part that thinks about organizing information in purely digital terms. But we can't take this point of view in isolation anymore. We are way past a world where somebody interacts with digital life sitting at a special computer in a special room. That container is not there. Luca and you brilliantly explored all of this in *Pervasive Information Architecture*. The dematerialization of our infrastructure cannot be stopped. Everything that can be automated or digitized is going to be if it hasn't yet, because it's cheaper and more scalable.

And the more abstracted and the more digitized everything becomes, the more critical it is to reel it back into who the person is and what are they doing and how are they situated. Whether this produces physical or digital artifacts is by and large irrelevant—what you have is an architectural process.

Andrea Resmini is associate professor of experience design and information architecture in the Department of Intelligent Systems and Digital Design at Halmstad University and the Director of Innovation and Research at the Center for Co-production, Jönköping Academy for Improvement of Health and Welfare at the School of Health and Welfare, Jönköping University. An architect turned information architect, Andrea is a two-time past president of the Information Architecture Institute, a founding member of Architecta, the Italian Society for Information Architecture, the Editor-in-chief of the Journal of Information Architecture, and the author of *Pervasive Information Architecture* (2011) and *Reframing Information Architecture* (2014).

Concepts for an Information Architecture of Time

Marsha Haverty and Marcia J. Bates

Abstract Our purpose here is to present a structure and a vocabulary for discussing time in relation to information architecture. Designers need a way to look across time to see the shapes of performances in order to design satisfactorily for human activities in relation to systems. We elaborate on what we mean by performance rhythms, and show through examples how these rhythms both arise out of and influence human behavior. We provide a vocabulary of timings, rhythms, and cadences to model the time aspect, and show how these behaviors develop in behavior settings within a domain. This analysis comes from an embodied perspective and a practice perspective, where human behavior is viewed as always being physically embodied in actual practices in the real world. Even online behaviors generate a social sense of embodied presence that captures participants in a collective sense of being in a common setting. While important for current design scenarios, addressing performance rhythms will become critical as information systems expand in intelligence and autonomy. The more automated systems become integrated into human life, the more human rhythms need to find resonance in human-system interactions and uses.

Introduction

Human behavior may be described as a performance that unfolds over time. The way in which a performance unfolds creates patterns. The shape of performance patterns materially impacts how performances are experienced by the actors engaging in them. Repeated performances often develop rhythms, which we call performance rhythms. Our purpose here is to provide designers a way to look across time to see the shapes of performances in order to address satisfactorily human activities

M. Haverty (✉)
Autodesk, Inc., Portland, OR 97214, USA
e-mail: marsha.haverty@autodesk.com

M. J. Bates
Department of Information Studies, University of California at Los Angeles (UCLA), GSEIS Building, 951520, Los Angeles, CA 90095, USA
e-mail: mjbates@ucla.edu

© The Author(s), under exclusive license to Springer Nature Switzerland AG 2021
A. Resmini et al. (eds.), *Advances in Information Architecture*,
Human–Computer Interaction Series, https://doi.org/10.1007/978-3-030-63205-2_24

in relation to systems. Examples in the next section build intuition for the ways in which performance rhythms both arise out of and influence human behavior in daily life. While important for current design scenarios, developing a framework for performance rhythms will become critical as information systems expand in intelligence and autonomy, gaining the ability to dictate rhythms for human actors, for good or ill.

To build our concepts of time, we start with everyday examples of performance rhythms to illustrate their nature and importance, then provide some theoretical background. Next, we define the core terms, "timings," "rhythms," and "cadences," along with "behavior setting" as the situation giving rise to them. After that, a variety of types of timings are discussed to reinforce our point that time and rhythm are not trivial considerations in analyzing human-system interaction. We conclude with a discussion of necessary next steps in the development of an information architecture of time.

A few points should be noted at the outset. While time is a general concern of experience design, modeling and influencing performance rhythms requires the structural approach of information architecture. We also note that this analysis comes from an embodied perspective and a practice perspective, where human behavior is viewed as always being physically embodied in practices in the real world, and where even online behaviors generate a social sense of embodied presence that captures participants in a collective sense of being in a common setting. Finally, though concepts such as "clock time" and "circadian rhythms" are relevant here, they are only a part of the larger project of integrating thinking about time into design, as should become evident during the following discussion.

Examples of Performance Rhythms in Daily Life

While we all recognize that human uses of and interactions with technology take place through time, and several authors address temporal[1] factors, an information architecture of time has not yet been developed and integrated into design. It remains easy to refer to "an action" like a singular event that takes place like the flash of a flashbulb and then is over. But, in fact, an interaction with a system usually involves numerous specific moves, as well as a pattern of shifting thought and movement through time. To truly design well for system actors, we need to understand these patterns-through-time—the whole pattern, or performance, not just a cross-sectional instant. When we actually observe these patterns-through-time, we see that the full sequence of behavior has a shape, and human beings feel better when they can move through these sequences with familiarity, even rhythm.

---

[1] Applications of Stewart Brand's pace layers model are common in information architecture (see Campbell and Fast [2006] for an early example), as are calls for taking a systems approach to design, in which designers consider behavior unfolding through time in terms of dynamics of interrelated parts (examples specific to information architecture include Resmini and Rosati [2009] and Morville [2014]).

This "flashbulb moment" sense of actions also leaves out the degree to which human beings subtly but persistently coordinate their behavior with other human beings. This coordination often takes place out of consciousness. For example, usually, when walking down the street toward another person, we jointly coordinate passing by each other so that we do not run into each other. We become aware of this coordination only on those occasional instances when we both swerve in the same direction so as almost to hit each other. We both recognize what we are doing, smile at each other, and then try again.

This type of coordination (or not, as it happens!) appears spontaneously in settings with humans moving about, their physical performances coming within reach of one another because human beings are highly social animals, who have developed a strong awareness of others of their own kind in their environment.

It is not hard to recognize that certain cooperative human activities involve intentional coordination through time. A sporting event such as a soccer match or a musical event such as a symphony performance both involve actors engaging in intricately coordinated performances to achieve desired outcomes—scoring the most goals (soccer), or evoking a work of art (symphony). Athletes and musicians drill on their respective action patterns in such detail and intensity that they develop great skill in picking up on and aligning with subtle shifts in the performance of their collaborators. For both settings, the entire group behaves together as a system, the actors continuously aligning with and influencing one another's actions, performing together toward their goals.

There are other social environments, however, that may not appear so obviously coordinated, yet they are. Munn (1992) describes a study identifying how the wait staffs of restaurants deliberately use timings of duration and tempo of table visits, carefully coordinated with the timings of the kitchen, to establish the rhythms of fine dining, distinct from the "harried industrial rhythm of food production" (p. 109).

To see the influence of these rhythms, let us compare rhythms of restaurant dining with rhythms of dining on a commercial aircraft. In a restaurant, the wait staff time table visits not for physical efficiency and scheduling, but on lulls in the *trajectory* of the clients' conversation; at the table, establishing a mindset of *exploring* the menu, which mobilizes *tempo* and *duration* in very specific ways. The rhythms of in-flight dining take a different shape with flight attendants timing meal orders (and distribution) for each client based on timings of *flight schedule* and physical *proximity* (one row after the next), mobilizing timings of *availability* (each passenger gets one visit for their order compared to ongoing *availability* of restaurant wait staff) and *tempo* (quick) and *duration* (short). Flight passengers pick up the shapes of these rhythms and mobilize timings to act in tune—quickly scanning the menu with *proximity* of the flight attendant, *prioritizing* and *finishing* food choices (as opposed to *exploring* and *relaxing*). Even when things get busy in fine restaurants, with *simultaneity* of needs across the tables, the wait staff does not shift to the *efficiency* rhythms of flight attendants, but rather engages timings like *sequencing*, adjusting *frequency*, and other timings of table visits in order to maintain the rhythms of fine dining for their clients.

Coordinating rhythms in electronic environments may be even more difficult, in part because we are all relatively new at such a process in comparison to the eons of physical presence with other people in cooperative endeavors that we had previously experienced. Yet our in-born social character as a species naturally leads us to try to create such coordination, difficult though it may be. To design for performance rhythms in information architecture, we need an awareness of these patterns, and a vocabulary with which to discuss them and design for them.

Theoretical Background

This chapter is constructed from the point of view of ecological psychology as well as a practice-theoretical approach to social science research on social timing. These two schools of research began from very different perspectives, and retain distinctive focuses. However, as we shall see, they have some overlap in that both emphasize the direct, on-the-ground experience of human beings, rather than studying human behavior from a theoretical position superimposed on human activities.

Ecological psychology During most of its history, the field of psychology has focused overwhelmingly on the individual, and the mind within the individual's head. For several decades, however, there has been a stream of psychological research that departs from that model by insisting on taking into consideration the relationship between the person and his or her environment. This is ecological psychology, most prominently associated with James Gibson ([1979] 2015) and others following his approach. This psychology focuses on the human being's direct experiences of his/her surroundings and the consequences of those experiences for understanding human behavior.

One concept famously associated with Gibson is that of *affordance*, that is, "a property of the environment that has perceived functional significance for an individual" (Heft, 2001, p. 124). As I am walking through a forest and see a downed log by the trail, I can see that it offers me the affordance of being able to sit down on it for a rest. Someone else, not in the least tired, may not notice that property of the downed tree. A deer wandering through the forest will also not see the downed tree as offering an affordance of sitting, because deer do not sit down in such a way as to be able to take advantage of the configuration of the felled tree and its relationship to the ground. However, if some tasty moss is growing on the side of the log, the deer may well notice the affordance of food provided by the tree. Recognizing an affordance provided by its environment is distinctive to each individual animal or human at each individual moment in time.

Following Gibson, Schmidt (2007) notes that social relationships also "property" the environment for individuals. In Schmidt's example, as I enjoy a morning coffee, I may perceive my coffee cup both in terms of affordances for picking up and sipping from the object, and if, for example, the cup came from a loved one, by a social property of "gift," with the "gift appreciation" relationship emerging in action in my using the cup every day (p. 139).

Roger Barker's work (Heft, 2001) complements Gibson's, because he studied at the level of the ecology's influence on the individual's behavior. He made a meticulous study of children's behavior in various environments, such as the schoolroom, soda fountain, and home, and found that both the range and limits of their behavior were often constrained by the environment they were in. Barker's team found that the actions of a given child were better predicted by noting *where* she was (school vs. playground) than by anything about her as an individual (Heft, 2018). Barker named these situations that gave rise to predictable kinds of behavior, *behavior settings*, and described how a setting is generated by the actions of those engaging it. It is this emergent structure that constrains what actions are appropriate. "By self-limiting their individual degrees of operating freedom in the context of collective action, new possibilities for experience can be realized for individuals that otherwise could not be realized," (Heft, 2013, p. 165).

In other words, human beings design environments in order to carry out various sorts of activities, and provide constraints and expectations for those environments that are generally mutually understood by the players within, who limit their behavior to certain types of actions that are suitable to the particular behavior setting. As children grow, they learn environmental expectations among their elders, and by the time a young person enters a restaurant as an adult, she/he usually knows how to act in one. Failure to know or confusion with contextual expectations is the stuff of countless stories and movies, both comedic and tragic, thus underlining the importance of these aspects of human association for people.

To capture the source of those mutually understood constraints, Hodges (2014) borrows and extends the term *good continuation*.

> Meaning…for two people who share a common history, and who care about each other, their present task, and their future together, have the real, potent possibility of directly resonating to this larger story of which they are a part—they feel it—in such a way that they know how the story should be continued. That is, together in concert with their culture, their place, and their purpose they can choose what Gestalt psychologists would call a "good continuation."

He concludes:

> *Whenever we act, including perceptual acts, we act prospectively*: We orient and move toward what we take to be good…The possibility that we can perceive directly, through conversing, the character of our surroundings, so that we can know better and worse directions in which to move, suggests that we might want to think of language itself, the activities of listening and speaking with each other over time, as a perceptual system. (p. 97, emphasis ours)

In the examples provided earlier of the soccer match, concert, and restaurant, the people involved were not carrying out their activities independently of their environments. In fact, other people previously had designed those environments to promote the effective conduct of the activities that the people wanted to engage in. For example, in the case of the restaurant, certain structures had to be built, certain resources had to be marshaled, and certain people with certain training had to be brought together in order to provide a suite of affordances around eating gourmet food and relaxing in a leisurely fashion. In fact, we as human beings move through a series of such planned environments throughout our lives.

When designers attend to information architecture, or "the structural design of shared information environments" (Rosenfeld et al., 2015, p. 24), they must orient prospective users to the kinds of places the environments are in terms of their suites of possibilities for meaningful action (Hinton, 2014). Because people have varied experiences, knowledge, and psychological makeup, it can be difficult to design environment properties that will be (1) immediately identifiable, (2) noticeable in circumstances where they can help the work of the human, and (3) blend well with the needs and rhythms of the person's work. It is the last of these requirements that is the focus of attention in this chapter.

Practice theory "(P)ractice theory is not a coherent theory, but consist[s] of several theoretical perspectives offering different analytical and interpretative 'lenses'" (Moring & Lloyd, 2013, p. 9). Research from a practice-theoretical perspective starts by looking at what people actually do, their daily practices, to better understand how they work together and how they might work better together. In the past, emphasis might have been on studying an organization after first dividing it up by organizational chart components and levels, or by formal processes. However, the actual on-the-ground functioning of the organization may work very differently from the formal model.

Huizing and Cavanagh (2011) review the history of practice theory and draw attention to several key theorists, each with a somewhat different emphasis or orientation, including these: Giddens (1984), Wenger (1998), Brown and Duguid (1991), Bourdieu (1977), Kaptelinin and Nardi (2006), Orlikowski (2000), and Schatzki (1996).

Our interest in practice theory comes from the perspective of Stanley Blue (2019), who applies Schatzki's approach to practice theory in combination with Lefebvre's (1992/2004) study of rhythm in social life. Lefebvre called this "rhythmanalysis." Though practices within a social group are central to the work of the several theorists listed above, their formulations, like so many other approaches, rather underplay the temporal element. Blue and Lefebvre, on the other hand, focus on it. Blue states:

> I argue that the concept of rhythms should be further developed in practice theory to better account for the emergence of particular organizations of practices and especially institutional configurations. (2019, p. 924)

Blue describes a characteristic pattern of social practices being repeated, but with some variation that may gradually change it. Rhythm is created by this repetition. The repetition with variation also gradually institutionalizes the practices, until they become well established and "natural" to the participants. It is the competition and coordination of practices that produces a rhythm. According to Lefebvre, these rhythms can be characterized as eurythmic or arrhythmic. "In eurythmia, rhythms mutually depend on, support, and reinforce each other," while in arrhythmia, rhythms are "desynchronizing, pathological, and different" (Blue, 2019, p. 940).

To complete our embodied view of organizational rhythms, we look to Barbara Adam's description of timing action as the source of rhythms. Actors judge the "right" time to engage certain activities based on timing, and which timings actors engage depends on specifics of the situation (Adam, 1995). Timing is not just the point in time at which an activity is initiated. As action unfolds, an actor assembles and balances a variety of timings to stay connected with timings in the environment (p. 21) (recall the different suites of timings used by restaurant wait staff and commercial flight attendants). Adam highlights that considering any one aspect of timing in a situation implicates the others since they act together in a complex (p. 51).

Thus, in the life of a group of associated people, rhythms, and the timings that generate them, need to be recognized, valued, and supported. In modern technical environments, that support inevitably comes, to a substantial degree, through the design and coordination of rhythms in technical systems and software. We need a mental framework and vocabulary to discuss design for rhythm support. Some such vocabulary is presented in the next section.

Terms for Time in Information Architecture

A way to assess and influence performance rhythms will be critical as information systems expand in agency and develop more autonomy and adaptability. The ability to instrument these systems to be sensitive to performance rhythms of human actors as well as reveal their own performance rhythms will help ensure that human-system performances remain aligned with what is good for the larger domain in which the human actors are performing. We need to find ways to design and synchronize healthy rhythms of performance for systems. In this section we describe and explain the vocabulary that can be used in this effort.

Human behavior unfolds over time as a performance. As humans, we do not simply decide ahead, then execute our actions in a series of discrete events. We perform by coordinating our actions with events in our surroundings and creating new actions to which our surroundings align.

Actors use *timings* to coordinate their actions with their physical, technical, and social surroundings. Timings create rhythms. When actors engage, they balance a tension between aligning with rhythms generated by other actors, and creating their own rhythms to which other actors align.

Timings are the moments of coordination when actors align with actions and events in their surroundings. Timings bundle into rhythms. To put it differently,

Rhythms are bundled timings that recur.

Cadences are rhythms that settle into steady states of performance for a given behavior setting.

Next, looking at the environments within which people conduct activities we introduce two more terms:

A *behavior setting* is a social environment that emerges naturally from the collective actions of a group of individuals. It is often, but not always, structured architecturally and socially in advance to support precisely the kinds of actions being taken in it. For example, a physician setting up a practice will likely use a building already designed for the activities of medical services. On the other hand, a group of hikers can set up camp de novo in the mountains and create their behavior setting, into which they fit their activities and communications for the evening. Though the camp is not designed in advance, it will nonetheless express a variety of social patterns and expectations that the hikers bring with them from their life experience.

A *domain* is a larger social context than a behavior setting, and is usually marked for the participants by being a highly structured social organization with evident boundaries. Domains often contain numerous behavior settings which are intended to produce the work or product for which the domain is designed. Examples are companies, academic disciplines, military units, government agencies, sports teams, etc., along with less formal but densely structured contexts such as large families and hobby communities (Hartel, 2010).

Because our interest is in timing within behavior settings, however, we provide a timing-oriented definition for behavior settings and domains, and add a third temporal term:

> *Behavior settings* are situations (physical, digital, or blended) which focus the performance rhythms of actors acting within them on moving toward good continuation for the domain which associates them.
>
> A *domain* is the conceptual space which provides values for good continuation, and sets the scope of behavior settings.
>
> *Good continuation* is about the effective attunements actors develop, through performing in a behavior setting, with the larger values of the domain in which they are acting.

Our mantra becomes: *timings bundle into rhythms which settle into cadences.* Figure 1 reiterates that performance rhythms should be considered as a system of interrelated parts (timings) behaving over time, not as a series of discrete events.

In Fig. 1, recall the timings the wait staff of restaurants assemble, and the timings clients adopt to hook into them. These timings influence each other to create rhythms of fine dining, which, repeated over time, settle into cadences.

Figure 2 shows that performance rhythms do not form randomly, but emerge in the situations of behavior settings, which are nested within domains, and constrained by the larger system of domain values.

For the domain of fine dining, we might zoom into focus on rhythms at the tables, or zoom out to see rhythms across the activities of the wait staff, kitchen, bar, reception, and others. Notice that even the highest-level behavior setting for a domain is not equal to the domain itself (Fig. 3).

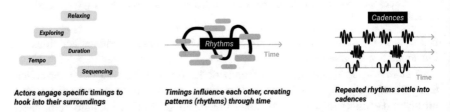

Fig. 1 Dynamics among timings create patterns (rhythms) through time which, when repeated, settle into cadences

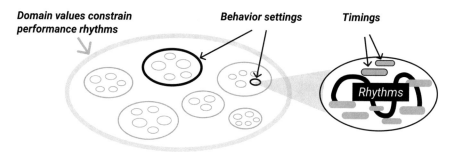

Fig. 2 A domain has nested behavior settings which exist because they are performed and aligned with domain values

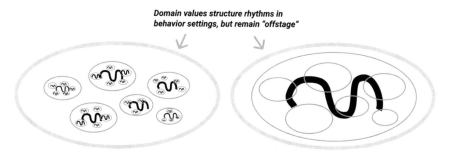

Fig. 3 Domain values constrain immediate performances in behavior settings, but are larger than the highest-level behavior setting

Behavior settings at any level of zoom point to domain values which constrain performances within, but domain values are always "offstage" in that they evoke the larger story of what is important to the domain across time and space. In the fine dining example, qualities of what fine dining ought to be like are offstage, but picked up by staff and clients alike in the rhythms of behavior that emerge in the restaurant. Domain values of fine dining, drawing from cultural history and refined by a particular restaurant, create very different rhythms from those guiding in-flight food service. The shape of performance rhythms in any given behavior setting is unique because it is formed partly by domain value constraints, and partly by local conditions and individuals (environmental dynamics unfolding together).

Behavior settings emerge when their performance rhythms emerge, yet rhythms are not things: "they are movings, forces, expenditures of energy that return with varying regularity in time and space," (Blue, 2019, p. 937). Behavior settings some-times emerge in scheduled times and places (a soccer match or a 9–5 office job). But, once actors have become attuned to cadences of a behavior setting, in certain situa-tions, they can perform "within them" simply by resonating with what *good contin-uation* is like and about, and moving in that direction, generating the shape of their rhythms, even without other environmental information present (the soccer player practicing footwork, or the office worker capturing a project idea from home). In cases of eurhythmia, the actors are attuning with the performance rhythms of these behavior settings by generating them. Arrhythmia develops if one or more individuals or teams prefers different rhythms or timings, or believes that different rhythms are necessary for success. Arrhythmia is not necessarily bad; it can be the impetus for needed change in an organization's or group's work patterns.

Modes of Alignment

Timings play different roles in the ways in which they influence rhythm dynamics. More work needs to be done to formally characterize modes of alignment for information architecture, but we offer some early thoughts here.

Mindset timings Qualities of an actor's attention and focus which serve as reference timings because of the ways in which they influence selection of other timings. Examples: *exploring, synthesizing, prioritizing, relaxing, rushing*, among many others, depending on the situation.

Trajectory timings Timing horizons which influence alignment based on where they are in their horizon as a behavior setting emerges. Trajectory timings may have natural sources, such as *seasonality*, biological sources, such as *circadian cycles*, and many physical and conventional sources. *Longevity* (physical for machines, conceptual for initiatives), *availability* (physical for beaches covered by tides, conventional for store open hours and train schedules), *maturation* (physical for raspberries, conventional for design teams), and many others. In our modern era of clock time, one of the most common trajectory timings is the *deadline*, which often influences many other timings, for good and ill.

Support timings The variety of timings that are mobilized to amplify and structure reference timings. It is easy to think there are only a few kinds of timings to support action, like *frequency* and *duration*, but there are many other structures for moments of alignment that include physical and abstract aspects of space and time. As a few examples, actors use and react to *sequencing, continuity, compartmentalization, concentration, distribution, proximity, simultaneity*, and aspects of *symmetry*, both physically and conceptually to organize action with their surroundings.

Clock time Quantified and measured units of time to coordinate action in complex or distributed situations. Clock time is a reference timing because it influences selection of other timings. It is singled out separately here, however, because unlike mindset and other modes of alignment, clock time is indifferent to change and, when overused, can dictate timing, stepping on all the other timings an actor may try to mobilize (Adam, 1995, p. 25). Examples include, *schedule, frequency, interval, speed, rate*, among others.

Knowing how mindset, trajectory, clock time, and all the various support timings mobilize and influence each other provides a powerful lens on the shape of rhythms.

Information technologies have created new ways of aligning based on digital events. Moran (2011) describes the way software settings and preferences let actors "configure the future by deciding in advance what to make of events yet to come," (p. 27), while "undo" lets actors experiment and take back action. Mackenzie (2007) describes the way algorithms fold together relations, concatenating past states and even all potential states into a microworld, or mosaic "now," "by solving all problems in order to solve a particular," (p. 104).

We will use the next section to put to work our terms for time using design examples.

Examples of Modeling Performance Rhythms for Design

To understand how performance rhythms may support design, let us look at two scenarios: a system to help people learn a new language for personal growth, and a system to help mechanical engineers design weed control machines for sustainable farming. To keep things interesting, we will look at this from the point of view of an actor engaged in both of these domains. As an individual, our actor resonates with a kaleidoscope of domains across her personal and professional life (Fig. 4).

When our actor engages the performance rhythms of a particular behavior setting at work, say modeling components of the weeding machine she is designing, her domain of influence becomes specific to her employer institution and her occupation of mechanical design (Fig. 4). Our actor resonates with rhythms of mechanical design, exploring geometric possibilities in rhythms she has picked up from mentors and colleagues, refined by rhythms she has picked up from coworkers and leadership at her institution. These rhythms of work time are guided by intertwined values of the larger practice of mechanical design and those of the actor's institution.

Suppose that designers of the system used by our actor had insight into these rhythms, and the values guiding them, because they had, through research and domain modeling, identified important behavior settings within equipment design for sustainable farming, and, for each, had identified important mindset, trajectory, and support timings. Because sustainability had emerged as an important concept in the domain model (a larger domain value), the system designers prioritized simulation tools with timings to represent rhythms of environmental impact. Further, because the designers had learned that formative evaluation throughout the design process is vastly preferable to holding off evaluation until the system is already completed, that simultaneity of timing was also captured in their domain model and prioritized in the system design. Instead of requiring actors to stop modeling in order to start evaluating, and stop-starting back again, suppose the system facilitated transitions between the mindset, support, and other timings of modeling and evaluating, amplifying the

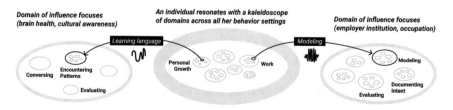

Fig. 4 Attuning with a particular behavior setting focuses the domain of influence for an individual

simultaneity of engaging in those settings. By facilitating performance rhythms, this system is participating in good continuation for the domain.

For another example, suppose modeling timings across behavior settings had revealed another simultaneity timing: mechanical engineers must document design intent for collaborators throughout the trajectory of design. This time, system designers realized that, unlike the way simultaneity of modeling and evaluating provide a generative creative tension for design, the rhythms of documenting intent (synthesizing, highlighting, sequencing, among others), compete with and destroy the rhythms of modeling and evaluating. In this case, suppose the designers prioritized automating documentation. The system could preserve simultaneity of modeling and documenting intent overall (important to ensure collaborators see design intent throughout a project), but offload the latter activity to digital agents, amplifying and reinforcing the timings of the other primary behavior settings for the human actors. Even notifications about documentation status and small decision points that need human input could have timings that are sensitive to and in tune with rhythms of modeling and evaluating.

Referring to Fig. 4, suppose our mechanical engineer is engaging in the rhythms of modeling at her office, when her personal device buzzes with a notification: her app is reminding her that it is time to practice Finnish. Our actor resonates with the values of personal growth, with keeping her brain challenged by the language's complexities, and the opportunity to experience a different culture by participating in it. She could open the app and start resonating with the behavior settings of encountering the language patterns, practicing conversing, taking quizzes, and all those timings orchestrated by the thoughtful architecture and design of the language learning system. Or, she could ignore the notification and keep modeling "at work," picking up the performance rhythms of language learning in some other moment.

This scenario exposes a challenge for systems that facilitate behavior settings for domains with more abstract boundaries and continuous availability timings. Practicing a language with small, intense doses is good continuation, but how to harmonize it with timings of behavior settings in other important domains? Currently, many systems rely on engaging actors with reminders timed only by clock time: remind the actor to practice at noon each day, for example. Unlike the system to support mechanical design, which had access to rhythms across key behavior settings and could orchestrate transitions among them, the designers of personal growth apps have no way to know what personal or professional behavior setting a given actor will be engaging when their app reminder pops up. Are there other timings that can help structure reminders in ways that reflect rhythms beyond time of day? What might those be? Further, this is not an edge case concern for performance rhythms. The boundaries of behaving within "work time" behavior settings and "personal time" behavior settings continue to blur. Personal devices, sensors, physical-digital displays, "always on" intelligent systems infuse all the behavior settings for a given individual with anytime availability timings. Even domains with more traditionally scheduled and focused behavior settings are becoming less so. Orchestrating performance rhythms across behavior settings and domains of influence is a challenge for us all.

Future Considerations on Performance Rhythms

In addition to establishing a way to talk about performance rhythms, we touch on considerations for a performance rhythms framework.

Modeling Performance Rhythms

Social science investigates the way practices bundle timings into rhythms "through a method of zooming in and zooming out to reveal processes and scales of entrenchment," (Blue, 2019, p. 931). Domain modeling, common in information architecture, is typically used to capture important concepts and relationships within a conceptual space at one level of zoom to drive content (Atherton & Hane, 2017), or data (Pope, 2016), but the technique can extend to capture nested behavior settings of interest. Timings actors engage with could be modeled in relation to other important objects. Simulating the system dynamics of timings is where domain modeling falls short.

Dynamics

One timing may be a reference for others, the other timings translating the structure of the reference timing and adopting its form (Moran, 2013). Our calendars translate the timings of the Earth's cycles around the Sun. A timing may amplify or dampen the effect of another timing. For example, a designer in early stages of a project adopts a mindset of exploring the problem space and associating to find interesting relationships; the designer mobilizes other timings of simultaneity (using sticky notes or other representations to capture ideas side by side), along with a certain intensity and continuity to amplify rhythms of exploration. The designer notes the unboundedness of the problem space and, when the trajectory of the project reaches the right timing, shifts mindset to prioritizing and synthesizing, with tempo shifting and simultaneity dampening as sequencing and compartmentalization are engaged. How might designers name and model these kinds of dynamics and see shape in the rhythms?

Language of Critique

It is not enough to discuss features of performance rhythms. Information architecture practice also needs a way to assess their health. Practice theory provides eurythmia for rhythms that hold together and arrhythmia for those that fall apart, but digital actors change the horizons of behavior settings. Because their processes are often hidden or inaccessible to human actors, algorithmic systems are not instrumented to notice the corrective force of being part of the collective performance, and can keep performances alive, even when rhythms move in directions misaligned with the values of the domains in which they operate. Healthy rhythms are performing toward good continuation, and adjust to stay in tune as good continuation is refined over time.

> While practices exhibit regularities, they are fundamentally open. As they are enacted in context-specific situations, they are forced through reinterpretation and therefore an innovation that represents more than pure reproduction. (Blue, 2019, p. 927)

From a performance rhythms point of view, we find three issues for a language of critique: (1) automations that are exact repetitions stand to impede the natural progression of a practice unless the human actors have ways to derive insights from and nudge performances in progressively better directions, (2) systems with agency need to reveal their performance rhythms so human actors may see their shapes unfolding through time, and (3) systems with agency need to have timings that are influenceable, aligning with timings of human actors, depending on the situation, keeping the domain moving together toward good continuation.

Conclusions

Without integrating time in the aforementioned ways, the incipient rhythms that actors are beginning to develop or impose on system interactions may be thwarted or clash with unacknowledged, or simply undeveloped, rhythms in system design. As the systems we are designing are truly systems—their behavior is not determined, but consists of dynamics expressed among interrelated parts—we need to design in ways that incorporate activity through time in order to produce a complete and genuinely supportive product.

References

Adam, B. (1995). *Timewatch: The social analysis of time.* Polity Press.
Atherton, M., & Hane, C. (2017). *Designing connected content: Plan and model digital products for today and tomorrow.* New Riders.
Blue, S. (2019). Institutional rhythms: Combining practice theory and rhythmanalysis to conceptualise processes of institutionalisation. *Time & Society, 28*(3), 922–950. https://doi.org/10.1177/0961463X17702165.
Bourdieu, P. (1977). *Outline of a theory of practice.* Cambridge University Press.
Brown, J. S., & Duguid, P. (1991). Organizational learning and communities-of-practice: Toward a unified view of working, learning, and innovation. *Organization Science, 2*(1), 40–57.
Campbell, G., & Fast, K. (2006). *From pace layering to resilience theory: The complex implications of tagging for information architecture.* Proceedings of IA Summit.
Gibson, J. J. ([1979] 2015). *The ecological approach to visual perception.* Psychology Press.

Giddens, A. (1984). *The constitution of society.* University of California Press.

Hartel, J. (2010). Time as a framework for information science: Insights from the hobby of gourmet cooking. *Information Research, 15*(4), colis715. http://InformationR.net/ir/15-4/colis715.html.

Heft, H. (2001). *Ecological psychology in context: James Gibson, Roger Barker, and the legacy of William James' radical empiricism.* Psychology Press.

Heft, H. (2013). An ecological approach to psychology. *Review of General Psychology, 17*(2), 162–167.

Heft, H. (2018, November 8). *Places as emergent dynamical structures in everyday life* [Video]. YouTube. https://www.youtube.com/watch?v=Eljsoaj0d44.

Hinton, A. (2014). *Understanding context: Environment, language, and information architecture.* O'Reilly.

Hodges, B. H. (2014). Righting language: The view from ecological psychology. *Language Sciences, 41,* 93–103.

Huizing, A., & Cavanagh, M. (2011). Planting contemporary practice theory in the garden of information science. *Information Research, 16*(4), paper 497. Available at http://InformationR.net/ir/16-4/paper497.html.

Kaptelinin, V., & Nardi, B. (2006). *Acting with technology: Activity theory and interaction design.* MIT Press.

LeFebvre, H. (1992/2004). *Rhythmanalysis: Space, time and everyday life.* Continuum.

Mackenzie, A. (2007). Protocols and the irreducible traces of embodiment: The Viterbi Algorithm and the mosaic of machine time. In R. Hassan & R. E. Purser (Eds.), *24|7: Time and temporality in the network society* (pp. 89–108). Stanford University Press.

Moran, C. (2011). Interactive time and "real time" in software and society. *Spectator, 31*(1), 23–28.

Moran, C. (2013). Time as social practice. *Time & Society, 24*(3), 283–303. https://doi.org/10.1177/096143X13478051.

Moring, C., & Lloyd, A. (2013). Analytical implications of using practice theory in workplace information literacy research. *Information Research, 18*(3), paper C35. http://InformationR.net/ir/18-3/colis/paperC35.html.

Morville, P. (2014). *Intertwingled: Information changes everything.* Semantic Studios.

Munn, N. D. (1992). The cultural anthropology of time: A critical essay. *Annual Review of Anthropology, 21,* 93–123. http://www.jstor.org/stable/2155982.

Orlikowski, W. J. (2000). Using technology and constituting structures: A practice lens for studying technology in organizations. *Organization Science, 11*(4), 404–428.

Pope, R. (2016, May 7). *Ontology dojo: Learn how to use ontology to define your information and supercharge your deliverables.* Conference Presentation, Information Architecture Summit, Atlanta, Georgia.

Resmini, A., & Rosati, L. (2009). *Information architecture for ubiquitous ecologies.* Conference Presentation, MEDES '09: International ACM Conference on Management of Emergent Digital EcoSystems, Lyon, France.

Rosenfeld, L., Morville, P., & Arango, J. (2015). *Information architecture: For the web and beyond.* O'Reilly Media, Inc.

Schatzki, T. R. (1996). *Social practices: A Wittgensteinian approach to human activity and the social.* Cambridge University Press.

Schmidt, R. C. (2007). Scaffolds for social meaning. *Ecological Psychology, 19*(2), 137–151.

Wenger, E. (1998). *Communities of practice: Learning, meaning, and identity.* Cambridge University Press.

Marsha Haverty is a veteran of information architecture, her experience ranging from early eCommerce websites to enterprise software. Her 2002 JASIST article is used in curricula at various institutions. Currently, she in bringing theory to practice in experience architecture at Autodesk.

Marcia J. Bates is Professor Emerita in the UCLA Department of Information Studies in Los Angeles, CA. She has taught, researched, published, and consulted in the areas of user-centered design of information systems, subject access, and information practices. She has been Associate Dean and Department Chair, and has consulted for government, foundations, and business, including technology start-ups. Her publications are widely cited, gaining an "h-index" of 42.

Afterword: In Conversation with Richard Saul Wurman

Dan Klyn

Richard Saul Wurman is recipient of the Smithsonian Cooper-Hewitt Design Museum lifetime achievement award, multiple Graham, Chandler, NEA, and Guggenheim grants. He was made a Fellow of the American Institute of Architects at the age of 41 served as the youngest-ever board member of the International Design Conference in Aspen, founded the interior design programs at Cal Poly Pomona and Otis Parsons in the 80s, invented the TED conference, and is the author and designer of more than a hundred books, including "Information Anxiety", "The Words of Louis I. Kahn", "Information Architects", "Understanding Healthcare", "Understanding Children", and "Understanding Understanding". He lives in Golden Beach, Florida with his wife, novelist Glory Nagy.

D. Klyn (✉)
The Understanding Group (TUG), Ann Arbor, MI, USA
e-mail: dan@understandinggroup.com

University of Michigan School of Information, Ann Arbor, MI, USA

© The Author(s), under exclusive license to Springer Nature Switzerland AG 2021
A. Resmini et al. (eds.), *Advances in Information Architecture*,
Human–Computer Interaction Series, https://doi.org/10.1007/978-3-030-63205-2_25

In May of 1976, the American Institute of Architects' national convention was convened in Philadelphia, Pennsylvania, and chaired by a freshly minted AIA Fellow and Philadelphia-based architect called Richard Saul Wurman. Wurman titled the conference "Architecture of Information," called himself an information architect, and went on in the mid-1980s to create a series of wildly successful ventures around making information understandable; including the Pacific Bell Yellow Pages, an award-winning series of city guides, and the now-eponymous TED conference. In the transcript that follows, Wurman elucidates an expansive viewpoint on the terminology and territory of information architecture, and ponders the connections between being able to sell an idea, and the advertising business, and the work of information architects.

In June of 2015, I traveled to Newport, Rhode Island to sit for a series of conversations with Wurman that were meant to generate some of the text for a book that was at that time called "80: Worship the God Of Understanding and the Angels of Clarity and Transparency of Source," and later published under the title "Understanding Understanding." What follows is a previously unpublished exchange that took place on June 26, 2015, that begins with Richard Saul Wurman and taking a look back at his career.

In the long night of my soul, about halfway through my life, I had a wrenching notion that I chose totally the wrong career. That I should have been an "ad biggie."

Which is not to say that I was your typical salesman, or ingratiating Madison Avenue type; but I felt I had the ability to "nuggetize" (a made-up word) an idea. So that in the curiosity of the bon mot, or of the acronym, there was a kind of alien curiosity that would elicit people to ask a question, or give me a natural way of launching into an explanation. Basically, advertising. And I thought I'd be good at it. And at different moments of my life, I had spurts of avarice and greed, as I saw people in advertising who actually could dress well, or had the accouterments that security gives one.

Fortunately, these were just flashes. And I still have some of that in me. One of the things I decided to do quite early on, that was totally against my nature initially, was to give talks and speeches that flowered inordinately out of control. So, I obviously had this propensity for grandiosity and stage presence and the impresario culture.

Now, this came at a huge price, because for years, let's say between maybe twenty five to thirty five, I tried to get invited to give talks. And these were kind of "five-dollar talks" within a university circuit, where I really didn't have much to say. And I got dry in the mouth. I was terrified. And the self-loathing and self-hatred after the public humiliation that I put myself through was unbearable.

I don't remember every one of the terrible speeches I gave, but I remember several of them even today, fifty years later. Where I would stop, dry mouthed, and not know where I was, and just wish I was someplace else. The humiliation, the phoniness of me, trying to get to speak someplace because I was so ambitious, and I knew that part and parcel of conventional success was being able to be in front of people, and talk. To sell an idea. Once again, we are back at advertising. Selling an idea. I knew that that was essential to me moving one step ahead.

And thus, I picked up this terror of being on a Zen-like path into deeper and deeper acceptance of my own stupidity; and at the same time, this desire and this ambition to sell. To make visible. To clarify an idea. So, one side was shutting down in an introverted way to accept the black hole in my stomach. And the other side was turning on, and toward the public. To explain things. To make the complex clear.

I realized—through Lou, and through the work of Paul Klee—that I felt the best when I understood something. That it was perhaps sexual. It was this warm feeling I got when I understood something, it couldn't be moved from my stomach. It was a satisfaction of not only understanding something, but to define and feel responsible for its raison d'être, its roots, its construct. The systemic way that I could explain how I could explain—understand how I understood.

And thus, when given the opportunity to develop my ideas in a fairly large-scale and public way, I said yes. I did the International Design Conference in Aspen in '72, and that was the proving ground. IDCA was the best conference in the world at that time. And the freest. And I was young—in my 30s still, I guess.

And after a succession of speeches, and meetings, came the oddity of my being asked to be the National Chairman of the American Institute of Architects Convention in the celebratory year of 1976, in Philadelphia. It seems natural now that I called the conference the "Architecture of Information." And then switched it, reversed it, to call myself an Information Architect. And however many years later, I've found that information architecture was a vessel that did contain, inherently, cartography, and the explaining of physical, three-dimensional space. The explaining of two-dimensional projections, and representation of ideas; the representation of time; the city, and the architecture of the city. And the understanding of the city.

And so that was really when the various things came together as far as information architecture. Now, the fact is, I had been doing information architecture long before then. I had done a bunch of books, and they all had in them—if you reverse engineer them—they all had the principles of the trade. Two of the three special issues I did with *Design Quarterly*, in 1971 and 1989, could be used as a kind of information architecture primer.

And in a sense, I provided the first definition of this field (it could be considered the first definition, because it was so popular), in *Design Quarterly* in 1971: "making the city observable." Making the city observable was about urban information in a broad sense. Not just a pretty map, or the primitive computer mapping that started to be done at Harvard at the time. It was 100 examples of the various ways you could make urban information clearer, and the various proponents of it; from history, and contemporary and experimental. And both in learning programs, as well as actual graphic design and architectural design. Giving a broad definition to the term of understanding, and beneath them, the kinds of rules that were represented in the choices I made in what was included, and what was not included.

The advertising part is that "information architecture" as a term has had staying power. I mean, it was a term that raged in controversy among graphic designers (which pleased me), because they were calling themselves—those that were partly interested in the field—"information designers," and objected hugely to my preferred term, thinking I wanted a royalty on the use of it. And who was I to call myself that?

Well, I call myself anything I want to. I wasn't asking anybody to call themselves an information architect. And I wasn't leading a movement (and am still not leading a movement), but it caught on. It caught on so much that today, you know, decades later, it's defined by people who put it on their business cards in many different ways. The explosion of people who just do web pages, calling themselves Information Architects, as opposed to what my definition is of making the complex clear.

And then I did the book Information Architects for Graphis, and Peter Bradford did that with me. And that was very popular, and it went out of print very fast, and was never reprinted because my deal with Graphis was that I got half the profits, and they couldn't bear it, so they wouldn't reprint it. They just couldn't bear me getting half of that much money. And there was a market for it! It sold out a paperback version and a hardback version right away. But they wouldn't reprint it.

Q: (Frowning)

It's okay. It gets a certain panache by being out of print. And then there was a group of architects in Texas that sent me a cease and desist letter, because they said I couldn't use the word "architecture." Because they were architects, and this wasn't licensed.

Q: Did they not know that you are a licensed architect?

Yes, but I couldn't make up the term information architect and have anybody who was "just a graphic designer" use it, because they are not licensed as an architect

Then a stream of communications with, I think, mostly German and Dutch graphic designers, who were angry. "Who is Wurman that he would do this? It's not right, and we are information designers, and ..." I didn't say anybody shouldn't be an information designer. But it got to be controversial. Well, of course, that helped it. And I kept on calling myself an information architect, but I never set up a club. Although a minor one has been set up since, a group that goes around calling themselves the Information Architecture Institute. I think they are pleasant people.

And the term is out there. And people seem to know the term. Enough that when people write stories on me, they say that he's "a self-styled Information Architect," that "he coined the term," or "he believed he coined the term," or something complimentary or something not complimentary about my relationship to the term, which makes it all the better. But it certainly is a term that's out there. And in the milieu of how I began to use it, I feel comfortable with saying I coined the term for contemporary society and gave it credibility. And if somebody comes up with some reason that I didn't, I will be happy to say I didn't, because my life isn't based on having coined that term. But I think I did.

Q: You did.

And I'm proud of that, because it helps me define what I do to people. And we're going all the way backwards to the beginning of this chat because it is a term that is memorable, that explains something, that allows for a description of what it means. My unhappiness with the term "design" is that, for most people, design means making something look good. Information architecture is more systemic in the populist sense and has to perform rather than just aesthetically in the popular sense, and therefore those terms go together. And I feel comfortable calling it architecture.

References

Wurman, R. S. (1971). *Making the city observable* (Design Quarterly No. 80). The MIT Press.

Wurman, R. S. (1986). *What will be has always been: The words of Louis I. Kahn.* New York: Access Press.

Wurman, R. S. (1989a). *Information anxiety.* Doubleday.

Wurman, R. S. (1989b). *Hats* (Design Quarterly No. 145). The MIT Press.

Wurman, R. S. (1997). *Information architects.* Graphis.

Wurman, R. S., & Feldman, E. (1973). *The notebooks and drawings of Louis I. Kahn.* The MIT Press.

Dan Klyn works as an information architecture and business management consultant at The Understanding Group (TUG), teaches information architecture at the University of Michigan School of Information, is a member of the core faculty in the architecture program at Building Beauty, and is writing the biography of Richard Saul Wurman. His research is focused on the spatiality of meaning, with an emphasis on the interplay of ontology, topology, and choreography in the built environment.

Index

© The Editor(s) (if applicable) and The Author(s), under exclusive license
to Springer Nature Switzerland AG 2021
A. Resmini et al. (eds.), *Advances in Information Architecture*,
Human–Computer Interaction Series, https://doi.org/10.1007/978-3-030-63205-2

Printed in the United States
by Baker & Taylor Publisher Services